# Psychological Assessment of Sexually Abused Children and Their Families

D0913646

## Interpersonal Violence:
## The Practice Series

### Jon R. Conte, Series Editor

# Psychological Assessment of Sexually Abused Children and Their Families

**William N. Friedrich**
*Mayo Medical School*

## IVPS

Interpersonal Violence:
The Practice Series

Sage Publications
*International Educational and Professional Publisher*
Thousand Oaks ▪ London ▪ New Delhi

*For information:*

Sage Publications, Inc.
2455 Teller Road
Thousand Oaks, California 91320
E-mail: order@sagepub.com

Sage Publications Ltd.
6 Bonhill Street
London EC2A 4PU
United Kingdom

Sage Publications India Pvt. Ltd.
M-32 Market
Greater Kailash I
New Delhi 110 048 India

Printed in the United States of America

*Library of Congress Cataloging-in-Publication Data*

Friedrich, William N.
  Psychological assessment of sexually abused children and their families / by William N. Friedrich.
    p.  cm. — (Interpersonal violence: the practice series)
  Includes bibliographical references and index.
    ISBN 0-7619-0310-0 (cloth: acid-free paper)
    ISBN 0-7619-0311-9 (pbk.: acid-free paper)
    1. Sexually abused children—Psychological testing.  2. Sexually abused teenagers—Psychological testing.  I. Title.  II. Interpersonal violence.
  RJ507.S49  F745  2001
  618.92'85836075—dc21                          2001003353


01  02  03  04  05  10  9  8  7  6  5  4  3  2  1

| | |
|---|---|
| *Acquiring Editor:* | Nancy S. Hale |
| *Editorial Assistant:* | Vonessa Vondera |
| *Production Editor:* | Diana E. Axelsen |
| *Editorial Assistant:* | Cindy Bear |
| *Typesetter/Designer:* | Janelle LeMaster |
| *Indexer.* | Rachel Rice |
| *Cover Designer:* | Michelle Lee |

# Contents

Appendixes

# Introduction

My book *Psychotherapy With Sexually Abused Boys,* published in 1995, introduced a conceptual framework to facilitate an understanding of sexually abused children and therapy, both in general and specifically for boys. The framework included the features of attachment, dysregulation, and self-perception. Each of these theoretical perspectives pointed to treatment issues that either were specific to the impact of abuse or addressed ways in which the impact of abuse can be lessened or exacerbated. It is clear that sexual victimization has a considerable impact over and above comorbid family and demographic variables (Boney-McCoy & Finkelhor, 1995). Yet, trauma-specific therapists too often ignore critical variables that moderate abuse impact in the lives of these children. A key moderator is the parent-child relationship, a feature subsumed under attachment theory.

My belief that assessment is a necessary part of treatment was reflected in the 1995 book. Several chapters concluded with a list of measurement tools and tests that addressed some aspect of the model. At that time, I intended to write a book on assessment that would parallel the book on treatment, and the end-of-chapter lists included in the latter served as small goads that kept at me until I was able to write this book. I strongly believe that an uninformed therapy is not likely to be productive. Formal assessment is on a par with and can surpass clinical intuition as a tool for keeping therapy both informed and sensitive to the needs of the client.

The first eight chapters of this book are intended to provide both a theoretical framework for assessment and an analysis of measurement tools for use with abused children and their families. Chapters 4 through 7 are linked together by case material on an 8-year-old boy, A. B., and his family. I chose this particular case because it was quite complex and allowed for the presentation of many different measures and their interpretation. I also had access to follow-up data on the outcome of the treatment interventions; such records are an excellent source of data to validate or invalidate initial hypotheses. Consequently, while atypical, this case does serve as an excellent teaching case.

Because the utility of clinical material as a teaching device is unsurpassed, I have included two other cases in this book (Chapters 9 and 10). Both these cases involved evaluations completed by psychologists. Each has had significant experience in evaluating maltreatment and has also contributed to the scientific literature in the area of child maltreatment and assessment. Diana Elliott, PhD, long served as the chief psychologist at the Harbor-UCLA child abuse program and, in addition, has an active forensic practice. Her paper on forensic evaluations and the combination of interview, self-report, and disclosure is a must-read (Elliott & Briere, 1994). W. Hobart Davies, PhD, is now on the faculty of the University of Wisconsin–Milwaukee, but he continues to work clinically. Prior to his academic position, he was at the Children's Hospital of Wisconsin in Milwaukee, where he directed a child abuse evaluation pro- gram. Both Elliot and Davies bring years of experience and an appreciation of the empirical requirements of assessment to their evaluations. I learned something about assessment and the integration of test results with clinical data when I read their reports, and I know you will also.

Chapter 1 outlines the purposes of psychological evaluations with maltreated children and adolescents. In addition to assisting with treatment planning, an evaluation provides useful information to the various agencies and caregivers involved with the child, typically with forensic cases. Although there is no psychological test that can answer the ultimate question regarding the validity of the child's abuse reports, there are interview protocols, observation strategies, and formal and informal measures that correspond to the abuse-related symptoms children and teens exhibit. These same devices can also help clinicians determine the viability of the parents and identify factors that interfere with their capacity to support their children (Elliott & Briere, 1994).

In Chapter 2, I present the theoretical literature necessary to understand the evaluation framework. Literature on attachment, dysregulation, and self-perception is briefly reviewed. In addition, readers may wish to refer to my 1995 book, as well as some of the latest writings of John Briere, to anchor themselves more firmly in this perspective (Briere, 1997, 2001b). The emphasis on attachment validates my belief that a book on assessment of maltreated children is insufficient if it fails to include information about the evaluation of their nonoffending parents, because family interaction is a critical dimension in understanding maltreatment (Burgess & Conger, 1978).

Sexually abused children present quite variably, and this is the focus of Chapter 3. Reasons for this variability, as well as the phenomenon of asymptomatic sexually abused children, are reviewed and discussed. Clinical data are presented suggesting that the overall number of asymptomatic sexually abused children, particularly those who come into our offices, may be lower than what is typically noted in the literature (Kendall-Tackett, Williams, & Finkelhor, 1993). However, psychotherapy with maltreated children and teens often fails to appreciate the fact that these children are extremely diverse. They can range from truly asymptomatic to enormously disturbed. In many cases, given the secretive nature of the abuse, they will appear to be much more competent than they are, and only later, or with more careful assessment, does the true extent of their symptoms become evident. In fact, their denial of victimization often parallels their denial of symptoms on objective self-reports, which further supports the need for a more comprehensive assessment (Elliott & Briere, 1994). Clinicians need to know how to recognize the potential for latent symptoms. They must also sort out what is specific to the abuse and the context variables that are either worsening or buffering the child's symptoms.

The next several chapters contain the meat of the book. Chapter 4 introduces the case material. I use this chapter to review strategies designed to assess the quality of the parent-child relationship, from both the parents' and the child's perspectives. I do not propose here that any of these measures directly assesses attachment as defined by John Bowlby and subsequently by his colleagues and followers (Cassidy & Shaver, 1999). However, the assessment is informed by the attachment literature, with disorganized attachment receiving special attention, given its relationship to unresolved trauma in the maternal figure (Main & Hesse, 1990; Schuengel, Bakermans-Kranenburg, & Van Ijzendoorn, 1999).

The assessment of dysregulation is reviewed in Chapter 5, with emphases on posttraumatic stress disorder, dissociation, and self-injurious behavior. Once again, the child's context cannot be ignored when considering these symptoms. For example, posttraumatic stress disorder in sexually abused children is best predicted not by the severity of the act, but by the child's context (Wolfe, Sas, & Wekerle, 1994). There is a range of dysregulation-related symptom clusters, including attention deficit hyperactivity (ADHD)-like symptoms related to trauma and self-injurious behavior.

Sexual behavior problems related to dysregulation are discussed in Chapter 6. Sexual behavior problems in children grab much attention in the current sociopolitical climate. In addition, they often are associated with comorbid family problems that should be considered for treatment to be effective. I believe the best way to inject a note of objectivity into the irrationality that surrounds these children is to discuss a logical and coherent assessment approach. The evaluation of these children has been greatly informed by recent NCCAN-sponsored research by Barbara Bonner, Eugene Walker, and Lucy Berliner (2000), as well as Alison Gray and Bill Pithers (Gray, Busconi, Houchens, & Pithers, 1997). In addition, Darlene Hall and Fred Mathews have conducted a line of research that is reviewed in this chapter and is likely to be extremely useful to the practitioner (Hall & Mathews, 1996).

The last part of the model, self-perception, and its evaluation in parents and children are reviewed in Chapter 7. Issues of self, including shame and the assumption of guilt, are rich treatment foci in teenagers, who have a greater capacity for self-perception than do children. Self-appraisal is distorted relative to sexual abuse (Spacarelli, 1994), and data on the negative appraisals by abuse victims can be enormously informative (Spacarelli, 1995). Chapter 8 outlines a number of measures that can be used if the goal is for much briefer assessment. Brief screening is the type of evaluation that is most commonly used by practicing clinicians. Suggested interview questions germane to brief screening are scattered throughout the book and in some of the appendixes. However, each of the screening strategies is related to the theoretical framework, and I encourage their utilization.

Chapter 9, by Elliott, provides additional insight on assessment through analysis of a case involving a teen-age girl and her family. Chapter 10, by Davies, Garwood, O'Conor and Carron, uses the case of a 10-year-old girl, Linda, to explore issues of truth and falsity in allegations of child abuse. The scope of this book is deliberately expansive, and I thank Jon Conte, series editor, for his permission to write a book of this length. Once I started to write, I was faced with a dilemma about the breadth and depth of the book. If I wrote only about children, I was ignoring the ecology of the child. It is impossible to write validly about the assessment of parent-child attachment by focusing only on children's perspectives on their parents. For example, insecure attachment predominates in maltreated children (Carlson, Cicchetti, Barnett, & Braunwald, 1989). One enormous risk factor for insecure attachment is a history of victimization in the parent. The potency of this risk factor is magnified when the parent has never had an opportunity to resolve it. A careful assessment of parental victimization is necessary as an adjunct to the evaluation of the child. I resolved the dilemma by including children and parents.

There is a maxim in fiction that you write what you know. The same is true for professional books. A large part of my practice is the provision of consultation and psychological assessment regarding maltreated children. These cases are both clinician referred and court ordered. Clinician-referred cases typically involve children and adolescents who seem treatment resistant or who have had a course of treatment and are still symptomatic, quite possibly more symptomatic than when they began therapy.

These referrals have taught me that therapy is also about goodness of fit. The most useful technique to maximize a good fit is to gather information about the child and his or her contexts. It is a rare sexually abused child who will make progress in supportive psychotherapy when his or her flashbacks are unaddressed and the parent continues subtly to blame or reject the child, or inaccurately perceives the child. Expressive language disorders and limited intellectual capabilities are not uncommon in sexually abused children (Erickson & Egeland, 1987); they interfere with progress in therapy and can be frustrating to the therapist if they are not diagnosed. Simply because a parent gets the child to the appointments does not mean the parent is without treatment issues that should also be put on the table.

A similar phenomenon occurs when a decision is made to use medication to manage symptoms in the child. Children are referred for ADHD treatment because of distorted attributions and perceptions by the parent as much as for any specific symptom cluster in the child. Parents with these distorted attributions often cut short the treatment efficacy of the stimulant by virtue of not changing their interactional patterns with the child. As a result, they expand the coercive cycle they have with this child to include arguments about the child taking the stimulant. Understanding this dynamic makes it completely sensible when the child starts skipping doses and then refuses to take the medication.

The next contributors to my practice are those evaluations that are court ordered and quite often involve the parents. In court-ordered cases, multiple types of maltreatment are typical. The issue is often one of the viability of the parent-child relationship. The evaluator is typically allowed to cast a broad net and include the parents and children. Over the years, I have developed a protocol that has been very useful for understanding children, parents, and the nature of the parent-child interaction. It is empirically and psychometrically driven and enables me to render reports to the court that address both abuse-specific and more generic issues. They typically have a profound impact on the family, for example, referral for treatment of the parents, and termination of parental rights. Because this is such an enormous issue and practitioners are often unprepared for its complexity, I wanted to use this book to address some of the issues involved.

An additional goal of this book is to provide a rich guide to the practice of assessment for both psychologists and other mental health professionals who are consumers of psychological reports. Interviews are the core component of the evaluation, and several outlines of interviews are provided to structure this process and make it more useful. However, clinical observations routinely occur during the interview, and the observations of small children can be made more systematic and valid by the use of parent-report and interviewer ratings, both of which are reviewed in the text.

Over the years, I have made it a practice to save data from every evaluation I have completed. One advantage is that when those cases involve therapy, I can also routinely obtain data on treatment outcome. At the very least, I have a data set that I can use in conjunction with clinical questions. Granted, these data are clinical and not random. Some readers may question the inclusion of projective measures in this text (Garb, Wood, & Nezworski, 2000; West, 1998), but I have several data sets that enable me to examine correlates of projective measures with objective reports and outcomes. For example, I know that with younger children, sexual content in drawings is significantly associated with sexual content to selected cards from the Roberts Apperception Test for Children (McArthur & Roberts, 1982) and elevations on the Child Sexual Behavior Inventory (Friedrich, 1997). It is also associated with boundary problems with the evaluator (Appendix K) and valid abuse reports. These behaviors are also associated with sexualized home environments, which potentiate this display of sexual behavior (Friedrich, Fisher, et al., 2001; Friedrich, Grambsch, et al., 1992). While this fact makes it a challenge to understand the origins of sexualized behavior, a challenge of this type requires systematic assessment. Because psychological assessment is often about the internal consistency of the measures, having these data is reassuring to me personally and enhances the validity of my assessment on a more professional level.

My practice has contributed to my developing a number of assessment devices and strategies (Friedrich, 1997). The field of child maltreatment is privileged to have practitioners who have been sensitive to abuse-specific issues and have developed valid measures. They include John Briere, Judith Cohen, Julian Ford, Tony Mannarino, Joel Milner, Frank Putnam, and Vicki Wolfe. A number of assessment tools that I have developed are contained in the Appendixes. Some of these guide interviews and can be utilized by practitioners not formally trained in psychological assessment but who desire to be more focused in their assessments. However, these interview protocols are flexible guides, and the interpretation of their results still relies on formal training and experience.

Papers are currently being written on the Adolescent Sexual Behavior Inventory (both self-report and parent-report versions; (Friedrich, Lysne, Shamos, & Kolko, 2001), the Child Behavior Checklist PTSD/Dissociation Scales (Friedrich, Fisher, Trane, Lengua, et al., 2001), and the Interviewer Rating Scale (Friedrich & Lui, 2001). Data are currently being gathered on the Safety Checklist and its predictive utility. All of these measures are presented in the Appendixes. I encourage readers to become clinical researchers with these scales and contribute to the knowledge base in the maltreatment literature.

I want to thank a number of people for their role in this book, beginning with many wonderful colleagues in APSAC and ATSA. They are too many to name individually, but I count on them for support, encouragement, and stimulation in a clinical field where these positives are often in short supply. I also greatly appreciate those colleagues who over the years have collaborated with me on the Child Sexual Behavior Inventory studies, including Lucy Berliner, Judith Cohen, Linda Damon, Hobart Davies, Alison Gray, Catherine Koverola, Tony Mannarino, and John Wright. John Briere is an inspiration by virtue of both his elegant theories and his continuing efforts to create abuse-specific assessment strategies. The entire field owes him an enormous debt for his many contributions.

I have been privileged to be associated with Barbara Bonner, Eugene Walker, and Lucy Berliner as well as Alison Gray and Bill Pithers and their seminal research on sexually aggressive children. Many other friends and colleagues in the field have provided support during the writing of this book. John Briere provided comments on an early draft, and Lucy Berliner's questions about its completion and her devotion to empirically informed practice continued to provide encouragement during my writing doldrums. The additional cases by Elliott and by Davies and colleagues were a chance for me to learn from experts, and their contributions are also greatly appreciated. I have been blessed with numerous students, fellows, and colleagues here at Mayo. Their support, intellectual curiosity, and clinical perspectives have informed my practice. My current postdoctoral fellow, Sarah Trane, deserves a special word of thanks for her tremendous assistance with reference checking and copy editing. My various editors at Sage, including Jon Conte, Terry Hendrix, and Nancy Hale, have also been very supportive.

Lastly, with each passing year, I gain more personal wisdom and increasingly realize the enormous debt that I owe to my family, who are alternately supportive and inspiring. I owe a particular debt to my wife and true friend, Wanda. She daily teaches me about the curative power of relationships and provides encouragement and support in many incalculable ways.

# 1

# The Purposes of the Psychological Evaluation of Sexually Abused Children and Adolescents

On one level, the sexual abuse of a minor represents something very simple—a serious wrong has been committed. However, children's adaptation to their victimization is a very complex process. If we expect to treat the consequences of trauma, we must be able to understand the complexity of victimization and its attendant features. An objective perspective is critical to understanding maltreatment and the diversity of its impact. Psychological evaluation can provide this critical perspective.

There are many challenges to the objective understanding of trauma and its impact. First, sexual trauma is highly variable across victims. Consequently, the assessor is never evaluating a consistent set of circumstances from one child to the next. Second, trauma is rarely an isolated event. Rather, it is couched within a number of individual and systemic contexts. Each of these contexts operates to make the child more or less vulnerable to the trauma. In addition, the child is also on a developmental trajectory that predates the victimization and carries the child beyond the moment of trauma. Although this can be protective, it does create the potential for a lifetime of aftereffects.

Given this complexity, it is logical that from the moment you first meet a sexual abuse victim, at least one part of you needs to function as an evaluator. You most likely bring to the evaluation a schema about victims and their symptoms. The first questions you ask are designed to gather data that confirm or disconfirm these theories. The information gathered in the assessment will illuminate the complexity of the victim and the victim's context. This information provides insight into what is needed to correct the presenting problems. Whoever functions as the child's or family's therapist can now be informed about the most suitable treatment approach.

This book is specifically about the evaluation of child and adolescent sexual abuse victims. The assessment of their parents is also ecologically relevant to understanding the children, and their evaluation is also discussed. The evaluative framework that is offered is built on conceptual underpinnings that reflect the complexity of maltreatment and adaptation. My goal is to improve your evaluative capacities and to provide a framework that makes your assessments efficient, rich, and directly relevant to empirically validated or supported therapy approaches.

Although I have written or edited several books on the treatment of sexually abused children (Friedrich, 1990, 1991a, 1995a), my therapeutic interactions reflect my objective assessment. I typically rely on formal assessment for at least a portion of every evaluation I complete. I believe that assessment is a precondition to therapy. I also believe that the more appropriate and targeted the assessment, the better the child's treatment prospects. An understanding of assessment is critical to treatment.

❑  **Why Should Anyone Need More Than Background Information?**

Why does any clinician need anything more than background data on children and the circumstances that brought them to see you? Many

therapeutic approaches have a primary focus on the presenting
plaint, for example, problem-solving therapy (Haley, 1987), or b
ior therapy (Bandura, 1977).

Background information is essential to the treatment process. These
children come from chaotic families, and you must know with whom
the children are living, what traumatic event brought them to you, and
how caregivers view their functioning. However, these data are insufficient. Risk literature is quite clear that the number, not the type, of
risk factors is critical to understanding immediate and long-term outcomes (Garbarino, 1999). The clinical literature is also clear about the
frequent bias that affects the caregiver's objectivity (Everson, Hunter,
Runyon, Edelsohn, & Coulter, 1989).

Therapists, however, exist along a continuum regarding the necessity of assessment. On one end are those who believe it is minimally
relevant and on the other are therapists who believe assessment to be
central to their therapy. Pragmatic individuals like me also agree that
not everyone who comes into the mental health system needs an
in-depth assessment.

Many very capable therapists cannot wait to get down to the business of therapy. They may have found that even brief assessment, and
certainly more extensive assessment, is not useful to them personally.
Assessment may be over after a few, well-chosen questions. They may
view assessment as a hindrance to treatment. Their view is certainly
more defensible when you consider the large number of relatively useless evaluations that are written each year.

Other therapists are positioned elsewhere on the continuum, some
realizing the need for evaluation but not sure what or how to assess.
Finally, other therapists are on the opposite end of the continuum,
where assessment is central to the treatment process.

While it is true that most victims are adequately served by brief assessment, it is also true that unfortunate consequences can occur without an evaluation. For example, because of the lack of an initial point of
reference, the clinician may never know if change has occurred. Simple
remedies may be overlooked. Complex problems may be misdiag-
nosed. Neglect or improper treatment with negative consequences
may produce legal liability. Without evaluation, you are never in a position to answer such important questions as, Is it useful to disclose?
What are the key ingredients for bringing about change? Can brief

therapy be helpful? and How do parents' abuse histories affect the course of therapy in their children?

Sexual abuse activates many emotions in the parents, victims, and service providers. As if this were not difficult enough, abuse typically occurs when the child is younger and the caregivers need to think developmentally. Objectivity, in the form of valid assessment, can make the circumstances more manageable for all parties. This is true whatever the outcome.

I have several reasons for writing this book. First, I have found that writing helps me understand better what I do as a clinician, in this case in my role as an evaluator. Although writing a book certainly is not the easiest vehicle for understanding a process that I practice every day, I have always come away from the writing process more clear about what I do, why I do what I do, and how I might practice even more effectively.

Good therapy is a balance of the intuitive and the analytic. This fact is relevant to all therapists on the "continuum of the utility of evaluation." You need ample quantities of both of these disparate components to succeed as a clinical practitioner. I certainly know that evaluation is an analytic process that has long complemented my more intuitive, therapeutic abilities, and I believe that is true for you as well.

A good evaluation also reflects an integrative process that goes far beyond any single test score or bit of data. Integration is a positive counterbalance to the fragmentation that many victims bring to the clinical arena (Putnam, 1985). Careful assessment enables us to integrate disparate pieces of information. If we understand the various features of victims' lives, and communicate this appropriately, victims have a chance to view their lives more accurately and positively.

For example, what if the therapeutic task given to you is to facilitate a reunion between nonoffending parents and their child? You then jump into this task unaware of how deeply the parents were affected by their own childhood deprivation. Months of frustrating therapy that is revictimizing to the child may occur before you realize the futility of reunification at this time. Helping parents address their own attachment and victimization history and how this interferes with parenting would have been a more useful initial attempt.

There are other examples as well. If your evaluation found abuse-specific behavioral reactions, including the identification of potential triggers, you would expect children's flashbacks to increase after they encounter a reminder of their past. It is something predicted by their posttraumatic stress disorder (PTSD; American Psychiatric Association [APA], 1994). A knowledgeable therapist could incorporate these data into the therapy, for example, stress inoculation, relaxation training, and so on. In this way children can more successfully counter these intrusions rather than react with increased symptoms.

Objective assessment is absolutely essential in cases involving sexuality and violence, for example, sexually aggressive children. There is an enormous push to criminalize all levels of this behavior (Chaffin & Bonner, 1998). Children as young as 7 and 8 are being charged with felonious sexual behavior (Chaffin & Friedrich, 2000). Children are then given age-inappropriate treatment that focuses on offender dynamics rather than on correcting parental monitoring, increasing positives, and addressing victim issues.

A developmentally sensitive evaluation could inform the court that a criminal justice approach that includes understanding offender dynamics is useless to preteens due to their cognitive developmental level. Accurate self-perception is difficult to do even in teenagers, who more often than not have the capacity for formal operational thinking. The case presented at the beginning of this book illustrates the evaluation of a child and the child's family in a case of sexual aggression.

A critical aspect of treatment planning is whether or not the parent has a history of sexual abuse. There are excellent data that indicate that an unresolved history of victimization in the mother is directly related to disorganized attachment in preschoolers (Main & Hesse, 1990). This attachment type has lasting sequelae in the form of greater vulnerability to anxiety/phobia in the child (Main, 1995) and dissociative experiences when older (Liotti, 1995). The child victim is part of a system, and we need to know whether the system can be the safe holding environment (Winnicott, 1965) the child needs. It does the therapist absolutely no good to ignore the parent's victim history and how that might interfere with the parent's stated wish to protect her child.

Equally as important as knowing the parents' abuse history is knowing the degree to which the parents have resolved their victimization (Egeland, Jacobvitz, & Sroufe, 1988). We can learn this critical information only via direct inquiry. Some questions I try to ask every parent are the following:

1. Have you ever been in therapy that has helped you?
2. Did you talk specifically about how badly your mom/dad treated you when you were younger?
3. What all did you share with them? Did you share even the really painful stuff?
4. How many sessions did you have with this therapist? At how many of those sessions did you talk about these deep hurts?
5. Think about how you felt about yourself before those sessions with the therapist. On a scale of 1 to 10, where would you have put yourself? How do you feel about yourself now? Where would you rate yourself on that same scale?
6. Do you feel that you left some issues buried?

You are freer to ask these important questions if you operate under the assumption that the child patient comes with a family that typically has therapy needs as well.

Knowledge about assessment also enables you to be an informed consumer of mental health evaluations. Even if you work only with victims, it is invaluable to know how to assess critically the evaluation of the offenders who victimized your patients. Being knowledgeable about such clinical issues as the risk to reoffend; the assessment of character disorders; the implications of unresolved PTSD on parenting; and the correct usage of standardized, widely used objective measures is very important in this field.

Assessment provides me a new set of lenses through which to view my clients. One lens that I use is attachment, an essential ingredient in parent-child relationships: If I cannot assess attachment quality, I cannot intervene precisely in the relationship. For example, how do I respond to a guardian ad litem or caseworker who misinterprets a child's behavioral response during visits with her mother? The mother is technically quite skillful over a 60-minute period, but her daughter wets and soils herself during or shortly after the visit. The child's behavior suggests that she does not find her parent to be a secure base.

If a teen victim hits her mother, does that reflect the mother's persisting victim stance in the family? Does it suggest coercive attachment? Is it indicative of oppositional-defiant disorder? Could it be related to the hyperarousal associated with PTSD?

What treatment foci are recommended for a teenager who comes in giddy and immature one session and sober and pseudomature the next? What does the caregiving behavior of parentified children suggest about the neglect they experienced when younger? What might be a pathway to correcting this caregiving stance?

Assessment enables me to "language" a child's life. By getting to know an individual extremely well, I am in a position to document another life that "deserves" to be written about. I want my reports to present the child to future workers in a way that instills hope. I think there is both value and utility in recounting a life accurately, and the benefits are pragmatic as well as more existential and humanistic (Pennebaker, 1995).

Evaluation is also about collecting data to understand what treatments work, who responds best to what type of therapeutic approach, and how much time it truly takes to make a lasting difference. In this day and age of reduced reimbursement for psychotherapy, clinicians have to argue forcefully for what works and how much time is needed. Data are your best allies in this endeavor. If you are given an initial 8 weeks by an HMO to treat a child who is sexually aggressive, you need to know the data from research studies that point to the need for significantly more time with not only the child, but also the child's system (Friedrich, 1995a).

For example, an agency-based study with several of my colleagues found that 6 to 8 months of therapy was needed simply to be initially successful with the majority of boys at the end of therapy (Friedrich, Luecke, Beilke, & Place, 1991). These were boys who had already received brief, structured interventions, but were continuing to be symptomatic. I have used this article several times to support my court testimony about what is needed for successful treatment for boys presenting with multiple abuse-related issues.

How did the data from the above study come about? They required instituting careful and routine intake assessments in an agency that had no history of using assessment as part of the treatment. A "culture of nonassessment" prevailed in the agency, but with persistence we were able not only to obtain the data but also to make them useful to the practicing clinicians.

Finally, the evaluative process can serve as an intervention. The effort to know children in their family contexts can be affirming to all those concerned, can be educative and prepare them for treatment, and can also uncover issues that would have gone unnoticed without your expert eye. For example, an assessment-driven intervention with high-risk families, which relied heavily on formal and informal assessment, resulted in a reduction of maltreatment and a larger number of cases where parental rights were terminated than a comparison group of families that were not evaluated as thoroughly (Zeanah et al., 2001).

## ❏ The Purposes of Psychological Evaluations

The results of psychological evaluations with sexually abused children can be used to plan for and assess treatment success. The data from these evaluations can also be used in forensic settings. Although the same evaluation process may occur, the clinical and forensic roles are completely different for the evaluator. I believe that while my assessments inform my therapy, I also agree that the roles of evaluator and therapist need to be kept separate as often as possible, but particularly in forensic cases (Myers, 1998; Pruett & Solnit, 1998). This reflects the need to "avoid performing multiple and potentially conflicting roles" (American Psychological Association, 1992, p. 14). A closely related statement from another document is, "during the course of a psychological evaluation in child protection matters, psychologists do not accept any of the participants involved in the evaluation as therapy clients" (American Psychological Association, 1998, p. 7). Although the material in this book can inform both the clinical and forensic roles of the evaluator, individuals who perform these evaluations must also inform themselves about how their data will be used and act accordingly and ethically.

For readers whose activities include forensic assessment, this text needs as a companion several other recent books that outline the legal issues in child sexual abuse. These include the second edition of John Myers's (1998) *Legal Issues in Child Abuse and Neglect;* the book edited by Steven Ceci and Helene Hembrooke (1998), *Expert Witnesses in Child Abuse Cases;* and Debra Poole and Michael Lamb's (1998) book, titled *Interviewing Children in the Forensic Context: A Developmental Approach.* In addition, there are other guidelines that I will mention throughout this book that are essential reading for the forensic evaluator.

In the next section of this chapter, I delineate several issues that can be addressed, at least in part, by psychological evaluations. These include assessing allegations of sexual abuse, helping the court to understand a child's testimony, determining overall adjustment and the related issue of identifying treatment needs, assessing risk in cases of sexual aggression, and, finally, evaluating treatment outcome.

## DETERMINING THE LIKELIHOOD OF SEXUAL ABUSE

Whether or not mental health professionals have any business testifying in cases of child maltreatment is a hotly debated topic (Myers, 1998). Positions on this issue range from one extreme to the other. This fact alone should caution any evaluator whose data are used in court settings. It suggests that the collection, interpretation, and presentation of the data need to be done ethically and with utmost attention to established practice guidelines.

The type of psychological evaluation suggested by this book could uncover very useful information that increases the likelihood of determining whether abuse has or has not occurred. In legal terms, symptoms in the child may be relevant or probative evidence that the child had been abused (Lyon & Koehler, 1998). In fact, the process of rendering an opinion or arriving at a diagnosis is a common professional practice. It is also a process supported by professional guidelines specifically relevant to child maltreatment, including sexual abuse (American Professional Society on the Abuse of Children, 1990).

There will be times when the data from the interview and the child's behavior as observed by different caregivers are extremely compelling, and you as the evaluator have a high degree of certainty that abuse has occurred. Although the fact of abuse is something that can be determined only by the court, as a skilled evaluator you can organize the data, present them in a context that is clear to the court, and thus help a decision be rendered that is beneficial to the child you have assessed.

This book is not about investigative interviewing. Forensic interviewing has been discussed thoroughly in other texts (Faller, 1996; Poole & Lamb, 1998). Typically the evaluations and the process used in

the evaluations described in this test are completed following a forensic interview. In my practice, these interviews most often have been
done by a mandated agency, that is, Child Protective Services (CPS).
My role is to complete a court-ordered assessment prior to the onset of
treatment.

Children with a high likelihood of abuse will come into your practice. Your evaluation may be useful in determining the likelihood that
abuse has occurred, particularly in those situations where the child has
not made a clear statement or has recanted. Although these psychological data are not proof that the child was sexually abused, they can
guide the therapist more accurately to help the child talk about maltreatment specifically. There are compelling reasons for this to occur.
Though clinicians have long felt the need to have victims acknowledge
the abuse events, recent research with a sample of teens has illustrated
how central this is to overall adjustment (McGee, Wolfe, & Wilson,
1997).

Forensic evaluations are typically comprehensive and the data obtained may be both confirmatory and contradictory. A clear indication
of an invalid evaluation is when a clinician points to a single bit of data
as proof of abuse, for example, a drawing that is sexually explicit.

Alhough it is true that a child drawing genitals on a human figure
drawing is unusual and that data indicate that sexually abused children draw genitals significantly more often than children who are not
sexually abused (Friedrich, 1998; Peterson & Hardin, 1997), by itself
the significance of such drawings wanes. Although Lyon and Koehler
(1998) write that "drawings of genitalia would be probative evidence
that abuse occurred," it is very important to note that sexual behavior,
including the drawing of genitalia, is influenced by a number of
nonabuse factors in the child's context" (Friedrich, 1998, p. 253). Consequently, the interpretation of a drawing without respect to the
child's context, such as exposure to pornography, is inappropriate.

For example, I was asked to evaluate a 9-year-old girl. Her parents
were suspicious that she had been sexually abused, but they had been
unable to convince the local authorities to interview her. The girl's
mother had recently discovered a sexually explicit picture drawn by
the girl. Several days later, the mother discovered her daughter putting a candle between her labia. In addition, the girl had suddenly developed troubled sleep. She was also newly phobic of the neighbors,

more particularly their 19-year-old son, who had returned home only in the past 6 months. She once blurted out a suspicious-sounding statement about the 19-year-old to her mother, but had since refused to elaborate. The girl is no longer allowed to play with his younger sister, a very good friend.

During my formal evaluation, I found a 3-month decline in grades despite above-average capabilities and no prior history of learning problems; significant sexual distress; and a sharp increase in symptoms related to anxiety, depression, and PTSD on the Child Behavior Checklist (CBCL; Achenbach, 1991a). My assessment also uncovered contextual evidence that there was no pornography in the home nor were there opportunities for the girl to witness sexuality. Her parents' marriage was stable, neither parent had a history of sexual abuse, and there were no apparent stressors.

My two attempts to interview the girl led to no disclosure of any sort, but I reported my concerns to the local authorities as mandated. She was then interviewed by a female detective and denied sexual contact by the 19-year-old or any other individual. However, she reported being punched and bullied by two 12-year-old boys at her school. Her mother later confirmed the veracity of her daughter's statement after a conversation with the principal. The girl was removed to another school and her symptoms stopped.

Imagine my chagrin when I was informed of this finding. Although I am aware that behavior has many origins, the very low frequency in a 9-year-old girl of two unusual sexual behaviors—drawing of genitals, placing an object in the genitals—in combination with her recent-onset phobia to a 19-year-old seemed very suspicious. I refer back to this case often because it helps me to ground my interpretations in forensic cases.

I am also reminded of the problems inherent in arriving at a diagnosis based solely on sexual behavior, for example, the parent report on the Child Sexual Behavior Inventory (CSBI), a measure that I developed (Friedrich, 1997). I believe the CSBI to be the best single measure currently available to screen sexual behavior in sexually abused children. It is comprehensive, well-normed, and valid. It has a high false-positive rate, however, and if used to screen a random sample of children for sexual abuse, it would identify more nonabused children as abused than abused children as abused (Friedrich, 1997).

It is inappropriate to decide that sexual abuse has occurred and base this conclusion on a single, highly unusual sexual behavior. Comprehensive evaluations are not based on single markers but are integrations of many indicators, some of which are contradictory and need to be explained.

A recent review of the literature on the consequences of sexual abuse in children pointed to two clusters of behavior that are reliably related to sexual abuse: sexual behavior and symptoms of PTSD (Kendall-Tackett, Williams, & Finkelhor, 1993). The studies reviewed in this paper relied on research that examined group differences, typically those of sexually abused children from children who neither were abused nor had other behavior problems. While group data are very important for reliable prediction (Meehl, 1954), on an individual basis there are behaviors that children exhibit that we could assume are related to their sexual abuse experience, for example, encopresis in a boy who reports sodomy. I point to this behavior— encopresis—since it falls into a cluster of behaviors—toileting problems—that do not discriminate sexually abused children from nonabused psychiatric outpatients (Kendall-Tackett et al., 1993). The specificity of the abuse to the behavior can be determined only if assessment, for example, a thorough interview, occurs.

For example, a girl might exhibit sleep problems subsequent to her molestation. Although this may be a direct effect of the abuse, it is important to realize that sleep problems are also common markers of generic distress in children (Horn & Dollinger, 1995). It is logical to argue that the victim formed a link between the molestation and the safety of her bed. But what if the girl was not abused in her bedroom, but rather in a remote area of a playground? The sleep problems are now more likely to be related to other associations, for example, feeling alone, reliving her fears, feeling overwhelmed, or to more general problems with self-regulation secondary to the trauma.

We need to have an appreciation for the individual characteristics of our clients (as in the girl above), but if we are going to predict behavior, now or into the future, it is more useful for us as evaluators to rely on empirically based group differences. This is true even if the differences characterize only a portion of sexually abused children. I hope that this is already beginning to sound complicated, since careful evaluation is a complex process, and anyone undertaking this task needs to appreciate this fact.

However, I believe there is a place where individual variation/differences must be appreciated. This is the context for forensic interviews. There is a clear trend in many states to prioritize abuse cases according to whether they warrant attention. Many protective services agencies cannot handle the influx of maltreatment cases given their staffing level. There is also a high level of concern about false allegations. Many social service agencies have adopted developmentally insensitive interview protocols to handle the volume and have less variability from one interviewer to the next, in order to make their practice less vulnerable to criticism.

Although I think this defensive posture around child welfare is completely asinine, what this now means is that children of all ages are being interviewed in a standard format, typically one brief interview. It is not surprising that the validation rate drops after the agency begins to utilize these more standardized and less individually sensitive interviews (Jones & Finkelhor, 2000).

Consequently, there are children who have been abused who are not being identified by the authorized investigatory agency. These children were unable to disclose, for one or more of the many reasons that interfere with the interview process. These include the inability of children, with their limited vocabulary for feelings, to talk about something they wish to avoid thinking about. Other factors include divided family loyalties and an often justified worldview that adults are not helpful. Knowing how to interview and how to document your interview process will be a critical adjunct to your evaluations and help you to interpret the data you do get in as valid a manner as possible.

## EXPERT TESTIMONY TO REHABILITATE CHILDREN'S CREDIBILITY

Myers (1998) writes that expert testimony from mental health professionals falls into two categories. The first category is testimony to provide an opinion that a child was abused. This was discussed in the previous section.

The second category is more limited and typically comes after a child has testified or has difficulty with testifying. The professional is now in a position to rehabilitate a child's credibility after the child has been cross-examined (Myers, 1998).

Let's say that you are the expert in a case. You provided testimony to the court about the child, as well as the degree to which the child's statements, context of disclosure, and symptoms are consistent with abuse. However, you now need to be able to talk about a number of other factors. These might include reasons why children are inconsistent, why they delay reporting the abuse, or why they might recant an earlier statement (Myers, 1998). You may also be asked why a child did or did not evidence certain behaviors or symptom clusters associated with trauma; for example, a child denied nightmares in court but had reported them to a therapist or to you. The defense attorney may have introduced a letter the child wrote to the perpetrator professing love for him, and you may now have to testify as to the ambivalent nature of parent-child relations in incest families.

This is a serious task and requires you, as a witness, to be completely objective and thoroughly grounded in the literature. However, an informed and objective approach presumably guided your evaluation and, if so, this is just one more arena for you as the professional.

## DETERMINING CHILDREN'S ABILITY TO TESTIFY

The two broad areas addressed in this section pertain to barriers that prevent a child from testifying in a valid fashion. These include special considerations regarding children's testimony, as well as a child's competence to testify validly.

An example of the first issue is reflected in the case of a 13-year-old girl recently raped by a 19-year-old male acquaintance. The county attorney contacted me for two reasons. First, he was concerned whether any special consideration should be given to the girl testifying in front of the rapist, who had made terroristic threats to her and family members after the rape. Second, he was also concerned because there were statements in her deposition that were not corroborated by witnesses.

My interview with the girl resulted in a diagnosis of PTSD. Her mother reported that her grades had dropped right after the rape, suggesting concentration problems. She was observed by two people to have blanched the one time she saw the perpetrator in the community. In addition, she was virtually housebound except for attending school during the day. My diagnosis provided a basis for the court to enable her to testify in this criminal trial but still feel protected.

The second issue was related to the girl's reporting that she had been dragged from an apartment to the scene of the rape. The county attorney assumed she had been dragged on her back, resisting the entire way, and this statement had never been supported by the two credible eyewitnesses. However, given her obvious agitation during these interviews, the county attorney had not asked the necessary questions to clarify this issue.

I simply asked the girl to demonstrate with dolls how she had been forced to accompany the rapist and one of his friends. She indicated that they had each taken one arm, put another behind her back, and walked her forward, despite her verbal protests. At no time was she being literally dragged. She reported the same sequence to the county attorney at a later pretrial interview, and this was consistent with witness reports.

Essentially, your expertise can be used to identify extenuating circumstances regarding a child's testimony, or help to interview a child more fully and hence more accurately. As long as the legal requirements are met, any strategy that enables the fullest and most valid recounting should be supported.

*Competence* is a legal term that has to do with a child's capacity to give testimony (Melton, Petrila, Poythress, & Slobogin, 1987). There are four criteria that are generally required to establish competence: the capacity to perceive facts accurately, the capacity to recollect and recall, the capacity to understand the oath, and the capacity to communicate based on personal knowledge of the facts (Weissman, 1991).

The issue of competence overlaps with the prior section on rehabilitative testimony. It is also quite relevant to other issues, such as whether or not 4- or 5-year-olds can and should give testimony.

The evaluator needs to consider the issues of perception and memory that may distort the testimony of any witness. Included here are the concerns regarding children's capacity to be influenced by repeated or inappropriate interviewing. Children are often viewed with suspicion about the reliability of their testimony. Issues of developmental immaturity need to be considered in establishing a child as competent to testify (Ceci & Bruck, 1993). The child may come to you after having given a statement whose validity is now being questioned. The evaluator needs to know the developmental literature on children so that a valid opinion can be rendered (Hewitt, 1999).

Courts typically presume that children may be less likely than adults to give testimony that is valid. Competency must be established on a case-by-case basis as to whether the child's testimony will help achieve justice. Primary emphasis is on the child's ability to comprehend the duty to tell the truth, to know truth from fiction, and to understand the consequences of not telling the truth. Typically it is sufficient that the child have a general understanding of his or her obligation to tell the truth.

It is also necessary that children have the cognitive abilities to understand what has happened to them and then to communicate their understanding when questioned in court. Children will need to remain composed and resist suggestion. They will also need to know the meaning of sexual terms and behavior (more on this in Chapter 6).

The forensic evaluator must also be aware of other aspects of competence. Although these may not reflect competence in the purely legal sense, they are related to children's developmental level/capacity. One example has to do with sexually aggressive children and adolescents who have a history of sexual abuse and are now offending. This becomes even more important as more states enact "three strikes" rules, and every "offense" begins to count toward that allotment of three.

For example, I evaluated an adolescent in a residential treatment program for juvenile sexual offenders. He molested a child while on leave from the facility. In addition, while on leave he had sexually touched an animal. Technically speaking, this left him with three offenses in his state, the first that brought him into the facility, and now these other two. It was critical that I understand his offenses, his frame of mind, the influence of prior victimization, and also his developmental level. I also had to appreciate the enormous difficulty in making accurate predictions about the future behavior of teenagers and inform the court that "three strikes" rules for adolescents have less support than they do for adults.

## DETERMINING OVERALL ADJUSTMENT

It is important to know a child's psychological adjustment. Since the severity of sexual abuse varies from one child to the next, it is reasonable that the psychological functioning of sexually abused children varies as well. In fact, the severity of sexual abuse is only one predictor, and often a lesser predictor, of a child's current functioning (Friedrich, 1988). There are typically two reasons why you want to know how well the child is doing: to determine whether formal intervention is needed, and if so for how long; to provide input to a civil lawsuit where the victim is suing for damages.

Determining the abused child's level of psychosocial adjustment is not an easy task. Confounds are introduced by the parents, the child victim, and the measurement tools and evaluative process itself. These will be addressed briefly below, and numerous examples of how these difficulties affect the assessment process will be provided in the text of the book.

Natural parents are typically and appropriately included in the evaluation of a sexually abused child. There are exceptions, and these are cases where the parent is clearly biased or cannot be contacted. In these cases, the foster or adoptive parent provides parental input. Parents need to be accurate observers and unbiased about their child's behavior for their information to be most useful (Everson et al., 1989). However, the parents of sexually abused children are often poor observers of their child. This is particularly true in those cases where the abuse has gone on for a long period of time, where the parents have their own psychological problems, they received inadequate parenting themselves, or where incest has occurred. Each of these scenarios suggests that parental bias is operative. Research shows that parents who are depressed report more symptoms in their child than teachers (Boyle & Pickles, 1997), and parents of aggressive children show bias in their reports as well (Patterson, 1982).

Parental bias shows up in both the over- and underreporting of symptoms. Incest will persist due in part to parental inattention. This parental inattention may be manifested in parents' underreporting of their children's behavior to you. Parents may also have reason to report that children are doing better than they actually are doing. If the abuse is incestuous, parents may be protecting a family member or protecting themselves from an overload of shame.

Parents seem to have even more problems objectively reporting sexual behavior in their child. I had an introduction to these blinders when I was first developing the Child Sexual Behavior Inventory (CSBI; Friedrich, 1997). Parents frequently did not notice overt sexual behavior I saw in my office. For example, a 7-year-old girl touched me numerous times during our first session, stood too close to me, and seemed at least one other time to be masturbating over her clothing. However, her biological mother endorsed none of these behaviors on the CSBI. After interviewing the mother, I came to believe that she was not deliberately misrepresenting her daughter. Rather, she was a very poor observer who did not have a reference for what was and was not appropriate. This poor observation was directly related to her daughter's prolonged victimization.

Research on behavior problems in sexually abused children typically notes a substantial percentage of children (30%-50%) who are not exhibiting a level of behavior problems that warrants clinical attention; that is, they are asymptomatic (Kendall-Tackett et al., 1993). The frequency of asymptomatic children is typically derived from research that relied on a single source for information regarding children's level of functioning. Most often, this was parent report. Whether this percentage of asymptomatic children is valid has never been studied in a systematic fashion utilizing multiple sources of input (asymptomatic children are reviewed in more detail in Chapter 3).

The little research that has utilized multiple reporters with sexually abused children illustrates that different assessment procedures reveal different percentages of asymptomatic children. This same research also indicates that parent- and child report can show minimal overlap (Shapiro, Leifer, Martone, & Kassem, 1990). Although all of these dilemmas add to the complexity of the evaluation process, children and their parents are served best when many sources of information are utilized.

Inaccurate data do not come only from parents of the sexually abused child. Evaluation typically obtains information from the child. The child is asked how she is feeling, as well as other questions about her activities and circle of friends. However, maltreated children are less able to describe their internal feelings than children who grow up feeling securely attached to their parents (Toth, Cicchetti, Macfie, & Emde, 1997). Some maltreated children not only learn to inhibit negative affect but also learn how to display false-positive affect (Crittenden & DiLalla, 1988) and report firmly held but completely false beliefs (Crittenden, 1995). These expressions of positive feelings are not reflections of how the child actually feels; rather, they are indicative of a false self (Winnicott, 1965).

Other research has found evidence of distortions in self-representations in sexually abused girls (Calverly, Fischer, & Ayoub, 1994). Calverly and colleagues' data found these girls to be inaccurate in their estimations of both self and others. Another example of this distortion is in British data on sexually abused children in foster care (Farmer & Pollock, 1998). Though you would expect their sense of self to be impaired, none of these children were in the problematic range on a measure of self-esteem. This is hardly because they were feeling so positive about themselves.

When children with PTSD are interviewed, their avoidant symptoms contribute to their denial of subjective distress. They will steer clear of any reminder of their trauma. All of these features make it likely that relying simply on self-report of the maltreated child or teen will result in distorted reports, often underreports of symptoms.

The measures used may also contribute to misperception about the child's status. Abuse-related evaluations that do not rely, at least in part, on abuse-specific symptoms or assessment procedures are not sufficient (Briere, 1997). Sexually abused children often avoid thinking about their distress and are overly compliant. It troubles me when the author of a report concludes that the child reports positive self-esteem but never reviews the reasons the child may not be able to report accurately. Children are likely to report their self-efficacy honestly if they grow up in families where they learn to talk about how they feel and are rewarded for being honest about their concerns. But a feelings-friendly environment is not the typical experience of maltreated children. In fact, severely abused children who report that they think positively of themselves are probably broadcasting to you that they either don't trust the outcome of the evaluation or use denial and/or rationalization as a primary defense.

## WHAT TYPE OF INTERVENTIONS ARE NEEDED?

I think every child who has been maltreated needs an opportunity to hear developmentally sensitive corrective and supportive feedback from concerned adults. Ideally, this can come from parents and, where appropriate, mental health professionals.

However, this type of feedback may never occur, or else be too brief. Sometimes there are good reasons for its brevity. For example, an evaluation may find that what the child needs most at this time are assurances of safety and increased availability of parental support. The concerned questioning and subsequent assurances that the child receives in the evaluation process may be sufficient at the time. Natural therapy does occur in many families, and its quality may be just what is needed (Kegan, 1982). There are no data that say that every abused child needs extensive therapy.

The questions that may be answered with a careful evaluation include the child's need for therapy; the length and focus of therapy; who should be involved and in what combinations; the mode of therapy; and the degree to which the child may need structured, trauma-specific therapy. The model of assessment presented in the next chapter is based on my belief that therapy for victims of sexual abuse involves several components. These are a combination of parent-child therapy to address their combined relational issues, abuse-specific intervention to aid all parties in learning how to deal with the traumatic sequelae, initiating steps to resolve the victim's self-perceptions vis-à-vis the maltreatment, and prevention of further abuse.

Each of the above treatment components will vary in its primacy and also in how difficult it is to address. A number of processes are influential, including the psychological health and support of the parent, the child's ability to talk without feeling internally or externally punished by the process, and the family's capacity to create a safe environment.

We have all seen situations in which the family is unsafe, parenting is inconsistent, parents do not see the need for treatment, and children feel disloyal if they talk about the abuse. Victims from these families come to you with very few resources.

If I were dealing with such a situation, I would not expand my focus. First, I'd try to enlist the parent as an ally in the child's treatment. If this failed, I'd enlist the support of protective services for the therapy. I would rather begin my therapy from an enlightened perspective than have an initial session with the child that goes nowhere and results in my never seeing the child again.

Assessment can determine the most appropriate modality. If children are poorly socialized, we might believe that they would benefit from group therapy. This is made even more of an automatic decision if group therapy is the primary intervention available at your agency.

However, group treatment is not the most appropriate modality for all victims. Inappropriately putting a child into a therapy group may impede the progress of the other children (Friedrich, 1995a). Groups for children must be composed primarily of children with reasonably appropriate social skills. Children who benefit from group are reasonably socialized, not overly reactive to other children's issues and histories, and able to control their anger. The last thing we would wish is for the group treatment to become one more maltreatment experience.

Assessment can identify the reasons why some children are very well defended. These children send messages that they do not need therapy or at best are ambivalent about therapy. They deny problems, they offer little in the way of conversation, and they quickly exit your schedule. It is important to know whether they are avoiding assistance because they truly are doing well or because there are individual and/or family contributors to their silence. This knowledge can guide your efforts to obtain family support so that these children can be more free to talk about what is important or to prepare a teenager for therapy that is more inviting and not overwhelming.

Therapy does not occur only in your office or via in-home counseling. One of the most important benefits I can provide some children is enhancing the type and range of supportive services they receive in the school setting. Maltreated children are more likely to have academic problems (Einbender & Friedrich, 1989; Erickson & Egeland, 1987). Evaluating the academic problems of a quiet female victim who is depressed and/or learning disabled can result in the provision of important school-based services. This assistance may open up a greater future for the child than what is provided in several supportive sessions. It is not likely that school personnel would have noticed her, since she was not a problem. However, she is in your office, and you realize she's struggling to read the self-report depression measure you are asking her to complete. As her therapist, you must find out if she is getting help for her reading. If she is not, you need to find a mechanism to help bring this about.

Your evaluation may have implications for other forms of intervention. These include the provision of protective supervision, such as supervised contact, to vulnerable children. Extremely reactive children will challenge any parent and make it harder for the parent to be supportive. It might be important to recommend no contact with the father until his therapist has reported treatment progress so that the child's reactivity is reduced.

Now imagine how much stronger and more valid your recommendation for no contact is if you ground the recommendation in a more formal assessment process. For example, you combine information about the precarious parent-child relationship with the victim's reactivity at home and school as assessed by teacher and day care provider ratings, and then argue that the offending father not have contact with his nonvictim children. This is far more compelling than a therapist's letter that is not supported by assessment data.

## TREATMENT PLANNING

In the section above, I outlined the typical foci of therapy with sexually abused children: Stabilize the parent-child relationship, address the traumatic aspects of the abuse, help children think of themselves and the abuse experience more accurately, and prevent further abuse. Assessment must be directly applicable to the treatment of the child. If we cannot provide guidance to therapy, the evaluation task is not useful (Hall, 1993).

Evaluation can identify a range of treatment needs, many of which are associated with a specific treatment modality. Sexual behavior is an excellent example. Because this is a common symptom, it needs to be assessed as part of any valid assessment. If present in one or more settings, then a behavioral plan that targets the behavior(s) can be put into place (Friedrich, 1990). Ideally, your assessment has also determined the capability of each setting to follow through with the behavior modification; for example, the parents' capacity to be consistent and affirming. It is very important to intervene quickly in the child's aberrant behavior patterns, since inappropriate sexual behavior can interfere with peer relations, affect the ability of adults to be positive, contribute to further victimization, and impact the child's future sexuality. Your assessment can also help to direct the degree to which children have both the capacity and the need to debate verbally about their sexual behavior, since some discussion about the behavior and why it is present is also important to treatment.

Hyperarousal and reexperiencing can also be addressed via cognitive-behavioral interventions, and in fact there are good data that this is also true for sexually abused children (Berliner & Saunders, 1996; Deblinger, Lippman, & Steer, 1996). Consequently, it is very important to determine to what degree these issues affect the child. This can be done via careful questioning or as part of a more formal evaluation.

Throughout this book, there are many references made to the simultaneous assessment of the parents of the children or teenagers you are evaluating. I believe that in many cases, significant parental issues need to be addressed in the treatment process so that intervention efforts with the child victim can be maximally effective. There are many times when treatment planning definitely is helped by some assessment of the parents as well.

## DETERMINING TREATMENT OUTCOME

There are many reasons why we want to know if children are benefiting from therapy. These kinds of variables can affect reunification planning, when to end treatment, whether or not to drop the protective services petition, and so on. Clearly, it is important to know whether the therapy is helping the child's symptoms.

At this nascent stage of knowledge regarding what is effective therapy for traumatized children, almost any outcome study that utilizes clearly defined approaches and a comparison group can add to our knowledge and guide future treatments. If you are certain that play therapy can be helpful and you want to be reimbursed for this in the future, then it would be helpful to establish that fact more fully than is currently done (Reams & Friedrich, 1994).

In this book, I will identify a range of assessment measures that not only can introduce the child to treatment, for example, asking relevant questions, but also can be used to determine whether the child is being helped and, if so, by what means. The combination of treatment and evaluation integrates in a wonderful manner the best work we can do as helping professionals. I will describe a number of assessment strategies that will be very complex and that are not necessary for the average child who uses the services of your clinic. However, I will also outline briefer compilations of measures that have some genuine clinical returns to you as a treatment professional (see Chapter 8 in particular).

For example, you could quickly assess the child's level of behavioral disturbance with a parent rating scale (CBCL, Achenbach, 1991a; CSBI, Friedrich, 1997). If you take an ecological view, you can also inquire about conflict (Conflict Tactics Scale; Straus, Hamby, Finkelhor, Moore, & Runyan, 1998) and safety in the home (Safety Checklist; Friedrich, 1996c). To be even more complete, you can directly ask children or teens about their own symptoms. By asking children directly about abuse-related feelings at the very beginning of treatment—for example, the items from the Children's Impact of Traumatic Events Scale (CITES-R; Wolfe, Gentile, Michienzi, Sas, & Wolfe, 1991) or the Trauma Symptom Checklist for Children (TSCC; Briere, 1996)—you are setting the stage for more successful therapy. What I mean by this statement is that you have exposed the child to the words and concepts used in treatment. She has been given a start in thinking about these important emotions and thoughts. Her answers can then be used to guide some of the content of early sessions.

## ❑ Guidelines for a Valid Evaluation

Because of my training as a clinical psychologist, the evaluation process that I describe in this book is reflective of my training in psychological assessment. I cannot teach this form of evaluation to the reader of this book. It is something that can be learned only with advanced training and supervised experiences. I will introduce a number of psychological tests, and users may be qualified to use some or all of them, depending on their training. I believe there is much utility in psychological testing, and the use of selected results can be very helpful for both planning and evaluating treatment. However, testing differs from psychological assessment. In assessment, the clinician's focus is not on obtaining a single test score or even a series of scores. Rather, the focus is on taking a variety of test-derived pieces of information obtained from multiple methods of assessment, and placing the data in the context of historical information, referral information, and behavioral observations made during the testing and interview process. This enables the psychologist to generate a cohesive and comprehensive understanding of the person being evaluated. The clinician must then communicate this understanding to the patient, the patient's significant others, and referral sources in a frank but interpersonally sensitive and therapeutic manner (Eisman et al., 2000). The key to successful psychological assessment is the knowledge, ability, and experience of the psychologist to integrate multiple sources of data to reach a professional judgment about the individual (Anastasi & Urbina, 1996).

Although interviews and observations can be efficient and generally effective ways to obtain information, there are limitations to this method of data gathering. When interviews are unstructured, it becomes easy for the clinician to overlook important areas of functioning and focus only on the presenting complaint. The patient is often a poor historian and interviews obtain biased data.

The evaluation of children and teenagers who have been sexually abused can be enormously assisted by psychological evaluations for a number of reasons. The confusion surrounding a case, the guardedness of the informants, and the need to be sensitive to forensic issues all combine to justify psychological evaluations. These evaluations usually assess a wide range of functional domains. They provide empirically quantified information, and tests are administered and scored in a standardized fashion. You are in a position to observe behaviors in a uniform context. Because the tests are normed, there is usually history that supports the utility of particular test scales apart from other clinical information (Eisman et al., 2000).

Some clinicians are unaware of their own stimulus value and fail to realize how they affect children. But when a child rests her or his shoe on yours during the administration of the WISC-III and displays other boundary problems in a setting that never pulls for this type of behavior, the clinical information derived is much more valid than data obtained in an unstructured play interview. The child's behavior in these more structured settings can be noted on the Evaluator Rating Scale (see Appendix K for a copy of the scale).

## IMPORTANT FORENSIC ISSUES

A careful review of the chapter on expert testimony in John Myers's (1998) excellent book on legal issues relevant to child maltreatment is a must for those evaluators who provide expert testimony. Guidelines published by the American Academy of Child and Adolescent Psychiatry (AACAP) outline a number of important forensic issues that all evaluators must be aware of (AACAP, 1997). Even if your assessment is solely to guide therapy and is technically not forensic, the above guidelines are very important nonetheless. I will list them first and then briefly define each one. They are role definition, clear communication, confidentiality, privilege, the problem of bias, awareness of limitations, degrees of certainty, and knowledge of the law.

Regarding role definition, it is important to reiterate that the child's therapist is preferably not the individual completing the forensic evaluation. The evaluator must have a clear understanding of what is expected. She must be willing to testify in court. All parties must have a clear awareness that this is an evaluation, not therapy, and is being done at the request of a specific agency or person. Parents and children need to know that the evaluation is not confidential but will be released to the court as well as to other mandated agencies and persons. Privilege is a special form of confidentiality, but in forensic cases the court can order the clinician to testify despite objections by the patient.

Bias affects the evaluator's perspective in two critical ways in forensic cases. First, it can create a distorted filter through which the clinician views the data. Second, the clinician may lack the capacity to be objective and therefore treat a forensic case as a therapy case. Extra caution needs to be used to guard against bias. For example, the evaluator may need to discuss the case with a colleague, indicate reasons for the conclusion in the report, and preserve the raw data so that another person can review it. Sometimes bias affects evaluators' abilities to appreciate the limitations of their expertise. The fact that clinicians can arrive at widely divergent opinions about sexual abuse cases is well documented (Horner, Guyer, & Kalter, 1993). The emotionality around these cases can also blind persons to the limitations of their role.

The last two forensic issues reflect the need to understand key aspects of the law. For example, *degrees of certainty* addresses the proof that must be established. Civil cases require the "preponderance of the evidence," whereas criminal cases require proof that is "beyond a reasonable doubt." Physicians and mental health professionals are often asked whether their opinions are given with "a reasonable degree of medical certainty," which has been defined as the level of certainty a physician uses when making a diagnosis and starting treatment. Finally, the evaluator needs to hear from the attorney the legal issue that is the original basis for the evaluation.

The guidelines listed below are related to the issues outlined above but are more generic and applicable to clinical assessment.

## CLEAR PURPOSE

The disorganized and chaotic life of maltreating families and the often muddled organizational system of those agencies working with maltreatment can create a vortex that will pull the evaluator in and spit her out as a befuddled clinician. That is an inevitable result unless you have a clear purpose to your evaluation and permission has been granted to proceed in a logical and organized manner.

A few examples can be helpful here. I occasionally am ordered by a court to complete a personality evaluation of a set of parents involved with a child and then find out that they are separated and someone else is doing the custody evaluation. When I ask how we are to work together, I am assured that I am to determine only a parent's potential to reabuse. I am further told that I won't be called on to render an opinion about the person's competence as custodial parent unless I uncover some data that illuminate the custody issue.

However, the likelihood of my uncovering something relevant is inevitable. A personality evaluation of a parent must be validated by data on how the parent behaves with his or her child(ren). The evaluator needs to be clarifying and delineating who, what, where, and what for, from the moment the referral source places the first call.

Another situation that can be quite muddy pertains to a parent who has performed poorly in the reunification process with her maltreated children. The caseworker is now asking whether the children should go home. The experienced evaluator knows that these kinds of questions have direct implications for permanency planning, including the possible termination of parental rights. This is likely to be the most important question that is ever asked. It is important to clarify what efforts at rehabilitation have been tried, as well as the unique issues of the children in question.

A related question has to do with the resumption of visits with the offending parent or parents. This is a very tough question to answer if you were not involved in the initial assessment and are unaware of possible progress. Like the issues involved in the other questions above, it could have been clarified if you had been involved from the beginning in shaping the case plan and lending some expertise to what can and cannot be expected of an evaluation. This suggests that it behooves many forensic evaluators to maintain a close but independent working relationship with the county social service agencies that are more closely involved with the families.

## USE MANY INFORMANTS

As if these evaluations were not complex enough, given the scant literature on predicting success in parenting and therapy in cases of sexual abuse, I am suggesting that there are cases where you should make the process even more complex. To evaluate complex cases successfully, your assessments cannot be limited to the individual party who is referred. If it is a teenager who is failing an adoption because of repeated running away, it is important to evaluate the adoptive parents and to speak to the adoption worker and personnel at the shelter where she is currently residing. Is the biological parent still in the picture? This additional information allows you to arrive at a reasoned explanation for why the adoption is unraveling and to identify the changes needed in both the teen and the adoptive parents for the adoption to succeed.

Sexual behavior in young children has clear abuse origins, but it is also influenced in its range and frequency by family factors that are not sexual-abuse specific (Friedrich, 1998). These include family violence, life stress, exposure to adult sexuality, family nudity, and other behavioral difficulties in the child (Friedrich, Fisher, et al., 2001). The assessment of a highly sexualized child will necessitate the gathering of information from all caregivers who have contact with this child. The differing information they provide will allow a valid opinion about the origins of the behavior and the need for intervention. These include the child's parents, teachers, and day care providers, as well as the child.

Children and teenagers are in school or day care. This is an important arena of their life, and every effort should be made to gather information that is relevant and still respects children's privacy.

Evaluations also rely on several sources of information. To be complete, the information assembled should include the developmental *history* of the child and the parent-child relationship, *interviews* with appropriate parties, and the utilization of normed measures and *tests*. This spells out the acronym HIT, borrowed from Meloy and Lewak (1998).

## FOCUS ON COMPETENCE

I appreciate the developmental psychopathology framework on which this book is built for many reasons. It is elegant and developmentally sensitive. It also routinely focuses on the competency-related aspects of individual behavior, including resilience.

For example, Main (1995) writes that the anxious attachment patterns (defended, coercive) are "strategies for maintaining self-organization" (p. 409) and creatively maintaining proximity to an inconstant caregiver. This is more useful than thinking about the child's behavior in pathological terms. One of the variations of defended attachment (caregiving) is certainly an adaptive (in the short run) strategy to organize a child's behavior. Crittenden (1995) reports that this pattern stabilizes children's relationship with their parent(s) and meets some relational needs as well.

However, a simple focus on competence becomes insufficient in cases where objective statements of pathology are needed, for example, when there is the risk of an older sibling molesting a vulnerable child in a home with inadequate supervision. In this time, when social services focus on family reunification—sometimes at any cost—an objective psychological evaluation that states the risk clearly may be even more essential to the protection of children.

## EVALUATIONS MUST BE ABUSE SPECIFIC AND RELATIONAL

The reader will hear a mantra many times before the end of the book. It goes as follows: An evaluation of a maltreated child that does not assess sexual behavior, PTSD, family safety, abuse history in the parents' background, and maltreatment potential in the parents is insufficient. The influence of parental behavior, such as agitation or unavailability related to unresolved trauma, on the security of a child's attachment has been documented (Main, 1995). Knowing whether the parent is struggling with unresolved abuse, which typically can be addressed, is very important to formulating an opinion about the viability of the parent-child relationship.

This leads to the other component of this section: Valid evaluations must examine the parent-child relationship. Knowing something about children's comfort with disclosure in their family will allow you to understand the meaning of one child's surprisingly low score on a self-report measure of distress. You may determine that the low score reflects the child's lifelong experience with unavailable caregiving. Why should the child, at this time and with a relative stranger, choose to be open and bare his or her soul and tell you the pain being experienced? You can put this in context only if you understand the parent-child relationship, a key aspect of all maltreatment evaluations.

## AVOID SIMPLE ANSWERS

Evaluators need to avoid providing simple answers to complex situations. This does not mean that they should avoid giving an answer, particularly if it can lead to a needed intervention, provisions of safety, or stability of a child. Rather, answers need to reflect children's individuality and their context. Questions about a child's functioning cannot be answered unless you also know the psychological resources of the parents. Simple answers often beg the question and fail to appreciate the complexity of children and their families.

## TOTAL SCORES DO NOT EQUAL DIAGNOSIS

Many screening measures are presented in this text. Many of the symptom clusters that children are struggling with are effectively evaluated by having the parent or the child complete behavioral ratings. However, the evaluator must resist the pull to overinterpret a single test score rather than place it in the larger context.

For example, a teenager completed a Beck Depression Inventory (BDI) during a recent evaluation. The total score was suggestive of very severe depression. However, this girl was primarily angry at her mother and intent on sending a message to anyone who would listen that her mother had failed as a parent. It was more therapeutic to return to the focus of her anger.

It is important that simply because children are significantly elevated on a certain scale, they are not necessarily diagnosable. Ratings plus follow-up interviews along with integration of these findings into a meaningful whole make the most valid assessment.

The evaluator must never lose track of the base-rate phenomenon (Melton & Limber, 1989). The behaviors associated with sexual abuse, with almost no exception, are also identified quite commonly in the general population and even more often in samples of troubled but not sexually abused children. A child's sleep problems or difficulty performing may be due more to chaotic family functioning than to one act of sexual abuse.

Dissociation is a symptom that is quite difficult to determine (see Chapter 5). Let's suggest that you are asked to determine if a sexually abused child is dissociative. The given reports are that the child exhibits two behaviors—memory gaps and sudden changes in mood and affect. Both of these are part of a dissociative diagnosis. However, both of these symptoms have a base rate, either separately or together, that is higher than the base rate of dissociation in children. This fact alone would suggest that a more parsimonious explanation might be in order for the child's symptoms.

## ASSESSMENT MUST BE RESPECTFUL

The evaluation process may be the child's and/or parents' first meeting ever with a mental health professional. I try to maintain this perspective in all my dealings with individuals I assess. I must appreciate that they may be talking about painful aspects of their lives for the first time. Although it is important not to merge the evaluator and therapist roles, you are not precluded from being respectful and attentive.

Each request we make of someone to answer questions, fill out forms, or take tests places a demand on a system that may have a short supply of emotional energy. Families may feel overwhelmed unless the clinician judiciously picks only those areas that are particularly relevant to understanding and treatment planning.

Sometimes you can communicate your understanding to the family that this is an arduous task by administering questionnaires over time. I also try to give direct and sympathetic feedback to all those I assess. Sometimes this is done with a final meeting or with a conjoint meeting with a therapist.

## ❑  The Process of Interpretation

A few comments to guide the integration and interpretation of disparate data sources are needed. It helps the process to begin with several themes that organize your interpretation. One theme might be validity of the test and interview data. Another could be nature of impact, while a third could be moderators of impact. A final theme focuses on the practicality of the evaluation or treatment specificity.

Validity is affected by several factors that come from the child, for example, developmental level, ability to self-report, support to disclose; from the parent, such as divided loyalties, unresolved issues, psychological mindedness; and from the context, for example, legal implications and competing alliances. A child or parent may minimize or exaggerate symptoms because of some combination of the above, but the evaluator should consider all of them as possibly operative.

We are still unsure how closely related the nature of the abuse is to the outcome of the child (Fergusson & Mullen, 1999). It helps to think about the abuse in terms of dose response in the context of both abuse-specific, PTSD, sexual behavior, and generic outcomes. However, it is very important to have a clear knowledge about the prevalence of generic symptoms in the population of children and teens so that long-standing attention problems do not suddenly become part of the abuse response. Moderators also have a variable relationship with outcome, but support of the child, safety in the home, the absence of other maltreatment, age-appropriate development, and secure attachment all buffer the child.

Several considerations about therapy guide me as I look at the evaluation data. A primary one pertains to the ability of the child to be supported, as well as the presence of some specific symptoms that can be targeted. I also think about the child's use of language and how that might help or hinder therapy. I also know that enhancing the parent-child relationship and having a sensitive but abuse-specific focus will serve the child best. Consequently, my next concerns deal with what parts of an ideal treatment plan the family can absorb and use.

In complex evaluations, there can be several hundred bits of information that need to be integrated and examined for consistency. To help me in this process, I have expanded on a worksheet developed by Beutler and Berren (1995) to integrate the findings of the evaluation. This allows me to examine what a range of interviews and measures indicates about key topics that are of typical concern in the assessment of sexual abuse impact.

At least 10 domains of patient functioning are assessed. These are arranged on the left side of the sheet; they are approach to task, reliability/validity of report, support of the child, accurate perception of the child's symptoms, abuse-specific symptoms (with specific categories for PTSD and sexual behavior), generic symptoms, moderators of impact, family safety, capacity for therapy, and treatment foci. The procedures are then entered across the top of the page; they reflect interviews, developmental assessment, self-reports, behavior ratings, and projectives.

I then have a simple method to examine for the consistency of a specific domain. For example, I might note sexualized behavior on the CSBI from the foster mother but not the biological mother, in the child's responses to the Roberts Apperception Test, and in the child's boundary problems with me as rated by the Evaluator Rating Scale (Appendix K). Obviously, the results on this domain would cause me to question the validity of the biological mother's report, as well as her capacity both to support the child and to perceive him accurately. A clear advantage of this method, over and above the organization of complex data and the opportunity to give it the time it deserves, is that internal consistency is more readily apparent.

## ❑  Summary

Psychological evaluation of the maltreated child and related family members allows for a careful consideration of the child and the circumstances that necessitated the referral, as well as the family in which the child lives. Whether the evaluation consists of interviews on the child's behavior and the quality of caregiving, or whether the evaluation relies on a combination of more and less formal approaches, including psychological tests and scales, assessment is the most appropriate entry into treatment for children and teenagers with a maltreatment history. These are complex cases, and valid and systematic assessment can help the therapist proceed in a more informed and appropriate manner.

Many times, the data from the evaluation will make their way into court, and clinicians need to be aware of the legal issues surrounding the case, their ability to testify, and also the bias they bring to such matters. Practicing in a structured and scientific manner and adhering to the standards of proof that are needed are essential aspects of the process.

At the same time, evaluators must appreciate that the best needs of the child are another important issue before them. Assessment can provide critical information about treatment and how to proceed in therapy. Should you support the child? Focus the treatment on the trauma? Should the treatment focus be on the child or the parent? A thorough and informed assessment can answer these questions. The examples throughout the text will illuminate more clearly the contribution to treatment from assessment.

# 2

# *Theoretical Framework for Assessment*

The mechanisms by which maltreatment produces pathology in the victim are not well understood. One common perspective is in terms of regression or fixation (Freud, 1966). This assumes that the trauma so derails the developmental course that the child is forever at some earlier stage of development. In fact, we have all heard people say something like, "Isn't he stuck at about 2 years old?"

However, fixation fails to appreciate the fact that the child is always developing. It is not as helpful or accurate a perception as one that views pathology as involving development along an unusual or atypical pathway, rather than as the child persisting in functioning at a primitive level. Maladaptation needs to be viewed as development rather than as disease (Sroufe, 1997). Maltreatment can shift a child from a more normative path onto one that is less adaptive, but development will still occur (Cicchetti & Toth, 1995).

It is impossible to write about the adjustment of children and adolescents without also describing their development, which is a process embedded in a family context. An approach that combines development as well as systems theory can be applied to all aspects of their behavior, including psychopathological behavior. "Development can be conceived of as a series of qualitative reorganizations among and within behavioral systems, which occur through the processes of differentiation and hierarchical integration" (Cicchetti, 1989, p. 379). The various behavioral systems that are operative include interlocking social, emotional, cognitive, and social-cognitive domains. Biological systems are also implicated in the process of development (Schore, 1994). Because this process involves the incorporation of prior patterns of functioning into subsequent reorganizations, continuity of functioning is maintained.

This is a different conceptualization than a deficit or medical model. A deficit model adheres to the belief that some flaw in the child is responsible for the behavior, and little consideration is given to input from the context or developmental processes. In a medical model, pathways to the etiology of behavior problems are assumed to lie primarily in neurophysiological pathology. With the tremendous recent focus on how stress alters neurophysiological processes, there is an even greater push to think primarily in terms of biologically based deficits, with the logical extension being biological therapy (Schore, 1997).

A perspective that emphasizes neurophysiology is both reductionistic and incorrect. Adhering to a deficit model suddenly simplifies a problem that must be viewed as complex. Evaluators must see the big picture if they are to work with the consequences of maltreatment. If one thinks in the developmental model, children and their contexts are inseparable. To paraphrase Winnicott (1965), there is no such thing as an infant, only an infant and its mother. Behavior is not solely an expression of some genetic or internal process. Normality and disturbance are similar in that both are products of a succession of context-influenced adaptations over time.

Various factors influence the course of children's development, either protecting them from deviation from the normal developmental course or potentiating their momentary or longer-term derailment from the developmental process. In fact, it is the unique combination of risk and protective factors that governs the emergence of maladaptation (Sroufe, 1997). This is particularly germane to the evaluation of the impact of sexual abuse. Sexual abuse is only one factor in a child's life, and all of the other aspects of the child's context need to be considered to identify the child's true level of functioning and potential for correcting his or her developmental path.

**Protective factors** decrease the risk of maltreatment or its transmission across generations. These include the following: a parent's history of good parenting, marital satisfaction, support network, adequate income, and problem-solving skills. **Potentiating factors** include medical problems in the child that make parenting unrewarding, parental history of maltreatment, poor frustration tolerance in the child or parent, chaotic/violent neighborhoods, and high stress levels (Cicchetti & Olsen, 1990). Some of these factors have been quantified into the Risk Factor Checklist (expanded from an article by David Jones, 1987, on the issue of untreatable families). This checklist provides a simple guide to the evaluator of risk factors that have been empirically related to poor outcome (see Appendix I).

Incorporating protective and potentiating factors into a model of development results in a transactional risk model that can be used to direct intervention with maltreating families (Kolko, 1996). This model can also be used to guide the evaluation process. Because the members of the child's system—parent, school, social environment—are interlocking, intervention in only one component is not as useful. Interventions must be multisystemic. A recent study of risk factors found that disruptive behavior at age 5 was predicted by the risk factors of disorganized attachment, maternal personality risk, and child-rearing disagreements (Shaw, Owens, Vondra, & Keenan, 1996).

From this developmental psychopathology framework come three domains of child functioning that I believe are critical to successful treatment (Friedrich, 1994, 1995a). These same domains are essential to an integrated assessment process. They are parent-child attachment, self-regulation, and self-development. These three domains are not only developmental; they also tap the various interlocking competencies outlined by Cicchetti (1989). Each of these will be briefly reviewed in the following sections. A more thorough review of these factors, with treatment suggestions for each, can be found in Friedrich (1995a).

❏  **Attachment**

The concept of attachment is a central element in many contemporary theories of child psychopathology and child treatment. Although originally developed and expanded with infants and toddlers, research has demonstrated its applicability as a construct across the life span (Crittenden, 1995). For example, children's prosocial inclinations are governed primarily by the quality of their relationships with their parents (Main, 1995), and romantic love in young adults also has origins in attachment history (Hazan & Shaver, 1987). This has implications for the emergence of peer relations, aggression, and the formation of social skills.

Attachment theory defines children's relationships with their parents as a biologically based bond, an instinctual connection. It first emerges because of a need to maintain proximity with a caregiver or a secure base (Bowlby, 1969). Ainsworth (1985) originally framed attachment as evidenced in patterns of behavior, but Crittenden (1995) has expanded this perception. She views attachment behavior as reflecting the utilization of an information processing style where the evaluation and integration of relational data can occur in either an accurate or a biased manner.

Although instinctual, the various permutations in attachment behavior become learned as a result of interactions with caregivers (Crittenden, 1995). Attachment behavior is most apparent in young children who are distressed, but it is integral to reciprocal and mutual relationships between parent and child across the life span. Over time, children's behavior toward their parents becomes internalized into mental frameworks called internal working models. Children in consistent and supportive relationships will develop a core self that views their self and others positively. As teenagers, they learn to integrate disparate relationships via a clearly established sense of self in relationships. Assessing these internal representations can give the clinician insight into the child's perception of the parent as available or not. Early experiences with the attachment figure allow the child to develop expectations about the behavior of his or her parents, as well as the nature of other relationship roles.

A fundamental conflict for children in abusive relationships is between the child's attachment to the caregiver, on the one hand, and the experience of that caregiver as abusive and uncaring, on the other (Finkelhor & Browne, 1985). This creates an internal conflict that is often impossible to integrate into a coherent internal working model. Research indicates that children in this dilemma learn to split themselves along emotional lines. They react in terms of the affective quality established by the adults with whom they are interacting (Calverly, Fischer, & Ayoub, 1994).

It follows naturally that since parental caregiving can vary from sensitive and skilled to insensitive and unskilled, attachment outcomes can also be quite varied. In fact, children's attachment behavior sorts into at least four broad categories: secure, insecure-coercive, insecure-defended, and insecure-disorganized (Crittenden, 1995). Further subdivisions of each of these four categories have been reported. For example, within the coercive type of insecure attachment, Crittenden (1995) suggests several subtypes, including threatening/disarming, aggressive/helpless, and punitive/seductive.

## SECURE ATTACHMENT

Secure attachment is the most optimal. Children who are securely attached have an internal working model of caregivers as consistent, supportive in times of stress, attuned to their needs, committed to the relationship, and reciprocal to the children. These children have the initiative to connect with supportive adults and accept the challenges of living.

## INSECURE ATTACHMENT

There are three types of insecure attachment—resistant/coercive, avoidant/defended, and disorganized (Main, 1995). Insecurely attached children operate from the assumption that different levels of unpredictability and unavailability, as well as reduced reciprocity and commitment, characterize interpersonal relationships. For example, they may have learned that punitiveness characterizes the parent-child interaction. The strategies the child has developed are quite adaptive and make the best of a painful parent-child relationship. For example, it is good reality testing for a child to be overly solicitous and compliant if that maximizes security in the face of minimal parental availability.

A defended or avoidantly attached child has learned that interactions with parents are consistently aversive. Infants who are labeled as avoidant by one year of age have typically experienced maternal rejection when they exhibited a desire for closeness (Ainsworth, 1979). This rejection may be overt or may result from withdrawn and unresponsive behavior on the part of the caregiver (Erickson, Sroufe, & Egeland, 1985). Such children have learned that if they protest the rejection or lack of nurturance, they may experience maternal anger or further withdrawal. As a result, they have learned to inhibit affective displays (Crittenden, 1995). These children often adopt an eventual stance that is self-protective and inhibited. When older, they seem to dismiss the importance of relationships. The avoidant stance keeps them distant from both caregivers and helping professionals. It often makes it hard for them to take the perspective of others, and they can be quite cruel (Cassidy & Shaver, 1999). However, they may also learn how to display false-positive affect, thus making themselves more rewarding and appealing to the withdrawn, downcast caregiver (Crittenden, 1995).

Coercive or resistantly attached children seem to come from families where the caregiving is characterized by intrusiveness and inconsistency. Caregivers often communicate mixed signals to these children, and the children have difficulty learning how to react. This seems to promote the development of anxiety and anger in the context of close relationships (Crittenden, 1995). In essence, children are left without an organizing strategy for how best to succeed in their interactions with caregivers. This is why these children are often called ambivalently attached, since there is an approach-avoidance, or push-pull, quality to some of their interactions. The lack of a consistent strategy for how best to maximize attachment behavior results in these children learning to manipulate their caregivers, for example, with coercive behavior. Crittenden (1995) writes, "the girl learns to display, selectively and in alternation, her anger on the one hand, and her fear and desire for nurturance, on the other" (p. 374). Though resistantly attached children are typically more interested in other people than avoidantly attached children, their interactions with adults are characterized by a range of passive to more actively oppositional features.

The echoes of maltreatment from one generation to another are reflected in disorganized attachment. This category was added only af-

ter the first three had been researched for some time. It was more difficult to recognize since these infants did not demonstrate a coherent attachment strategy. Their behavior was often contradictory and incom-
plete (Main, 1995). More than any of the other types of attachment, this
style reflects the maltreatment history of the parent and is a manifestation of "ghosts in the nursery" (Fraiberg, Adelson, & Shapiro, 1975).
The parent becomes alarming or frightening to the child because the
parent's distress is palpably evident to the permeable infant. The child
is paradoxically frightened by the parent and needful of the parent.

Consequently, the disorganized child's behavior with caregivers is
quite inconsistent and unintegrated (Main, 1995). The child may exhibit simultaneous approach/avoidance, with lapses into stereotyped
and even bizarre interaction, such as momentary "stilling" or freezing
when the caregiver enters the room during the Strange Situation.
Typically, the disorganized type is coded with another attachment
strategy that reflects the more predominant style: disorganized with
avoidant (Main, 1995).

Attachment security has been shown to be directly related to the issue of victimizing behavior in children. Troy and Sroufe (1987) found
that securely attached children were neither victimized by nor victimizing of other children. Avoidantly attached children were most likely
to victimize others, and their targets were most often the resistantly attached children. Teachers have reported that avoidantly attached children were the most likely to make them angry, securely attached children pulled for matter-of-fact treatment, and they treated resistantly
attached children as helpless (Sroufe & Fleeson, 1986).

## ATTACHMENT AS INFORMATION PROCESSING

It is essential to go beyond the four broad patterns of attachment (secure, insecure-defended, insecure-coercive, and insecure-disorganized)
and appreciate the mental representations, or internal working models, that individuals create on the basis of their experience. Crittenden
(1994, 1995) has developed an information-processing model of attachment wherein the child learns to integrate both the affect and the
cognition associated with the parental relationship. This integration
includes the utilization of different memory systems, some of which

are accessed preconsciously. A careful review of her two chapters is recommended to the readers of this book.

Securely attached children have learned that when they feel distress (true affect), this distress is labeled accurately and responded to appropriately (true cognition) by the mother (Crittenden, 1995). A defended child learns that distress does not elicit parental attention (false affect) and learns quite accurately that adults cannot be relied on (true cognition). Consequently, you may have a defended child who exhibits false-positive affect around other people (Fischer et al., 1997). A coercive child learns only unpredictability (false cognition) but feels terribly distressed and agitated when with the caregiver (true affect).

It is in this domain of mental representations that intervention can occur. For example, the parent of a defended child is quite likely to have the same false affect that the child is now developing. One question on the Adult Attachment Interview (AAI; George, Kaplan, & Main, 1985) asks adults to generate five adjectives that describe their parent. Defended adults are likely to give truncated descriptions of their parents that are not directly related to their relationship, for example, "hard-working," "had a lot of hobbies," and so on. These descriptors downplay the emotional distress they may have experienced. They are dismissive of emotional pain, even if that is suggested in a supportive manner by the evaluator.

Knowledge that parents are avoidant can help your therapy. They understand when you preface your comments to them with, "I know that you may wonder why I am making such a fuss about your son's connection with you." By beginning with a validation of their view of relationships, you can help them begin to see how they stay emotionally distant from their child. This may help them arrive at a point where they can describe one or more painful experiences with their own parent. The therapist can then validate this emergence of true affect and help them look for more genuine experiences in their interactions with their child.

Although there is little research on the parent-child interaction of sexually abused children, a recent study found that mothers with a history of incest were more self-focused and relied more on their children for emotional support than a comparison sample (Burkett, 1991). If reinterpreted through the lens of attachment theory, self-focused parents are less available to their child. Parental reliance on the child results in role reversal. The child may learn that interactions with the parent are frustrating, possibly overexciting, and unpredictable.

While early research on attachment has focused on young children, it has been concluded that adults have attachment styles that parallel the styles they had as children and that are related to their child's attachment security. The AAI (George et al., 1985), which was briefly introduced above, is used to inquire of adults their perceptions of their relationship with their parent through the use of a number of open-ended questions. The resulting narratives can be scored and result in the following attachment classifications: secure/autonomous, dismissing, preoccupied, and unresolved/disorganized. These adult attachment classifications depend in part on the coherency and balance of the narratives they provide on the AAI. For example, brief and unelaborated narratives—"my mom was a good person, end of discussion" —are seen as reflective of a dismissing type of attachment in the adult. This reflects a history of insecure attachment and is now seen in compromised parenting with the child in question.

## ATTACHMENT AND MALTREATMENT

Alexander (1992) has summarized the attachment difficulties in maltreating families into three themes: rejection, role reversal, and the multigenerational transmission of unresolved trauma. These are clinically relevant, since they can be used as a guide for interviewing the parents of molested children and teens. The clinician needs to inquire about aspects of the child that the parent dislikes, even hates, along with whether the parent relies on the child for emotional or relational/sexual gratification. Lastly, knowledge about the parents' own abuse history, and whether they have taken steps to resolve it, will be critical to the treatment and will inform prognosis.

The role of attachment and the necessity of its careful assessment are illustrated quite clearly in an abundance of research on the effects of maltreatment and attachment. Maltreated children are significantly more likely to be insecurely attached (Beeghly & Cicchetti, 1994). Attachment insecurity has been related to individual differences in visual self-recognition, executive function and pride in mastery, empa-

**Table 2.1**   Behavioral Manifestations of Attachment Insecurity

1. Child seems unable to receive support from caregiver
2. Child is preoccupied with caregiver's availability
3. Child is victimized in relationships
4. Child bullies others in relationships
5. Child is compulsively compliant
6. Child has assumed a parental role in the family
7. Child has impaired peer relationships
8. Child is unable to be soothed by the primary caregiver
9. Child indiscriminately seeks affection
10. Child's mood varies quickly in the relationship, for example, punishing to charming

thy and prosocial behavior, affect regulation, use of emotional language and emotional awareness, and interpersonal planning capabilities (Cicchetti & Toth, 1995). The parenting styles of maltreating parents have been labeled as overly controlling, hostile/punitive, neglecting, and/or inconsistent (Alexander, 1992).

After evaluating a parent of a maltreated child, the evaluator is left with the dilemma of what to recommend. Parent training is a frequently utilized resource, but the effectiveness of that intervention seems related to attachment quality (Wahler & Meginnis, 1997). The key factor predicting change in parenting effectiveness was a variable of maternal responsiveness, which the authors saw as related to attachment, not to the behavioral interventions they were teaching the mothers.

The framework provided by attachment theory aids the therapist and evaluator in appreciating (a) the origin and diversity of relationships between children and their parents; (b) the influence the internal working model plays in the formation of all social relationships, including the treatment relationship; and (c) the need to improve the attachment relationships if the therapist is to alter the fundamental perceptions the child and parent have about each other. Refer to Table 2.1 for a listing of behaviors that presumably have origins in attachment insecurity. See also Appendix A for a copy of the AAI.

## ❑ Dysregulation

Risk factors common to psychopathology in children typically share a tendency to produce high levels of arousal or to interfere with the development of strategies for regulating arousal (Bradley, 2000). Problems with the regulation of arousal are manifest in such diverse symptoms as PTSD, depression, and aggressive behavior. Specific to trauma, the symptoms most often are emotional.

Thompson (1994) has defined emotional regulation as follows: "Emotion regulation consists of the extrinsic and intrinsic processes responsible for monitoring, evaluating, and modifying emotional reactions, especially their intensive and temporal features, to accomplish one's goals" (pp. 27-28). There are a number of aspects of this definition that warrant further discussion. The first is that emotions are managed both by the person (intrinsic) and by others (extrinsic). An example of appropriate extrinsic regulation comes from the secure-base behavior of children, where children seek soothing from overwhelming distress by gaining closer proximity to their parent.

Emotion regulation is also goal-directed. Sometimes the child can have conflicting goals, since emotions are managed for many reasons. Thompson and Calkins (1996) give the example of a child who feels wronged and has to struggle between restoring the peace (controlling anger), getting back at the offender (expressing anger), or getting support from some other authority to resolve the matter. Clearly this is a complex piece of decision making, and one can expect that emotion regulation is a capacity that improves with age.

As part of emotion regulation, children need to learn how to monitor their internal emotions and modify them so they can respond accordingly. The capacity to recognize one's internal cues plays a central role in the development of self-regulation. But for a very young child, the cues related to self-control come from external sources. These cues can be very confusing to the child, particularly if in a maltreating home environment. At other times emotional regulation comes about by maintaining, enhancing, or inhibiting arousal. Children throwing temper tantrums are enhancing their arousal.

From the above, one can realize the number of tasks children have to master as they learn to manage arousal. They must develop the ability to modulate their arousal level, maintain physiologic homeostasis, and differentiate between a broad range of both positive and negative affect. They also need to integrate different aspects of arousal, including affect, behavior, and cognition. Failure to do so can result in feelings of unreality and even fragmentation.

Thompson and Calkins (1996) state that children must learn a number of strategies for managing their discrete emotions. Children who are not given permission or models for the honest expression of feeling learn few strategies. Other children gradually learn a number of seemingly dialectical strategies: to diminish/accentuate the intensity of an experienced emotion, to slow/accelerate its speed of onset, to limit/enhance its persistence over time, and to reduce/increase emotional range or lability. The increasing ability to influence the qualitative experience of emotion reflects increasing maturity.

Maltreatment of all types interferes with children's developing capacity for self-regulation. For example, sexually abused children are likely to feel confused about their feelings and prone to subsequent dysregulation for several reasons. First, they may not be allowed to express distress in response to the maltreatment. Second, their distress can continue unceasingly, even after the abuse is over. This may be due to the absence of support. An intellectual understanding of what happened may also be absent. This could result in part from the children's inability to link their distress cognitively to the abuse and thus be able to modify its intensity.

In a study that specifically examined the cognitive-affective link in self-regulation, subjects with unexplained arousal produced elevated self-reported and physiologic measures of arousal, increased negative mood, and misattribution about the cause of their arousal when compared with subjects with explained arousal (Pennebaker, 1995). Sexual abuse that cannot be articulated because of family strictures is certainly an example of unexplained arousal and can be expected to lead to the same behaviors noted by Pennebaker (1995). In fact, expressive language is a moderator of dysregulation (Beitchman, Cohen, Konstantareas, & Tannock, 1996).

Maltreatment is dysregulating for many reasons. First, there are the traumatic features of the abuse, which can be overwhelming to the child. Second, abuse most often arises in the context of a family environment that is characterized by other stressors that are typically over-

**Table 2.2**    Behavioral Manifestations of Dysregulation

1. Stereotypic trauma play
2. Sexual behavior difficulties
3. Sleep problems
4. Anxiety
5. Aggression
6. Compulsivity
7. Depression
8. Dissociation
9. ADHD (with its attendant features of impulsivity, inattentiveness, and  overactivity)
10. Panic attacks
11. PTSD (with its attendant features of hyperarousal, numbing, avoidance, and intrusive remembering)
12. Social withdrawal
13. Somatic complaints
14. Agitation
15. Rage outbursts
16. Conversion disorders

whelming to the child. These potentiating factors include marital conflict, reduced economic status and its attendant stressors, frequent moves and losses, psychiatric problems in the parents, and greater unpredictability and chaos in general. In fact, given the heterogeneity of maltreatment, for many children the major contributors to their dysregulation are not abuse specific—they are context specific, such as family support and family conflict (Friedrich, 1988a).

## BEHAVIORAL MANIFESTATIONS
## OF DYSREGULATION

Hall (1993) has suggested that "trauma signs" (p. 7) fall into three broad categories based on the types of behaviors seen in PTSD. These are reexperiencing behaviors, avoidant behaviors, and increases in arousal. The behaviors listed in Table 2.2 also sort fairly neatly into these same three groups, even though only some of them are primary symptoms of PTSD.

There are several reexperiencing behaviors. One that seems most directly related to sexual abuse is sexualized behaviors directly reminiscent of the abuse. Younger children seem to exhibit sexual behavior that is quite abuse specific. They often translate the abuse quite concretely, for example, the child inserting objects into his rectum following sodomy (Friedrich & Luecke, 1988). Sexual behavior problems are discussed in more detail in Chapter 6.

Another behavior whose connections are transparent is stereotypic trauma play (Terr, 1981). The play may have themes that are clearly sexual or violent. Other themes include fantasies of rescue or undoing of the trauma. Often the play is driven and lacks the type of creativity for which children's play is known (Hall, 1993).

The reexperiencing aspect of PTSD shows up in flashbacks, which may be difficult for very young children to report. Nightmares and night terrors are quite common, and there are data to support this connection with sexual abuse, particularly in very young children (Hewitt & Friedrich, 1991). Victimized children may not have learned self-soothing capacities since their internalized working model is that interactions are overwhelming. Many of them live in a heightened state of arousal, sometimes chronic arousal. This can manifest itself in nightmares and night terrors.

Sometimes children will display intense distress at events that evoke similar emotions, for example, threatened loss, smells, large men, and so on. These triggers can create setbacks in the therapy of these children.

Avoidant behaviors most directly tied to the sexual abuse trauma include children's withdrawing from any activity that reminds them of the abuse or its related emotions. Over time this can evolve into generalized social withdrawal. Children whose perpetrator was male may avoid male teachers. Other victims drop out of athletic activities and are unable to take part in physical education, because these activities involve undressing and feeling physically vulnerable.

Other avoidant behaviors include dissociation, substance abuse, self-injurious behavior, and suicidal acts. Dissociation is not a frequent outcome in younger children and when present often reflects the sexual abuse as well as a lifetime of chaos and rejection. It presents some unique diagnostic issues as well, including the task of sorting out normative dissociation from pathological dissociation. Both substance abuse and self-injurious behavior can distract victims from their internal distress.

The last category identified by Hall (1993) is related to increases in arousal. Children with PTSD will at times exhibit behavior reminiscent of agitation and difficulties with self-soothing. They report problems falling asleep and may be up and down throughout the night. Inattentiveness/overactivity in the classroom setting is a related manifestation in this third category of increased arousal. This may earn the child a diagnosis of attention deficit hyperactivity disorder (ADHD), even though physiologically the child is likely to be quite different from a child who arrives at that diagnosis on a nontraumatic pathway. In addition, stimulant medication for a child who does not have ADHD may have some treatment implications that are not desirable.

It is quite sobering to read a study by Carlson, Jacobvitz, and Sroufe (1995) that illustrated the fact that a diagnosis of ADHD by age 6 was not related to medical or physical factors in the child. The key features in the prediction of these behaviors were contextual variables, such as intrusive parenting and life stress. Their study explains that there are many environmental pathways available to children that make them look as if they are impulsive, overactive, and inattentive, the cardinal features of ADHD. This contributes to many children ending up with this diagnosis. Regrettably, the most common focus of the treatment for these children is the child's neurophysiology, not the environment he lives in. In addition, the parent often walks away with the message that ADHD is simply a chemical imbalance and is given little direction about the need to create more safety and predictability.

Hinshaw (1994) has plotted that the half-life of effectiveness of a solely pharmacological intervention is only 6 to 12 months. This effectiveness is directly related to qualities of the family, among other variables. This is a very brief time span when you consider that the child's difficulties are part of an environment that is lifelong.

Although I initially included dysregulation as a component in this model because of the dysregulating aspects of trauma or maltreatment, disruptions in attachment are also dysregulating to children. Schore (1996) has written that the developing brain of infants who experience frequent, intense disruptions in their attachment relationship is routinely exposed to states of impaired autonomic homeostasis. The withdrawal of support from the attachment figure is already experienced by the child as shame prior to the age of 2 years. Shame is an example of a profoundly dysregulating process that has both cognitive and affective components.

There are many symptoms that fall under the rubric of dysregulation-related manifestations. These are outlined in Table 2.2, and their assessment will be discussed in the chapters ahead.

## ❑ Self-Perception

While developmental psychopathology routinely considers the child's context, individual children and their developing sense of self and self-efficacy are also very important considerations. In fact, the emergence of an integrated sense of self is one of the most important outcomes of development. The child's understanding of himself, his ability to perceive himself accurately, and finally his capacity to behave in an organized and consistent manner follows a developmental course and contains affective, cognitive, and behavioral processes (Fonagy & Target, 1997).

This developmental course includes a number of shifts as the child matures. Children's sense of who they are will initially rest entirely on physical attributes and be derived from the sensations they receive from their internal and external environment (Fonagy & Target, 1997). The finding of increased somatic symptoms in young sexually abused children may reflect the heightened focus on physical integrity in the young abused child (Friedrich & Schafer, 1995). Given the mixture of contrasting bodily sensations that accompany sexual abuse, one has to wonder if young children are at greater risk for developing a disordered self, given the primacy of bodily sensations at this early age.

After this initial phase, a transition to a "self in activity" occurs, and children come to have an appreciation for their ability to move and behave purposefully. The next transition includes the social self, and the importance of mutual peer relations sharply increases. This shifts to the psychological self, the latter including one's emotions and cognitions. Children are interested in talking about the how and why of feelings, as well as the feelings and meanings of another person's behavior. In fact, Fonagy and Target (1997) suggest that it is this aspect of the reflective function that is very important to self-organization. They define reflective function as the "mental function which organizes the experience of one's own and others' behavior in terms of mental state constructs" (p. 680).

The accuracy with which a child views himself is certainly a critical component of self-perception. Young children are egocentric, and their assumptions often reflect wishes rather than accuracy. Harter (1990) writes that environmental changes produce inaccuracies in one's judgment of one's abilities. She also has stated that children who consistently view themselves inaccurately, by either overestimating or underestimating their competence, expose themselves to less challenging problems. Avoidant coping strategies are an example of this dynamic.

Even children's capacity to view themselves is not automatic but nurtured by the environment. Fonagy and Target (1997) state that the securely attached infant becomes the mentalizing child.

Maltreatment is related to a range of symptoms regarding the self, including fragmentations in sense of self and malignant feelings and thoughts about self and the world (Calverly et al., 1994). Children may see themselves inaccurately and have a reduced self-efficacy. They may have problems separating their own issues and perceptions from those of others.

Numerous contributors to inaccurate self-perception exist in the world of the maltreated child. Examples of these inaccuracies include all-or-none thinking, overgeneralizations, and shifts from one extreme of self-perception to another. In the presence of increased stress and reduced support, an abused child is more likely to continue on a developmental path where these inaccuracies in self-perception are not routinely corrected. This has profound implications for resilience, since self-confidence has been shown to be a major predictor of resilient adaptation in maltreated children (Cicchetti & Rogosch, 1997). In fact, the authors of this study suggest that therapy focus on enhancing self-system processes such as "autonomy, mastery, and self-determination" (p. 813).

Children who live in families that do not talk about feelings have a reduced vocabulary for emotions. This is similar to children who live in families whose parents rarely verbalize their observations of their children. The result is children who are unclear about who they are and who have a difficult time describing their feelings. Directly related to this problem is a statement by Fonagy (1998) that psychotherapy with attachment impaired individuals should have as a goal the "recovery of reflective function" (p. 163), not the achievement of insight. By this he means the ability to "step beyond immediate experience (physical reality) and to try to identify the mental state that might underpin the observed behavior of the caregiver" (p. 154).

The stability of the child's self-perception across a number of settings or in the face of contradiction is another dimension of self-perception that should be considered. Attribution theory has illustrated how individuals attribute responsibility for life's vagaries to internal or external sources (Spacarelli, 1994). Internally focused children are not as bothered by the fluctuations in their life, since they tend to view themselves as having the capacity to act on the world rather than having the world act on them. The latter is not true of externally focused individuals.

Attribution theory forms the basis of the assessment techniques utilized in the Children's Attributions and Perceptions Scale (CAPS; Mannarino, Cohen, & Berman, 1994). For example, one of the item reads, "Children naturally fractionate, or 'split' their observations of themselves and others into categories, beginning with good and bad" (Calverly et al., 1994). This is not the "splitting" that is associated with severe psychopathology. Rather this is a normal cognitive process of construction of self and other that progresses into more and more complex formulations. One place that splitting remains and grows more complex is the formation of a self-concept. Healthy, nonmaltreated children increasingly emphasize the positive aspects in their self, that is, a "positivity bias." Affective splitting refers to the separation along this dimension of positive and negative (Fischer et al., 1997). Maltreatment is thought to reverse the usual pattern of developing a positivity bias, and in fact one of the most important characteristics of maltreated children is that they show a bias toward a negative view of self rather than a positive view.

By adolescence, maltreated children have constructed darkly negative views of themselves and their world. In a very clever study, using a combination of graphic and interview-derived data, Calverley et al. (1994) found that depressed, sexually abused girls had a negative bias that was central to their self-concept, while depressed, nonabused girls had positive attributes as central to their self-concept. The sexu-

**Table 2.3**  Behavioral Manifestations of Self-Perception Difficulties

1. Body image distortions
2. Reduced self-efficacy
3. Problems with identity
4. Depersonalization
5. Persisting guilt/shame over their abuse
6. Impaired reflective functioning

ally abused girls also split their representation for their parents—strongly negative for their mother and the opposite for their father. The capacity to maintain contradictory self-descriptions without apparent conflict was labeled as "polarized affective splitting" (p. 205).

Despite the centrality of self-perception in the formation of the self, children usually have little interest in self-examination or introspection (Harter, 1983). They typically view their problems as outside of themselves, given their embeddedness in the family context. Interesting research on the child's use of an internal state lexicon and its relation to maltreatment history has clarified this point (Beeghly & Cicchetti, 1994). The effects of maltreatment could be identified over the effects of poverty, with maltreated toddlers clearly impaired in their capacity to make statements about their internal state. This has tremendous implications for the utility of self-report with maltreated children and the difficulties therapists have in helping young maltreated children talk about their distress.

In the earlier section on dysregulation, dissociation was described as one of its behavioral symptoms. Since dissociation is associated with overwhelming trauma, this is quite understandable. However, a case could be made as well that dissociation is a disorder of the self (Ogawa, Sroufe, Weinfeld, Carlson, & Egeland, 1997). Since the mature self is the cumulative product of numerous integrative efforts, the lack of integration reflected in dissociation is suggestive of a disorder in self-development. Dissociation is utilized by the maltreated child to ignore, discount, and forget critical life experiences. In fact, it serves "as a protective mechanism for the integrity of the self in the face of catastrophic trauma" (Ogawa et al., 1997, p. 877). See Table 2.3 for a review of self-perception behavioral problems.

## ❏ Summary

The model described in these pages is composed of three fields of study that are also inseparably connected. For example, in the section on attachment theory it was noted that Crittenden (1995) had identified the phenomenon of false affect in defended children. This is related to the "false self" described later in the section on self-development. Attachment research has also illustrated the fact that self-regulation is increased in children with secure attachment, and research has illustrated that the emergence of PTSD in children is a function in part of the supportive context of the child (McLeer, Deblinger, Henry, & Orvaschel, 1992). One more example of the interconnectedness of the various components of this model is the fact that the representational mapping that is part of the attachment system is intimately related to the reflective function of the self (Fonagy & Target, 1997). This interrelatedness is for me both validating of the framework and suggestive of the integration that comes with complexity, a factor to value in the evaluation of complex problems.

# 3

# *Variability in Sexually Abused Children*

A central difficulty in the assessment of sexually abused children and adolescents is the fact that their emotional and behavioral presentation is quite variable. There is no single "profile" of a sexually abused child, nor is there a single profile of an incestuous father or a sex offender. Rather, there are clusters of symptoms that on examination can appear related. With the passage of time, they may be transformed into something that can appear unrelated—for example, an angry boy with numerous peer conflicts and sleep problems at age 5 may become an isolated underachiever at age 12. Thus, variability and complexity of response are central aspects to a child's response to maltreatment.

In this chapter, I review the reasons why sexually abused children vary so widely in terms of behavioral presentation from one victim to the next. Because family dynamics contribute greatly to this variability, the literature on the commonalities shared by maltreating and chaotic families is selectively reviewed. This material is critical to understanding the diversity in behavioral and symptom presentation. My hope is that the data presented here will provide you with another set of lenses through which to review the data you derive from your evaluations.

## ❏ Contributions to Variability

### SEXUAL ABUSE IS NOT A SYNDROME

Unlike depression or anxiety disorders in children, sexual abuse is not a disorder characterized by a discrete cluster of symptoms. Rather, it is an experience with widely diverse manifestations. A recent review of behavioral sequelae in sexually abused children found that any individual symptom characterized no more than 30% to 40% of the abused children in the samples studied (Kendall-Tackett, Williams, & Finkelhor, 1993). The same is true for physical abuse, a similar trauma that also varies in terms of severity and frequency and is modified by child-context variables (Kolko, 1996).

Consequently, variability in sexually abused children is a given. There is no prototype of a sexually abused child, and developmental progression only adds to the variability. The composed, asymptomatic 6-year-old girl can present as an angry, self-destructive, and sexually focused 14-year-old.

One example of developmental differences in the trauma-behavior relationship pertains to sexual behavior. Although no research has followed a sample of sexually abused children into adolescence, I have data on samples of sexually abused children and adolescents. Depending on age, the children were assessed with either the Child Sexual Behavior Inventory (CSBI; Friedrich, 1997) or the somewhat similar Adolescent Sexual Behavior Inventory (ASBI; Friedrich, 1996a; see Appendixes L, M). Sexual abuse was identified as the single best predictor of total sexual behavior problems in children 12 years of age and under (Friedrich, 1997). However, it was only one of several predictors in adolescents, with such variables as family conflict and emotional abuse being equally or even more important than a history of sexual abuse (Friedrich, Lysne, Shamos, & Kolko, 2001).

Although there are some relatively predictable outcomes, including increased sexualized behavior, posttraumatic symptoms, and, to a lesser degree, dissociation, they are not universal (Friedrich, 1998). The fact that certain familial variables are related to many of the same outcomes as child maltreatment is clearly indicative that child abuse must also be viewed as a child-family phenomenon. For example, children in chaotic home environments were relatively indistinguishable from abused children, at least on parent report with the Child Behavior Checklist (CBCL; Wolfe & Mosk, 1983). Children who witness parental violence also demonstrate many of the same symptoms represented in sexually abused children, such as hyperarousal, and aggressiveness (Allan, Kashani, & Reid, 1998).

A recent study by Friedrich, Lengua, et al. (2001), using parent input, illustrates the difficulty in discriminating sexually abused children from children with psychiatric problems. Confirmatory factor analysis was used to identify items from the CBCL (Achenbach, 1991a) that were related to dissociation or posttraumatic stress disorder (PTSD). The items utilized are listed in Table 5.2. Sexually abused children differed significantly from a nonpsychiatric, nonabused, sample of children on both the PTSD and Dissociation scales. However, these children did not differ from children who were being evaluated in an outpatient psychiatric clinic. This is a sobering finding and a further reason not to attribute a single symptom, for example, fear of certain situations or places (Item 29 from the CBCL), to a specific traumatic event. Though there are qualifications to these findings, including the psychometric qualities of the CBCL (Perrin, Stein, & Drotar, 1991) or the validity of parental report, the absence of discrimination between the abused and psychiatric samples is further evidence for the relative lack of specificity of discrete behaviors or even clusters of behaviors in sexually abused children.

## VARIATIONS IN THE SEVERITY OF SEXUAL ABUSE

In a developmental model of childhood traumatic stress, the trauma is conceptualized as having both objective and subjective features (Pynoos, Steinberg, & Wraith, 1995). Research with children has elucidated some of the objective features of disasters and transportation accidents that are strongly associated with PTSD. These include exposure to direct life-threat, injury to self, witnessing of grotesque death or mutilation, and hearing cries of distress (Pynoos et al., 1995). The authors of this model suggest a dose of exposure experimental model, and they further suggest that there is a direct relationship between dose of exposure and the severity of posttraumatic stress reactions.

Sexual abuse is an often-traumatic event that varies on numerous dimensions. These dimensions include severity of the abuse, with penetration typically deemed the most severe; duration of abuse as a percentage of the child's age; intensity, or the frequency of the victimization; status of the perpetrator, with intrafamilial abuse thought to be more severe; nature and number of perpetrators; the emotional closeness of the perpetrator to the child; developmental age at abuse onset; accompanying force or coercion; and accompanying medical injury (Finkelhor, 1995). Although these variables are often related to the quality of the child's holding environment, each has the potential to leave a stamp on the victim's psyche.

Some of these dimensions are more specific to the act of abuse, whereas others are related to the child or the child-perpetrator relationship. The latter variables may be even more important. They include the familial response to the child's victimization. A positive response may include the provision of support, acceptance, prevention of further abuse, and opportunities for disclosure.

However, research is inconsistent regarding the degree to which abuse factors are directly related to emotional and behavioral sequelae (Beitchman, Zucker, Hood, Da Costa, & Akman, 1991; Beitchman et al., 1992; Kendall-Tackett et al., 1993). The abuse-specific variables that have been most clearly supported by empirical data include penetration, the duration and frequency of the abuse, force, and the relationship of the perpetrator to the child (Kendall-Tackett et al., 1993).

The variability in relationship of abuse factors to behavioral outcome certainly does not negate the severity of the abuse. Rather, it etches more clearly the fact that abuse is an act that occurs in a developing context (Pynoos et al., 1995). A central component of this context is the child and her ability to report accurately what occurred and over how long a period of time. This contributes error variance to the analyses that examine the relationship of abuse to outcome. Data on the reports of child victims indicate that they typically underreport severity and often have cognitive limitations that interfere with their ability to report duration and frequency (Hewitt, 1999).

The child victim is continually transforming, moving from one developmental era to another. A child who behaves in one way at the time of the abuse may behave in a completely different manner a few years later. That does not necessarily mean the sequelae are absent. Only a careful assessment can help the clinician understand the consistency or relationship between Time 1 and the present.

A critical context is the family and its premorbid functioning and subsequent response to the abuse. For example, I found that family conflict and support of the child were more directly related to reported child symptoms than were abuse features (Friedrich, 1988a). The variable of support of the child has been validated in subsequent research (Kendall-Tackett et al., 1993). Ann Burgess and colleagues followed a sample of children involved in sex-rings and also noted family variables as critical to predicting outcome. She noted that families who blamed the child for the abuse and used physically harsh discipline had children who later went on to offend against other children (Burgess, Hartman, & McCormack, 1987).

Finkelhor and Browne (1985) appreciated the variability of response and proposed four traumagenic factors: betrayal, powerlessness, stigmatization, and traumatic sexualization. This conceptualization is extremely useful, although they do blur the distinction between the act, the victim of the acts, and the context of the victim. The traumagenic factors are also related to the subjective features of trauma suggested by Pynoos and colleagues (1995).

For example, the act by itself does not need to be stigmatizing, but it becomes stigmatizing by virtue of the child's cognition and the response of the family. Stigma and shame are closely related, and Schore (1996) has defined shame as first triggered by the withdrawal of anticipated parental support. Another factor may be more clearly related to the act, that is, powerlessness. It seems that powerlessness is as much a component of the coercion, frequency, and duration of the abuse as it is due to the child's construction of the meaning around the abuse.

However, powerlessness cannot be separated from the family context. There are data that suggest that duration of the abuse is directly related to greater pathology in the mother as measured by the Minnesota Multiphasic Personality Inventory (MMPI; Friedrich, 1991b). The same is true for traumatic sexualization, which reflects the child's precocious introduction to adult sexuality. Traumatic sexualization is reflected in the child's subsequent sexualized style of relating. However, there are data suggesting that sexually intrusive behavior in the child is directly related not just to sexual abuse, but also to comorbid physical abuse, family conflict, and externalizing behavior in the child (Friedrich, Fisher, et al., 1998; Hall & Mathews, 1996).

Trauma carries with it both external and internal threats (Pynoos et al., 1995). The experience of external threat involves children's appraisal of the magnitude of the threat, the degree to which they view their efforts at protection as being helpful, and the experience of being physically helpless. Internal threat includes whether children feel they can tolerate their affective and physiological responses ("I couldn't breathe") and their sense of catastrophe ("My heart was going to blow up").

The evaluator needs to be aware of the inconsistent relationship of abuse severity to behavioral sequelae. However, a careful assessment of the specifics of the abuse is a central component of the overall evaluation. This assessment helps to determine the trauma "dose" that the child has experienced. In addition, the information obtained provides valuable information about the family's response to the abuse, a critical variable to consider.

## DEVELOPMENTAL CHANGES

Development makes an understanding of traumatic experiences more complex (Pynoos et al., 1995). For example, the degree to which children reference attachment figures on how to respond to situations will vary with age, with younger children's responses presumably more closely related to parental response. The experience of emotions, including rage and shame, will also vary with age. Trauma that is experienced while children are going through a period of compensatory invulnerability, for example, early school age years, may result in a failure to acquire a specific developmentally related experience. The 6-year-old boy who proudly reports he is "the fastest runner" will be prematurely humbled if he is victimized at this time period.

Each childhood transition offers opportunities for a child to negotiate previous trauma. Younger children may have a less than accurate perception of what sexual act has been perpetrated on them than older children have. However, the child's appraisal of the event is critical to coping. What happens when a child processes a trauma inaccurately? Internal models of relationships may be formed that are incompatible with other models. This creates conflict. A trauma experienced in preschool by a socially inhibited child may have a persisting effect in that the child does not follow a normal developmental course toward less inhibition. The child may persist in being fearful and asocial, thus reinforcing vulnerability that maturation usually resolves (Pynoos et al., 1995).

Trauma has been shown to affect a central personality axis that involves the dimension of fear and fearlessness, as well as courage (Van der Kolk, McFarlane, & Weisaeth, 1996). The way traumatized children integrate their experiences into their developing self can have lifelong effects. There is much speculation but little large group data on the effects of trauma on the nervous system. It is thought that the impact of maltreatment has both physiological and psychological aspects that need to be integrated (Schore, 1994, 1997). Ideally, there will be concrete data that emerge in the next years that could possibly guide treatment.

Specific to sexual abuse is how children deal with the sexual aspects of their abuse and their resulting sexuality. For example, childhood masturbation fantasies may incorporate persisting traumatic themes that insert themselves into the adult's sexual life (Stoller, 1989). Pynoos and his colleagues have suggested that sexual perversions may represent a "reparative" process and incorporate fantasies about being rescued and exacting revenge (Pynoos et al., 1995).

The need for a developmental frame is quite apparent in the evaluation of sexual behavior problems related to sexual victimization. Excessive sexual behavior in preschool victims may no longer be visible in latency-aged children, but can then show up in teens in terms of fantasies (that are not volunteered to the evaluator), sexual preoccupation, and also being sexually used/victimized (Friedrich, Lysne, et al., 2001). Latency-aged children may also be very good about hiding their behavior from their ineptly monitoring parents, for example, the initial case presented in this book.

A child's contexts also change over the course of development and may protect the child from the full emergence of trauma impact. School may provide a refuge and source of social support as the child learns that academic capabilities can bring curative experiences. While some transitions are positive, others can be negative as well. Avoidant, overly controlled children may become more angry and self-destructive as they move through adolescence and are confronted by sexual coercion from peers or the modeling of substance use and abuse.

In order to make this discussion more relevant to clinical practice, an example reflecting different stages in a victim's life warrants further discussion and questioning at this point. An often disheartening phenomenon is that of girls who seem to do well with the initial intervention, usually during latency age, but then seemingly get derailed in adolescence. As young women, they show up again, involved in drugs and exhibiting eating problems and self-defeating sexual behavior. Who are these children, what processes were not corrected, and how might assessment identify them so that more appropriate therapy be applied?

These children often seem to fall into the compulsively compliant category of defended attachment as outlined by Crittenden (1995). When they walk into your office at the age of 9, following the discovery of a year or more of sexual abuse, they may evidence a range of symptoms typically described as internalizing and reflected in depression and agitation. However, they may be quite circumscribed about the true nature of their thoughts and feelings. They are likely to endorse few symptoms on self-report measures, but because of the duration and severity of their abuse, you initiate treatment. They respond superficially well to support, given their compliance, and rather quickly may appear to have returned to a more positive developmental course. They are then back at 14 because they are bingeing and purging at such a level that their family cannot ignore what is going on. When you interview them, you find out that their eating disorder symptoms are most acute after dates with their 17-year-old boyfriend. They may appear depressed but deny most symptoms, and their grades are reasonable.

What has transpired in the intervening 5 years? A defended female who has a history of compulsively compliant behavior is likely to have an internal working model in which other people are deserving of care, not her. She is also capable of detaching herself from her true feelings and presenting herself more positively because the words she uses seem to be coherent. The compulsivity at one age becomes another type of compulsive behavior—bulimia. The same may be true of sexual behavior, although determining that will require resolve on the part of the interviewer as well as careful questioning about sexual practices. The inability of self-report measures to identify these latent problems is more evidence for the fact that overt symptoms, on which adjustment is typically based, are only one manifestation of psychological integrity.

## VARIABILITY RELATED TO MEASUREMENT FACTORS

Psychological assessments look for internal consistency. The combination of asymptomatic and defended behavior despite severe abuse should have produced some very negative symptoms. A severely abused girl who denies most symptoms and appears defended should not be internally consistent to the clinician. A warning light needs to go off that says this girl will deny distress. While she may recompensate rapidly, that does not mean that she does not need treatment or that everything is fine in her world. This child is an example of why brief screening is often inadequate and fails to identify these children. Whether or not more extensive individual assessment would have uncovered her true distress is not a given. It is likely that a careful assessment of parent-child relations would have indicated that this girl was in all likelihood being raised in a home with little in the way of emotional sustenance. She was precociously alone, and her internal model of relationships is that they are frustrating and support is unavailable. It now makes complete sense that she smiles and acts as if all is right in the world.

A second example is a 15-year-old boy who is now sexually offending against other children. It is not too surprising that his victims are of an age similar to his when he was victimized. Unlike the girl in the above example, he admitted to a lot of distress when he was seen after having been abused. He also was open in therapy of longer duration. He demonstrated a considerable amount of anger at the perpetrator, and his abuse was briefer than the girl's. What happened? Why are both continuing to exhibit behavior related to their abuse?

One has to wonder if the boy was also unavailable to therapy but in a different manner than the girl. He encapsulated a type of coercive attachment style that combined angry-helpless features (Crittenden, 1995). Adults were frustrating to him and never seemed to hear what he had to say. This could also have occurred in therapy. Despite his apparent openness, he "knew" that he wouldn't be heard. When this attachment style is combined with adolescent sexuality and unresolved abuse in a male, a potent mixture is operative. Coercive but inadequate behavior toward others is likely to continue to be his primary relational style.

The boy captures a combination of behaviors that are also not internally consistent for the assessing clinician, particularly if you are also familiar with the parent-child relationship. Immature boys may be open but not in a helpful way. Parents of these children are not accurate reporters of events and are quite rejecting on the whole. Boys in these families should be even less likely to report their feelings accurately. In fact, their self-report is often an overstatement of their distress in order to affect the behavior of others. Only by knowing the context of this child does the clinician know how the child uses words and feelings and how that affects the validity of his reported distress. Social immaturity is also more likely, thus decreasing the likelihood that he will have a corrective emotional experience with peers as he gets older.

Developmental considerations are absolutely critical and must be considered in any assessment. Because we are often asked to make predictions about children and their prognosis, knowing how they might process their trauma at one developmental level can help to inform our decision making. Psychoanalytic approaches argue for worse outcomes with earlier onset, because this increases the likelihood of fixation. Developmental psychopathology theory suggests a more complex explanation than simple age at the time of abuse. This model states that children continue to develop, varying in the degree to which the trauma is incorporated into their developing self. There are protective factors that may be operating at earlier onset, further complicating the prediction process. For example, a very young child may be buffered in terms of outcome, particularly with very minimal abuse, more so than an older child with the same abuse. This is because the child is less likely to appraise the abuse in a stigmatizing way and less likely to react to the abuse in a prolonged and persistent fashion.

## NONSYMPTOMATIC CHILDREN

I do not dispute the fact that a large percentage of sexually abused children are not symptomatic. Often they are children who have experienced minimal abuse or whose family context was not disrupted because of the abuse. However, there are other data that suggest that the issue of nonsymptomatic children needs to be revisited more carefully (Wright et al., 1998). For example, symptoms are only one way to measure outcome, as is very well indicated in a study of competent professional women with a history of sexual abuse (Elliott, 1994).

*Parent Report Validity.* Information about a child's symptoms comes most often from the child's caregiver. There are two broad factors separate from the validity of parent report measures themselves that interfere with the validity of parent report. These include the demand characteristics of the situation, as well as the ability of parents to report objectively about their child's behavior.

With regard to demand characteristics, there are several as well. The first pertains to the accuracy of parents in reporting about their child now that they have reason to believe their child was sexually abused. This cognitive set represents the filters parents use to make sense of behavior that prior to the disclosure they found confusing or were oblivious to. The mother might remember her daughter's nightmares, and the abuse is now the reason for these. Other demand characteristics have to do with parents realizing that their information may have clear implications for family members who are accused of the abuse. The parent may be trying to avoid the removal of the child from the home, the imprisonment of a spouse, or a change in economic circumstances, as well as a tacit admission of having been a failure in ability to protect the child.

Parental factors that may interfere with their validity at recognizing their child's symptoms include a prior history of abuse, rejection of the child by the parents, parents' psychological mindedness, and their capacity and/or interest in observing and reporting accurately. Parents who have a prior history of abuse that was never resolved may be projecting their own feelings into the report they are providing, and the symptoms they indicate may not be seen by other caregivers. Other parents with an abuse history may be sensitized to their child's experiences, and this may make them more accurate reporters. Parents who are defended against their own abuse may be underreporters in the same way they avoid reminders of their past trauma. The same is true of depressed parents whose reports of their child's behavior differ from those of parents who are not depressed (Walker, Ortiz-Valdes, & Newbrough, 1989).

Sexual abuse is often about rejection, and rejecting parents may endorse more negative behaviors in their child than parents who are not rejecting. Insecure attachment, which characterizes 80% of maltreated children (Carlson, Cicchetti, Barnett, & Braunwald, 1989), is characterized by insensitivity, including rejection by the parent. Consequently, the parent may view the child's behavior as cruel or deliberately mean, and not reactive to the child's abuse. There are empirical data that will be reported in the next chapter about a measure that I developed, the Parentification of Children Scale (Friedrich & Reams, 1986). One subscale, titled Negative Projection, has items that include, "This child knows how to bug me," and "I feel better when this child is out of the room." Parental endorsement of these items was associated with elevated scores on the CBCL, and in fact predicted more of the variance of both the Internalizing and Externalizing scales than such variables as family conflict, life stress, marital discord, and maternal depression. This has powerful implications for validity of parental report of child behavior problems.

Everson and his colleagues have studied the phenomenon of maternal support of the child victim and the relationship of this variable to the parents' accuracy of report of the child's symptoms (Everson, Hunter, Runyon, Edelsohn, & Coulter, 1989). This much-needed study found a clear relationship between support and symptom level.

Fathers also have a reputation for underreporting that is well documented in the research literature on parent report (Achenbach, McConaughey, & Howell, 1987). Why parents correlate with each other only .3 to .4 is reflective of a number of factors, including their differential involvement and roles with their child, as well as gender differences in the observation of behavior.

*Child Self-Report.* Although the validity of adult self-report is typically considered a given, developmental literature should tell us that children vary, depending in part on age, in terms of their ability to report their feelings accurately. This is even more likely to be the case with maltreated children, particularly those who have been neglected as well as sexually and/or physically abused (Friedrich, Jaworski, Huxsahl, & Bengtson, 1997).

I think it is this difficulty with accurately reporting their interior emotional world that explains the lack of utility of self-report measures of self-esteem with sexually abused children. The same is true for depression, where despite the seemingly obvious, some studies have found no differences between sexually abused and nonabused children (Kendall-Tackett et al., 1993).

The capacity to self-report accurately is a complex task that has numerous elements. Children have to have the cognitive capacity of self-reflection, they need to have words for their feelings, they need to have permission to express these feelings; then they can become more accurate in comparing themselves to others. Self-report is also an interpersonal activity, and, as such, it reflects a child's internal working model about how to relate to caregivers who may be punitive or rejecting. A child who is dealing with PTSD may become upset by the sex items on the Trauma Symptom Checklist for Children (TSCC; Briere, 1996) and refuse to answer, even though they reflect a large source of distress.

Human movement on the Rorschach is a function of the capacity for introspection and reflection before acting (Exner, 1991). This is a variable that improves after therapy, and it is not surprising to find maltreated children lacking any human movement in their Rorschach protocols.

*Multimethod assessment.* Psychologists are typically taught that multimethod assessment adds to the validity of an evaluation. Comprehensive assessment of maltreated children and teenagers will rely on information obtained in several modalities. This could include self- and other report of a range of symptoms, including those that are abuse specific. Research that includes several sources of data can be quite illuminating. One example is a study by Shapiro and colleagues (Shapiro, Leifer, Martone, & Kassem, 1990). They assessed depression in a sample of sexually abused black girls, utilizing three standardized measures: the Internalization scale from the CBCL (parent report), the Child Depression Inventory (CDI; self-report), and the Rorschach Depression Index. Despite their experience with both sexual abuse and poverty, the subjects did not report significant levels of depression on the CDI when compared with a normative group, but were more depressed according to both parent report and projective testing. None of the independent variables were significantly correlated with one another, although the correlations were all positive. Depression also seemed to be more apparent in girls who were active processors of their thoughts and feelings and not as apparent in those girls who were constricted. Each source of data provided unique and useful information. The CDI was related to guardedness, the Internalizing scale reflected parental perceptions of child maladjustment that varied in accuracy, and the Rorschach was ideally able both to circumvent the guardedness and to provide information about the manner in which the girls processed their trauma and emotions.

Wright and colleagues (1998) used a standard assessment protocol that obtained input from 40 parents and 48 child victims. When elevated scores across all measures were combined, the rate of symptom-free children was 19%, certainly lower than is typically reported.

In an ongoing multimethod study, I attempted to collect systematic data on a consecutive sample ($N$ = 88) of sexually abused children (ages 6-15) referred for evaluation. Four sources of information were available: parent report (CBCL, CSBI, Child Dissociative Checklist [CDC]); self-report/objective (MMPI, TSCC, Youth Self-Report [YSR], CDI); projective testing (Rorschach, Human Figure Drawing [HFD], Kinetic Family Drawing [KFD], Roberts Apperception Test for Children); and teacher report (Conners Parent and Teacher Rating Scales, Teacher's Report Form [TRF]). The projective data were scored empirically, for example, Exner system for Rorschach.

I had at least one measure from each of the four sources for each child, although the children varied on the total number of measures; for instance, the CSBI was administered only to children less than or equal to 12 years of age. The median for the sample was five data sources per child.

Although these were consecutive, clinical referrals, and I expected that most of them would be exhibiting symptomatic behavior, only 59.1% had a $T$ score of $\geq$ 65 on at least one subscale of the CBCL. I chose a $T$ score of 65 as an indication of clinically elevated symptoms, since this is 1.5 standard deviations above the mean and is at the 93rd percentile.

Using 59.1% as a base rate for symptoms, I then calculated how many additional children were identified as symptomatic on one or more of the other measures I completed. Other parent reports identified another 9.1%, projective testing identified another 12.5%, and teacher report and self-report another 3.5% each over the base rate of 59.1%. The results suggest a comprehensive assessment will find that at referral 87.7% of these children exhibited clinically significant levels of distress. This leaves 12.3% not identified, which is certainly lower than the asymptomatic 30% to 40% usually suggested in the literature. Although this is not a random sample, the sample size is similar to those in studies reviewed by Kendall-Tackett et al. (1993), which is the source of the rate of asymptomatic children with a sexual abuse history. In addition, these data are cross-sectional, so there are no data that follow these children over time to determine who went from symptomatic to asymptomatic and vice versa. Although the results need to be confirmed with an independent sample, it is important to realize that asymptomatic on one method or on one behavior does not have to mean asymptomatic after a more thorough evaluation across several settings.

*Consistent Sources of Input.* Clinicians also stand to learn even more about the people they are evaluating if they adhere to an assortment of tests, even two or three that they learn quite well and utilize routinely. For example, in a recent paper, John Wright described a battery of tests and checklists used in the province of Quebec (Wright et al., 1998). These measures were utilized with both the parent and the child. They were assembled with the thought that they could provide an excellent springboard to therapy and also help to document the initial symptoms of abused children and their system and then document any improvement over time.

*Abuse-Specific Measures.* There is now convincing evidence that the use of abuse-specific measures of sexual behavior and PTSD and/or dissociative behavior is a must for valid assessment. While these domains do not comprise a full assessment, they need to be evaluated for a report to carry the type of weight that you would wish for any patient in your care. In recent years, a number of valid measures for children and adolescents have been developed, including the CDC, CSBI,

**Table 3.1** Variations Over Time in Self-Report on the TSCC (*t* scores)

| Subscale | A1 | A2 | B1 | B2 | C1 | C2 |
|---|---|---|---|---|---|---|
| Anxiety | 47 | 63 | 74 | 55 | 53 | 60 |
| Depression | 50 | 66 | 78 | 59 | 44 | 61 |
| Anger | 51 | 60 | 75 | 55 | 70 | 53 |
| PTSD | 53 | 61 | 79 | 56 | 49 | 60 |
| Dissociation | 55 | 62 | 78 | 50 | 46 | 61 |
| Sex Concerns | 48 | 55 | 77 | 61 | 49 | 56 |

TSCC, and the Children's Impact of Traumatic Events Scale (CITES-R). Other research has focused on creating more abuse-specific subscales from exiting measures, that is, PTSD subscale of the CBCL (Friedrich, Lengua, et al., 2001).

*Trauma-Person Interaction.* Perhaps the best way to interpret this phenomenon is to turn to clinical data on three similarly aged sexually abused boys (11-13 years old). I had pretherapy and posttherapy data from the TSCC on each. Each boy completed the TSCC at the end of therapy without reference to the first TSCC he'd completed. I then brought his first response in and discussed both as part of therapy. The boys' scores are reported in Table 3.1.

The first boy, A, was quite defended the first time he answered the TSCC. He denied significant levels of symptoms in most domains at the beginning of treatment, and he actually endorsed more problems at the end of treatment than at the beginning. Did he deteriorate over the course of treatment? In actuality, he was now more honest about his feelings and had less of a need to deny the lingering distress he continued to feel. In fact, the continued distress was secondary to the original trauma and related more to family-related loss.

The second boy, B, did the opposite, admitting distress quite freely at the first assessment. He needed people to be aware of how much he was hurting and wasn't convinced that people would believe him. His placement in a supportive relative's house was what he needed at the moment, and his decrease in reported stress suggests that he had come to some resolution by the end of therapy.

The third boy, C, exhibited a different pattern. At the onset of therapy, he was quite angry. By the end of therapy, he was more depressed and anxious. He was most comfortable with his angry feelings initially, and as he developed more awareness of sadness related to the abuse, he could express it more easily. In each case, I felt that reasonably good progress had been made and, in fact, parent reports supported that.

A more careful review of these three boys can help inform the assessment process, however. They also articulate how assessment measures can be incorporated into the treatment process to make the process more meaningful to the patient.

*Delayed Effects.* The developmental psychopathology model on which this book is based has room for the very real possibility that symptoms may emerge later as the child becomes older and encounters new ways of relating to others or experiences other stressors that capture the same old feelings of being out of control. I try to inform parents and patients that development brings new challenges of intimacy and parenting that will test their resolution of the abuse.

In summary, there are many reasons why sexually abused children present variably to the clinician. Some contributors are due to the variability of sexual abuse, but many more are a function of the vagaries of the assessment process, which relies on information from children and caregivers who are often severely compromised in their ability to report accurately on measures that may be suspect.

## ❑ Summary

There are many contributors to the variability in sexually abused children, the least consistent of which is the nature of the abusive experience. This means that there is no "typical profile" of a sexually abused child, and there are data that suggest that for developmental reasons, adolescents are even more variable. The clinical implications that emerge from this fact are several and include that how a child presents to the evaluator may occur for many different reasons that are a function of the person and the environment. Children with PTSD may appear different upon questioning, and sexual behavior problems may not emerge until months later, sometimes for reasons that are very difficult to identify. Children who talk in a detached manner about their abuse experience are no less believable than children who seem clearly distressed, and conventional reasoning about how the former must be untrue or have less of an effect may need to be reconsidered.

Children may be reluctant or have difficulty admitting to symptoms because of guilt, perceived threat to family intactness, and/or avoidant aspects of PTSD. Other contributors include dissociation and inability to identify accurately their own emotions. These types of confounds are not typical in other aspects of child psychopathology and make the task of the evaluator even more difficult. Consequently, an appreciation of diversity in the individual patient, while relying on group-derived assessment strategies, becomes the rule in the psychological evaluation of these children and their parents.

# 4

# *Attachment-Related Assessment*

The quality of parent-child attachment is directly related to the overall adjustment of the sexually abused child. In fact, there is a growing body of research that indicates the centrality of parent-child relationships in the adjustment of sexually abused children (Friedrich, 1988a; Rind, Tromovitch, & Bauserman, 1998). For this reason, the assessment of relationship quality is critical to a valid evaluation. The importance of attachment is why it is the first dimension reviewed in this text.

This chapter reviews a range of assessment strategies designed to evaluate the quality of the parent-child relationship and assist the clinician in making inferences about attachment security. The tools include an interview protocol and observation procedures. A number of self-report and projective measures that assess the quality and strength of relationships—parent-child, parent-parent, and child-peer—are also highlighted. These various strategies and measures are listed in Table 4.1 in the order in which they are reviewed. This chapter, as well as the next three chapters, reviews assessment strategies for

**Table 4.1**    Measures and Techniques to Assess Attachment

---

I. Parent-Completed
   A. Attachment Interview (Table 4.3)
   B. Working Model of the Child Interview (Zeanah, Benoit, & Barton, 1996)
   C. Observation of Parent-Child Interaction
      1. Informal
      2. Formal
         a. Crowell, Feldman, and Ginsberg (1988)
         b. Response-Class matrix (Mash, Terdal, & Anderson, 1981)
         c. Family interview (Appendix C)
         d. Weekly Behavior Report (Cohen & Mannarino, 1996)
   D. Parent Personality-Generic
      1. MMPI/MMPI-2
      2. MCMI
   E. Parent-Personality-Abuse Specific
      1. Child Abuse Potential Inventory (Milner, 1986)
      2. Conflict Tactics Scale (Straus, Hamby, Finkelhor, Moore, & Runyan, 1998)
      3. Parenting Stress Index (Abidin, 1995)
      4. Parental Support Questionnaire (Mannarino & Cohen, 1996)
      5. Trauma Symptom Inventory (Briere, 1995)
   F. Marital Relationships
      1. Locke-Wallace (Locke & Wallace, 1959)
      2. Dyadic Adjustment Scale (Spanier, 1976)
      3. Relational Interview (Appendix E)
   G. Family Relationships
      1. Family Relations Index (Moos, 1990)
II. Child/Teen Completed
   A. Family Relationships—Generic
      1. Roberts Apperception Test for Children
      2. Thematic Apperception Test
      3. Family Relations Test
      4. Kinetic Family Drawing (Burns & Kaufman, 1972)
      5. Attachment Stories (Bretherton, Ridgeway, & Cassidy, 1990)
      6. Adolescent Attachment Inventory
      7. Rorschach
   B. Family Relationships—Abuse Specific
      1. CITES-R (Wolfe, Gentile, Michienzi, Sas, & Wolfe, 1991)
   C. Peer Relations
      1. CBCL Social Competence
      2. TRF Social Competence

---

each of the three areas subsumed in this book: attachment; dysregulation, sexual behavior (a subset of dysregulation); and self-perception.

The format for each chapter is the same: Each chapter begins with a review of the information derived from nonoffending parents in three categories: themselves, the parent-child relationship, and their child. Child-report techniques then follow. Generic measures are followed by abuse-specific strategies in each area.

The specific domains reviewed in this chapter include the parent-child relationship, the parents' marital relationship, and the overall quality of family functioning. The child's perspective on the quality of parent-child relations is then reviewed, followed by child-peer relations. The available measures and techniques vary widely in their validity and ease of interpretation, and hence the review is selective rather than exhaustive.

Case material is presented in each chapter in an effort to breathe life into the review of particular measures. Chapter 4 presents both the background information on the case and the attachment-related material from the evaluation. Subsequent chapters present the pertinent test data: PTSD and family safety in Chapter 5, sexual behavior problems in Chapter 6, and self-efficacy in Chapter 7.

The chapters conclude with two additional sections. The first is a discussion of clinically and forensically relevant assessment questions that face the clinician and that are pertinent to each domain. The second is a discussion of specific treatment suggestions that flow from the evaluation.

❑  **Attachment-Related Case Material**

## Background Information

A. B. is a boy, aged 8 years, 1 month, who was referred for an evaluation following his admission to an inpatient psychiatric setting. His admission was on an emergency basis following two attempts at self-harm and an attempted assault on his mother.

Ten days prior to admission, A. B. had been found lying down in the street in front of his house. When asked by his mother, he stated that he wanted to die. His next suicide attempt, 5 days later, consisted of his swallowing 10 or 12 aspirins in front of his older sister. He again reported that he wanted to die. On the day of admission, he cornered his mother in the kitchen with a knife. A maternal aunt subdued him, and she reported that A. B. then asked her to kill him.

A. B. lives with his 32-year-old mother, his two older sisters (B. B., age 14, and C. B., age 12). His mother's boyfriend of 1 year lives in the house on most weekends and is reported to be a recovering alcoholic. A. B.'s parents divorced 4 years ago. Their marriage was characterized by domestic violence. Prior to the marriage, A. B.'s father served jail time for two nonfamily assault convictions. The father continues to see his three children on random weekends, is nearly up to date in his child support payments, but is relatively uninvolved in his children's lives. Mrs. B. is steadily employed as a legal secretary and has worked with this firm for approximately 10 years.

The mother reports that A. B.'s self-destructive behavior coincides closely with visitation to the father. She states that all three children have witnessed his violence toward her, and they continue to be exposed to yelling and screaming between the parents at least several times per year.

Both of the older sisters have made substantiated allegations of sexual abuse. A different maternal uncle molested each sister. Each uncle was court ordered into outpatient treatment. Between the two of them, B. B. and C. B. received a total of nine therapy sessions, with therapy apparently ending prior to any resolution of symptoms in either girl. The mother admitted that she is having some difficulty with her oldest daughter, but she attributes this to her adolescence and does not believe that her prior abuse is a contributing factor. Apparently B. B. is coming home after curfew, staying away from home without permission, and drinking to excess. Mrs. B. described C. B. and A. B. as being "extremely close," and views C. B. as "well behaved."

A. B. is struggling in third grade and recently was found eligible to receive supplemental assistance in reading and math. He is reported to have no friends, either at school or in the community. His mother attributes this to his temper and "angry attitude." A telephone call to his school counselor revealed that A. B. is seen as an unpredictable boy, sometimes sad, other times extremely angry and confrontational with peers and teachers. The counselor reports that his school progress has "completely stopped."

I interviewed A. B. on the second and third day of his inpatient stay to elicit information about possible sexual and/or physical abuse. I used a cognitive interview format in combination with a human figure drawing. He was able to correctly identify all body parts and could tell the difference between a truth and a lie. He indicated that sister C. B. touches his genitals frequently, and that she comes into his bed at night and "scares him." C. B. was interviewed the following day. After initial denial, she admitted to having touched A. B. "more than five times" and having him touch her "more than five times."

Mrs. B. initially disbelieved A. B.'s report and her daughter's admission. She informed me that both of them have a problem with lying and watch "too much" TV. She was certain that A. B. mistook his sister for the daughter of one of his father's girlfriends. However, she later queried C. B. and decided that the sexual touching had occurred. At the time of A. B.'s discharge into foster care on Day 8, Mrs. B. informed us that she believed her son's statement but could not parent him at this time.

The referral questions that guided my evaluation were developed in concert with the CPS worker involved in the family, the child psychiatrist for the unit on which A. B. was currently placed, and the school counselor. The attachment-related question required an evaluation of the parent-child relationship in order to determine if A. B. could be kept safe if discharged to his home. Given concerns regarding his sisters and their abuse history, A. B.'s relationship with them, peers, and other adults in his life were related issues. If attachment-related issues were identified, then appropriate treatment goals needed to be identified.

## Assessment of Attachment

### Interview With Mother

Mrs. B. was interviewed with the Attachment Interview found in Appendix A. She was minimally elaborative regarding questions about her pregnancy with A. B. but did indicate that she was seeking to end her marriage to Mr. B. when she found out she was pregnant. She smoked but did not drink during the pregnancy, which was described as uneventful. The maternal grandmother was "happy" about having grandchildren, but "took over" the parenting of A. B. because Mrs. B. became quite depressed after the delivery. The maternal grandmother was the primary maternal figure for A. B. for the first 2 to 3 months of his life.

Her descriptors of A. B. were "angry," "confusing," and "used to be good in school." The examples that she used were all immediate and related to his hospital admission. She believed he took after his father in terms of his anger and stated that A. B. was a parenting challenge from early on. However, she then denied that he was demanding of her time or that he would turn into a criminal.

Mrs. B. reported that B. B. was closer to her son than she was due to her employment. Other than the first few months after the delivery, and a 1-month-long period the prior summer when A. B. had stayed with his father, she had been his full-time mother. She doubted her son's report of abuse at the time of this interview. Mrs. B. stated that she had been loved by her father but not her mother, but then went on to report that her father had "gotten weird" with her when she started high school. She did not elaborate on this statement but flatly denied a history of any maltreatment as a child or teenager. Her primary support at this time is reported to be her boyfriend and a coworker in whom she had confided about A. B.'s hospitalization.

Although I did not spend as much time with Mrs. B. regarding her relationship with her two daughters, she was asked to describe each one briefly and state any worries or concerns she had about them. Again her descriptions were brief, although she seemed to exhibit the most positive affect when discussing B. B. Although she had first described the 14-year-old as a typical teen, Mrs. B. then brightened and recounted her having won a spelling contest in fourth grade. She stated that both she and B. B. were good spellers and that this was very handy in her work as a legal secretary.

C. B. was described as a "tomboy" who loved animals. However, she then added that occasionally C. B. was " too rough" with the family dog and that lately it had taken to shying away from C. B. when she approached. Mrs. B. said that she could not recall anyone in her family or her ex-husband's family who had any features similar to C. B's. She did not believe that either of her daughters had continuing issues related to their molestation. When I asked if either had seen the offending uncle since the abuse, she commented that as far as she was concerned, her brothers "were no longer part of my family."

Because of her initial denial that either B. B. or C. B. had lingering problems related to their past sexual abuse, I then asked Mrs. B. directly if she believed that C. B. may have molested A. B. because of her past abuse. She paused and replied by saying, "that's a possibility. I see where you are coming from." However, even after I assured her that the past abuse was most definitely an issue that warranted attention and that we needed a more thorough assessment of C. B. as well as getting her into therapy, she replied that C. B. was doing well in school.

In summary, the data from this interview suggest that the mother's relationship with her son has been less than optimal from the beginning. His birth continued an unwanted marriage for another several years, A. B. reminds her of an ex-husband with whom she is still in conflict, and her views of her son are quite negative. She does not seem to have had a good relationship with her mother and thus lacked a model of close mother-daughter relating. Her ambivalent relationship with her father appears to be the model of relationships she has with males.

Similar concerns regarding Mrs. B.'s attachment with her two daughters were evident, although neither seems to be seen as negatively by her as A. B. Of concern is the report of C. B. being cruel to the family dog, since this lack of empathy seems to be related to the sexual touching of A. B. she had done.

### Parent-Child Observation

As part of my evaluation of A. B., I observed him for 1 hour during a structured parent-child interaction with his mother. This was on Day 3 of his hospitalization. The observation occurred in a playroom on the inpatient unit, and I observed the interaction through a one-way mirror.

The mother was instructed that the first half-hour would be free play and that A. B. would be allowed to dictate the parameters of the play. I would then come in and ask them to participate in a structured task. This was to be followed by more free play. The free play was followed by cleanup, and both parties were expected to cooperate. I observed the interaction for the entire 60 minutes, and I also rated the frequencies of eight behaviors noted in their interaction over five 2-minute time blocks. See Appendix B.

The mother exhibited neither positive verbal statements nor positive physical contact with her son over the course of the five time blocks. A. B. did not comply with his mother's requests nor did he respond to her initiations during these same five time blocks. The mother criticized her son a total of eight times. Both of them appeared completely disengaged by the last time block and failed to initiate any interaction with each other. This last period occurred during the cleanup process and had been preceded by a standoff in which neither party could agree to begin the cleanup.

By 20 minutes past the hour, the mother appeared disengaged, and she was sitting turned away from her son. The quality of assistance she provided to her son was poor. She never gave a straight command or set limits on his behavior. Neither of them could agree to cooperate with the cleanup. When A. B. became frustrated during the structured task, his mother provided no support, either emotionally or in terms of modeling.

A. B.'s behavior reflected a boy whose initial enthusiasm upon seeing his mother waned quickly. He persisted at each activity for roughly 30 seconds. His self-reliance was reflected in that he asked his mother for assistance only one time. He exhibited no affection toward his mother although he did attempt to involve his mother early on in the observation, usually by showing her a small toy. He then completely stopped doing so. A. B. did attempt to order her around the room, typically asking her to pick up toys that he wanted. He also swore at her on four occasions. A. B. became increasingly anxious over the course of the observation and, in fact, urinated in his pants. This was never mentioned by A. B. His mother's response consisted of her wrinkling her face and looking away, without comment.

By way of contrast, I attempted to observe A. B. with his father, but he was unavailable while his son was hospitalized. Consequently, A. B. was observed in an identical format with his primary nurse on the following day. The nurse was noted to praise A. B. eight times over the five time blocks, and touched him supportively on one occasion. A. B. complied with both requests that were made and initiated interaction with the nurse on six instances. No criticism was noticed, and during both the structured task and the cleanup, A. B. persisted with the task through completion.

In summary, during a structured parent-child observation, passive rejection and lack of involvement characterized Mrs. B.'s behavior. She was not a supportive presence, and the quality of her assistance was poor. In fact, she seemed unable to be positive with her son and had few skills to enlist him in cooperative activities. A. B. does not seem used to individual time with his mother and quickly found it anxiety provoking. Consequently, rather than being a secure base for her son, she appears to be unavailable to him and likely to be an impaired monitor of him and his behavior. The burden for the failure of this interaction seems to reside primarily in Mrs. B., given her son's much more positive response to his nurse of the past 3 days.

## Maternal Ratings

A. B.'s mother completed three rating scales that indirectly reflect the quality of attachment and her parenting of her son. On the Child Abuse Potential Inventory (CAP), she was above the cutoff on scales measuring stress, unhappiness, problems with child and self, and problems with family. She obtained a total score on the Abuse Scale of 223, which is also above the cutoff and suggestive of a significant potential for physical abuse.

On the Family Relations Index, the mother rated her family as above average on cohesion and conflict, and in the average range on expression. For example, she reported that family members frequently lose their temper, hit each other, and become openly angry.

On the Conflict Tactics Scale, which I used as a structured interview, Mrs. B.'s responses validated the findings from the CAP. She reported that in the past she had threatened to throw things at him, had kicked, shoved, slapped, spanked, and punched him.

These results suggest that the family is characterized by considerably more conflict, including physical conflict, than appropriate. Mrs. B.'s elevated potential for physical child abuse makes her at risk for continued abusive parenting. It may also explain her avoidant parenting strategies with her son, for example, reduced involvement results in less physical conflict.

### Child Self-Report

A. B.'s attachment was assessed with several measures. His first attempt at a Kinetic Family Drawing (KFD) was of himself and his older sister C. B. He drew her as an extremely large and threatening figure with elongated fingers, toes, and extremities. The figure of himself was approximately one seventh the size of his sister's, and he positioned himself overlapping her abdomen. I then asked him to include everyone in his family, and his second drawing was of his family "playing volleyball." He positioned himself to the far left of the drawing, with both of his sisters between himself and his mother.

A. B.'s responses to five Attachment Stories reflect his perception of punitive parenting and insecure attachment. In "The Monster in the Bedroom" story, A. B. reported that his mother says, "I don't want to hear you or see you until morning." In "The Departure" story, A. B. stated that the boy "jumps out the window onto the roof. They have a deck under the roof. He jumps off to the deck and then onto the motor home. Then he runs away." In "The Reunion," A. B. reported the kids "are all angry cuz they didn't get anything they wanted. They slammed the door behind them."

On the Roberts Apperception Test for Children, three of A. B.'s eight stories are reflective of abusive parenting by both mother and father. On Card 14B, which pictures a boy who has misbehaved, he described the mother figure as "mad. She is going to spank, spank, spank him. Later he will be spanked again. She might just put his butt in the frying pan." The theme of being spanked continued for Cards 15 (which pulls for sexual detail) and 16B, which is of a father and son. On a positive note, A. B.'s response to Card 2 concluded with the boy and mother "hugging."

On the Rorschach, relevant attachment-related themes emerged. Although A. B.'s human content was within normal limits, he was more than two standard deviations above the mean on the number of responses that were scored as containing aggressive content. The clinical interpretation is that he anticipates that interpersonal interaction will be characterized by conflict and anger.

In summary, A. B.'s exclusion of his mother in the KFD and his view of the world and parents more specifically as aggressive support the results of the Attachment Stories, which suggest insecure attachment.

His mother does not appear to be seen by him as a consistently supportive presence.

### Attachment-Related Treatment Recommendations

1. Refer Mrs. B. to outpatient group therapy with mothers of other sexually abused children. This will allow her to receive support, correct her understanding of the behavior of sexually abused children, and begin to address her own maltreatment.
2. Begin Parent-Child Interaction Therapy (PCIT) with Mrs. B. and her son.
3. Request a temporary stop to A. B.'s visits with his father.
4. Request a temporary placement of C. B. in foster care, so that A. B. can return home from the hospital. This will allow for some increase in safety at home and create a chance to initiate the PCIT.

## ❏  Parent-Child Relationship

Since research has illustrated the clinical relevance of attachment theory, clinicians have struggled with how to measure it validly. Although research on attachment typically utilizes the Strange Situation (Ainsworth, Blehar, Waters, & Wall, 1978) with infants and preschoolers, and the Q-sort following observation of parent-child interaction with older children (Waters & Deane, 1985), the typical clinician cannot use these observation-intensive strategies in his or her practice. In addition, no classification schemes are available for primary school children (Goldberg, 1995). Consequently, the measures suggested in this chapter are less direct in their assessment of attachment relationships. However, I believe that if interpreted appropriately, they can be assumed to be closely related and clinically relevant.

The security and overall quality of the attachment relationship is more typically inferred from parents' responses to direct questions about their relationship with their child. The quality of parents' narrative regarding their child is central to the inference process, and the coherence of the narrative is a key component of the narrative's quality. Attachment researchers have suggested that the coherence of the parents' narrative regarding their child is one feature that is related to security of attachment. In fact, coherency ratings are used to score the Adult Attachment Interview (George, Kaplan, & Main, 1985), which enables one to determine the security of adults' attachment to their own parent.

Coherence is characterized by a well-organized and logical flow of ideas and feelings regarding the child and the parent's relationship with the child. Incoherences include descriptions that are contradictory, confused, or irrelevant and even bizarre. Contradictions often reflect relational ambivalence. For example, despite Mrs. B.'s reporting being closest to her father, she then said that he had "gotten weird" when she started high school. Her inability to describe what this meant is an example of incoherence.

Particularly troublesome reports are when the parent does not realize the contradictions. An example is a parent who begins by stating to you that his or her child "behaves okay" but then goes on to express the worry that "one day I'll wake up and he'll have a knife at my throat."

Sometimes parents will have tremendous difficulty responding to questions about their child, choosing instead to turn the conversation to their own experiences. This illustrates their difficulty in permitting their child to be the focus of attention and is reflective of another example of incoherence, for example, irrelevance. Coherence also refers to the believability of caregivers' descriptions of both the child and their relationship, such as a mother of an extremely angry boy describing him as "just a darling." Parents who speak in generalities and fail to back up their statements with specifics are also less coherent. With coherence in mind, let's now turn to a suggested interview format.

## ATTACHMENT INTERVIEW

Alexander (1992) presented three broad domains of impaired attachment in maltreating families. These include rejection of the child, which can be both active and passive; role-reversal, wherein the child takes on parental responsibilities; and the multigenerational transmission of unresolved trauma. These three areas can be assessed with a combination of self-report, including interview, as well as observation of the parent-child relationship.

Taking a history of the parent-child relationship is a central component of most intake evaluations. The history can be made more useful and attachment related by asking a group of questions designed to arrive at the parent's perceptions of the child, as well as the parent's relationship with the child's grandparents.

Interviews designed to assess attachment security need to address the three domains suggested by Alexander (1992). The format outlined in Appendix A includes the following relational domains: Pregnancy/Delivery; Grandparental Acceptance/Rejection; Acceptance of Child; Secure Base; Ruptures in Parenting; Abuse-Related Acceptance; Perspectives on Their History of Being Parented; Trauma/Abuse Interruptions; and Current Attachments.

Questions about pregnancy, which is a time that should be happy for the parent, often reveal strained circumstances that linger years later. If the child was unwanted, is born at a time of marital tension, for example, A. B., or the grandparent disapproved, the transition to parenthood can be quite difficult. Parents who fail to think about their child during the pregnancy, or whose memories are vague, will likely not be the secure base the child needs.

There is literature that indicates that teenage pregnancy, and more particularly illegitimacy, is a risk factor for parenting problems (Maughan & Pickles, 1990; Miller-Johnson et al., 1999). Teen mothers are more likely to act out and have a history of excessive aggression (Woodward & Fergusson, 1999).

Questions about the degree to which the grandparents accept their adult-child as a parent are also useful. This often turns up a history in which parents have a history of being "entrapped" in their family. They may be multiply entrapped and the recipient of constant bickering and criticism about their parenting by a number of sources—biological parents, in-laws, siblings, social services, and so on (Wahler, 1980).

Another cluster of questions in the interview outlined in Appendix A provides parents an opportunity to describe their child in more detail. Ideally, they will provide answers that are rich, specific, and positive. For example, in a manner very similar to the Adult Attachment Interview (AAI), parents are asked to generate descriptors of their child along with examples related to each descriptor. I make it a point to ask who the child reminds the parent of, since this can reveal projective identification, such as a boy reminding an abused mother of her abusive father or brother (Wachtel & Wachtel, 1986).

The concept of the secure base is central to attachment theory, and I believe that it is assessed with the next group of questions. It is not uncommon to hear from the parents of a clinically referred child that they are demanding. By itself, this may simply capture a difficult temperament. The parent may also report that the child turns to a sibling or someone outside of the family for support. Both of these resolutions suggest the parent is not a secure base, or is not as attuned to the child as would be maximally optimal to thwart the display of difficult temperament. Other parents communicate their unavailability to the child by informing you that they are tired and have little to give.

Parents who are quite guarded or vague about their children often provide answers that lack detail and hence are difficult to quantify. For example, one mother initially responded with a vague, "She's active, always on the go." Only with some difficulty did she finally elaborate enough for me to understand that she actually appreciated her daughter's energy level relative to a niece's lethargy. Because I evaluate many parents of limited intelligence, I have wondered to what degree their problems with expressive language confound the results of my assessment with an interview such as the AAI (George et al., 1985). Though I agree that the sample that I serve is skewed, the reduced coherence seems to be a function of the impaired attachment as much as it is of their expressive language, and I do not feel they are unfairly penalized via this format.

Sometimes the clearest indicators of attachment problems are the ruptures in continuous parenting due to long illness in the parent or to unofficial "foster care," such as a boy being sent to relatives when he acts up. A rupture in those cases where parents also report that their relationship with the child is "fine, but it has its ups and downs" and then cannot provide examples, suggests that the vagueness in the parents' report of the child is related to rejection.

It is very important to ask about parents' belief in children's veracity in reporting the abuse and its details. This reflects acceptance, a component measured in a study by Mark Everson and his colleagues (Everson et al., 1989). They found that parents who were supportive of their child's disclosure were more valid in their reports of their child's distress levels.

Valuable insight is gained with the group of questions that focuses on parents' relationship with their own parents and their history of being parented. When parents who are struggling with their own lives are unable to speak about their parents in anything but vague and/or overly positive terms, it is likely that they have not been parented adequately. The same is true of parents who are obviously troubled and continue to become agitated when they speak of their parents. An unresolved history of poor parenting increases the likelihood of insecure attachment in this generation (Main, 1995).

Attachment researchers have identified people who have acquired secure attachment despite adverse life circumstances and negative rearing experiences (Phelps, Belsky, & Crnic, 1998). These people developed a coherent perspective on their negative, early attachment relationships and were observed not to reenact poor parenting practices with their own children. This was true even when facing the pressure of aversive environmental conditions, for example, increased daily hassles.

The quality of parents' social support network may reflect their attachment quality with their child. This fact makes it useful to inquire whether they have someone in their life to whom they feel they can turn for "real help in time of need." Sometimes parents' initially benign answers to questions about friends are countered by their vehement agreement that they get used in relationships. This contradiction is important to note in the evaluation. The role of support in helping parents be more available to their child is documented in a number of studies examining the role of social support from marriages and friends on attachment security and parenting quality (Belsky, Rosenberger, & Crnic, 1995).

How do you interpret the data from this interview? Some guidelines come from the Working Model of the Child Interview (WMCI; Zeanah, Benoit, & Barton, 1996). This is a structured interview that was developed to understand better parents' mental representation of the very young child. Some of the question probes that it uses are closely related to the AAI (George et al., 1985), and, in fact, the content of these two interviews is reflected in a number of the questions in the interview outlined in Appendix A.

For example, both the WMCI and the AAI ask the parent to generate up to five adjectives that describe the personality of the individual in question, either the parent's mother or father in the AAI or the referred child in the WMCI. Other questions from the WMCI cover the pregnancy, reasons for the child's name, features of the child's behavior that make him or her difficult to manage, and projections regarding the future of the child, for example, how does the parent see the child's outcome as a teen and as an adult.

The WMCI can be scored on six scales that include the following: richness of detail, openness to change, intensity of involvement, coherence of the narrative, caregiving sensitivity, and acceptance. *Richness of detail* reflects the poverty or richness of caregivers' perceptions of their child and the relationship they share. Parents high on this scale describe the child as an individual in full and vivid detail throughout the interview. You leave the interview knowing some clear particulars about the child's life.

Parents who are low on the *openness to change* dimension do not welcome new interpretations of their child's behavior. They are the type of parent who persists in maintaining a biased view of the child, often negative, or less often, naively positive and unbalanced.

Involved parents are engrossed with their child on an emotional as well as an intellectual level. While the *intensity of involvement* may be primarily positive—joyful—or tinged with negative—anxious preoccupation—involved parents are not likely to be neglectful. *Coherence* has been described in more detail above and reflects the organized and logical flow of ideas and feelings parents have about their child. The descriptors they provide are not contradictory. *Sensitive caregiving* is based on caregivers' descriptions of different instances in which they have responded sensitively to their child, for example, disclosure of the abuse, peer conflict, and so on. Neglectful parents often have few instances to describe, and you leave your interview with them wondering whether they think very often about their child or whether they are concerned enough to know what is going on in the child's life. These are parents who have a difficult time creating a safe environment, and their children are subsequently victimized.

Finally, *acceptance* is used to assess the degree of parents' ability to subordinate their own needs to those of the child. Substance abuse during pregnancy, for example, drugs, alcohol, and/or tobacco, is one example of limited to no acceptance. These WMCI criteria can be used as you analyze the responses that are derived from the interview outlined in Appendix A.

Using Mrs. B.'s responses as a basis for analysis, I observed in my report that she provided little detail, and her account of her son was contradictory and hence not coherent. The initial failure to believe her son and the early rupture in parenting strongly suggest a lack of involvement and insensitive caregiving. Her failure to accept her son's account of sexual abuse indicates her failure to accept him as he is. Regrettably, her problems with attachment are not limited to her son but are similarly evident with her younger daughter. Although she seems more positive about her older daughter, for example, recognizes a positive similarity between them, she has not been the advocate for her therapy that is needed.

## OBSERVATION OF THE
## PARENT-CHILD RELATIONSHIP

The physical abuse literature contains studies that utilized parent-child observation (Reid, 1978; Trickett, 1993). Observations conducted in physically abusive families during mealtime identified greater levels of verbal and physical conflict than in comparison families. While the observational schema and coding systems used in research are far more complex than can be used by the clinician, the observation of the parent with the child can provide rich data about the quality of the parent-child relationship.

There are few studies of families of sexually abused children. In addition, the great variability of families of sexually abused children reduces the likelihood of finding consistent patterns across families. Burkett (1991) did identify that mothers of sexually abused children were more self-absorbed and relied on their children for emotional support. Her findings suggest that during parent-child observation, the evaluator should note those instances where parents have difficulty interacting directly with the child. Parents of clinically referred children may actively compete with the child for favorite toys, whereas others are unable to allow their child to direct the first period of play, even after you have actively instructed them in the process.

The consistency whereby incest families exhibited stereotypical features was recently examined with 49 families (Trepper, Niedner, Mika, & Barrett, 1996). The incest was characterized as affection-exchange for the largest group of these families. Less than one third of the fathers were authoritarian, and less than one third had primarily pedophile fantasies. Despite this variability, the findings supported the relevance of some family variables that have long been assumed in the clinical literature. These include social isolation, enmeshment, and rigidity, and the researchers found these features to be present in a significant majority of their families. Communication was characterized by secrets, lack of clarity, and little attentive listening. More than three fourths of the offending fathers reported minimal nurturing of the victim when she was a baby.

Seductive behavior in mothers of toddlers was described in 16 of 173 mothers followed as part of a longitudinal study of lower socioeconomic status (SES) mothers and children (Sroufe & Ward, 1980). This type of behavior was described as sensual physical contact, sensual teasing, promises of affection, and maternal requests for affection. The behavior (a) was directed almost exclusively to males; (b) was associated with significantly more physical punishment and threats of punishment; and (c) was not related to cooperation, encouragement, and emotional support. In general, these mothers were rated as less supportive and effective. The majority of these mothers reported a history suggestive of incest. This research has great clinical relevance in understanding the occasional sexualization of relationships I see in the nonperpetrating mother of a sexually abused child, usually a boy that I am evaluating or treating.

Claire Haynes-Seman (Haynes-Seman & Baumgarten, 1994) was the primary author of a book that presented the Kempe Interactional Assessment system. This qualitative system of parent-child observation was designed to determine if incestuous abuse had occurred in the dyad being observed. The authors of this system suggest that the clinician look for a number of variables that emerge in the session, including avoidance of eye contact, the nature of spatial relationships, physical proximities including touching, discordant affect, and a reduced willingness to engage each other fully. However, the criteria are never well operationalized, and this limits the ability of an independent evaluator to measure the same constructs.

The variables outlined in the Kempe Interactional Assessment system do have a great deal of face validity. I certainly wish that a foolproof system existed to identify incestuous dyads reliably. Regrettably, there are absolutely no empirical data to support the Kempe Interactional system as valid (Friedrich, 1995b). Clinicians who observe incestuous father-child dyads might note the father's behavior with the child as circumscribed and stilted. Although you could assume that the father behaves in this way because he wants to conceal the sexual aspects of his relationship, nonincestuous fathers also behave in this way as well because of the anxiety of being observed and their genuine inability to be more open and spontaneous.

It is highly unlikely that either party will exhibit sexualized behavior or comments, either overtly or covertly. For example, in dozens of observations of incestuous fathers and mothers, I have seen only four instances of clearly sexualized interaction, and one of them I detected only on a videotape review, not during the actual observation. You cannot determine if abuse has occurred with parent-child observation. Observation is quite useful at illuminating the quality of the parent-child relationship, and occasionally some sexualized interaction or unhealthy discordance can be noted. Not only are these processes unusual, they may be reflective of a number of parent-child processes other than incest.

*Informal Observation.* The informal assessment of the parent-child relationship should begin when you first meet the child and parent(s). Note the following when you first meet the family: Are they sitting together or are they dispersed all over the waiting room, are they engaged in interaction, is the affect between them positive, does the nonoffending parent initiate the interaction with you (suggesting that she is the family head), and can the parent exert appropriate control over the child's behavior?

Parents who cannot manage their children in a structured setting for even a brief duration typically have numerous problems exercising appropriate parental authority. For example, during the course of my evaluation of a very neglectful parent and her children, I could always expect her to "lose" one or more of her children. This young mother had very little idea of where her children might be in the building. She also seemed to lack the motivation to keep them close or to find them once lost. This was an important piece of information, because adults the children had met casually while wandering unsupervised around their town had molested both of her children.

The waiting room is a useful arena to informally observe the reunion between a parent and a child. This may be in situations where the parent has been accused of sexual abuse and has not seen the child for some time, or the child is in foster care and the quality of the parent-child relationship is in question. Research with the Strange Situation (Ainsworth et al., 1978) has clearly indicated that separations and reunions are important with infants and toddlers. While older children are more capable of suppressing their attachment anxiety, there are some behaviors worth noting. They include behavior that indicates the child is anxious (suddenly has to go to the bathroom), finds the parent overwhelming (looks away or to a caregiver in the area), or reflects ambivalence (approach and then avoidance, a smile and then an insult or act of aggression). Reunions are the scene of behavior that reflects disorganized attachment, for example, stilling or freezing, self-injurious behavior, staring blankly (Main, 1995). It is extremely important to document these occurrences and interpret their significance in light of other data that also pertain to the security of the parent-child relationship.

The caregiver may also exhibit instances of hesitancy, verbal aggression, and insensitivity to the child's distress, as well as avoidance. Eye contact, mirroring, and physical touch are markers of security in the relationship. Leave-takings between the parent and child are observed for ease of separation as well as sensitivity by the caregiver to any distress the child might exhibit. None of these behaviors by themselves is sufficient to indicate the actual quality of the parent-child relationship, but your observation is most complete when it begins with the reunion and continues through the leave-taking.

Observation of the family continues in other settings as well. The parent is typically available at early interviews with the child, particularly if I need the parent to support the child in being open with me, and gives the child assurances that there is nothing to fear. Parents who have a difficult time communicating support to their children, either nonverbally or verbally, will have children who are reluctant to open up and tell you how they are feeling. Other parents send contradictory messages to the child about their support, for example, turning their back as the child starts talking, looking away, and so on. Other parents will use this time to talk about their own issues, seemingly unable to allow their child the time to talk about his or her problems.


*Formal Observation.* The formal observation of parent-child interaction can be a central part of your assessment. This is typically conducted in an observation room or a similar setting. You may be challenged in court that these formal observations are unnatural and not ecologically sensitive. Your best defense to these challenges is to create a situation that allows you to sample rich and diverse interactions. Simply playing together for 50 minutes is not enough. The best evaluations utilize a combination of activities, including free and structured play.

For example, the observation system developed by Crowell and her colleagues was adapted from a problem-solving procedure, and mother-child dyads (children aged 24 to 54 months) were scored on their approach to tasks, relationship, and separation-reunion behavior (Crowell, Feldman, & Ginsburg, 1988). The 45- to 60-minute session consists of 10 minutes of free play, a 5-minute cleanup, a series of four tasks graded by difficulty, and a 4-minute separation-reunion. Mothers are rated on supportive presence and quality of assistance, and children are scored on nine variables: enthusiasm, persistence, self-reliance, affection, negativity, avoidance, controlling behavior, anxiety, and compliance with mother's requests.

Although the separation-reunion component of the Crowell system may not be very illuminating with children who are older, it presents a challenge to parents of young children who might appear to be reasonably capable and positive if the observation is simply a time to "play with your child" for 50 minutes. The free play portion of the session may go well, but when the parent then asks the child to help with the cleanup or the child faces the threat of separation, an entirely new set of behaviors may emerge, including oppositionality in the face of inept parenting.

A parent-child observation strategy that was originally designed to tease out ADHD from oppositionality is the Response Class Matrix

(Mash, Terdal, & Anderson, 1981). This system has been used with physically abusive parents and their children (Mash, Johnston, & Kovitz, 1983). A central component is for the parent to get the child to comply with a series of inane requests, like taking off his or her shoes. The data from research with this measure indicate that young ADHD children will more often than not comply with parental requests, but oppositional children will not.

Lizette Peterson and her colleagues have also developed a method of observation, the Maternal Observation Matrix (MOM; Tuteur, Ewigman, Peterson, & Hosokawa, 1995). It contains a task that is similar to one of those utilized in the Response-Class Matrix. The mother is instructed to help her child draw as many circles on one piece of paper as the child can in 10 minutes. During this task the quality and intensity of maternal behavior is recorded. The validity of both the MOM and the Response-Class Matrix has been determined with maltreating parent-child dyads, such as physically abusive mothers. The developers of the MOM found that abusive dyads could be identified with this procedure, with nonabusive mothers significantly higher in the use of positive control.

Clinicians typically become better at interpreting the results of standardized measures the more frequently they use these assessment strategies. The same is true of parent-child observation. My current observation system for parents and one or two children under the age of 10 includes portions of the free play, cleanup, and separation-reunion tasks from the Crowell system (Crowell et al., 1988) and tasks from the Response-Class Matrix (Mash et al., 1981) and the Peterson system (Tuteur et al., 1995). The observation runs a total of 45 to 60 minutes in length. After repeatedly using the same protocol, I am better able to know what I can expect and what is clearly deviant.

My observation system consists of several phases, including a lengthy period of child-directed play, followed by a parent-directed task and then by more free play. The final phase is a parent-directed cleanup. The playroom should be reasonably well equipped with age-appropriate toys, particularly those that invite parent-child interaction.

After I instruct parents in what is expected of them, I can remain in the room, but I do not talk to any family member unless I clearly need to intervene. Usually I try to observe from behind a one-way mirror or with a video monitor. The parent is informed prior to the evaluation not to bring up any sensitive issues, for example, the sexual abuse allegations, the ongoing investigation, and so on.

Once in the observation room, I allow for a period of acclimation before I do my more formal observational ratings. The different dimensions that I tally are listed in Appendix B and are designed to be rated after an initial 5- or 10-minute warm-up. I typically choose four or five different 2-minute segments in order to more systematically rate the frequency with which a parent exhibits behaviors such as positive verbal and physical manifestations of support, initiation of social interaction, and parent and child complying with each other's requests.

A range of behavioral responses is seen. Sometimes the interaction quickly becomes parallel play, with both child and parent enjoying the toys but not interacting. Other times children are quite dependent and regressed, and the play they exhibit is nonsustained and below their developmental level. Other children exhibit signs of steadily increasing distress. This can be manifested in a number of ways. Children might request to leave and go to the bathroom. They may become more and more intrusive, even physically or verbally aggressive with the parent. They may shut down completely. These behaviors are indicative of the parent being associated with distress and not being a secure base to the child.

These are rare behaviors and are not specifically listed on the rating scale. Behaviors of this type should be noted. It is also important to rate the overall mood of the observation period as well as the quality of parent-child connection, such as supportive presence from the mother, or enthusiasm from the child. These are global assessments that come at the end of the observation, but as summary ratings they capture the overall quality of the interaction. It is here that you can note a common pattern of relationship, that is, a depressed but well-meaning parent who starts off energetically with the child but quickly fades over the course of the observation.

Although the rating scale has no norms, it provides a rich set of data by which to compare one parent with another, or the foster mother with the biological mother, and so on. More important, it provides an organizational schema that helps observers to anchor their observations. For example, I often observe parents with another observer, for example, a child protective services caseworker. This person is typically less skilled at observation and certainly is less compulsive than I am. The caseworker's observations are usually more subjective, and in fact, there are times when our summary impressions can differ significantly. However, when I point out that there were at least three opportunities where the parent could have praised the child but did not, it adds validity to a system that contains quantifiable observations.

The suggested framework does not preclude rich, qualitative observations that are central to understanding the parent-child relationship (James, 1994). The observer should note any occurrences of physical intrusiveness, stereotypic play by the child that may be trauma related, subtle distancing or rejecting, and the emergence of role reversal in the child. If more than one child is observed, favoritism can also be noted.

Gross disturbances in attachment security can be noted best via direct observation. Disorganized attachment was reflected in one observation when the older child stumbled and then fell to the floor when her mother entered the room. Both this girl and her younger brother had been molested by a number of the mother's boyfriends and were now in foster care. The mother had made superficial progress and was meeting roughly half of the expectations of the case plan. At the 6-month review, the caseworker had opted to close the case, but the guardian ad litem had asked for a more formal assessment of the parent-child relationship. My assessment indicated quite clearly how impaired the mother-daughter relationship was. This prompted the caseworker to require Parent-Child Interaction Therapy (PCIT; Hembree-Kigin & McNeil, 1995), which the mother did not even begin. The mother then rapidly deteriorated in her functioning, and two drug screens were positive for illicit narcotics.

Parent-child observations are where examples of attunement or lack thereof may be noted. An attuned parent remains interested while allowing the child to direct the play in the first portion of the observation.

For example, the child may start off with some comment that the parent steers it in a completely different path than the child might have intended. An attuned parent would have detected the child's need to converse about a topic and been flexible enough to realize that her own agenda needed to be tabled. How well the parent creates a secure, attuned base with the child and alters herself to make this brief time optimal for the child is a critical issue to assess.

When I evaluate families with more than two children, or where one of the children is above the age of 10, I utilize a family interview to understand some key processes in families. For example, when decisions are being made about resuming contact with an offending parent or teenage sibling, the ability of the family to speak openly about what has happened and the need to maintain safety are critical considerations. For the family evaluation to be valid, it must have as one focus the abuse that got the family into treatment, and whether or not the nonoffending parent can provide safety from further abuse.

Another important focus is to determine the competence of parents and their capacity to create environments where children can speak freely. Families who balk at a topic, even after supportive comments about how important it is to be able to talk about the referral issue, should raise concern in the evaluator. Other concerns emerge when the children begin to wind out of control, and the parent cannot exert appropriate parental authority to foster a discussion or quiet the children. These are key features of safety. Because family evaluations are complex and the amount of data accumulated is confusing, I keep track on a simple checklist of the important areas that I am trying to assess. See Appendix C for more information.

At times the evaluation is best served in the home of the child. One way this can be done is to assign the parent some homework in between evaluation appointments. The homework should be specific and afford you a week of data from the parent's observation of the child. This can be done via the Weekly Behavior Report (Cohen & Mannarino, 1996), a simple monitoring sheet designed to assess behavior in sexually abused children while in treatment. From one appointment to the next, parents are asked to rate for a range of behaviors they observe in their child. How well parents comply with this request speaks not only to their capacity to observe but also to their ability to follow through with treatment recommendations that will emerge from your report. For this reason, a functional assessment of this type is likely to have more validity than the results of a personality measure.

**Table 4.2**    Operationalization of Alexander's (1992) Attachment Domains

| Domain | Subscale/Measure |
| --- | --- |
| **Rejection** | |
| Passive | Anxiety |
| | Depression |
| | Alienation |
| | Avoidant |
| | Negative Projection |
| Active | Anger |
| | Paranoia |
| | Control |
| | Insensitivity |
| **Role Reversal** | Dependent |
| | Somatoform |
| | Low IQ |
| | Dissociation |
| **Multigenerational Transmission** | Victim History |
| | PTSD |

## PARENT PERSONALITY

Alexander (1992) described three aspects of insecure attachment in the families of sexually abused children: rejection, role reversal, and the transmission of traumatic issues multigenerationally. I have operationalized these three areas regarding the related psychological assessment measure. This is reported in Table 4.2. For example, MMPI/MMPI-2 and Millon Clinical Multiaxial Inventory (MCMI) subscales that suggest problems with anxiety, depression, avoidant personality, or alienation from self and others would directly relate to the phenomenon of passive rejection (Dyer, 1997). While more subtle than overt rejection, it is the inability of the parent to be available to the child despite their reported intentions.

Active rejection is purportedly related to MMPI/MCMI subscales that are related to anger, unpredictability, and the aggressive-sadistic, antisocial, and paranoid personality types. Parents who are struggling with dependency or reduced problem-solving capacities related to low IQ, as well as dissociation, will often rely on their child to meet many more needs than the child should be asked to, as in role reversal. Finally, chronic PTSD or an extensive victim history in the parent is likely to be related to the multigenerational transmission of victimization.

Although the personality measures, including the MMPI/MMPI-2 (Caldwell, 1997) and the MCMI (McCann & Dyer, 1996), are useful for generating hypotheses about possible attachment difficulties and are often used in the forensic assessment of parents with maltreated children, they are typically interpreted in terms of individual psychopathology. Consequently, the literature on the MMPI and the MCMI and their relevance to the quality of parenting is somewhat scant (McCann & Dyer, 1996).

*MMPI/MMPI-2.* I believe that the subscales of these instruments can be interpreted from an attachment perspective. The central features of attachment include secure base, commitment, attunement, and reciprocity with the child. A parent who is struggling with impulsive and angry outbursts, which might be reflected in elevated MMPI scales 4, 6, and 9, would have difficulty providing a secure base to the child. The detached quality seen in elevations on MMPI scales 8 and 0 might also suggest that the parent would have problems with commitment and attunement to the child. See Table 4.3 for MMPI scales and their reputed relationship to attachment.

Typically, the MMPI is interpreted in terms of 2-point codetypes. Some of the codetypes that have been reported in physically abusive parents include 2-4/4-2, 2-8/8-2, 3-4/4-3, 4-6/6-4, 4-8/8-4, 4-9/9-4, 6-8/8-6, and 8-9/9-8 (Friedrich, 1988b). Anger (scales 4 and 6), Alienation (scale 8), and Impulsivity (scale 9) are components of most of these codetypes. These codetypes suggest unpredictable parenting that is counter to secure attachment.

Several MMPI studies of mothers of sexual abuse victims have also been completed (Friedrich, 1988b; Scott & Stone, 1986), as well as of mothers who themselves were victims of sexual abuse (Meiselman, 1980). The resulting codetypes overlap to some degree with those noted for physically abusive mothers.

**Table 4.3**   MMPI/MMPI-2 Scale Elevations and Their Relationship
                to Parent-Child Relationships

| Scale | Attachment Implications |
|-------|-------------------------|
| L | Rigidly unattuned to their child |
| F | Too distressed to be a secure base |
| K | No clear implications |
| 1/Hs | Somatic focus/denial of feelings |
| 2/D | Depression keeps parents unavailable |
| 3/Hy | Unable to accurately identify feelings/intrusive |
| 4/Pd | Angry, impulsive, family of origin issues |
| 5/Mf | Atypical anger if elevated in mothers |
| 6/Pa | Angrily rejecting of child |
| 7/Pt | Controlling, emotionally constricted |
| 8/Sc | Decreased empathy, alienated |
| 9/Ma | Self-centered, intrusive, inconsistent |
| 0/Si | Disconnected, lonely |

In a study of mothers of sexually abused children, it was noted that some of the subscales from the parent's MMPI profile correlated with several aspects of the abuse, particularly length of abuse and maternal history of sexual abuse (Friedrich, 1991b). Parents with a history of sexual abuse will routinely exhibit more elevated profiles (Scott & Stone, 1986).

The more common MMPI codetypes seen in these parents are subclinical ($T < 65$), but elevations can certainly offer insight into the parenting dynamics present in the home. For example, the 4-3/3-4 codetype has very clear parenting implications (Patterson, 1982). The mixture of anger and repression suggested by these two scales can contribute to a parent's behaving inconsistently, provocatively, and angrily. She is unlikely to be a good observer of her child's behavior and is also likely to lack insight into how she behaves with her children. Parents with this profile are often initially gregarious, and clinicians

**Table 4.4** Common MMPI Codetypes and Their Relation to Parenting Behavior

| Codetype | Behavior |
| --- | --- |
| 1-3 | Poor monitoring, somatically focused, child is caregiver |
| 2-1-3 | Poor monitor, ignores the obvious, inconsistent |
| 2-6 | Bitter and resentful, "my child has a better life than I do" |
| 2-7 | Difficulty showing affection |
| 2-7-8 | Alienated, uncomfortable with closeness |
| 3-4 | Inconsistent, poor monitor, unaware of anger |
| 3-6 | Provocative, unaware of anger |
| 4-6 | Edgy, reactive |
| 4-8 | Angry, alienated, distant |
| 4-9 | Impulsive, inconsistent, child may become caregiver |

may perceive them as more capable than the average parent. However, they fail to follow through with parenting homework. The relatively poor monitoring skills in these parents make it difficult for them to observe their child accurately or to detect maltreatment that may be occurring in the family. Poor monitors are inconsistent nurturers and often intrusive in their children's lives. The children they raise are presumably more resistantly and coercively attached. See Table 4.4 for more information and a summary of relevant codetypes.

The 4-8/8-4 profile, which is seen with some frequency in parents with a sexual abuse history (Friedrich, 1988b), suggests parents with another set of issues. The anger and impulsivity common to individuals with elevations on scale 4 are likely to be present, but an elevation on scale 8 also suggests a parent who has problems with intimacy and empathy for the child. Relationships are characterized by alienation. Consistent empathy for the child's victimization may be lacking, and you may hear cruel comments made about the child. Negative projection, such as describing the child as cold and angry when those are the parent's own characteristics, may be present. The child victim may be coping with the parent via a defended attachment strategy. These are parents who are skittish about therapy because they have found caregiving to be so frustrating in the past.

Parents who are elevated on scale 2, Depression, are also common. Some of their depression may be a natural (and even welcome) response to their child's situation. However, it may be a more chronic condition. Parents who are depressed and angry (2-4/4-2 or 2-6/6-2) may also have some problems with disordered eating, for example, bulimia (Root & Friedrich, 1989). Another codetype (2-3/3-2) is often called "smiling depression," and these parents may deny their depression despite their elevated score on this scale. Because a somatic focus is typically present with this elevation, parents may be disappointed that you can't prescribe a medication for the somatic complaints that seem to incapacitate them and make them less available for their child. Somatizers also lack insight into their own and their child's situation.

*MCMI.* The MCMI, in its various permutations (MCMI-II, MCMI-III), measures dimensions that are useful for the evaluation of parenting fitness (McCann & Dyer, 1996). It results in subscale scores that range across the *DSM-IV* Axis II personality disorders and includes, as well, the Axis I disorders that many parents bring to the office: dysthymia, substance abuse problems, and so on. The parenting implications of a person who is elevated on the Aggressive-Sadistic subscale are not too difficult to surmise. In my clinical experience, mothers of sexually abused children, with some regularity score highly on the subscales related to dependent, histrionic, avoidant, and compulsive personality patterns. If there is also a history of sexual abuse, the likelihood of elevations on self-defeating, passive-aggressive, and borderline scales is increased. However, there are few empirical data on this measure relating it either to parenting quality or to a sexual abuse history. In addition, the MCMI has a tendency to pathologize some of the nonoffending parents that I see, for example, those with no sexual abuse history and a normal profile on the MMPI-2.

The above comments are restricted to the assessment of the personality of nonoffending parents. Personality assessment can be useful in documenting the treatment needs of sex offenders, particularly those offenders who have admitted their guilt and are willing to be involved in treatment. A framework for this assessment is outlined in Hall (1996).

## ABUSE-SPECIFIC INFORMATION

Sexual abuse often occurs in the context of physical abuse. In these cases, it can be quite illuminating for the parents to complete the Child Abuse Potential Inventory (CAP; Milner, 1986), and be interviewed with the Conflict Tactics Scale (CTS; Straus, Hamby, Finkelhor, Moore, & Runyan, 1995). The CAP inventory is a 160-item measure that is quite useful at predicting parents' potential for physical abuse. It contains a total of 10 scales, and the primary clinical scale is the 77-item Physical Child Abuse Scale. This abuse scale can be divided into six factor scales: distress, rigidity, unhappiness, problems with child and self, problems with family, and problems with others. In addition, there are three validity scales, including the Lie Scale, the Random Response Scale, and the Inconsistency Scale. Although it is useful to examine the subscales, which can illuminate some of the individual contributors to abuse potential, only the total score of the 77-item Physical Child Abuse Scale is used for screening purposes. The information from the CAP can be used to guide parents into interventions that address their inaccurate perception of their child, as well as the internal distress that increases the potential for abuse.

Elevations on the Physical Child Abuse Scale certainly reflect problems with attachment. Even if that scale is not elevated to the cutoff point, the factor "Problems with child and self" is reflective of parents who "describe their children in a negative manner" (Milner, 1986, p. 3). I have found that elevations on this scale are related to resistant attachment in the child.

Conflict Tactics Scales (CTS) are a series of scales originally developed for use by family violence researchers (Gelles & Straus, 1988). A number of them have been developed to assess violence between couples, elder abuse, and conflict with children. The CTS-Child Form R (Gelles & Straus, 1988) and its more user-friendly version, the Parent-Child Conflict Tactics Scales, Form A (CTSPC; Straus et al., 1998), is structured to identify conflicts between parents and children that have occurred over the past year.

The CTSPC is printed in the article cited above and is extremely handy during your parent interviews. It contains 22 behaviors and provides an excellent format for asking very specific questions about parenting practices that may end in conflict, including the following: explained why something was wrong; put child in time-out; spanked, swore, or cursed; knocked the child down; took away privileges; and so on. Parents are not likely to acknowledge poor parenting practices if simply asked generically about their parenting. The CTSPC enables you to ask more specifically and to develop a more valid assessment of their parenting.

The Parenting Stress Index (PSI; Abidin, 1995) can also be useful with preteen children. The 120 items are divided into Parent (7 scales) and Child (6 scales) Domains. A Total Stress score as well as Domain scores are calculated. If both Parent Domain and Child Domain scores are high, it suggests a dysfunctional family that is in a crisis situation and has an elevated potential for child abuse. Parents who view their child as the primary source of the problems they are experiencing are often elevated on the child subscales but not elevated on the parent subscales. I have found that this variability in elevations is clinically significant and, in terms of therapy, means that you will have to work extra hard to correct the parents' biases against their child.

In addition to giving parents a chance to relay to you aspects of children that make them difficult to rear, or other stresses parents are experiencing, it has a specific Parent Domain scale that is labeled Attachment. Abidin (1995) writes that this scale is related to the parent's ability to read and interpret the child's feelings. Research has compared the CAP with the PSI and found that they complement each other in detecting physical abuse (Holden & Banez, 1996). My clinical experience with this scale is that when problems are reported, the child more often appears resistantly attached. Parents of avoidantly attached children are less likely to report problems in this domain.

The Parental Support Questionnaire (PSQ; Mannarino & Cohen, 1996) is abuse specific and has a definite clinical role. It was designed so that changes in parental support of the abused child could be assessed over the course of therapy. The PSQ is a 19-item rating scale with a 5-point Likert scale format. Sample items include, "Do you ever feel the sexual abuse was your child's fault?" and "Have you encouraged your child to tell you how they feel about the abuse?"

The PSQ examines the degree and kind of perceived parental support provided to the sexually abused child as well as the nature of attributions that parents make regarding responsibility for the abuse. The

Support subscale consists of eight items and the Blame subscale consists of 11 items. A higher total score reflects greater support and less blame of the child. The measure is face valid, and parents can chose to be deceptive. However, I have found it to be a very useful instrument for the initial clinical assessment of both the child and the teen, since the content is directly related to treatment, and targets can be immediately identified.

Specific to the parent's abuse history is the Trauma Symptom Inventory (TSI; Briere, 1995), a 100-item scale that provides an overview of the parent's trauma-related symptoms. Although it assesses general distress with such scales as Depression and Anger/Irritability, some of the scales are much more specific to prior trauma. These include the following: Intrusive Experiences, Defensive Avoidance, Sexual Concerns, Impaired Self-Reference, and Tension Reduction Behavior. While empirical research has not been published on scale elevations and parenting problems, parents who score high on Intrusive Experiences or Defensive Avoidance will be struggling with their own abuse. These parents are likely to find it even more difficult to be available to the child you have been asked to evaluate. Although these parents need to be referred for their own therapy, I have found that parents who have more than two or three of the abuse-specific scales in the clinical range, that is, $T > 65$, are more likely to struggle in therapy and be variable in their attendance. Given the importance of maternal history of prior, unresolved victimization in the etiology of disorganized attachment, assessing symptoms related to its presence is critical.

## ❑ Marital Relationship

The quality of the marital relationships of the parents that you evaluate must also be assessed, since the marital dyad is part of the child's secure base. Although many of the mothers I see are not married or are separated, they will have a history with significant others, and a review of the quality of those relationships can be very informative. Marital relationships show the adult resolution of attachment problems when younger. Since most parent-child relationships in maltreating families are insecure, it is likely that current marital relationships will be fraught with difficulty. While it is possible to use one or more marital satisfaction scales, such as Locke-Wallace (1959) or the Dyadic Adjustment Scale (Spanier, 1976), in the interests of keeping the evaluation organic and simple, a list of questions will typically elucidate a great deal of information. In the same way that the parent's coherence is rated in attachment assessment with the child, it is useful to examine for contradictions or overly brief and stereotypically positive descriptions backed up by few examples.

I start my interview by determining if the nonoffending parent has a history with a consistent partner. I also ask about domestic abuse in these relationships. Questions about the sexual relationship between the offending and nonoffending partners can also be very illuminating, not only about the abuse the child experienced, but also about the parents' own sexual problems. It is also useful to inquire further whether the parent ever detected warning signs that the partner might have been abusive. The decision that led to the parent's choice of a partner with a history of criminal sexual activity is also important to review. See Appendix D for suggested topics to cover in an interview.

## ❑ Family Functioning

Numerous family assessment devises have been developed, but with typically less than desired validity. The material obtained on the CAP (Milner, 1986) or the CTSPC (Straus et al., 1998) can shed some light on a narrow aspect of family functioning. More light is cast via the observation of parent-child interaction, either formally or informally. However, for those clinicians who are determined to be thorough or who wish to monitor the quality of the family relationship and how it is affected by treatment, the suitability of broad family measures is a continuing weakness in the assessment field.

I routinely use the Family Relations Inventory (FRI; Moos, 1990) with all the families I see. It is derived from the Family Environment Scale (Moos & Moos, 1986). The FRI is the sum of three of the subscales from this longer measure. Each subscale is nine items in length. They are Cohesion, Expressiveness, and Conflict, with the latter scale reverse-scored (Moos, 1990). While the items are face valid and lend themselves to deception, I find the subscale information more often useful than not.

For example, in analyses with a consecutive sample of families, I found the FRI to be significantly related to the behavioral elevations on the CBCL of the sexually abused child reported by the mother. The Conflict subscale was also significantly related to sexually intrusive behavior on the CSBI, and this finding illustrates the extra degree of aggression modeling that I think is necessary for a child to become sexually aggressive.

Considerable information emerges via a review of the parents' comments on the behavior rating scales that they complete on the referred child. The CBCL (Achenbach, 1991a) invites parents to write what they like about their child. Some parents leave this blank, use it to criticize the child, or write confusing and/or contradictory statements. This is consistent with the negative parental bias that has been demonstrated by abusive parents when rating their child's behavior on parental report measures (Reid, Kavanagh, & Baldwin, 1987). The written comments at the end of the CBCL communicate volumes about the coherence and integrity of their relationship with their child.

The Behavior Assessment System for Children (BASC; Reynolds & Kamphaus, 1998) is another parent-report measure that has several advantages over the CBCL, including a validity index, the F index. It assesses the possibility that the parent or teacher rated the child in an inordinately negative fashion. When it is elevated, the clinician needs to be prepared for a parent who has no qualms about excoriating the child, even in front of other people. The parent's report is often a marked contrast to the well-behaved child seen by the teacher.

## ❏ Child-Parent Relationships

### GENERIC INFORMATION

It is extremely useful to organize parental comments into the behavioral categories developed by Crittenden (1995; see also Table 4.5). She developed 11 attachment categories, typified by the child's behavior, that emerge over time. The number of categories range from 8 by preschool, to 9 by school age, and 11 by adolescence and adulthood. The Integrated (Secure) categories are labeled as follows: Comfortable, Reserved, and Reactive. The Defended (Avoidant) are labeled Inhibited, Compulsive Caregiving, Compulsive Compliant, and Isolated/

**Table 4.5**　Attachment Security Classification Security System
　　　　　　　(derived from Crittenden, 1995)

| Type | Descriptors |
| --- | --- |
| **Integrated (Secure)** | Capacity for closeness and exploration in new settings is always present to a greater or lesser degree |
| Comfortable | Relaxed with new people and events; takes things in stride |
| Reserved | Slower to warm up to new relationships |
| Reactive | Genuine feelings are more easily registered |
| **Defended (Avoidant)** | Distance in relationships and dismissal of emotions are typical of these categories |
| Inhibited | More extreme of Reserved (above) |
| Compulsive Caregiving | Meets relationship by providing care and nurturance; maintains detached control in this manner |
| Compulsive Compliant | Overly eager to please and meet your needs |
| Isolated/Promiscuous | Indiscriminate affection seeking |
| **Coercive (Resistant)** | Ambivalence in relationships, strong emotionality |
| Threatening/Disarming | Intimidation followed by charm and deflection of blame |
| Aggressive/Helpless | Alternates between angry/rejecting and helpless/inadequate; Passive-aggressive |
| Punitive/Seductive | Uses those around him but accompanies this with charm and pizzazz |
| Menacing/Paranoid | Perceives world as out to get him; anger keeps people away |

Promiscuous. The Coercive (Resistant) are labeled Threatening/Dis-arming, Aggressive/Helpless, Punitive/Seductive, and Menacing/Paranoid.

The dual styles for all of the Coercive types reflect the ambivalence in the young, coercively attached child. These are children who often move from approach to avoidance in the course of a single interaction. For example, the threatening/disarming types may be very controlling and intimidating to the parent, but when confronted about their behavior, they state that they were "only pretending."

Although these categories have not been clearly operationalized by Crittenden, their labels suggest the types of behavior that warrant that categorization. For example, when I see a boy threaten and then hit his mother and then react with agitation and even panic when she leaves, I think that he is exhibiting insecure attachment of the coercive type. His behavior may be most closely related to the category labeled Aggressive/Helpless.

Another example is the sexually abused child who has had a very disrupted and chaotic life, and has often been exploited. However, this child seems always eager to help clean up the playroom after each session. In addition, she can be counted on to inquire in a concerned way about any "sniffle" or sign of fatigue from the examiner. The category that best suits her is Compulsive Caregiving, a defended subtype. I do have to admire that a child found a mechanism to obtain support but remain in control of the course of the relationship. For more information, please refer to Table 4.5.

Children's working models for attachment relationships can be difficult to assess separate from observing the parent-child interaction. However, their view of parental emotional and physical availability along with support around the abuse is an important component of a broad-based assessment. It is difficult to ask children if they like their parents or feel liked by them. It is also difficult to get valid answers to these hard questions. These difficulties the child has with self-disclosure can sometimes be overcome through the use of well-crafted questions, particularly those that rely on contrasts or ask for input about another person's feelings rather than the child's. A nonexhaustive list of questions, presented in no particular order but that I find more useful than not, is presented in Appendix E.

Projective storytelling tasks, such as the Roberts Apperception Test for Children (McArthur & Roberts, 1982) and the Thematic Apperception Test (TAT; Bellak, 1986), are widely distributed assessment devices that have long been used to arrive indirectly at the child's view of parental relationships. The Roberts manual contains a scoring protocol with clear instructions on scoring such attachment-relevant scales as Reliance on Others, Support-Other, Support-Child, Limit Setting, and Rejection. There are norms for these scales as well. Particularly when they buttress what you observe in the parent-child observation, the child's deviation from the norm has been very useful to cite in legal settings, when your conclusions about the parent-child relationship are being confronted. Westen's work developing an attachment-related scoring system for the TAT is also an important resource (Westen, Lohr, Silk, Gold, & Kerber, 1990).

There has also been a recent resurgence in the use of the Family Relations Test now that it is more readily available in the United States (Bene & Anthony, 1976). It is a standardized and semi-projective device that allows for the assessment of the child's feelings about various family members as well as the reciprocal feelings of these family members as perceived by the child. For example, with this test, children can describe hateful feelings that they have toward parents and siblings or their perception that they are disliked by family members. Children are still cautious in the degree to which they disclose to a stranger, but the format of the test seems to make some children more open about these negative feelings.

Some progress has also been made with family drawings and tying various features of the drawings to attachment security. For example, attachment quality in a sample of 8- to 9-year-old children drawn from a prospective study was related to variables derived from a family drawing completed by each child (Fury, Carlson, & Sroufe, 1997). The authors found that the family drawings were a "window to representational models" of the child. A number of individual signs of attachment quality were found to discriminate significantly between secure and insecure attachment types, and a global rating of the drawing did as well. Maternal attachment quality accounted for the most variance of the family drawing, along with life stress and a teacher rating of emotional functioning. The individual signs are listed in Table 4.6.

The Kinetic Family Drawing (KFD) differs from the family drawing described in the study by Fury et al. (1997). This task is structured so that children are asked to draw a picture of everyone in their family do-

**Table 4.6**    Family Drawing Variables From Fury, Carlson, and Sroufe (1997)

1. Signs related to anxious-resistant attachment
     figures separated by barriers
     unusually small figures
     exaggeration of soft body parts
     crowded figures
     lack of individuation
2. Sign related to anxious-avoidant attachment
     arms downward
3. Sign related to nonsecure attachment
     neutral/negative facial affect

**Table 4.7**    Family Drawing Variables From Spinetta and Deasy-Spinetta
                        (1981)

| Communication | Self-Image | Emotional Tone |
| --- | --- | --- |
| Compartmentalization | Incompleteness of body | Conditions of nature |
| Barriers | Frequency of missing body parts | Use of color |
| Used front-back of paper | Cross-outs | Use of space on paper |
| Exclusions | Subject portrayal | Developmental level |
| Body position-patient | Figure size | Use of stick figures |
| Body position-mother | Facial completeness | |
| Facial position-patient | | |
| Facial position-mother | | |

ing something. The KFD has a long clinical history (Burns & Kaufman, 1972). Spinetta published a study on the use of the KFD with pediatric cancer patients (Spinetta & Deasy-Spinetta, 1981). The authors developed three subscales, based on 19 items, related to communication, self-image, and emotional tone. These items are listed in Table 4.7.

The drawing features that seem most illuminating in the clinical evaluation of sexually abused children are the child's use of barriers as well as the exclusion of figures. When foster children draw a picture of the foster family that they have only briefly lived with, rather than their own, the possible implications warrant further examination and may be related to these children's feeling rejected by their parents.

Recent work by Peterson and Hardin (1997) has focused on identifying indicators of sexual abuse in the drawings of children, including human figure drawings (reviewed in Chapter 7) and KFDs. A total of 24 variables are scored, resulting in a score ranging from zero to between 0.5 and 2.0 per variable. The authors suggest that a drawing is "suspicious" if the child obtains a score of 6.0 or greater. An independent validation of the authors' findings is needed in order to make their findings even more useful than they are currently. At this time, however, the drawings may suggest possible maltreatment, including sexual abuse; they may simply reflect the disturbed family the child is living in; or they may mean nothing.

Attachment stories (Bretherton, Ridgeway, & Cassidy, 1990) were developed for use with preschoolers. The child is oriented to a play setting, with small props, including human figures, furniture, and so on. The interviewer reads the introduction to five different scenarios, inviting the child to act out the end with the dolls, all the while providing a narrative. For example, one of the stories depicts a reunion between parents and children after the children spent a night with the grandmother. Most of the children in this study described their parents as empathetic, nonpunitive, and protective, and the stories were significantly related to attachment security, although not as robustly as earlier research had led the authors to believe. Regrettably, a corresponding technique is not available for older children. See Appendix F for a copy of these stories.

The Inventory of Parent and Peer Attachment (IPPA) was developed to assess the security of teenagers' relationship with their parents (Armsden & Greenberg, 1987). Although it has been used in a number of studies, it has never been anchored to an acceptable criterion such as the Strange Situation. Consequently its utility as a true measure of attachment is uncertain.

There are several variables from the Rorschach that are correlated with relationship quality (Weiner, 1998). The Isolate score is one such measure, as are the scores related to perceptions of relationships as cooperative (COP) and aggressive (AG). The Texture response is also presumed to be related to the child's overt need for relationships. Responses that suggest either the lack of boundaries or an overconcern with safety, including penetration and barrier responses (Kelly, 1999), are also in this category. The significance of any of these responses is best determined in light of other data that pertain to relationships.

The reader might wonder what happens if the evaluator simply asks children questions to determine the quality of their relationship with their family and skips the indirect methods described above. It is very difficult for children, who have little permission or opportunity to think about or talk about their relationship with their parents, to know what to say to open-ended questions like, "What is it like to live with your parents?" Questions like this typically result in noncommittal shrugs, half-smiles, and stereotypic responses. It is much more useful to ask questions along the lines of the probes in the AAI, such as words that come to mind when they think of their parent. For example, one girl, when asked to come up with three words that described her father, who was accused of molesting her, generated one word, "nice." She then went on to recount a story where he took her pet back to the pet store as evidence of that. This was a perfect example of a lack of coherence, and when I asked later if he was confusing to her, she assented by beginning to cry.

### ABUSE-SPECIFIC INFORMATION

The Children's Impact of Traumatic Events Scale-Revised (CITES-R) is a 78-item measure that has 11 subscales that fall along four dimensions (Wolfe, Gentile, Michienzi, Sas, & Wolfe, 1991). One of the dimensions, Social Reactions, includes two scales that are related to the child's working model of adults as supportive: Negative Reactions from others, and Social Support. In addition, another dimension, Eroticism, captures children's view that they have more sexual feelings than their peers and in this way is related to impaired relating. Although this measure is face valid and lends itself to denial by the child, the instrument becomes very useful as a transition from the evaluation into the therapy process.

Although there is no research literature on this next strategy, having children draw the perpetrator has long provided useful information about the nature of their relationship. In the majority of the cases that I evaluate, children have a history with the perpetrator, and their treatment of the drawing can indicate some important therapy issues. I have seen stick drawings with exaggerated penises from boys who are sexually aggressive to extremely detailed drawings by children who both blame themselves for the abuse and deny any symptoms related to the abuse.

## ❑ Child-Peer Relationship

Social Competence scales from the CBCL (Achenbach, 1991a) and the Teacher Report Form (Achenbach, 1991b), or the Adaptive Scales from the BASC (Reynolds & Kamphaus, 1998), provide information on the child's social relationships. It has been suggested that social competence has five sequential processing steps that are assumed to occur in real time and are necessary for competent social behavior (Dodge, Pettit, McClaskey, & Brown, 1986). The child first encodes the social cues, and second, represents mentally the encoded cues and interprets them in a meaningful way. In the third step, the child accesses a social response to the cue, and in the fourth step, evaluates the likely outcome of the behavior. Finally, the child enacts the social behavior. Clearly, this is a complex process.

Information on social competence was very useful in a child who had been fondled by her grandfather over an extended period of time. The child quickly regrouped, and I thought that her symptom relief was possibly reflective of suppression. However, both the teacher and the mother saw the girl as having resumed her prior social competence, and this supported what appeared to be some genuine progress in therapy, even though the positive changes being reported seemed too rapid to me.

There is some interesting research that examines the relationship of bullying and victim behavior in children to their attachment quality (Troy & Sroufe, 1987). Bullying seems to be related to avoidant attachment, and victim behavior seems to be related to resistant attachment. It is important to ask either children or their caregivers if they have been harassed by their peers or if they have been accused of bullying behavior themselves.

Bullying is consistent with interpersonal cruelty and is reflective of impaired empathy. Regrettably, interpersonal cruelty is an all-too-frequent outcome of maltreatment. In a recent paper that explored children whose parents reported that they were cruel to others and cruel to animals (two items from the CBC; Achenbach, 1991a), physical abuse was the best predictor of these behaviors (Friedrich, Ascione, Heath, & Hayashi, 2001). Children who are bullies and/or cruel do not make good participants in group therapy.

The degree to which a child sexualizes relationships following sexual abuse can be viewed both as an attachment issue and as one reflecting rule-violating behavior that has potentially long-term consequences. Peer relationships in preteens are not typically characterized by intense sexual interest. This certainly changes in at least some adolescents. To determine if the teenage girl's interest in "boys" is developmentally appropriate or related to prior sexual abuse is thus much more difficult.

Whatever your perspective, it is important to find out if a sexually abused child is now precociously "boy-crazy" or talking sexually with younger or same-aged children. This is very hard to do with young children using direct interview, and input from the caregiver is critical. Ideally, the parent is a good monitor and an accurate reporter of the child's behavior with peers.

## ❏  Common Clinical Assessment Dilemmas

There are five common questions that emerge in this domain: (a) What is the quality of the child's attachment to the nonoffending parent? (b) What is the quality of the child's attachment to the perpetrating parent in cases of incest? (c) Does the parent have the capacity to be securely attached to this child and keep the child safe from further victimization? (d) Is this a parent-child relationship that is healthy enough to try to salvage? and (e) To what degree are the child's difficulties related to poor attachment?

The first question is relevant in all cases of sexual abuse, including extrafamilial. Typically, the assessment of this relationship occurs as part of the intake interview as the child or teen is entering treatment. Parents' relationships with their own parents and a history of maltreatment with subsequent therapy of lack thereof are two critical areas that may tell you most of what you need to know in the way of future treatment planning. Sensitive and supportive parenting relationships will buffer all adversity, and the lack of these characteristics makes abuse-specific therapy longer and even contraindicated. In addition to the above questions, I also take into consideration parents' comments about positive features of the child. These cursory observations are typically not sufficient for forensic cases, and so a more thorough evaluation is conducted.

A question of this type reflects concern about reactive attachment disorder and typically is raised with children facing adoption or if the child is failing an adoptive placement. This diagnosis includes children who display two broad types of behavior problems related to insecure attachment. The first are children who are indiscriminately affectionate, and the second are the avoidant, detached children seemingly content to be by themselves. A feature of this diagnosis is the assumption of pathogenic parenting. Of concern to me is that children receive this diagnosis because they have experienced very poor parenting but their behaviors are more reflective of PTSD, oppositional defiant disorder, or ADHD than they are of the behavior problems outlined above. I have no easy answers regarding the assessment related to this diagnosis and would rather describe the child in terms of attachment theory, that is, one of three types of insecure attachment.

My assessment strategy is to search for indices suggesting that the child has the capacity to be interested in people and to view them accurately, the child has the potential for a reflective capacity, and the match with the parent figure is a good fit. This latter aspect is critical, since attachment insecurity is resolved only as part of a process with sensitive caregivers who know how not to overwhelm the child. I have never found it useful to refer the child for "attachment therapy" that involves rage-induction, and agree with James (1994) that the theoretical underpinnings of this strategy are suspect.

The second question assumes that the perpetrator is a parent figure of the child's, and the family or the perpetrator wishes to continue his involvement in the child's life. The perpetrator may be finishing treatment. He may feel that he wants to continue a relationship with the child he has wronged and genuinely hopes that this can be done with only regular involvement. However, the relationship a child has with one parent figure is partially related to the child's relationship with the other, and each relationship affects the security of the other. As you can see, the question immediately becomes more complex.

In these cases, I recommend that the evaluator obtain permission from the court to expand the assessment process to include a number of parties, not just the offending parent-child relationship. The people to be assessed include both the perpetrator and the child, as well as the nonoffending parent and the child. The evaluator should not settle for the narrow question of the unilateral quality of the child's relationship to the perpetrator. The child may actually state a wish for a continuation of the interrupted relationship with the perpetrator. This could stem from loyalty, because of a reaction formation, or the child's perception that the nonoffending parent wishes for this to be true.

An evaluation of this type necessitates getting access to perpetrators' treatment records. You need to determine if they have had a reasonable treatment experience, and if there has been a genuine reduction in future abuse potential. This may require consulting with a colleague who is an expert in treatment of sex offenders.

Incestuous fathers with no other sex-related violations or felonies on their record are at relatively lower risk to reoffend than non-incest perpetrators (Marshall & Barbaree, 1990). In addition, for this to be a valid referral question, some attempt at family reunification should have been suggested or attempted. The evaluator needs to determine whether this attempt followed an acceptable sequence, such as that outlined in Trepper and Barrett's (1989) book on treating incestuous families. It is also critical to determine the degree to which the nonoffending parent and the child have developed a healthier relationship since the abuse disclosure. Can the mother point to aspects of the therapy that have led to a new and more accurate appreciation of the child? Does she have the child's safety as an utmost priority?

There are times when, of the two parents, the perpetrator had the more positive and affirming relationship with the child victim. In these cases, supporting the parent-child relationship is probably worthwhile, as long as the mother-child relationship is not adversely affected.

Parents' competence to raise their children and keep them safe from further victimization is reflected in the parents' competence in a number of broad arenas of parenting. Sometimes this is referred to as a bonding evaluation, which is actually a misnomer. Bonding simply refers to an emotional involvement or connection between parties. A chronically alcoholic parent can report loving his or her child and thinking about the child all the time. This may refer to a bond and be held up by an attorney as proof of attachment, but it is not secure attachment. Bonding describes a connection that is nowhere as complex as an attachment relationship.

First and foremost in these evaluations is the quality of the parent-child attachment. The quality and coherence of the parent's narrative in response to the Parent Interview (Appendix A), as well as the parent's behavior in the parent-child observation, is critical. Evaluations of parental permanence that could lead to the termination of parental rights must be approached with a great deal of seriousness and thoroughness. The absence of psychopathology that would reduce parents' emotional availability and interfere with attunement and the resolution of their own victimization is another important set of criteria.

A determining factor in termination cases is the suitability of alternatives to living in the family. Is adoption or long-term foster care truly helpful to a child? Or is the child better off remaining in the home where the abuse occurred? What if the child has disorganized attachment, some organicity due to prenatal exposure to drugs/alcohol, and the likelihood of never making significant improvement? There are data from studies of long-term outcomes of adoptions and that illustrate that it is an empirically defensible suggestion and that children as a group do better being reared in a more positive environment (Maughan & Pickles, 1990).

The fourth question is very tough to answer and one that makes me doubly pleased simply to advise the court, not be the one who answers the ultimate question. The answer certainly rests on the quality of the attachment, as defined in the two paragraphs above. It also requires an understanding of what it takes to resolve a history of victimization, knowing that the answer varies from one person to the next. Parents with reduced intelligence as well as malignant Axis II diagnoses are very unlikely to change, and certainly not in the time needed for children to have the family they need. Similarly bleak prognoses are likely for individuals with dissociative diagnoses, or parents who persist in abusive relationships. Parents who cannot follow through with a simple self-monitoring request between one appointment and the next with you are also not likely to change.

Regarding the final question, attachment problems and child disturbance go hand in hand and feed each other (Crittenden, 1995). Although they may be more easily demonstrable with younger children, the connection remains at all ages.

## ❏ Summary

The clinical assessment of attachment is made difficult in that the technical assessment of attachment quality, via the Strange Situation (Ainsworth et al., 1978) or the Attachment Q-Sort (Waters & Deane, 1985), is not available to the clinician. Consequently, we are left to assess the quality of the relationship via strategies that are related to but are not the same as the research devices described above. Therefore, reports based on these nonresearch measures assess the quality of the parent-child relationship, and the degree to which this is related to attachment security is not certain.

In addition, the quality of the parent-child relationship, more than any other variable, defines the child's ability to change and rebound from victimization. Consequently, critical questions are answered by strategies that provide approximations, not exact answers.

However, understanding the quality of the child's attachment to the parent can make the child's symptoms easier to understand and make you more specific and targeted in your treatment recommendations. You are then in a position to advise the court as to the true best interests of the child.

When it comes to attachment-related treatment recommendations, a logical choice is Parent-Child Interaction Therapy (Hembree-Kigin & McNeil, 1995). Several cases utilizing this approach with maltreating families have been reported in the literature (Borrego, Urquiza, Rasmussen, & Zebell, 1999; Urquiza & McNeil, 1996). Although developed to enhance the parent-child relationship with younger children and thus increase child compliance, the upper age of children for whom it appears helpful has been extended into the early teens.

The approach outlined by Esther Deblinger in her research with nonoffending mothers relies on a cognitive therapy approach. To the degree that this alters the negative perception of the child by the parent, it is related to attachment security (Deblinger & Hefflin, 1996). This is also true of Azar's (1997) and Kolko's (1996) work with physically abusive parents.

# 5

# *Assessment of Dysregulation*

This chapter reviews measures used to assess a range of dysregulation issues in both child and parent (see Table 5.1). Dysregulation subsumes the two most common sequelae of maltreatment, posttraumatic stress disorder (PTSD) and sexual behavior problems, with the latter cluster of behavior problems discussed in Chapter 6. Chronic dysregulation has also been associated with dissociation (Ogawa, Sroufe, Weinfeld, Carlson, & Egeland, 1997). However, that does not exclude the role of affect regulation problems in the etiology of a range of internalizing and externalizing disorders (Bradley, 2000).

The case that was initially presented in Chapter 4 is continued here. A number of dysregulation-specific issues were relevant and related to A. B.'s overall level of distress, particularly his suicidality, possible PTSD, and sexual behavior difficulties. The child psychiatrist and his school counselor had also raised the question of attention deficit hyperactivity disorder (ADHD). Similar questions pertained to the adjustment of both of his older sisters, but because the sisters were not

**Table 5.1**    Measures and Techniques to Assess Dysregulation

---

   I. Parent-Rated—Self, Generic
      A. Life Stress
  II. Parent-Rated—Self, Abuse Specific
      A. Trauma Symptom Inventory (Briere, 1995)
      B. Dissociative Experiences Schedule (Bernstein & Putnam, 1986)
      C. Lifetime Victimization Questionnaire
 III. Parent-Rated—Family
      A. Safety Checklist
  IV. Parent-Rated—Child, Generic
      A. IOWA Conners Rating Scale (Loney & Milich, 1982)
   V. Parent-Rated—Child, Abuse Specific
      A. Child Sexual Behavior Inventory (Friedrich, 1997)
      B. Child Dissociative Checklist
      C. Child Behavior Checklist (Achenbach, 1991a)
         1. Sleep problems
         2. Anxiety/Depression
         3. Attention problems
         4. Somatic complaints
  VI. Teacher-Rated—Child
      A. Teacher Report Form (Achenbach, 1991b)
      B. Children's Attention/Activity Problems Scale (Edelbrock, 1991)
 VII. Child-Rated Measures—Generic
      A. Child Depression Inventory (Kovacs, 1991)
      B. Revised Children's Manifest Anxiety Scale (Reynolds & Richmond, 1978)
      C. Trauma Symptom Checklist for Children (Briere, 1995)
         1. Anxiety
         2. Depression
         3. Anger
      D. Rorschach
VIII. Child-Rated Measures—Abuse Specific
      A. Sexual Abuse Fear Survey Schedule (Wolfe & Wolfe, 1988)
      B. CITES-R (Wolfe, Gentile, Michienzi, Sas, & Wolfe, 1991)
      C. Trauma Symptom Checklist Children (Briere, 1995)
      D. Adolescent Dissociative Experiences Schedule
      E. Self-Injurious Behavior Questionnaire (Appendix R)
      F. Suicide Potential Rating Scale (Cull & Gill, 1982)

---

available, their problems were assessed more briefly and via parent report. Other dysregulation relevant family issues pertained to the safety in the home from further victimization, the presence of family characteristics that were stabilizing, and also Mrs. B.'s psychiatric problems.

## ❏ Dysregulation-Related Case Material

### Parent/Family

The Safety Checklist (Appendix G) was the basis of my interview with A. B.'s mother. She reported a number of areas of concern that contribute to A. B.'s feeling out of control. The safety issues include cosleeping (A. B. and C. B.), family nudity, and family violence. In addition, Mrs. B. has difficulty with monitoring the children's activities, given the amount of overtime she puts in. With regard to family nudity, the mother reports that both of the older girls are occasionally nude or partially nude, and more often they wear only underwear in the house. The children regularly fight with each other, and this includes punching and biting.

When I asked Mrs. B. about these problems with safety, she was at first dismissive, stating that as a single parent she could not be home that much, that she needed her personal life, and that her immediate family was far healthier than her family of origin. I then explained to her that safety was a major issue in stopping further victimization. Safety in the home was her way of sending a clear message about being sensitive to the needs of the other. Although she became more subdued, she did indicate that she would think about safety from this perspective. Her ability to begin considering this is positive.

I summarized the risk factors present in the B. family household using the Risk Factor Checklist (Appendix I), and 14 of 21 factors were identified. These included the following: disruption in A. B.'s parenting; maternal history of sexual abuse (for which the mother has not received treatment); rejection of the child; abuse duration of more than 1 month; child's report of abuse not believed by parent; child experiencing other abuses; criminal history in either parent; substance abuse in either parent; conflict with extended family; marital instability; pregnant prior to age of 18; inconsistent parenting; parent cannot use child management skills; and violence in the home. Each of these contributes to the family's difficulties in making progress in therapy. The sheer number clearly indicates that these problems are multigenerational and underscore the need for Mrs. B to receive therapy to address her ambivalence toward her children, particularly A. B.

Mrs. B. completed the MMPI-2. Although she answered in a some-what defensive manner, her overall profile was valid. She obtained elevations above $T = 65$ on scales 4, 8, and 3, respectively. This profile suggests longer-standing problems with distrust, impatience, reduced empathy, moodiness, impaired monitoring capacity and inconsistent response to child behaviors, and reduced insight, despite a superficially gregarious and sociable veneer. Given her life circumstances, the absence of acute depressive or anxious symptomatology is a concern. In fact, A. B.'s primary nurse described Mrs. B. as very friendly over the phone. However, immediately after the intake interview, the same nurse found her to be cold and angry. In addition, Mrs. B. showed no interest in a brief visit with A. B. before she returned to work.

### Child

A. B. was evaluated with the Trauma Symptom Checklist for Children (TSCC; Briere, 1996). He was read each question and responded minimally, with his predominant response a very quick, unemotional "Never." In fact, he was significantly elevated on the Under Response Validity Scale, with a $T$ score of 66. This response style contributed to his being below the mean on all clinical scales and subscales of the TSCC. However, he did endorse four critical items: wanting to hurt myself, wanting to hurt other people, getting into fights, and wanting to kill myself. Unlike the dismissive stance he took with the majority of the other questions on the TSCC, he looked quite sober and subdued when he answered these items.

A. B. had been placed on Ritalin by his family physician in second grade but had become "hyper" according to his mother's report, and the medication trial was stopped at that time. However, the concerns about possible ADHD had persisted, and A. B. was noticed to be quite inattentive and preoccupied in his first few days in the hospital. Consequently, A. B. was observed during the Barkley Academic Observation Schedule (Barkley, 1991). This is a 15-minute observation in which a child is observed from behind a one-way mirror while working on academically related tasks. Behaviors are rated every 30 seconds. A. B. was given several reading and math worksheets. For example, he was asked to write short answers to questions and then complete grade-appropriate math sheets. He was off task 97% of the time and fidgeting 83% of the time. He was also vocalizing 80% of the time. In fact, he was unable to complete any of the worksheets provided. He impressed me as emotionally depleted and agitated, which accounted for much of his off-task behavior.

Mrs. B rated her son on several behavior rating scales. On the Child Behavior Checklist (CBCL; Achenbach, 1991a) she reported significant problems in all areas assessed, including the three Social Competence scales. *T* scores of 70 or higher were noted for Anxious/Depressed, Attention Problems, Aggressive Behavior, Delinquent Behavior, Social Problems, Thought Problems, Somatic Complaints, and Withdrawn. On the Experimental PTSD and Dissociation subscales (see Table 5.2), A. B. was between 3 and 5 standard deviations above the mean across dissociation, PTSD, and combined PTSD/dissociation when community norms were used. When contrasted with a clinical sample of children, he ranged between 1 and 2 standard deviations above the mean on dissociation, combined PTSD/dissociation, and PTSD, respectively.

A. B.'s third-grade teacher rated him on the Teacher Report Form (Achenbach, 1991b). This enabled a comparison of his behavior in the school setting versus his behavior at home. In keeping with the verbal report from the school counselor, A. B. was rated by his teacher as significantly ($T > 65$) anxious/depressed, withdrawn, and socially immature. She did not report the aggression his mother indicated, or the attention problems. She indicated that he had been doing well in school until several months earlier. Her ratings actually corresponded more closely to our observations of him on the inpatient unit and were far more positive than Mrs. B.'s ratings indicated. In fact, they more clearly indicated Mrs. B.'s clear negative bias regarding her son.

The Rorschach also suggested significant problems with A. B.'s expression of feelings. His protocol was devoid of chromatic responses, suggesting the lack of appropriate channels to express his feelings. His lack of comfort with strong feelings and his reduced psychological complexity are also reflected in his significantly elevated lambda (Exner, 1991).

### Siblings

Mrs. B. rated both daughters regarding generic behavior problems on the CBCL (Achenbach, 1991a). On the CBCL, B. B. had problems on

**Table 5.2**    CBCL Items Related to PTSD and Dissociation

*Dissociation*: 13, 17, 80

*PTSD*: 9, 29, 45, 47, 50, 76, 100

*Combined PTSD/Dissociation*:  8, 9, 13, 17, 29, 45, 47, 50, 66, 76, 80, 84,
                                 87, 92, 100

school-competency and was also elevated (*T* > 65) on the Aggressive and Delinquent subscales. C. B. was within normal limits on the Social Competency subscales but elevated (*T* > 65) on Aggressive and Somatic Complaints. The elevations on the Externalizing scales are quite concerning and are associated with the increased risk for drug and alcohol abuse, teenage pregnancy, and early school dropout.

### Dysregulation-Related Treatment Recommendations

1. As part of the therapy recommended in Chapter 4, Mrs. B. must address the distorted thinking and impulse control problems reflected in her elevated score on the Child Abuse Potential Inventory.
2. A. B. is not yet ready to talk about the victimization he experienced, but he has some awareness of his angry impulses. Individual therapy that respects his ambivalence but offers a chance to expose these feelings gently and discuss them is recommended. It is likely that after several sessions the therapist will be able to assess more accurately for other dysregulating symptoms.
3. Mrs. B. needs to be educated about safety, trauma, and triggers. This may help her be more empathetic to A. B.'s difficulties with anger control. Tying this to her own past is likely to help her take his perspective more readily.
4. Consideration is needed about how to help Mrs. B. with more appropriate monitoring.

❏ **Overview of Dysregulation**

Symptoms of dysregulation can fall into a number of categories, including reexperiencing, avoidant behaviors and diminished responsiveness, and increased arousal (Hall, 1993). Although these categories reflect PTSD symptoms, they include clinical phenomena other than PTSD. For example, panic attacks related to trauma reflect both reexperiencing and heightened arousal. Separation anxiety in the child made insecure by abuse may reflect increased arousal, as well as avoidance of potentially threatening situations.

The careful assessment of dysregulation requires input from parents, teachers, and the child in question. These data often come from traumatized individuals, for example, parents. Research on mothers of severely maltreated children found that in a sample of 109 cases, 15.6% of the mothers currently had PTSD and 36.7% had a prior history of PTSD (Famularo, Fenton, Kinscherff, Ayoub, & Barnum, 1994). The PTSD diagnosis was also significantly overrepresented in those children whose mothers were diagnosed with PTSD. A second study found that mothers appeared to be traumatized by the abuse of their children, and this activation persisted over time (Newberger, Gremy, Waternaux, & Newberger, 1993). It is difficult to imagine how parents can easily be supportive if their children become a reminder of trauma and a trigger for their own reactivity.

The questions that are addressed by an evaluation of dysregulation are many. They include whether the referred child is demonstrating one of the dysregulation-related symptom clusters, and if so, whether this is related to the abusive experience. Other questions include whether parents are struggling with their own dysregulation-related symptoms, whether parents' problems in this domain aggravate parenting problems, and whether or not the child's environment is safe from further abuse and can facilitate the child's recovery.

A frequent manifestation of dysregulation is PTSD or its closely related disorder, acute stress disorder (ASD), which typically is used to describe the earliest (one month) response by the individual (Briere, 1997). The measurement of PTSD has been the basis of some controversy that bears review prior to the remainder of the chapter. For a more detailed review of the arguments, refer to Carlson (1997). In addition, a comprehensive set of practice parameters in the assessment of PTSD is also available from the American Academy of Child and Adolescent Psychiatry (AACAP, 1998).

For a diagnosis of PTSD to be made, the clinician has to identify a trauma, which is Criterion A in the diagnosis (American Psychiatric

Association [APA], 1994). There are two components to this criterion, the first is that the trauma be extreme and must involve "actual or threatened death . . . or a threat to the physical integrity of self or others" (p. 427) and "the person's response involved intense fear or horror" (p. 428). The second component is modified in the case of children to include "disorganized or agitated behavior" (AACAP, 1998, p. 55).

There are also several subtypes of PTSD. Symptoms that appear within a month of Criterion A and do not last (or have not yet persisted beyond 1 month) are given diagnoses of ASD. The acute type has symptoms for less than 3 months. Chronic types have symptoms that have lasted for at least 3 months. Delayed onset is often 6 months later, although careful questioning may reveal that it is chronic.

The first issue in the above-referenced controversy pertains to whether the criteria are broad enough to accommodate all of the events that could produce PTSD. Very young children who were molested in an erotic manner may not have feared death, nor can they state that they experienced horror, but yet they may have the behaviors subsumed under Criteria B (reexperiencing), C (avoidance), and D (increased arousal) that are required for the diagnosis. Older children also have developmental limitations that interfere with the clinician being able to substantiate the full range of symptoms. A primary one is an inability to articulate their trauma-relevant emotions. Children who blame themselves, as do children of this age, may choose to deny the severity of incestuous abuse.

There may be a number of traumatic experiences in the child's history, all of which predispose him to PTSD, but together they may not measure up to the criteria required by Criterion A. In fact, most abused children have other abuses or family problems that characterize their lives (Cicchetti, 1989).

Another dilemma emerges if the child reports reexperiencing something other than the abuse, such as a drive-by shooting. The parent may have noticed increased arousal and avoidance only after the disclosure of the incest. Does the clinician assign the abuse or the drive-by shooting to Criterion A?

A further controversy, again seemingly affected by developmental level, pertains to whether the patient has to connect both C and D symptoms to the traumatic event. A child who has been kept away from the perpetrator since her disclosure is unlikely to have exhibited avoidant behavior. In addition, I have never interviewed a preschooler who could validly answer a question such as, "Have you been trying not to feel or think about what happened?" And what young child can actually make the decision "not to go places" that are reminders of what happened? Is it valid to surmise that if the child saw the offend-ing parent and then exhibited a burst of separation-anxiety, then this child has Criterion C symptoms?

Finally, Carlson (1997) reviewed another controversy related to the adequacy of the criteria that describe PTSD. For example, dissociative symptoms are part of the diagnosis of acute stress disorder (ASD; APA, 1994), a common precursor to PTSD, but they are not part of the PTSD diagnosis. There is no logic to this, particularly when research suggests that dissociation may be more likely to emerge after chronic trauma (Putnam, 1994).

The debate behind these questions is reflected in two alternate frameworks. The first is by Terr (1991), who proposes a Type 1 (sudden blow) and Type 2 (long-standing) form of PTSD. The second is by Famularo, Fenton, Augustyn, and Zuckerman (1996), who describe acute and chronic with the latter having more dissociative and affective symptoms.

Traumatic experiences may have a profound impact on self-perception, for example, rape, but these sequelae are not represented in the B, C, and D criteria. It is very important to remind ourselves that the diagnostic category of PTSD was developed on veterans, not rape victims or children. This conundrum may need to be spelled out in your evaluation when you are explaining whether or not the child meets criteria for PTSD. This does not mean that you should be less precise in diagnosing PTSD in children. Rather, you might state what criteria of PTSD the child meets fully, what developmentally related behaviors may be approximations of these criteria, and what behaviors could be related to the traumatic event in question or even to other family circumstances, for example, chronic domestic violence. Finally, you could state that if the diagnosis cannot be made, what excludes this from happening. Only as children mature are they capable of exhibiting adult-like PTSD symptoms (Scheeringa, Zeanah, Drell, & Larrieu, 1995).

It is also critical to keep in mind the three factors that have been found consistently to mediate the development of PTSD in children: severity of trauma exposure, trauma-related parental distress, and temporal proximity to the traumatic event (Foy, Madoig, Pynoos, & Camilleri, 1996). It is interesting to note that there are data that suggest in cases of maltreatment, either physical or sexual abuse, the anticipation that the trauma might reoccur was related to minimal drop-off in PTSD symptoms over time (Green, 1985; McLeer, Deblinger, Henry, & Orvaschel, 1992).

Since this text's primary focus is on the assessment of children and teenagers, a developmental perspective on PTSD is also needed. Very young children are typically not diagnosed as having PTSD using the *DSM-IV* criteria (Zeanah, Boris, & Scheeringa, 1997). At least 8 of 18 of the PTSD criteria require verbal descriptions of both the experience and the internal states (Scheeringa et al., 1995). This is an impossible task for preschoolers and many early elementary-school-aged children. Some researchers have suggested that diagnostic play sessions will be critical in the assessment of PTSD in preschoolers (Almqvist & Brandell- Forsberg, 1997). In fact, the direct reenactment of the trauma was used in the diagnostic assessment of PTSD in children who were all younger than 48 months (Scheeringa, Peebles, Cook, & Zeanah, 2001). Due to the limited verbal and cognitive skills of children ages 0 to 3, the authors developed behaviorally anchored criteria that were more developmentally appropriate (Scheeringa et al., 1995) and that have been validated in a subsequent study (Scheeringa et al., 2001). In these children, PTSD may be seen in symptoms of generalized anxiety, sleep disturbance, and idiosyncratic avoidant and preoccupied behaviors (AACAP, 1998). The alternate criteria for young children exhibited more criterion validity than the *DSM-IV* criteria. See Appendix S for the alternative PTSD criteria developed by Scheeringa and colleagues (Scheeringa et al., 2001).

As an ancillary to this text, I would suggest the excellent book on the behavioral assessment of children by Mash and Terdal (1988), which has outstanding chapters on depression and anxiety. Two excellent recent texts on assessing PTSD and trauma (Briere, 1997; Wilson & Keane, 1997) are also very useful companions to this chapter.

## ❑ Parent Rating—Self

### GENERIC MEASURES

To evaluate the significance of dysregulation-related symptoms in the child or teenager, you must pay close attention to the child's contexts, that is, parent-child relationships, family functioning, and so on. The child's symptoms are best understood after evaluating the contribution of each of these contexts.

The parent is predisposed to dysregulation-related symptoms by the cumulative buildup of distress in life. The sexual abuse of the child is one more of these experiences that can both interfere with parenting and contribute to agitation, a recurrence of PTSD, and other arousal-related problems, such as sleep difficulties, anxiety, panic, and depression. An evaluation of dysregulation-related symptoms in the parent necessitates questions about prior maltreatment and stressful experiences in the parent's life. In addition, the relationship between child and parent symptoms may be bilateral, with each one having the potential to trigger or stress the other.

A logical place to start is to assess the parent's experience with a range of stressful life events. If you already have the parent completing either the longer PSI (Abidin, 1995) or its 36-item counterpart, you will have a sense of the parenting-specific stress being experienced. Other strategies include having the parent complete the Daily Hassles Checklist (Crnic & Greenberg, 1990) or any one of several published life stress checklists (Johnson, 1986) as part of the intake process.

The Risk Factor Checklist (Appendix I) is one mechanism for tallying up the cumulative stress load of the parent-child relationship. These factors grew out of the Untreatable Family Checklist, which I modeled in part on David Jones's excellent paper on the untreatable family (Jones, 1987). It includes variables that are empirically related to compromised parenting.

A review of the items from the Risk Factor Checklist suggests that the risk factors are related to any threat to the security of the parent-child relationship (e.g., 1-6, 9, etc.), upsetting events in the home (e.g., 11, 15, 21, etc.), or those factors associated with an increase in parenting problems (e.g., 7-8, 10, 16-17, etc.). The likelihood of continued foster care placement, treatment failures, and termination of parental rights is directly related to the total number of risk items (Friedrich, 1995a).

Many of the preexisting life stress checklists are problematic for disadvantaged families. A central failing is that the unique stressors these families experience are not listed in the inventory. Items pertaining to violence in the community, evictions by landlords, experiences with racism, unsafe housing, and involvement with the law are needed to make the checklist complete and valid for families that live in unsafe neighborhoods. For that reason, Vaughn, Egeland, and Sroufe (1979) modified a preexisting life stress measure that has been utilized in some of the studies cited in this text, such as Fury, Carlson, and Sroufe (1997). For example, in their paper on precursors to ADHD, a closely related measure of the child's life stress was a useful predictor of the diagnosis at the age of 6 years (Jacobvitz & Sroufe, 1987).

Since prior victimization is a key contributor to parents' ability to parent their abused child effectively, an assessment of the emotional, physical, and sexual abuse parents have experienced is a very important component of your evaluation. A victimization screening device that can be completed by the parent and that was developed by Briere (1991) and modified for several research studies (Springs & Friedrich, 1992) is included in Appendix C. For a briefer alternative, I recommend the revised Conflict Tactics Scale, which has some excellent questions for the parent on prior maltreatment (Straus, Hamby, Finkelhor, Moore, & Runyan, 1998).

Substance abuse problems are often a direct reflection of early dysregulating experiences in the parent's life (Stewart, 1996; Wilsnack, 1991). Chronic substance abuse is also a direct contributor to dysregulation in the current home environment. Chemical dependency is more common in individuals with a history of sexual abuse (Springs & Friedrich, 1992) and also in the parents of sexually abused children (Daro, 1988). When present, it compromises parental support (Leifer, Shapiro, & Kassem, 1993). It is critically important that alcoholism and substance abuse be assessed in a systematic manner, using a screening device such as the Self-Administered Alcoholism Screening Test (SAAST; Colligan, Davis, & Morse, 1988) or its close cousin, the Michigan Alcoholism Screening Test, reprinted in Salter (1988).

*Personality Functioning.* Many of the same personality variables that interfere with attachment quality are also important to dysregulation-related assessment. The concept of secure base, which is so germane to attachment security, also depicts the degree to which the parent can provide a soothing, supportive, and nonreactive home environment to the abused child. For example, a parent who is an accurate observer of her or his child's behavior is in a better position to create safety for the child and to monitor the child's level of distress and make adjustments so that the child does not become overwhelmed. For this reason, such issues as depression, hysteria, and paranoia clearly detract from parental attunement. Other symptom clusters, including PTSD and dissociation, are also deleterious to the parenting process.

Generic measures include the MMPI-2 (Butcher, Dahlstrom, Graham, Tellegen, & Kaemmer, 1989), MCMI (Millon, 1987), and other increasingly utilized measures of adult personality variables, such as the Personality Assessment Inventory (PAI; Morrey, 1991) or its derivative, the 22-item Personality Assessment Screener (PAS; Morrey, 1997). The evaluator should look for elevations that suggest the parent is overwhelmed or has the type of personality problems that detract from observing her child accurately or creating a secure base.

If you are using a longer measure—MMPI-2, MCMI, and so on—scales 2, 3, 4, 6, and 8 from the MMPI-2 are logical ones to examine. If the concerns expressed by the referral source, for example, county attorney, are of a magnitude that affects the future of the parent-child relationship, it is very important that the evaluation be anchored by one or more broad-based personality measures.

At times I have elected to be more parsimonious and assessed variables that were narrowband, for example, depression with the Beck Depression Inventory (BDI-II; Beck, 1996) or agitation/anxiety with the Symptom Checklist (SCL-90-R; Derogatis, 1983). In fact, Saunders and colleagues (Saunders, Arata, & Kilpatrick, 1990) have identified more than 25 items from the SCL-90-R that are empirically related to a diagnosis of PTSD. These efforts helped the SCL-90-R yield additional information.

More recently, I have found the PAS (Morrey, 1997) to be very useful and, given its brevity, quite user friendly. In addition to a total score, which can prompt a more extensive evaluation, it has 10 other ele-

ments, including negative affect, acting out, anger control, and suicidal thinking. The items are face valid and as a result are open to deception, but data from these brief measures can be quite useful, that is,
they can identify a parent with an atypical but chronic affective disorder not immediately evident during interview.

## ABUSE-SPECIFIC MEASURES

Parents with an admitted or suspected abuse history need to be systematically evaluated. This is accomplished with selected questions
during the interview or via rating scales that they complete while you
talk to their child. It is quite likely that defensive parents will deny that
their child's abuse interferes with parenting. While this may reflect actual reality, it may be due to denial and their wish to succeed as the
child's parents. In these cases, measures such as the TSC-40 (Trauma
Symptom Checklist; Briere & Runtz, 1989) or the TSI (Trauma Symptom Inventory; Briere, 1995) may suggest otherwise.

For example, it was only after administering the TSI that I realized
that one mother was engaging in a significant amount of Tension Reducing Behavior (one of the subscales of the TSI). Further interviewing revealed that she engaged in self-cutting, a typically secretive behavior. She also revealed considerable substance use, and she would
alternate these two "coping strategies." The frequency of these two behaviors had increased after the disclosure of her child's abuse. This information was very important to the treatment process, since follow-
up questions about how these behaviors were affecting her parenting
illuminated how separate the mother and daughter had become after
the disclosure. Both were actively avoiding the other, and this was related to the mother's preference for avoidant coping strategies, for example, substance abuse.

More specific assessment of PTSD and/or dissociation, which are
assessed with a range of subscales from the TSI, may need to be completed either informally or via a more structured PTSD interview
(Davidson, Smith, & Kudler, 1989; Weiss & Marmar, 1997) and the
Dissociative Experiences Schedule (DES; Bernstein & Putnam, 1986),
respectively. The DES has been shown to be valid (Kihlstrom, Glisky, &

Anguilo, 1994), but I have found that its reading level makes it somewhat difficult for many of the parents I evaluate.

Both the DES and its adolescent counterpart, the Adolescent-Dissociative Experiences Schedule (A-DES; Armstrong, Putnam, & Carlson, 1993), are face valid. A high score on either does not mean the patient is dissociative. First, these measures are screening tools and are not diagnostic. Second, a high score can be interpreted much like an elevation on Scale F of the MMPI and is reflective of patients' distress level, their experience of unusual events in their life, and a willingness to endorse unusual behaviors. Either the DES or the A-DES is best used to support your diagnosis of dissociation. I will administer one clinically only after I have asked questions about gaps in memory, depersonalization, and derealization. I have not found them useful as stand-alone screening devices.

Dissociation and its assessment and treatment have met with considerable controversy. Some clinicians wonder if it is an actual phenomenon, or if it is generated solely by the interaction of the eager clinician and the passive and suggestible client (Carlson, 1997). Others accept its validity without question and diagnose it frequently.

Since dissociation is best viewed as a continuum disorder, there are five core issues that are typically but variably associated with a diagnosis of dissociation. These include amnesia, depersonalization, derealization, identity confusion, and identity alteration (Steinberg, 1996). The lack of integration among the emotions, behaviors, and thoughts displayed by the dissociative parent is of grave concern. Chronically dissociated parents are likely to be inconsistent and are experienced as rejecting and often unavailable by their children.

It is important to assess other forms of child maltreatment that parents have experienced and that could interfere with their parenting. There are several mechanisms to do so, beginning with the interview. It is important to remember that directly asking parents if they have been physically or sexually abused may result in a negative response, even though more careful and specific questioning may reveal that they have been abused as well as raped or beaten. The interpretation by the individual of what is and what is not "abuse" is extremely variable and highly subjective. The Victim Screen found in Appendix P is a structured interview that can be used to assess prior history and is based on an earlier measure (Briere, 1991). Rather than asking a blanket question about abuse, it asks more specific questions about emotionally, physically, and sexually abusive acts that the parent may have experienced while growing up. Asking about specific acts increases the validity of the evaluation.

The Parental Emotional Reaction Questionnaire (PERQ) was designed by its authors to measure parents' emotional reactions to their child being sexually abused (Mannarino & Cohen, 1996). The PERQ contains 15 items and examines such reactions as fear, sadness, guilt, anger, embarrassment, shame, and emotional preoccupation. Mothers are asked to rate each item on a 5-point scale ranging from "never" to "always" regarding how well it describes their emotional response to their child's sexual abuse. The higher the total score, the more intense and severe is the parent's emotional reaction to the abuse. It has been shown to have good inter-item and test-retest reliabilities.

## ❑ Parent/Caregiver Rating of Child

Parents need to rate their child's level of behavioral distress both broadly and more specifically. Because of the considerable range of behaviors included in dysregulation, a general measure of child behavior problems is useful. The CBCL (Achenbach, 1991a) and the parallel Teacher's Report Form (TRF; Achenbach, 1991b) are the two measures that have been utilized the most in research on sexually abused children. This does not mean the CBCL is as useful as other measures, for example, the Behavior Assessment System for Children (BASC; Reynolds & Kamphaus, 1998), and in fact a great deal of very appropriate criticism has been leveled against the CBCL (Perrin, et al., 1991). The reasons for the criticism are several and include the scale's insensitivity in identifying mild adjustment problems. The items are at times too easily subject to parental bias and misinterpretation, subscale names are misleading, and domains of behavior are not adequately sampled, for example, social competence. Because the CBCL uses age-related norms, it becomes difficult to determine children's true improvement over time when they move from one age level to the next.

Using parent and teacher report forms that are parallel can help the clinician become aware of how generalized the problems are, for example, at both home and school, academic and behavioral, social relationship problems, and so on. If a child is doing better at school than at home, this may suggest different demand characteristics in one setting over another. Although teachers often seem to minimize children's behavior difficulties, the parent-teacher discrepancy could also indicate a negative bias by the parent compared with the teacher and/or address the need for greater structure and support at home. This bias is quite genuine in the parents of abused children, given the finding that parents who have problems with their children are likely to perceive them in a different manner from parents who do not (Reid, Kavanagh, & Baldwin, 1987). Reid has found that some parents have "an axe to grind" with their child and overreport symptoms, others simply have a low tolerance for essentially normal behavior, and other parents are poor monitors and are not aware of all the behaviors their child is exhibiting.

In an effort to make the CBCL more directly applicable to those situations where trauma-assessment is an issue, several researchers have attempted to identify those items from the CBCL that appear to be more content-specific to PTSD, Dissociation, or both. For example, Vicki Wolfe and her colleagues have identified 20 items from the CBCL to measure PTSD. This subscale has an alpha coefficient of .89 (Wolfe, Gentile, & Wolfe, 1989). Subsequent research with the derived scale found it to correlate significantly with the child's report of sexual abuse-specific fears and with sexual behavior problems in the child (Wolfe, Gentile, Michienzi, Sas, & Wolfe, 1991). However, the scale does not measure the full range of PTSD symptoms, and it includes other symptoms that are at best associated features of the disorder, such as "sadness."

Confirmatory factor analysis was utilized in another study to identify other CBCL-derived scales, including PTSD (7 items), Dissociation (3 items), and a combined PTSD and Dissociation scale (16 items; Friedrich, Lengua, et al., 2001). These items satisfy a number of research criteria and when used to distinguish between abused and normative children, they succeed quite nicely. In addition, they correspond closely to specific CBCL items (Achenbach, 1991a) identified in

Table 5.3    Means and Standard Deviations of CBC Scales for PTSD
             and Dissociation (Friedrich, Lengua, et al., 1999)

| Variable | Community Sample | | | Clinic Sample | | | F | p |
|---|---|---|---|---|---|---|---|---|
|  | Mean | S.D. | Range | Mean | S.D. | Range |  |  |
| Dissociation | 0.34 | 0.70 | 0-5 | 1.28 | 1.64 | 0-6 | 182.4 | .0001 |
| PTSD | 1.44 | 1.64 | 0-12 | 3.99 | 3.34 | 0-14 | 291.0 | .0001 |
| Combined | 2.70 | 2.68 | 0-20 | 8.21 | 6.23 | 0-25 | 434.9 | .0001 |

a separate study (Ogawa et al., 1997). However, in the Friedrich et al.
study above, when abused children are contrasted with a psychiatric-
nonabused sample, the two groups do not differ with any useful regularity. A central failing of parent-report scales that purportedly assess
PTSD is that unless the rated behaviors are anchored to specific traumatic events (Criterion A), you have an index only of arousal/agita-
tion, not of PTSD. See Table 5.3 for the items utilized and mean values
for each scale.

GENERIC SYMPTOMS

There are several symptom clusters that are repeatedly reported in
sexually abused children but are common to many other groups of
children and teens as well. These include ADHD, affective distress including anxiety and depression, and impulsive and aggressive behavior. A recent review article reiterates that there is a high rate of co-
occurrence of anxiety and depression in both children and adolescents
(Seligman & Ollendick, 1998). For this reason alone, there are problems
sorting one syndrome from the other. This can be a problem, since children with predominantly negative affectivity may need a different initial focus in therapy than children who are not predominantly negative in their agitation.

The cluster of behaviors that falls under an ADHD diagnosis, including inattentiveness, impulsivity, and overactivity, may be the primary "trigger" that forces a parent to seek an evaluation. There is no
"test" of ADHD, as there is no single "test" of any behavioral syn-

drome. Elevations on any of the three primary domains of ADHD—inattentiveness, overactivity, and impulsivity—may be correlated more closely with a diagnosis of conduct disorder, affective disorder, or PTSD than with ADHD (Ford et al., 2000). For example, the occasional blank staring seen in some children who are dissociative can be misread by a teacher as an example of the inattentiveness aspect of ADHD.

In addition, I believe that many measures, though popular, do a relatively poor job of identifying the core ADHD symptoms in a manner that allows you to contrast them with other behaviors and make a distinction, for example, the Conners Parent and Teacher Rating Scales (Goyette, Conners, & Ulrich, 1978). The two measures that I find to be both brief and routinely useful are the IOWA Conners Rating Scale for Parents and Teachers (10 items; Loney & Milich, 1982) and the Children's Attention Profile (CAP, 12 items; Edelbrock, 1991), which is derived from the TRF (Achenbach, 1991b).

The IOWA has two 5-item scales, Inattention-Overactivity and Oppositional-Defiant. In young children with elevations on both, the likelihood of a primary oppositional stance is quite high. However, if the child you are evaluating is not significantly elevated on either scale based on teacher report, but is reported as inattentive by the parent, a contributor may be the abuse. If this is the case, it may prove to be illuminating to ask the child if he or she ever thinks about what happened, or even "goes away" in his or her mind and tries "not to think."

The CAP also has two subscales, Inattentiveness (seven items) and Overactivity (five items). One of the Inattentiveness items is Item 17 from the TRF: "Daydreams or gets lost in his/her thoughts." A second-grade teacher endorsed that item and then told me that the girl I was evaluating was "always daydreaming." The teacher also reported that when she finally asked the second grader what she was thinking about, the girl replied, "My boyfriend." As it turned out, "the boyfriend" was the 16-year-old perpetrator. This suggested that the girl's inattentiveness was clearly abuse related.

An advantage of the CAP is that the child's relative elevation on this scale can be contrasted with the Aggression Scale of the TRF or with parent report on the CBCL. This enables a determination of the primacy of inattentiveness or overactivity to aggression or other behaviors that the teacher reports.

## ABUSE-SPECIFIC SYMPTOMS

It would be malpractice if the evaluator did not assess the abuse-specific symptoms that are associated with sexual abuse. These include sexual behavior problems, posttraumatic stress, and dissociation. Parent-report measures exist for both children and adolescents in each of these domains although their empirical and clinical utility are often still being sorted out. Given the importance of understanding sexual behavior problems that may arise as a result of sexual abuse, a sepa- rate chapter is devoted to this issue (Chapter 6). This section will fo- cus on other domains that are abuse specific, particularly PTSD and dissociation.

Parent input is critical regarding behaviors related to both PTSD and dissociation. However, their input must be placed in the context of other behavior problems assessed by such broadband measures as the CBCL or the BASC. These data are essential to inform the evaluator so that internalizing and externalizing problems are not missed by structured interviews or rating scales that evaluate only core PTSD symptoms. At the same time, however, if your intent is to reach a diagnosis, it is essential to review each of the 17 *DSM-IV* PTSD symptoms, via either structured interview or parental rating.

### PTSD

The evaluator now has several options available. Julian Ford and his colleagues (Ford et al., 2000) have developed the PTSD Checklist for Children-Parent Report. It notes the extent to which, in the past month, the child has exhibited 17 PTSD symptoms. It is reported to have very adequate psychometrics. Ford's Traumatic Events Screening Inventory-Parent can be used as a companion to establish Criterion A. Ford and his colleagues (Ford et al., 2000) used these measures in a study that illustrated the comorbidity of physical and sexual maltreatment in children with adjustment disorder (10%, 0%), ADHD only (26%, 11%), oppositional defiant disorder (ODD) only (48%, 18%), and ADHD/ODD (73%, 31%). These measures can be obtained directly from Ford at the University of Connecticut School of Medicine.

Kenneth E. Fletcher's efforts in this field are also appreciated. His Parent Report of Child's Reaction to Stress (PR-CRS) is a 79-item measure completed by caregivers on the child (Fletcher, 1996). Although no upper age limit is posited, the available data are primarily with younger, school-aged children. All of the *DSM-IV* criteria for PTSD are assessed by more than one item. Fletcher has also developed an interview for parents, the Childhood PTSD Interview-Parent Form, which meets *DSM-IV* criteria and assesses associated symptoms as well. He suggests that given children's difficulty with self-report, a diagnosis of PTSD be given if either parents or children report a level of symptomatology that meets criteria. (He is a willing correspondent and can be reached at Kenneth.Fletcher@Banyon.UMMED.edu.)

The PTSD Symptom Scale (Dancu, Riggs, Rothbaum, & Foa, 1991) can also be used as an interview with parents. It assesses all 17 of the PTSD criteria in *DSM-IV*, and has excellent convergent validity with other structured interviews. It is also quite brief.

## DISSOCIATION

Resources in this domain are more limited (Carlson, 1997). The Child Dissociative Checklist (CDC; Putnam, Helmers, & Trickett, 1993) is a 20-item measure whose items are related to dissociative disorder, although the child's score is not necessarily diagnostic. The parent rates the child over the past 12 months on a 3-point format (0, 1, and 2). The authors have arrived at a cutoff score of 12 that is suggestive of dissociation.

The use of this cutoff score to signify dissociation has a number of problems. First, since dissociation has an extremely low base rate, you are likely to make more false diagnoses than true ones on the basis of that cutoff alone. In addition, many of the CDC items are confounded with such syndromes as ADHD. Consequently, you must interview the parent to determine if any of the endorsed items are actually suggestive of dissociation or are related to ADHD-like behaviors. The items that are most clinically useful include Item 2, "Goes into a daze"; Item 7, "Rapid regressions"; and Item 13, "Unexplained injuries and self-injurious behavior."

In a study of adolescent sex offenders in a residential setting, staff ratings on the CDC discriminated between those who were diagnosed as dissociative and those who were not (Friedrich, Gerber, et al., 2001).

## ❏ Parent Rating—Family

The family is the arena in which trauma impact is either ameliorated or potentiated. There are both family (Friedrich, 1988a) and individual variables (Wolfe, Sas, & Wekerle, 1994) that can mitigate the dysregulation response. In significantly disadvantaged families, where insight-oriented or purely behavioral approaches are not possible, the simple creation of greater safety and more effective monitoring can be a significant treatment advance (Dishion & McMahon, 1998). Therapists realize that safety is a basic need when they see that families improve once they have moved to safer housing, or after weekends have been structured with respite care. In one case, encouraging the mom to change shifts so she could stay home in the evenings helped to reduce sibling aggression that had escalated in her absence. This aggression was retraumatizing the only sister, a sexual abuse victim. Shortly after the reduction in sibling conflict the child made an important step in therapy, due most likely to increased safety.

The above reasons prompted my development of the Safety Checklist, a very useful screening device that covers a number of aspects of family functioning that can be disruptive to recovery from trauma (Friedrich, 1996c). The dimensions assessed by this checklist are the following: cosleeping, cobathing, family nudity, family sexuality, availability of pornography, family violence, community violence, PTSD triggers, and monitoring problems. The measure is structured to arrive at both positive and negative safety features of the family. I have found that it can easily be incorporated into an early interview with the parent or even as part of an early family session with the non-offending parent and the siblings. There are times when the children can provide even more immediately useful and valid information about sibling violence and family nudity than the parent(s). A further benefit is that the questions on the Safety Checklist "make sense" to the parent.

I view the Safety Checklist as both an evaluative strategy and a therapeutic intervention. For the first time ever, parents are given a framework of the concrete features of their family that are related to their child's behavior. I have seen many of them develop their first, significant awareness that there are features about the home environment that are important and that they can correct. See Appendix G for a copy of the Safety Checklist.

The questions asked by the Safety Checklist are quite personal, however, and defensive parents will minimize safety problems. A strategy that partially ameliorates this tendency is to preface the first set of questions with a brief discourse that goes something like the following:

> I am now going to ask you some very personal questions. They can make you squirm and even make you want to deny to me that you have any problems in this area. But I'll be very frank with you and tell you that your child cannot have the problems he has (say in the case of a child with sexual behavior problems) if everything is perfect in your house. So if we go through and you tell me nothing is wrong, then I will know that you are not being honest, and I will have to write that in my report. Not being honest is a bigger strike against you than being honest, because if you are straight with me, then we have a place to start to help you and your family. Here's an example. If I ask you about (insert a behavior that you are reasonably certain goes on in the family, e.g., yelling), and you say that never happens, I know you aren't being completely honest.
>
> Here's another example. You already told me that you were sexually abused. One of the questions in this interview is whether any sexually abused people live in your house. You will want to say yes to that one. That way you will be honest. Is this clear?

By using this preface with even resistant families and feeling free to be gently confrontive, the validity of the interview is vastly improved.

## ❑ Child Rating—Self

### GENERIC MEASURES

Before I begin a discussion of the range of self-report measures available for children and adolescents in the areas of depression, anxiety, and anger, it is important to review issues related to the validity of these self-reports. Children who are struggling with guilt and shame or who are avoidant regarding their abuse will not be valid reporters of their symptoms. Children who are not given permission or appropriate modeling to talk honestly and accurately about emotions—for example, children who are somatizers—will also be poor reporters.

There is even some suggestion that clinically referred children seem to give less severe ratings about themselves to questionnaire and interview items than their parents, whereas control children provide more severe ratings than their parents (Stone & Lemanek, 1990). This may be a partial reason for the repeated failure of self-report measures to discriminate between group differences in the research on affective symptoms of sexually abused children (Cohen & Mannarino, 1988; Kendall-Tackett, Williams, & Finkelhor, 1993).

Stone and Lemanek (1990) suggest that parents and teachers may be more accurate about objective behavioral symptoms than children, but children may be more accurate about the subjective experience. Since the child is also the focus of therapy, which typically focuses on subjective experiences, there is a place for self-report, particularly self-report that serves to introduce the child to the process of therapy. However, a self-report by children 11 and under is often an underreport and reflects their lack of language for feelings at this age (Aldridge & Wood, 1997; Edelbrock, Costello, Dulcan, Kalas, & Conover, 1985).

There are many measures to choose from, but I will address only those that have an empirical basis and that I am familiar with and find useful. Depression in children is often assessed via the Child Depression Inventory (CDI; Kovacs, 1991), a 27-item measure that yields a total score as well as subscale scores for the following domains: Negative Mood, Interpersonal Problems, Ineffectiveness, Anhedonia, and Negative Self-Esteem. Although it is one of the better-researched measures in this area, it has been suggested that it does not necessarily predict depression scores from other measures (Kazdin, 1990). I have seen several situations more specific to sexual abuse, where a child may score quite low on the CDI but turn around and have a significantly higher score on the Depression subscale of the TSCC (Briere, 1996). Most likely, this is related to the greater abuse specificity of the TSCC.

Interest in the objective assessment of anxiety in children has spawned the development of more than 100 measures, with close to half of them relying on self-report (Barrios & Hartmann, 1988). The Children's Manifest Anxiety Scale-Revised (Reynolds & Richmond, 1978) has 37 items, with most of them assessing the child's general anxiety state and the remainder examining the child's tendency to falsify reports. The format of the Fear Survey Schedule for Children-Revised (Ollendick, 1983), an 80-item measure, prompted the development of the 27-item Sexual Abuse Fear Survey (Wolfe & Wolfe, 1988), which is reported on later.

Anger is another useful dysregulation-related concept to assess, but self-report measures in this area are relatively few. This is due in part to the fact that oppositional and conduct-disordered children are not valid reporters of their internal states (McMahon & Forehand, 1988). It is useful to report that angry children do not seem to appreciate that they are angry. But due to their defensiveness, I seldom see the utility in assessing for anger in 10- to 15-year-olds any more thoroughly than via parent report or via the Anger subscale of the TSCC.

General measures of pathology as well as anger include the self-report version of the BASC (Reynolds & Kamphaus, 1998), the Youth Self-Report (Achenbach, 1991c), the Millon Adolescent Clinical Inventory (MACI; Millon, 1993), or the MMPI-A (Archer, 1992). However, the user of the MMPI-A should be aware of the cautions regarding its validity that are discussed in Caldwell (1997). I have similar reservations about the pathologizing tendencies of the MACI, although the interpretation guidelines suggested by McCann (1999) are quite useful in this regard.

## PROJECTIVES

Although most of the measures discussed in this book are self-report and behavioral in nature, projectives have their place in the comprehensive assessment of sexually abused children and teenagers (West, 1998). This is particularly true of the Rorschach (Exner, 1991). I am very intrigued by how children approach ambiguous and complex stimuli. In keeping with the spirit of the Exner system, I primarily view the Rorschach as a perceptual task. As an adjunct, I'd suggest a chapter on the use of the Rorschach to assess PTSD with adults (Levin & Reis, 1997), particularly Levin and Reis's summary of the Rorschach variables relevant to *DSM-IV* diagnoses.

There are a number of indices or content scores from the Rorschach that have some empirical utility in the overall evaluation of dysregulation. Coping resources are reflected both in the Coping Deficit Index and in the D score (Weiner, 1998). Possible problems in the child's affect modulation can be quickly noted in the color balance (FC: CF + C) ratio, and the form of the affective discharge is suggested by either the amount of anger evident (AG; Space) or the depression that is indicated. The child's tendency to view the world selectively in terms of violent and sexual stimuli is reflected in the content categories of Sex, Blood, AG, and the absence of cooperation (COP). In fact, data indicate that sexually abused young girls give more sexual content on the Rorschach than their nonabused counterparts (Friedrich, Einbender, & McCarty, 1999). However, the frequency was quite low.

The child's approach to stimuli/interpersonal settings in either an intratensive (thoughtful, inhibited) or extratensive (impulsive, emotion-based) manner is evident in the Erlebnistypus (EB). As much as any measure, the Rorschach gives me insight into the therapy approach that might be useful to the child.

For example, a therapist asked for my input regarding her difficulties getting a teenaged girl to talk in therapy. The girl had experienced considerable prior victimization but was finally in a stable home. However, the girl was extremely uncomfortable with any emotionally tinged topic, such as sexual abuse, physical abuse by her mother, and so on. An earlier evaluation with a brief measure of intelligence suggested average verbal expression and intellectual abilities in the upper half of the average range. Thus, cognitive problems interfering with verbal expression were not likely. The Rorschach revealed a very strong stylistic tendency to avoid emotion (lambda = 6.0) and a high degree of passive oppositionality (5 Space responses in the absence of AG). I suggested that the therapist avoid direct discussion about painful topics and focus instead on joining with the girl via her passive oppositionality, for example, making snide remarks about people they both knew. An alliance developed quickly, and the girl was far more vocal about past traumas. I do not believe either of us would have arrived at this solution as quickly if we had not had the Rorschach available.

The Dissociation Index derived from the Rorschach and developed by Armstrong (Armstrong, 1991) was not validated in a study with adolescents (Friedrich, Jaworski, Huxsahl, & Bengston, 1997). It is the sum of Anatomy, Blood, Sex, Morbid, and Aggressive content divided by the total number of responses. Scores above .20 are worth noting and suggest several possibilities. The first is that individuals perceive the world to be a very dangerous and hostile environment. A second possibility is that they have problems editing their perceptions well enough to block these responses. Sexually aggressive children who score high on this index appear to be more impulsive, traumatized, and immature. Their worldview is dominated by morbid and violent themes. They can be difficult to manage in group therapy, and their individual therapist may need to help them selectively edit these perceptions with a cognitive approach.

## ABUSE-SPECIFIC ASSESSMENT

Abuse-related fears, PTSD symptoms, dissociation, and sexual concerns can all be assessed via self-report, and the child's responses can be imported into the therapy office. The Sexual Abuse Fear Survey Schedule (Wolfe & Wolfe, 1988) was developed to complement generic anxiety assessment with the Fear Survey Schedule for Children-Revised (Ollendick, 1983). It is a 27-item inventory that includes situation-based items that are more closely related to the child's abuse experience and the attendant fear, for example, "taking a bath," "taking my clothes off."

## PTSD SELF-REPORT

A self-report of affective and behavioral symptoms, particularly when these measures assess symptoms that appear irrelevant in the mind of a sexually abused child, often results in a normal limits profile. A measure that is directly tied to the child's experience has a greater likelihood of being sensible to the victim. The TSCC, a 54-item self-report measure, meets this need quite well (Briere, 1996).

The TSCC items, even on the more generic subscales of Anxiety, Anger, and Depression, were developed with trauma in mind, for example, Item 24, "Feeling afraid of men"; Item 16, "Getting mad and can't calm down"; and Item 28, "Feeling like I did something wrong," respectively. Children who are within normal limits on the Revised Children's Manifest Anxiety Scale (RCMAS) may be elevated on the Anxiety subscale of the TSCC because the items are more immediately relevant to their abuse experience. In addition, the TSCC information can easily form the first step in the therapy process with sexually abused children. By this, I mean that important, abuse-related topics are introduced to the child via the TSCC and can be directly followed up in treatment.

A number of validational studies of the TSCC have been published, and the most recent titles can be obtained via John Briere's Web site: http://members.aol.com/jbriere. For example, a recent study explored the convergent and discriminant validity between the CITES-R and the TSCC (Crouch, Smith, Ezzell, & Saunders, 1999). The reliability of individual scales on the TSCC was higher on average than for the CITES-R, although the TSCC was not as strong in assessing the avoidance aspects of PTSD. Another recent study found that the PTS (Posttraumatic Stress) subscale did discriminate sexually abused from nonabused teens. This finding is made even stronger by the fact that all of the teens studied had psychiatric problems (Sadowski & Friedrich, 2000). I believe the utility of the TSCC could be maximized if the evaluator revisits the items and reinterviews the child by anchoring the PTS items to a specific event, for example, "You told me that you have bad dreams and nightmares (Item No. 1). Now, are any of them about what your (fill in the blank) did to you?"

The TSCC provides a one-instrument vehicle to assess most of the above areas of concern with the subscales of PTS, Dissociation, and Sexual Concerns (Briere, 1996). In addition, it has norms, something that is lacking in the CITES-R. Each scale is 8 to 10 items in length, and both Dissociation and Sexual concerns have two subscales: Overt and Fantasy, and Sexual Preoccupation and Sexual Distress, respectively. The child is not anchored to a criterion event, which is required for a PTSD diagnosis, so translating an elevated PTS score into a PTSD diagnosis cannot be done without further questioning. Two more important features of the TSCC are two validity scales, Underresponse and Hyperresponse; their relative elevation can suggest how the child or teen approached these questions.

A PTSD-specific measure for children has been developed that corrects some of the problems of the TSCC, but it does not cover the range of symptoms that the TSCC does. This is the 43-item Children's PTSD Inventory (Saigh et al., 2000). The test questions correspond closely to the *DSM-IV* criteria, it is suitable for children 7 to 18 years of age, it has good reliability and validity, and it takes roughly 15 to 20 minutes to administer as a structured interview.

The CITES-R (Wolfe et al., 1991) contains numerous items that are useful, since they anchor the child to the specific abuse event in question. The largest dimension, labeled PTSD, contains the subscales of

Intrusive Thoughts, for example, "I think about what happened to me even when I don't want to"; Avoidance, for example, "I try not to think about what happened"; Hyperarousal, for example, "I often feel restless or jumpy"; and Sexual Anxiety, for example, "Thinking about sex upsets me." Regrettably, the CITES-R is not normed.

Although it can be administered in a self-report format, the CITES-R is most useful and valid to me as a semistructured interview. For example, I was asked whether a child needed therapy. The young girl denied a significant number of symptoms on the TSCC, which she completed while I spoke to her mom. Her mother reported generally positive adaptation in the girl. But the CITES-R items allowed me to engage the girl in a conversation about her feelings related to the abuse. I also had a chance to observe the girl's body language and emotionality during this process. By the end of the interview, the girl also could see that she needed to talk further to a therapist.

## DISSOCIATION

The assessment of dissociation is difficult with adults and even more difficult with children and adolescents. There are several reasons why this is true. The first is that younger people are less capable at self-reporting. The second is that if your life has been so traumatic that you are beginning to utilize dissociation, your self-report capabilities are even more likely to be impaired. Third, there are data that suggest that the emergence of dissociation is associated with reduced intelligence, with the consequence that symptom description is even more difficult (Ogawa et al., 1997). Finally, the occurrence of dissociation is quite unusual.

The Adolescent-Dissociative Experiences Schedule (A-DES), which is a downward extension of the adult version of the same measure (Armstrong, Putnam, & Carlson, 1993), can be useful for exploring this dimension in teens, particularly if there are other data to suggest the possibility of dissociation. It contains 30 items that are answered on a scale ranging from 0 to 10. The total score is then divided by 30. While the items it contains correspond to *DSM-IV* criteria, it does not specifically assess *DSM-IV* criteria for any specific disorder. For example, Item 6 reads as follows: "I feel like I am in a fog or spaced out and things around me seem unreal."

In a study that I did with adolescent sex offenders and psychiatrically hospitalized inpatient adolescents, the mean score on the A-DES for the dissociative subgroup was 3.1 ($S.D. = 1.3$), but it did not differ significantly from the nondissociative group (Friedrich, Gerber, et al., 2001). A further note of caution is that in this same sample, the A-DES correlated significantly with the Hyperresponse scale of the TSCC, also used in this study. However, the A-DES did correlate significantly with the caregiver rating on the CDC. The most useful scales for discriminating dissociation in this study were the CDC (Putnam, Helmers, & Trickett, 1993), completed by the staff on the units where the teens were being treated, and the self-report Dissociation Research Scale (Sanders, 1986).

A diagnosis of Dissociation at age 19 was related to data from two different projective measures gathered when the child was in elementary school (Ogawa et al., 1997). The authors found that dissociation was related to drawings that were fragmented/incongruous and stories where there were sudden shifts/affective tones. It is likely that some of these children had disorganized attachment. The fragmented quality of their productions suggests the implicit memory level at which a confusing world gets stored (Siegel, 1999). Although there is a lot of skepticism about the validity of dissociation as a diagnostic entity, the data from Ogawa et al. (1997) come from a premier prospective longitudinal study of children at the University of Minnesota, the Minnesota Parent-Child Project (Cassidy & Shaver, 1999).

Forensic reasons at times require the accurate assessment of dissociation. I have completed forensic evaluations on incarcerated teenagers with very extensive maltreatment histories. Typically, their caregivers as well as the referred teens report gaps in memory and feelings of detachment that preceded the crime they committed. Each has shown evidence for some or all of the features of Dissociative disorder NOS, and this information was found to be helpful, usually during the sentencing phase.

## TENSION-REDUCING BEHAVIORS

There are several other dysregulation behaviors that fall into the category of "tension-reducing behaviors" (Briere, 1995). These include self-injurious behaviors, suicidality, and substance abuse. While these are more commonly noted in adolescents, the evaluator should be aware that maltreated children may exhibit self-injurious behavior and report suicidal ideation and behavior as well. For example, several studies have identified a relationship between physical abuse and suicidal ideation (Kaplan, Pelcovitz, Salzinger, Mandel, & Weiner, 1997; Stone, 1993).

The phenomenon of self-injurious behavior (SIB) in teenage abuse victims has been noted (Brand, King, Olson, Ghaziuddin, & Naylor, 1996) and has been clinically observed in children. SIB is related to a history of trauma and thought to be an aspect of reexperiencing (Carlson, 1997). At times it is the most salient clue to the investigator about possible abuse, and a recent paper noted the strongest connections with sexual abuse (Briere & Gil, 1998).

The literature on SIB indicates that it is not a unitary phenomenon and serves many purposes. For example, it may be reflective of anger, depression, loneliness, and feelings of emptiness or numbness. However, the use of SIB has been associated with increased shame (Briere & Gil, 1998). Knowing which of the above feelings is primary at the time of the SIB can be useful as a guide to treatment.

If the SIB is serious and a focus of treatment, knowledge about its frequency, range, and associated emotions and cognitions can be assessed with the Self-Injurious Behavior Questionnaire (SIBQ), a 28-item checklist assembled by one of my colleagues, Christine M. Sadowski. I follow the SIBQ with a structured interview that teases out the origins and motivators of the behavior. Both of these are included in the Appendixes (Q, R).

Related to SIB is the full range of eating disorders and their reflection of dysregulation in the teenager. Although there is debate about the traumatic origins of anorexia, I believe the data are clearer about the bulimia-trauma relationship (Root & Fallon, 1988, 1989). It is very important as part of a full evaluation of a sexually abused teenager that you ask about bingeing and purging and, if necessary, follow this up with the Eating Disorder Inventory-2 (Garner, 1991).

Suicidality may need to be assessed with a more standard measure than simply a suicide interview. The one with which I am most familiar is the Suicide Potential Scale (SPS; Cull & Gill, 1982), which, in addition to a total score, has four subscales: Hopelessness, Suicidal Ideation, Negative Self-Evaluation, and Hostility. There are also specific items about ideation and intent on the TSCC that, if endorsed, can be followed up with selected questions. However, I know of no way validly to predict such low-rate behavior as suicide, although elevations on the SPS, along with a score of 8 or higher on the Suicide Constellation score from the Rorschach, are very worrisome in older teenagers.

Substance abuse in teenagers is also related to a sexual abuse history, particularly in females (Dembo et al., 1989; Singer, Petchers, & Hussey, 1989). It is typically a hidden problem in a patient coming into your clinic and thus is not usually volunteered. In addition to asking care-givers about a family history of chemical dependency, you need to ask if they have concerns about their child's substance abuse. I also ask the teenager three questions: (a) "Do you feel you are a normal drinker?" (b) "Has anyone asked you to cut down on your use of substances?" and (c) "Is your use causing any problems at home or school?"

❑  **Common Clinical**
   **Assessment Dilemmas**

Psychological evaluations are often requested when the referring therapist is concerned about dissociation. A recent referral of an 8-year-old with a history of sexual abuse was prompted by his out-bursts of rage that were thought by his therapist to be "odd" and possibly suggestive of dissociation. Before I address this complicated diag-nostic question, I need to state that I believe that dissociative behavior occurs in and can be observed in children and adolescents.

However, a careful review of the referral source's thinking and moti-vation is warranted. Are they due to attendance at a recent workshop on dissociation? Is the client "stuck" in therapy? Have specific behav-iors or comments by the client been reported? If so, what are the spe-cific behaviors?

It is also useful to review your own beliefs and expectations concern-ing dissociation. Do you believe it exists? How often has it been your diagnosis? If your rate of diagnosis is more than a few percentage points, is there an explanation for this higher-than-expected fre-quency? Do you have accurate information about the abuse and privation the child has experienced? Do you have a sense of what is "normative" dissociative behavior and what is pathological? Is it important for treatment to know this answer at this time, or is it something that can be deferred until more data are in?

Dissociative behavior that is pathological has at times been observed by caregivers other than parents. Careful consideration of their input is important. Self-reported feelings of depersonalization, by themselves, do not mean dissociation nor does a report that some specific aspects of the traumatic event were forgotten. There are more parsimonious explanations for this than dissociation, for example, suppression of painful awareness. High reports on the A-DES and the CDC are only suggestive of dissociation, not diagnostic. The intellectual rigor one brings to all evaluations should not stop when you hear the word *dissociation*.

Below is a brief review of information related to my eventual diagnosis of dissociation in a 17-year-old girl. She initially received a rule-out diagnosis of psychosis, based in part on her report of hearing voices. Her reality testing was adequate on the Rorschach, although the Armstrong Dissociative Index was highly elevated at .47. In addition, on inquiry, she denied that she had provided two Rorschach responses, both with morbid sexual detail. Her A-DES score was quite elevated at 7.1, her Dissociation score on the MMPI was 20, and her Overt Dissociation subscale on the TSCC was $T = 72$. Despite average intelligence and no learning problems, she obtained a Freedom From Distractibility standard score of 69 on the Wechsler Intelligence Scales for Children, 3rd edition (WISC-III). Both her mother and stepmother rated her independently on the CDC with resulting total scores of 19 and 18, respectively, and on the 3-item CBCL Dissociation subscale she obtained scores of 5 and 6 (maximum score = 6), respectively. The voices were inside her head and identified as different "parts" of her talking to her or each other. Finally, she had a documented history of severe physical abuse and sexual abuse and, based on her mother's report, evidenced symptoms of PTSD for several years prior to becoming an adolescent. The outcome was that she was removed from antipsychotic medication and has benefited from therapy that has focused on both cognitive and imagery-based strategies to reduce her overt symptoms. In addition, her mother has taken steps to improve the actual safety of the home.

A second dilemma pertains to the differentiation between abuse re-active behavior and other behavior problems. Relevant abuse reactive diagnoses include ASD, PTSD, and Dissociation NOS. The most com-mon rule-outs are usually one or another form of anxiety-related disor-der, ADHD, depression, and oppositionality. In this section, I will sug-gest some strategies to reduce the diagnostic difficulties. In addition, a referral question for A. B. was ADHD.

There are several points on a decision tree I will suggest therapists use. The first point is the preabuse level of pathology in the parent and family. If the preabuse pathology is low, then the child's current symp-toms are less likely to stem from the confounding factors of parent and family pathology. (However, if the parent is unable to be objective—for example, if there is contested custody—the parent's input needs to be weighed with that in mind.)

If the preabuse pathology is high, I suggest that the clinician attempt to sort out this complex question by focusing first on the symptom clusters related to PTSD and sexual behavior.

Information about PTSD-related symptoms must come primarily from the child unless the child is very young or compromised intellec-tually and cannot be assumed to report accurately. The teacher or day care provider should also be able to rate the child's behavior in a set-ting other than the home on a scale such as the IOWA, which sorts out the Inattentive-Overactive subset from the Oppositional-Defiant sub-set of behaviors (Loney & Milich, 1982). Parent input is also critical, since parents are in a position to provide additional information about PTSD-related signs.

However, while there are no data that specifically have measured this issue, it is likely that parents with a history of traumatic experi-ences, especially those that are unresolved, have problems accurately reporting their child's signs separate from their own. This is not an in-surmountable obstacle, especially if you are specific and orient the parent at the beginning of the evaluation, and other times if need be, to report the child's specific symptoms and not the parent's own assump-tions.

When the diagnostic dilemma has to do with oppositional behavior versus PTSD or ADHD behavior, parent-child observation is needed. I use the structured observational approach contained in the Response-Class Matrix (Mash, Terdal, & Anderson, 1981). It is invaluable for sorting out the diagnosis, since it gets at the degree to which inept parenting and oppositionality are at play in the child's symptom presentation. This observation schema is not useful with older children and teenagers. However, criminal acting out in teenagers with a history of victimization does not have to reflect PTSD. A sexually abused teenager who steals her parent's car may have PTSD, but may more validly be viewed as conduct disordered.

If children endorse a significant number of symptoms on the PTSD Symptom Scale (Dancu et al., 1991), and parents are competent reporters, the likelihood that their ADHD-related symptoms and/or oppositionality is related to their victimization is quite high.

There will be many times when you cannot make a determination as to the origins of the child's symptoms. This is even more so the case with preschoolers. Hewitt and Friedrich (1991) sorted a sample of preschoolers into three categories: abused, nonabused, and uncertain. The uncertain category was children who came from very chaotic families. We believed this factor made substantiation more difficult since there were so many other potential contributors to their behavior, and they were less able to express their concerns.

The last differential diagnostic dilemma is related to the new "craze" for bipolar disorder in children and adolescents. Biederman's research largely ignores the role of trauma in the lives of these multiproblematic children who are seen in his clinic (1998). The most "efficient" way to have a child exhibit intensely dysregulated behavior is recurrent trauma. It is imperative that you carefully assess the presence of Criterion A of PTSD in the lives of patients where bipolar disorder is being considered. Not only will a careful interview typically find trauma, it is also very likely that there is unresolved trauma in the lives of at least one of the parents. In fact, that parent may have a history of affective disorder or a variant of same, for example, substance abuse. There is then a sudden leap that goes something like the following: "Wow, she has symptoms suggesting a serious affective disorder, and her mom drinks too much, so she is probably depressed, so this must be bipolar since that has a genetic component. Okay, where is the Depakote?"

This line of reasoning hardly means that there is a "genetic" basis to this patient's racing thoughts, hypersexuality, and recent onset auditory hallucinations that have their locus inside her head and are temporally related to an unwanted sexual experience. But there is such a reductionistic urge in the face of complexity. Professionals rush to find something biological, that is, bipolar, so the diagnosis of bipolar is now more common. An equally valid conceptualization for the above symptoms is to consider impaired attachment mixed with trauma, and the result is severe PTSD.

## ❑ Translating the Evaluation Into Treatment Recommendations

Treatment recommendations derived from the evaluation will include both short-term and long-term goals. The recommendations can address the parent, the child, and/or some aspect of their relationship. In addition, these suggestions can vary in their abuse specificity.

A constant guideline is to reduce the parent and family context issues that continue to interfere with the child's resolving the effects of the abuse. Short-term parent goals may include a referral for psychiatric medication, involving themselves in Alcoholics Anonymous, or referral to group therapy for anger management. If domestic violence is occurring, a referral to curb this behavior is also needed. Parents struggling with a prior and untreated abuse history need to be referred into group or individual therapy. The generically upsetting aspects of having a child experience abuse can be addressed with a cognitive protocol (Stauffer & Deblinger, 1996). If any salient issues emerge on the Safety Checklist, the family must take steps to address the most critical lapses in family safety, such as increasing monitoring.

The symptoms in the child can be targeted once there is movement to create a more modulated home environment. There are therapy protocols that can assist with the majority of possible symptoms, including a cognitive behavioral approach to PTSD (Berliner & Saunders, 1996; Mannarino & Cohen, 1996) or anxiety and aggression (Finch, Nelson, & Ott, 1993). Children whose behavior has been disrupted by the traumatic experience can be treated with a cognitive-play approach (Bodiford-McNeil, Hembree-Kigin, & Eyberg, 1996). Additional testing may indicate cognitive limitations or the need to be less direct in the therapy approach, for example, reduced resilience that makes brief therapy unsuccessful.

## ❑ Summary

A number of points warrant review. The most valid assessment of the significance of the child's symptoms requires a simultaneous evaluation of the cumulative stressor load on all family members, as well as an assessment of those features that can buffer the victim's experience of trauma.

More specifically, the evaluation must consider the parental experience of trauma, other abusive circumstances in the home separate from sexual abuse, family conflict, and violence, as well as the self-report (depending on age) and parent report of symptoms. Although a wide range of measures was reviewed in this chapter, some combination of generic and abuse-specific strategies is recommended.

The evaluation of dysregulation-related symptoms is made difficult by the lack of differentiation in the behavioral response of the young child. You are often left puzzled by how best to make sense of the child's quite variable distress. For example, anger, agitation, anxiety, and depression can overlap a great deal in younger children, and the difficulties with differentiation are compounded by the lack of valid self-report measures. I have also been frustrated by a common phenomenon in the lives of young traumatized children, which is that the younger the abused child, the more likely the parent's own issues are directly related to the child's problems and influence the parent's ability to report accurately. The clinician is faced with a child who is developmentally unable to report internal symptoms accurately and a caregiver who is typically deficient at objectively perceiving the child.

Another set of problems emerges with older children, who can exhibit a much wider range of reactions to trauma. Some teenagers will also exhibit behavior surprisingly at odds with earlier behavior, for example, the compulsively compliant 11-year-old who now, at 14 years of age, is running away from home and engaging in promiscuous behavior. However, both are related to the underlying dimension of self-regulation.

The older child or teenager may now display avoidant behavior (related to PTSD) primarily through substance abuse or SIB. Although there are many associated symptoms in a PTSD diagnosis, their presence is not equivalent to a diagnosis of PTSD, even if teens' alcohol abuse is temporally related to their trauma. There are many other behaviors that can mean dysregulation in teenagers. The frequency of self-injurious behavior, as well as its relative lethality and origins, warrants careful assessment since therapy can be helpful in these cases. Eating disorders may emerge at this time, together with the attendant body-image problems. Questions that establish the time line of these problems may be the first awareness the teen has of the trauma-symptoms link and ideally set the stage for therapy.

Dissociation is also difficult to diagnose since the very utilization of dissociation by traumatized children contributes to their being poor self-reporters. The variability and fragmentation common in children and teenagers does not mean they are dissociating. The base rate of this symptom cluster is quite low, and as a result my informal rule of thumb is that if I begin to diagnose more than a few percent of my new patients as dissociative, I most likely have lost my objectivity.

Finally, clinical data suggest that dysregulation-related symptoms are more readily corrected than family-related relational issues (Friedrich, 1995a). By evaluating these symptoms, these problems can be more easily addressed, and therapy efficacy can be more easily established.

# 6

# Evaluation of Sexual
# Behavior Problems

Sexual behavior must be assessed in the sexually abused child or teenager referred to you. Failure to examine this critical, abuse-specific domain yields a less than comprehensive assessment. Typically this will
be done via interview with the referred patient and the parent or caregiver, since there are few standardized measures available. Consequently, the evaluator must be comfortable with asking questions
about sexuality.

Sexual behavior in children has generated considerable confusion
over the past few years. One reason is that sexual behavior problems
are often reported in sexually abused children. This correlation has
created a perception that childhood sexual behavior is primarily related to sexual abuse. A corollary view is that children who exhibit persisting or intrusive sexual behavior problems must have been particularly scarred by their abuse. New data suggest these assumptions are
not completely valid (Pithers, Gray, Busconi, & Houchens, 1998).

Compromising the objective understanding of sexual behavior in children is the fact that very little empirical data on this topic existed prior to the discovery that sexual behavior is such a consistent and valid marker of sexual abuse (Kendall-Tackett, Williams, & Finkelhor, 1993). Consequently, the field of child maltreatment has moved from an area of relative ignorance to one of narrow enlightenment—sexual behavior occurs in sexually abused children—rather than broad enlightenment—sexual behavior problems occur not only in sexually abused children but also in other children who have not been sexually abused.

The consistent finding of sexual behavior problems in sexually abused children and adolescents warrants in-depth treatment in a book on the evaluation of the sexually abused child and adolescent. (This chapter does not address the evaluation of adolescent sexual offenders; the reader is referred to either Barbaree, Marshall, & Hudson, 1999, or Ryan & Lane, 1997.)

However, the assessment of sexual behavior lacks the research findings and methodology that have supported the investigation of most other behavior problems in these children. For example, the assessment of PTSD is more advanced in terms of instrumentation and research. Even though the diagnosis of PTSD is more variably identified in sexually abused children, there are enough assessment strategies, for example, interviews and self-report measures for both children and adults, that three recent reference books are now available (Briere, 1997; Carlson, 1997; Wilson & Keane, 1997).

The surprising lack of research on sexual behavior in children reflects in part the anxiety and ambivalence that parents and professionals experience when they hear reports of sexual behavior problems in children. This is regrettable, since parents who are confused about their child's sexual behavior are likely to respond to the behavior with either uncertainty or rigidity. This response could subsequently influence parents' response to general behavior problems as well as more specific sexual behavior problems.

Parents have many questions about both the origins of sexual behavior and their response to sexual behavior. Parents ask, (a) How should I respond when I observe sexual behavior in my child? Should I treat it as I would any other behavior problem? (b) Do I run the risk of scarring my child's future sexual adjustment if I set limits on this behavior? (c)

My child suddenly started to touch himself. Does this mean he was sexually abused?

The lack of clarity about how to respond to and interpret children's sexual behavior has led both parents and professionals to postulate sexual abuse when it has not occurred.

Recent research indicates what parents have long known, and that is that children do have sexual thoughts and are sexual beings.

Children without a history of sexual abuse will exhibit a broad range of sexual behavior, even unusual sexual behavior (Friedrich, Grambsch, Broughton, Kuiper, & Beilke, 1991; Friedrich, Fisher, Broughton, Houston, & Shafran, 1998). However, the nonabused child is typically compliant when asked not to exhibit this behavior in public, is not overly focused on the behavior to the exclusion of other activities, and the behavior submerges when the child gets older.

Much less is known about the relationship of sexual abuse to sexual behavior in teens. In fact, of the 25 studies on sexual behavior that were reviewed by Kendall-Tackett et al. (1993), only three were empirical studies of adolescent sexual behavior. Recent research does indicate that risky sexual behavior resulting in sexual misuse, deviant sexual interests, and fear/discomfort with sexual behavior are significantly related to sexual abuse.

While these new data have helped to normalize sexual behavior and place it in a developmental context, these same data have made our understanding of sexual behavior suddenly more complicated. Modeling is a powerful shaper of behavior. Why can't it have a role in the origins of sexual behavior in children? This is obvious to any student of social learning theory (Bandura, 1977), but it requires objective thinking about the origins of sexual behavior in children. And objectivity in this domain is often lacking in both parents and professionals.

This chapter begins with additional case material related to A. B. This is followed by a discussion of empirical research on the origins of sexual behavior problems in children, particularly the role of abuse and family factors that contribute to the initial emergence and then persistence of these behaviors. I will then discuss the variability in children with sexual behavior problems, including new research on sexually aggressive children. I then turn to a review of assessment devices and their utilization in a clinical assessment. Finally, the assessment information is translated into treatment recommendations.

❑  **Sexualization-Related Case Material**

### Child

My initial evaluation with A. B. consisted of face-to-face conversation as well as a brief play interaction in a separate, well-equipped playroom. During these periods, he exhibited a number of behaviors, which I noted on the Evaluator Rating Scale (Appendix K). He exhibited all five boundary variables and two of five sexual variables, including the following: child physically touches examiner, is physically destructive, moves about the office, bumps into examiner aggressively, and touches objects in office without asking. Sexual behaviors were putting his hand inside his underwear and spontaneous talk about his penis. This level of boundary and sexual behavior is higher than average for boys his age who have been sexually abused. They indicate that his personal boundaries are unclear and easily broached. He also has difficulty inhibiting his sexual thoughts, and his thought content has a sexual focus.

On the Child Sexual Behavior Inventory, which was completed by Mrs. B., A. B. was significantly elevated on Total Sexual Behavior ($T =$ 87) and Sexual Abuse Specific items ($T = 99$). These scores are above the 99th percentile. Mrs. B. endorsed items related to poor personal boundaries, sexual interest, sexual knowledge, self-stimulation, and sexual intrusiveness. The endorsed behaviors were reviewed with Mrs. B., and she was able to give an appropriate example for each behavior in the prior 6 months. Mrs. B. reported other family factors that are related to the reported frequency of the sexual behavior. These included domestic violence, family sexuality, recent stressful events, physical abuse, and modeling of sexuality by siblings. At the same time, Mrs. B. tends to be a poor monitor of her son and is more likely to underreport his behavior, so these elevations indicate a very sexualized boy.

The Sexual Concerns items from the TSCC were read to A. B. Although he admitted to occasional urges to "say dirty words," he typically looked away and denied the subsequent Sexual Concerns items. For example, he paused before responding to the last item of this scale,

"Getting upset when people talk about sex," and again answered, "Never."

Evidence for dysregulation with regard to sexuality emerged in A. B.'s response to Card 15 from the Roberts Apperception Test for Children. It went as follows: "The mother is taking a bath and the boy is looking at her. I don't know how he feels because I don't see his face. The mom looks sad. If she finds out that the boy was peeking at her, she will get out of the tub, get dressed, and spank his butt again and again." The specific mention of the boy "peeking" at his mom is the type of response more often reported in both sexually abused and oppositional children (Friedrich & Share, 1997). His pairing of the "peeking" with harsh physical punishment also reflects the anxiety and reduced safety he associates with sexuality.

### Siblings

Mrs. B. also rated B. B. on the Adolescent Sexual Behavior Inventory (ASBI; Friedrich, 1996a) and C. B. on the Child Sexual Behavior Inventory (CSBI; Friedrich, 1997). At this point no norms are available on the ASBI, and it is recommended that the responses be examined qualitatively. Mrs. B. reported a number of concerning behaviors on the ASBI, for example, stays away from home overnight without permission, runs away to unsafe places, and becomes sexual quickly in relationships. These are behaviors that have been identified more often in sexually abused female teens (Friedrich, Lysne, Shamos, & Kolko, 2001). Also concerning was Mrs. B.'s ambiguous response regarding B. B.'s past sexual abuse: She rated it as "possibly" having occurred, rather than "definitely." This is despite the fact that her brother was convicted of the offense.

C. B. obtained $T$ scores of 70, 59, and 76 on the CSBI subscales of Total Sexual Behavior, Developmentally Related Sexual Behavior, and Sexual Abuse Specific Items, respectively. Surprisingly, Mrs. B. did not endorse any items related to C. B.'s molestation of her brother, such as, "Touches another child's sexual parts." The elevations on C. B.'s CSBI are largely a result of her heightened sexual interest, for example, "Very interested in the opposite sex," "Talks flirtatiously," "Overly friendly with men," and so on. These elevations quite clearly indicate that C. B. persists in sexual behavior problems, most likely related to her past abuse. As a result, she continues to be vulnerable to sexualizing relationships with her brother and possibly other similarly aged males.

**Sexual Behavior—Related Recommendations**

1. Specific attention must be paid by the foster parents to A. B.'s boundary problems. A behavioral plan needs to be established, more appropriate boundaries role-played, and rules about personal boundaries and sexual talk established. His success in this domain can then be generalized to his home environment by working conjointly with Mrs. B.

2. C. B. continues to exhibit excessive sexual interest and consequently is vulnerable to revictimization as well as to behaving in a sexually coercive manner with her younger brother upon his return home. Abuse-specific therapy, with a focus on her sexual behavior, is needed.

3. Mrs. B.'s ambivalence about her daughter's sexual abuse by the uncle must be confronted. She also continues to passively deny that her younger daughter has molested her son. Given this level of defensiveness, having her accept the fact that her brother molested her child will present a challenge. In the meantime, helping her to manage her daughter's sexual behavior better and keep B. B. safe from teen-age pregnancy is needed. Mrs. B. will need to demonstrate her acceptance of the fact that her children have sexual behavior problems prior to the creation of a plan to return A. B. home.

4. Individual therapy with A. B. is also recommended. His sexual behavior and its link to prior victimization are an initial focus. The therapist could explore the degree to which he has intrusive thoughts that correspond to his behavior. If so, addressing his PTSD is warranted.

## ❏  Origins of Sexual Behavior Problems

Children typically exhibit sexual behavior over the course of their first few years of life. Observed behavior generally peaks during the ages of 4 or 5 years (Rutter, 1971). These behaviors are usually related to self-stimulation, learning personal boundaries, and sexual curiosity.

Sexual behaviors cause concern for the following reasons, which are presented in no particular order of frequency: (a) a discrete behavior, for example, insertion of object into rectum, that is directly reflective of the child's abuse experience; (b) misinterpretation of a behavior by a caregiver who decides that the behavior is similar to adult behavior and hence is related to sexual abuse; (c) misinterpretation of the behavior by a caregiver as bad and then negatively reinforced. There is often a preexisting pattern of coercive parenting occurring in these families, and a range of child behaviors is misinterpreted in an overly critical and punitive manner; (d) eroticizing sexual abuse, which introduces the child to an overly stimulating repertoire of behaviors, and the child persists in behaving this way because some aspects of the abuse were pleasurable; (e) traumatizing sexual abuse, which introduces the child to a confusing repertoire of behaviors and feelings, and the child is now acting out in a manner reflective of this confusion, for example, mixing aggression with sexuality; (f) overly stimulating parental practices, including the child witnessing sexual and aggressive acts between adults or teenaged siblings; and (g) the child having already developed a more persistent oppositional stance and because the child is getting older, has overheard peers, or has witnessed adult sexuality, now adds sexually provocative behavior to the lying, stealing, truancy, and physical aggression already exhibited.

Two studies shed much needed light on the relationship between sexual behavior and sexual abuse. Diana Elliott noted that the highest levels of sexual behavior of the children in her sample were not the children who had been sexually abused, but the children who had been exposed to pornography (Elliott, Kim, & Mull, 1997). She theorized that pornography was eroticizing to the child. Since the exposure was not associated with trauma, which might have inhibited the eroticization, sexual behaviors were more frequent.

Hall and Mathews (1996) also found that eroticizing sexual abuse was associated with more sexual behavior problems than abuse that was not. (They also found that abuse that was more sadistic was related to persisting sexual behavior problems, suggesting another pathway to the emergence of sexual behavior problems.)

More than half of sexually abused children do not exhibit immediate sexual behavior problems (Friedrich, 1994; Wright et al., 1998). A paper by Down (1993) also suggested that there are two trajectories for abused females, some becoming hyposexual and withdrawn, others becoming hypersexual and promiscuous. Consequently, the propensity to behave sexually is likely to reflect some interplay of abuse characteristics and the child's behavioral style and family strictures (Kendall-Tackett et al., 1993). Data also indicate that sexual behavior is significantly correlated with generic behavior problems (Friedrich et al., 1991; Friedrich et al., 1998). Sexual behavior in many children is best seen as the behavioral manifestation of an abusive experience combined with a tendency in the child to act out behaviorally (Friedrich, 1995a).

Two hypotheses about the origins of sexual behavior problems currently hold sway. The first is that sexual behavior is primarily related to the experience of sexual abuse. The second would argue that sexual behavior is related to other behavior problems, particularly externalizing problems.

The relative veracity of these hypotheses can be assessed by examining the relationship between sexual behavior and a range of behavior problems. If sexual behavior is more closely related to PTSD symptoms, then it might be more accurate to perceive it as a comorbid sexual abuse-related behavior. If sexual behavior is more closely related to externalizing behavior than it is to either internalizing behavior or PTSD symptoms, then one can construe sexual behavior as a general tendency to "act out" rather than "act in."

In an effort to evaluate the above hypotheses, I utilized three samples of children from 4 to 12 years of age, whose parents had completed both the Child Sexual Behavior Inventory (CSBI; Friedrich, 1997) and the Child Behavior Checklist (CBCL; Achenbach, 1991a). There were a total of 1,604 children, including 629 normative, 409 sexually abused, and 431 psychiatric outpatients without a history of sexual abuse. Factor analysis of the CSBI has consistently identified several factors, like sexually intrusive behavior, self-stimulation, and so on (Friedrich, Trane, & Wright, 2001; Schoentjes, Deboutte, & Friedrich, 1999).

From a theoretical perspective, sexually intrusive behaviors are likely to be more closely related to externalizing behaviors, for example, aggression. Self-stimulation is likely to be more reflective of anxiety, an internalizing behavior.

The two CSBI factors of self-stimulation and sexual intrusiveness were then correlated with the PTSD scale derived from the CBCL

**Table 6.1** Correlations of Sexual Behavior With CBCL Subscales

|                  | PTSD | Internalizing | Externalizing |
|------------------|------|---------------|---------------|
| Self Stimulating | .32  | .23           | .32           |
| Intrusive        | .28  | .20           | .30           |

(Friedrich, Lengua, et al., 2001) and the Internalizing and External-izing subscales from the CBCL. There are obvious limitations to these analyses, given that the information comes from one source, the parent, and the PTSD scale is not a true test of PTSD but simply the degree to which the child exhibits behaviors consistent with that diagnosis.

The results indicated that all three scales from the CBCL—Internal-izing, Externalizing, and PTSD—correlated equally well with both sexually intrusive and self-stimulating behaviors. The correlations are presented in Table 6.1 and are typically modest in terms of size, but all are significant at greater than $p = .0001$.

I believe these data suggest that there are many pathways to the emergence of sexual behavior problems in children. These behaviors are not simply reflections of a tendency to act out, but are also related to the child's developmental level, agitation, PTSD-related symptoms, and generalized distress. Given the modest size of the correlations, there are likely to be many other pathways such as eroticizing experi-ences, and also moderators like gender and family conflict. To help the clinician, I have assembled these moderator variables into a checklist that is associated with higher or lower scores. After the parent has completed the CSBI, complete the checklist in order to guide your in-terpretation of other contributors to the higher (family violence) or lower (lower parental education) scores. See Appendix J for this check-list.

## ❑ How Does Sexually Aggressive Behavior Emerge?

An increasingly important clinical issue pertains to children who are sexually aggressive. The balance of referrals into my assessment prac-tice has now changed from almost exclusively victims to at least 50%

preteen children who are accused of sexual activity against another child.

Early research suggested that sexually aggressive children were more often than not sexually abused (Friedrich & Luecke, 1988; Johnson, 1988, 1989). Research with larger samples suggests that sexual abuse is a likely but not necessary condition in the lives of sexually aggressive children (Pithers et al., 1998). Physical abuse, exposure to family violence, and relaxed sexual standards are other contributors (Pithers et al., 1998).

Sexually aggressive children do not have to puzzle the clinician. Excessive sexual behavior emerges via a process that is no different from that of other behavior problems. Research with aggressive children is directly applicable to understanding the emergence of sexually aggressive behavior. It is likely that some of the same individual and family variables related to oppositional and provocative behavior are relevant to understanding sexual behavior problems (Patterson, 1982). If you look over the seven nonexhaustive reasons provided above as to why sexual behavior problems develop, you'll find that family variables are central to many of them, for example, parents reading behaviors inaccurately, responding coercively, and allowing or fostering a sexualized family environment. The child is now reflecting this context.

Family variables that contribute to the emergence of aggression in children include modeling of aggression in the home, rejection of the child, inconsistent parenting, and poor or variable monitoring of the child by the parent (Morton, 1987; Patterson, 1982). The parents of these children are often isolated and caught up in coercive traps with both their children and extended family members (Wahler, 1980). The empirical validation of contributory context variables in the families of sexually aggressive children is just now emerging. The data suggest that the sexual abuse experience, in combination with a number of individual and family variables, interacts synergistically in the emergence of sexually inappropriate behaviors (Hall, Mathews, & Pearce, 1998). In many cases the child is reactive to the abuse and exhibits a spurt of increased sexuality. However, the behavior fades because it is not reinforced, or the child is supported and the trauma resolves.

Some of the microsocial issues that Patterson (1982) has identified are echoed in an attachment-based paper that gives a broader context to the development of disruptive behavior problems (Greenberg, Speltz, & DeKleyen, 1993). Greenberg and colleagues found that the interaction among risk factors in four areas contributes to the development of disruptive behavior. These include biologic factors in the child, for example, activity level; family ecology, such as negative factors active in the life of the family; parenting variables, such as ineffective and punitive parenting practices; and attachment security. Attachment security can be separate from the quality of parental management and socialization processes. Each of the above domains represents a legitimate focus of assessment.

Hall and Mathews (1996) studied sexually abused children referred to a treatment agency in Toronto. The children were grouped into three categories based on their sexual behavior: developmentally expected, sexualized, and sexually intrusive. The authors identified the "top 25 factors." These are variables most associated with interpersonal sexual behavior problems among sexually abused children and best distinguish the three groups. These factors were all statistically significant at the $p = .001$ level. The factors cluster into five categories—sexual abuse experience of the child, child characteristics, child's history, parent-child relationship, and caregiver characteristics—and are listed in Table 6.2. Only 20 of these 25 factors are identified in a related paper (Hall et al., 1998).

These factors reveal few surprises, and they confirm assessment and treatment foci. Many of the factors are congruent with the assessment framework reported in this book. All of the attachment features reported by Alexander (1992) are present: rejection, parentification, and multigenerational maltreatment. In addition, most of these children had experienced another form of maltreatment as well. These children also struggle with blaming themselves, an issue discussed in Chapter 7.

In addition, there are a number of factors of the abuse, as well as subsequent behaviors that clearly indicate the degree to which the child has become sexualized. Sexualized children seem to have learned to expect relationships to have a sexual component.

Each of these factors should be weighed when assessing children who have been sexually abused and for whom there are concerns about their potential to be sexually intrusive. It is also important to note that children without a history of sexual abuse, particularly boys,

**Table 6.2**    Top 25 Factors Associated With Interpersonal Sexual Behavior
Problems (Hall & Mathews, 1996)

---

**Sexual Experience of the Child**
  1. Sexual arousal of the child during the abuse
  2. Sadistic abuse
  3. Active involvement of the child in the sexual activity
  4. Child acted in "offender" role during child-to-child sex acts
  5. Child blames self or is ambivalent about who to blame for the sexual
     abuse
**Child**
  6. Lack of warmth/empathy
  7. Restricted range of affective expression
  8. Hopelessness/depression
  9. Poor internalization of right and wrong
 10. Blames others/denial of responsibility
 11. General boundary problems (non-sexual)
 12. "Sexualized gestures" and/or frequent or compulsive masturbation
**Child's History**
 13. Frequent moves
 14. Physical abuse
 15. Emotional abuse
 16. Permanent loss of father (males)
**Parent-Child Relationship**
 17. Intrusive/enmeshed mother-child relationship
 18. "Sexualized" interaction style within the family
 19. Role reversal, inappropriate parent-child roles
**Caregiver Characteristics**
 20. Mother shows PTSD symptoms
 21. Mother competes with child/high level of neediness
 22. Mother has history of physical neglect
 23. Father observed family violence in own parents during his childhood
 24. Mother experienced childhood separation/loss of own parents
 25. Maternal boundary problems with child

---

may act out sexually with other children. However, other maltreatment is typically identified in the child's history (Friedrich & Luecke,
1988; Gray et al., 1997).

To summarize, the emergence of sexual behavior problems, particularly sexually aggressive behavior, shares the same family pathways

that lead to aggressive acting out in children: parental rejection, inadequate monitoring, inconsistent parental response, and the modeling of aggression. Unique to sexual aggression in children, and to a lesser degree in teens, is the component of sexual abuse and/or sexually overly stimulating parenting, that is, exposure to adult sexuality, domestic violence, and physical abuse. Your evaluation must include a careful assessment of the referred child and, more important, the family context, including prior sexual abuse in the parent(s), the level of overt violence and sexuality in the home, and the context of the child's sexual acting out, such as mutuality/nonmutuality.

## ❑ Types of Sexual Behavior Problems

Sexual behavior problems in children vary on a number of axes. The first reflects a self-other dimension, for example, masturbation-sexual touching of others. Another dimension pertains to the immediacy of onset, with behavior that develops shortly after maltreatment more likely to reflect the impact of the abuse. Presumably, stopping the abuse and providing support to the child will ease these problems. A third axis pertains to the presence of coercion, with a greater degree of mutuality different from a high level of coercion and even physical force.

Another critical dimension relates to the comorbidity of sexual behavior problems with other behavioral and emotional difficulties. Sexually aggressive children often have well-established aberrant behavioral pathways and more uniformly will have problems in parent-child relationships as well.

Two federally funded research studies designed to evaluate treatment modalities with children exhibiting sexual behavior problems have been completed (Bonner, Walker, & Berliner, 2000; Pithers et al., 1998). Both studies reported that these children are quite diverse, and both utilized cluster analytic techniques to sort them into groups.

The Vermont-based group studied 127 children, and five groups were identified and labeled as follows: Nondisordered, Sexually Aggressive, Highly Traumatized, Rule Breakers, and Abuse Reactive (Pithers et al., 1998). The children in the Nondisordered group were overrepresented by females, appeared to have no true psychopathology, and had typically committed the least severe offenses. However, they had sexually touched another child and/or exhibited sexual behavior deemed excessive. They generally had low levels of other behavior problems.

Sexually Aggressive children were more often male, had the highest percentage of conduct disorder (CD) diagnoses, had the highest average number of penetrative acts, and seldom acknowledged their own maltreatment. The Highly Traumatized group had the highest number of psychiatric diagnoses and the highest percentage of PTSD diagnoses. They typically had an extensive history of child maltreatment, including multiple perpetrators of both physical and sexual abuse. Rule Breakers were overrepresented by females and typically had psychiatric diagnoses related to oppositional-defiant disorder (ODD), CD, or ADHD. Finally, the Abuse Reactive group had the shortest latency from their own abuse to problematic sexual behavior and were overrepresented in the ODD diagnostic category. The clusters seemed to be derived from two axes of variables, one based on the severity of the sexual act committed by the child, and the other on the degree of disturbance in the child, with ODD and CD children over-represented.

Despite several efforts, the Oklahoma-Seattle group failed to identify consistent subgroups of sexually aggressive children with cluster analysis (Bonner et al., 2000). The researchers finally categorized the children in their sample into three groups. The ordering was done on the basis of the severity and coercive aspects of the children's sexual behavior (Bonner et al., 2000). An interesting finding was that the most severe group, Group 3, did not differ from Group 2 in terms of overall sexual behavior as measured by the CSBI. Mothers of these sexually aggressive children do not necessarily report an inordinate amount of sexual behavior, nor do they have to be sexually abused.

A combination of sorting techniques led to the five-group typology developed with 100 3- to 7-year-old sexually abused children from two Canadian provinces (Hall et al., 1998). These children exhibited at least some level of sexual behavior problem. The five distinct groups, arranged in order of severity, were (a) developmentally expected; (b) interpersonal, unplanned; (c) self-focused; (d) interpersonal, planned; and (e) interpersonal, coercive.

A simple but useful schema developed by Down (1993) helps to explain a wider range of behavior in sexually abused children: avoidant asexual versus hypersexual. Although this dichotomy has not been the subject of research, my clinical impression over the years is that teens in the first group seem to have a history of avoidant attachment prior to their sexual abuse, and teens in the second group have a resistant or coercive attachment history.

Early efforts at classifying children with sexual behavior problems speak quite loudly that this is a diverse group. In the same way that there is no "profile" for an adolescent or adult sex offender, there is no "profile" for a child who is sexually intrusive.

## ❑  Developmental Differences

A developmental perspective on sexual behavior in children is essential, and this includes sexually intrusive behaviors. It is inappropriate to use adolescent or adult perspectives with these children. For example, it is inappropriate to view these children as having a paraphilia or to assume that their arousal patterns are fixed and that recidivism is likely (Chaffin & Bonner, 1998).

There are data to suggest that only 10% of adolescents who have been charged with a sexual offense reoffend sexually (Barbaree et al., 1999). This is certainly lower than adult rates (Chaffin & Bonner, 1998). A natural extension of these data is that there is a similar diminution in the likelihood that a child who exhibits intrusive sexual behavior will go on either to reoffend or to become an adult who sexually offends.

However, in a study that questions the conclusion in the above paragraph, Burton (2000) examined three groups of incarcerated teens ($N = 263$): one group with a history of sexual aggression only before the age of 12, another with a history after the age of 12, and a third with a pattern of offending before and after the age of 12 (labeled continuous offenders). More than 46% of the sexually aggressive teens began their deviant behaviors before the age of 12, and level and complexity of perpetration acts were more severe for the continuous offenders than for the other two groups. The earlier and more continuous the pattern of offending, the more likely the preteen goes on to more severe activities. This finding is also true for conduct-disordered youth who are labeled as life-course-persistent as opposed to adolescent-limited (Moffitt, 1993).

Recidivism data in teens need to be considered when you are assessing a child with sexual behavior problems. There are no data supporting a court finding a 10-year-old to be a juvenile sex offender and ordering the child to a sex offender treatment program. Although I have evaluated some sexually aggressive preteens about whose future I am very pessimistic, developmentally sensitive alternatives to their treatment are still warranted. We must be aware of our adultocentric perspectives on sexuality and separate those from what are developmentally more appropriate perspectives. Rather than criminalize these children, we must argue for sensitive responses (Chaffin & Bonner, 1998).

An example is two preschool boys who put their mouths on each other's penis. They laughingly reported it to the older brother of one, who then told his mother. After an extensive evaluation, it was determined that these were two impulsive, nonabused boys who engaged in this behavior because to them, penises did look like "popsicles." This was a far cry from the sexual motives that were first impugned.

There are other developmental considerations in childhood sexual behavior. One of these is related to age trends in overt behavior. Although it is true that some of the drop-off in reported sexual behavior is due to children being increasingly better able to be discrete and hidden from their parents, latency-aged children are less overt about sexual behavior. Latency-aged children who are more overt are outliers and come to our attention, sometimes because they have been abused.

Another critical assessment dimension is the context of the sexually aggressive behavior. By itself, a behavior says little absent a consideration of the behavioral context. Hall et al. (1998) suggest nine contextual characteristics to use in assessing the severity of the individual behavior. These are (a) nonmutuality, (b) harm/discomfort caused in others or self, (c) complaints by others, (d) differential power/not peers, (e) persistence despite limit setting by others, (f) coercion/bribery, (g) force/threat of force, (h) premeditation/planning, and (i) extensive adult-type sexual behavior.

What happens if you take the behavior, "Touches another child's sex parts" (CSBI Item 9), reported by the mother of a 10-year-old boy, and examine it along several of these contexts? The behavior in question was directed at a 9-year-old stepsister who just prior to the event insulted him, and he retaliated by grabbing the front of her T-shirt. The context variables described above, particularly if this were a one-time incident, would minimize the severity of this behavior.

Earlier in this chapter I mentioned the dearth of studies with teens who had a sexual abuse history. Promiscuity was a finding for 38% of sexually abused adolescents in two of three studies reviewed by Kendall-Tacket et al. (1993). Since that review, several other studies have been published. Sexually abused boys who were psychiatric inpatients had significantly more sexual concerns (Hussey, Strom, & Singer, 1992). A recent longitudinal study found that sexually abused teenagers were significantly more likely to have become pregnant than their nonabused counterparts after 5 years had elapsed (Swanston, Tebbutt, O'Toole, & Oates, 1997).

## ❑  Assessment

Sexually abused children vary in their nature and degree of sexual reactivity. For example, "children's trauma-based sexualized responses may be gender-specific, i.e. children may behave in certain sexually inappropriate ways only with one sex or another" (Hall, 1993, p. 10). This explains why female children, molested by a male, may engage in highly sexualized behaviors with a male but behave appropriately with women. Consequently, the perspectives of both male and female caregivers can be useful.

There are also other maltreatment experiences that seem important in predicting who becomes sexually aggressive. Sexually intrusive children are likely to be more aggressive, and their families of origin are more troubled (Hall et al., 1998). Consequently, their assessment must take into consideration some variables that are not as commonly evaluated in sexually abused but nonaggressive children. These include the nature of their abuse experiences; their history of rule-violating behavior; contextual limits on future behavior; parent discipline practices; and the quality of the parent-child relationship. The assessment of these children does not necessarily involve any new approaches that are not already defined in the other three chapters. However, the evaluator must have a sharp appreciation of the abuse-aggression link, the variability of these children, and the problems inherent in predicting behavior, particularly aggressive behavior.

Finally, more so than in other areas of assessment described in this book, the evaluator must be comfortable asking very personal and sexual questions. Can you ask a 10-year-old boy who has sexually touched several other children such questions as, "Do you ever rub your penis to make it feel good?" "To make it get hard?" "What do you think about when you rub your penis?" "What did it feel like to touch so and so's private parts?" Questions of this type can yield information useful to the evaluator. They also begin the important process of examining and discussing the child's experiences and help correct behavior and thinking.

## ❑ Parent Rating—Self

The generic measures completed by the parent include those discussed in Chapters 4, 5, and 7. The quality of the parent-child relationship, the parent's unresolved trauma, and parental competence and problem-solving capabilities are appropriate evaluation foci. The clinician needs to determine if the parent is motivated to improve the parent-child relationship, can keep her or his own issues from intruding on the child's adjustment, and can monitor the child and administer behavior management plans designed to reduce the child's aggressive and sexual behavior.

Recent research indicates that the majority of mothers of sexually aggressive boys (ages 11-15) were sexually victimized as children (Gray et al., 1997; Hall et al., 1998; New, Stevenson, & Skuse, 1999). Consequently, it behooves the clinician to determine the parents' level of compromise from earlier trauma, their attitudes toward sexuality, whether these attitudes make them less objective about their child's sexual behavior, and their sexual satisfaction in their current relationship. A measure that efficiently addresses these issues is the TSI (Briere, 1995). The scales Anger/Irritability, Intrusive Experiences, Defensive Avoidance, and Sexual Concerns specifically address the above questions. If a parent is elevated on any of these subscales, it is important to assess the degree to which these issues interfere with the monitoring and management of the child.

Defensive/antagonistic parents, that is, the parents of children with ODD and CD diagnoses, will disclose minimally (Pithers et al., 1998) and will yield normal limits on TSI profiles. If the evaluation is court ordered and there is concern about a parent's ability to care for the child, it may be more appropriate to administer an MMPI. In these cases, I look for codetypes that suggest modeling of aggression, for example, 4-9, 4-6, 3-6; victimization, for example, 4-8; and poor monitoring, for example, 4-3.

A semistructured clinical interview with the parents of sexually aggressive children would include the following:

1. Is it okay if we talk about sexuality? Does that make you uncomfortable?
2. You have told me that you were sexually abused. So what does it feel like to have a son who does sexual things to other children?
3. Are you thinking even more about your past abuse?
4. Is he ever sexual with you? Even in subtle ways?
5. Do you worry about him being sexual with your other children?
6. Do you worry that he will be sexual with children in the neighborhood?
7. Do you ever think he's doing this to "get you"? That he knows this is a weak spot?
8. How often do you hug him?
9. Is it as easy to hug him now that you know what he has done to other kids?
10. How often do you get angry at him when you see him doing these sexual things?
11. When you get angry, what do you do?
12. How do you control your feelings of being hurt? Of being angry?
13. Does his having been sexually abused interfere with your ability to be sexual with your significant other?

The parents' responses to the above questions cannot be scored systematically. However, parents with an unresolved history of victimization who then deny distress, minimize any natural worries about their child, and claim not to be affected are parents who cannot respond adequately to the child's problems. A sexual abuse history in the mother was associated with more negative attributions about her child's behavior (New et al., 1999). This suggests that the parents' response to Question 7 is worth examining. A positive answer to this question strongly suggests that parents interact with their child as if he were deliberately victimizing them.

## ❏ Parent Rating—Child

Parents are not used to thinking about their children being sexual. I am regularly impressed with the blind spot parents and caregivers have about sexual behavior of a child in their care. Inability to report this behavior objectively becomes more likely if they are troubled, have reduced income, and have fewer years of education than is average (Friedrich, Jaworski, Huxsahl, & Bengston, 1997). Consequently, if you ask about sexual behavior in their child, they may draw a blank since they are not organized to think in that manner. A study of children in foster care found that using the CSBI revealed more incidents of sexual behavior than had been described in an open-ended interview with the care provider (Farmer & Pollock, 1998). This is one reason why it is useful to have parents complete a CSBI (Friedrich, 1997) or an Adolescent Sexual Behavior Inventory (ASBI; Friedrich, 1996a). Critical information about the scope of the problem and the capacity of the parent both to monitor and to report accurately on the child's behavior is gained by using either of these measures.

The CSBI manual contains detailed information on administration, scoring, and interpretation (Friedrich, 1997). Briefly, the CSBI is a 38-item rating scale that screens for the presence of sexual behavior in the 6 months before the appointment. It works best if you have a chance to review the results with the parent to clarify any issues that emerge. It assesses a broad range of sexual behavior, including self-stimulation, boundary problems, sexually intrusive behavior, and sexual knowledge and interest, as well as gender-specific behavior.

In addition to the 38-item CSBI, it is useful to ask parents four additional questions that more precisely assess sexually aggressive behavior. They are listed in Table 6.3 and follow the same format as the CSBI. Data with a normative sample collected as part of the test-retest reli-

**Table 6.3**  Sexual Aggression Items to Add to the CSBI
(Ask the parent about the frequency in the past 6 months
on a 0, 1, 2, and 3 scale)

---

1. Touches other children's private parts after being told not to
2. Plans how to sexually touch other children
3. Forces other children to do sexual acts
4. Puts finger or object in other child's vagina or rectum

---

ability study with the CSBI found that no parents ($N$ = 131) of the nonabused children endorsed these items. Until recently, they have been reported only in children with a sexual abuse history, but Jane Silovsky of the University of Oklahoma Health Sciences Center has found that parents of preschool age sexually aggressive children without a clear history of sexual abuse report these behaviors (personal communication, September 2, 1999).

Although the norms were developed with female caregivers, it is useful to have male caregivers complete the CSBI as well. This enables you to examine any discrepancies between caregivers. If a male abused the child, the male caregiver may report more sexualized behavior. Though male caregivers typically report fewer sexual behaviors, this is not always the case, and in those instances where they report more, the discrepancy is worth noting and clarifying.

In addition to the discrete behaviors contained on the CSBI, it is critical that the evaluator also ask about the context in which these behaviors occur, as well as the parent's typical response to the behavior. Does the 8-year-old girl put on her bikini only when strange men come to the house? Does the parent have a difficult time responding calmly and in a nonpunitive manner to the sexual behaviors observed in the child? One question that I have found useful is, "Have you ever found yourself very angry because you are scared about your child's behavior?"

An example of the clarifying process is outlined in this next case. I was asked to evaluate a child whose mother had reported numerous instances of unusual behavior, much of it directed at her. The boy's total score on the CSBI was 67, an extremely high score even for children with very severe and eroticizing abuse experiences.

When I asked the mother to tell me when, in the prior 6 months, her 5-year-old boy had exhibited these behaviors, the score dropped immediately, since she had failed to use the 6-month time line as a gauge. For the majority of the other behaviors, she often could report only one instance rather than the greater frequency she endorsed. Finally, I was impressed that she was subtly reinforcing of the boy's behavior with her style of dress and her exaggerated emotional responses to his behavior.

What was helpful to my understanding of this case was the almost total absence of sexual behavior addressed toward other women in his life. This included several female preschool teachers. This does not mean that sexualized behavior that is exhibited in only one context and not another is solely a function of the observer's behavior. Children are quite context bound, and if abuse occurred at bedtime, they may not display much sexual talk or behavior except at bedtime, particularly if they are younger (Hewitt, 1999). Bedtime is not likely to be observed by a day care provider.

The parent should be asked about other critical aspects of context. For example, data suggest that sexual behavior is related to a number of predisposing factors, including family stress, family violence, physical abuse, and family sexuality (Friedrich, 1997; Friedrich, Grambsch, et al., 1992). You need to ask about each predisposing factor and weigh its possible contribution to the child's behavior. These factors are reviewed if you interview the parent using the Safety Checklist (see Appendix G).

The context of abuse disclosure is also very informative. Parents of younger children will report that the child's first disclosure was when the child was undressing or in the bathtub (Hewitt, 1999). Young children think concretely and being naked takes them back to the event, so disclosures at these times seem the most valid. As a way to organize the data from your interview with the parent of a preschooler, please refer to the preschool screening questionnaire that I developed with Sandra Hewitt and that is presented in Appendix H.

If the evaluation is scheduled over two or more appointments, and the parent appears to view the child positively and is relatively effective, it is helpful to enlist the parent's cooperation and then teach how to set limits on the child's sexual behavior. I typically teach the parent how to ignore the behavior, redirect the child, or apply a mild consequence. The parent's cooperation with this task—the amount of follow-through, keeping a chart—and the child's responses provide very useful information regarding future treatment needs and the parent's amenability to therapy.

The CSBI generates $T$ scores that indicate the degree to which the child's total sexual behavior (TSB), developmentally related sexual behavior (DRSB), and sexual-abuse-specific sexual behaviors (SASI) are of concern. $T$ scores of 65 and above are considered to be clinically elevated, since they are 1.5 standard deviations above the mean and place the child at the 93rd percentile. Although this information can be very useful in planning for treatment, many referrals come with the expectation that the clinician determine whether the child was sexually abused. Consequently, the CSBI is turned to as a "cutting tool." Using the CSBI in this manner is inappropriate. It can never indicate absolutely whether a child has or has not been sexually abused; too many false positives result.

Evaluators come under pressure to reach conclusions of fact. However, this question cannot be definitively answered on the basis of behavioral data alone. The task is made easier if there is reliability among several objective reporters who report excessive sexual behavior, particularly the type captured in the SASI subscale of the CSBI. If a child has also made a statement, the behavioral data certainly buttress it to the point that I have stated that the preponderance of the evidence supports the child's having been sexually abused. However, I also go on to state the various context variables that may also be related to the elevated sexual behavior, such as family sexuality.

In a study that examined the CSBI with three groups of children, normative, psychiatric-nonabused, and sexually abused, the TSB score from the CSBI varied widely in terms of sensitivity and specificity, depending on the age and gender of the groups being contrasted (Friedrich, Fisher, et al., 2001). For example, the sensitivity (true positives) ranges from .87 to .95 for the normative versus sexually abused groups. These are the types of scores that one wants from a population screening measure, and in fact most of the misclassified children were from the asymptomatic sexual abuse group.

However, the sensitivities are much lower and range from .40 to .55 for the psychiatric-nonabused versus sexually abused groups. Although the sensitivity clearly drops when the contrast is between one disturbed group (psychiatric) and another (sexually abused), the specificity (true negatives) goes up when the sexually abused group is contrasted with the psychiatric group, .78 to .87, respectively.

This finding raises the issue of cutoff scores with the CSBI. The advantage of cutoff scores is that one can increase the sensitivity or specificity, depending on the cutoff score. If you didn't want to miss any sexually abused children, you would set the score very low, with the end result that you would lower the sensitivity. If you wanted to identify only sexually abused children, you would set the score quite high and miss many sexually abused children but not include many nonabused children. This increases the specificity and lowers the sensitivity. For example, if the SASI score has a cutoff at $T = 70$, the specificity (between the sexually abused and psychiatric outpatient samples) increases from .92 to .97, respectively, for each age and gender grouping. This means that very few psychiatric children would be included in the sexual abuse sample. This finding can be very useful if you are trying to determine whether the child in front of you is more likely to be behaviorally disordered or sexually abused. However, no official cutoff scores have been published, and the sensitivity and specificity of the CSBI and its subscales must be validated with independent samples.

A related construct is parental attributions about the child's sexual behavior problems. I ask several questions to illuminate the parent-child relationship and whether the parent can apply sexual rules or benign consequences in ways that aren't coercive or shaming. Here are some examples from an interview with a mother whose son was a compulsive masturbator following sexual abuse.

> What happens to your gut when you see him do that?
> What's your theory about why he does that?
> Do you think he'll just stop on his own?
> Is there a part of him that is just doing this to drive you nuts?
> What would happen if you just told him to stop?
> Do you think he'll grow into a sexual offender?
> What would it take to get the point across that he just can't do that?

These questions can be tailored for other behaviors and expanded as you see fit. They naturally fall into the categories of parents' powerlessness over their child, willfulness on the child's part, and negative future outcome.

## ❑ Adolescents

I developed the Adolescent Sexual Behavior Inventory (ASBI) after initial success with the CSBI. Another measure for teens is the Adolescent Concerns Questionnaire (Hussey & Singer, 1989), but it assesses a smaller range of sexual behaviors and feelings. Research has found a correlation of some dimensions of adolescent sexual behavior with sexual abuse (Fergusson, Horwood, & Lynskey, 1997; Rotheram-Borus, Mahler, Koopman, & Langabeer, 1996). However, I believe that sexual behavior in teenagers is less related to a sexual abuse history than it is for children. While that is true, sexual abuse is related to sexual behavior problems, although there are other family and maltreatment variables that contribute significantly to problems in teenagers (Friedrich, Lysne, et al., 2001). For example, while body image distortion is greater in sexually abused females (Dansky et al., 1997), most females with psychiatric problems report difficulties in this domain on the ASBI. The same is true for many nonclinical females.

The ASBI has both a parent and a self-report version, and the 45 items seem to load most sensibly into five factors: sexual interest, risky sexual behavior/misuse, body image concerns, deviant sexual behavior, and sexual knowledge (Friedrich, Lysne, et al., 2001). A revised version is being developed and studied at this time.

If teens can be honest with you, their input is quite valuable. First, it introduces them early on to a very relevant treatment topic. Second, parents often have little idea about the sexual activity and perceptions of their teenage children. (Actually, in the first sample of 140 13- to 18-year-old teenagers, all with a psychiatric or sexual abuse history, the correlation between parent- and self-report on total number of sexual partners was significant ($r = .6$). This surprisingly high correlation was largely due to the high number of teens and parents who overlapped in their report of no prior sexual partner.) However, caregiver input on such behaviors as "Gets used sexually by others" may be something the parent can observe more objectively. Preliminary analyses suggest that such items as running away to unsafe places, promiscuity, and getting used sexually are significantly correlated with a sexual abuse history in both females and males. The current forms of the parent- and self-report versions are presented in Appendixes L and M, respectively.

Evaluators of sexually aggressive children get asked whether the child will develop into a sex offender. Your reply should be that this type of prediction is impossible to make with any validity. You might go on to state that the literature indicates that early onset CD and ODD have the worst long-term outcome in children and include a significant percentage of individuals who go on to more criminal behavior (Moffitt, 1993). My assessments are also informed by the Psychopathy Checklist- Revised (PCL-R; Hare, 1991) or the related Hare P-Scan (Hare & Herve, 1999).

The PCL-R evaluates for two domains of functioning: selfish, callous, and remorseless use of others, and chronically unstable and antisocial lifestyle. An adolescent version is currently being studied. Some of the Factor One behaviors that seem most relevant to children and adolescents include glibness, need for stimulation, pathological lying, manipulativeness, lack of remorse or guilt, shallow affect, and lack of empathy. Factor Two behaviors include early behavioral problems, impulsivity, and juvenile delinquency. These variables are useful to keep in mind while organizing your evaluation data. However, the most thorough evaluation of a preteen does not make you significantly better at predicting rare behaviors.

## ❑ Evaluator Rating of Sexual Behavior

In order to help the evaluator keep track of the child's behavior in a more systematic manner, I developed a 10-item rating scale with a former graduate student, Barbara Lui (Friedrich, 1990). Two categories of behaviors are rated, one pertaining to boundary problems and the other to sexualized comments/behaviors. Research with young children coming into an outpatient psychiatry clinic for their first appointment found that sexually abused children exhibited more problems in both of these categories than other children. The most commonly endorsed items were the sexual items. However, no norms exist, and the boundary items are endorsed for children with other maltreatment, for example, neglect, physical abuse, and children with ADHD. Foster parents often report that female children who are rated high on this scale make the foster father and brothers nervous. This suggests the behavior is also present in the home setting. The items are listed in Appendix K.

## ❏  Parent Rating—Family

The most appropriate rating scale in this domain is the Safety Checklist, since that actually targets specific triggers to sexual behavior: family nudity, cosleeping, and so on. Information from this measure can be very useful in planning treatment goals. The Family Events Checklist (Maddock, 1990), a checklist of sexual behaviors having occurred in the immediate and extended family, like illegitimate pregnancies, incest in relatives' families, and so on, is empirically related to sexual acting out in families (Seabloom, 1998). I am currently researching the relationship of these family sexual behaviors, in combination with family discipline practices and behavior problems in the child with the emergence of sexual behavior problems in preteen children. Preliminary data strongly suggest that separate from sexual abuse, a combination of family sexual practices and conduct problems as measured by the Strengths and Difficulties Questionnaire (Goodman, 1997) accounts for the majority of the variance of intrusive sexual behaviors in these children. Harsh discipline is also significantly correlated, but it is accounted for by conduct problems in the regression analysis.

Questions about sexuality in the home are quite useful. I typically introduce this portion of the Safety Checklist with a general question about what sexual material the child has been exposed to. Regardless of the parents' answer, I then list magazines, videos, TV shows, and Internet sites. I also again ask if anyone in the home rents X-rated videos. I directly ask about real-life exposure to sexual behavior between the parents, beginning with hugging and kissing, and moving to sexual grabbing and groping. After these questions, I believe parents are more likely to answer honestly such questions as witnessing parental or sibling nudity and intercourse. If you are going to help a sexually reactive child, you absolutely must know what sexual modeling goes on in the home. This knowledge can be obtained only with direct questioning; for example, if a child is inserting objects between her labia or, more rarely, into her vagina, I specifically ask if the child has ever seen the mother or teenage sister insert a tampon.

## ❏ Child Report—Self

Children's drawings have some documented utility with younger sexually abused children, particularly the degree to which they indicate discomfort with gender as well as the child's perception of others as sexual, such as sexual detail in the drawing (Peterson & Hardin, 1997). Interpretation of drawings is best done cautiously, and evidence needs to be balanced with other data that emerge. In addition, it is highly irregular for a child older than early elementary grades to add sexual detail in drawings.

Although the best use of the Rorschach is as a perception task (Exner, 1991), the content of the child's responses can be illuminating, even if none of the ratios and constellation summary scores are significant. Sexual responses are more common in sexually abused children and adolescents (Einbender & Friedrich, 1989; Friedrich et al., 1997; Friedrich, Einbender, & McCarty, 1999). The inconsistency of this finding is reflected in a finding that sex content on the Rorschach is not related to the TSCC Sex Concerns scale (Sadowski & Friedrich, 2000). There is some clinical lore as well regarding penetration responses being more common in individuals with a history of sexual abuse, but that has not been empirically validated (Kelly, 1999).

Rorschachs were obtained on the children in the study funded by the National Center on Child Abuse and Neglect (NCCAN) on children with sexual behavior problems that was conducted jointly at Oklahoma City and Seattle (Bonner et al., 2000). As a consultant to the grant, I was asked to review the Exner-scored (1991) Rorschach findings. My summary review was that the sexual behavior problem group was more intense and unmodulated in their emotional outbursts, less interested in people, more avoidant of affect, less likely to anticipate that people are cooperative, and more likely to view the world as aggressive.

Children's responses to the Roberts Apperception Test for Children have been studied in two separate projects (Friedrich & Share, 1997; Smith, 1992). Both found that sexually abused children are more likely to give sexualized responses to the Roberts stimuli cards, particularly Card 15 (a small boy looking at a woman in a bathtub). Card 5 is also useful, since it depicts a romantic moment between two parent figures. However, oppositional boys also were more prone to give sexualized responses, although not as often as the sexual abuse sample. Again, these results are with preteens.

The Thematic Apperception Test (TAT; Bellak, 1986) has been more thoroughly studied with samples of sexually abused children and adolescents. Though I prefer to use the Roberts for preteens, the TAT is my preferred measure with teenagers, despite the dated appearance of the stimulus cards. Hen- derson (1990) found sexually abused girls to differ from nonabused girls in characterizing relationships with fathers as being more sexualized. Stovall and Craig (1990) also found the TAT responses of physically and sexually abused girls to differ from nonabused children from distressed homes.

Westen and his colleagues in their development of a scoring system based in object-relations theory have completed truly impressive research with the TAT (Westen, Lohr, Silk, Gold, & Kerber, 1990; see also Ornduff & Kelsey, 1996). The complexity of representations of people, the affect-tone of relationship paradigms, the capacity for emotional investment in relationships, moral standards, and understanding of social causality can be derived from the analysis of TAT responses, with obvious implications for therapy. However, this scoring system is very complex and not easily mastered.

Caruso (1987) developed the Projective Storytelling Test, a series of quite explicit stimulus pictures with the same response format as the TAT and Roberts. The cards were published with no supporting research as to their utility for diagnostic evaluations. In an effort to understand if they could be useful, I completed an unpublished study. The sample size was small ($N = 19$), and six of the cards were used with consecutively referred preadolescent outpatients. ADHD was the most common referral question, followed by learning disability. All but one of the children provided at least one story that mentioned sexual abuse. Only three of the children had a sexual abuse history. My impression was that these cards may be too explicit to truly measure the projection to subtle stimuli seen more often in sexually abused children.

It is possible to get comfortable using sexual terms and talking about sexual behavior by using objective self-report measures such as the CITES-R (Wolfe, Gentile, Michienzi, Sas, & Wolfe, 1991) and the TSCC (Briere, 1996) as structured interviews. This format has unknown effects on TSCC validity, but valuable information is obtained during an interview about such a sensitive topic.

The CITES-R is not normed, but asks about a broader range of sexual behaviors and allows you to talk to the child in considerable detail about sexual matters. There are two scales, Sexual Anxiety and Eroticism, that are the most useful. However, the children who answer in the affirmative on the Eroticism subscale often seem to be the ones who feel considerable shame about their abuse and seem unable to deny distress as oppositional boys are able to do. At the same time, given Hall and Mathews's (1996) findings about shame and guilt and their relation to further sexual aggression, the information can be useful in a number of ways, including guiding treatment.

A recent study examined subscales from the CITES-R and the Sexual Abuse Fear Survey Schedule (SAFE) with two samples of children, one with a history of sexual abuse (Cohen, Deblinger, Maedel, & Stauffer, 1999). The researchers found that sexually abused children reported significantly more sexual anxiety than did their nonabused peers. This finding was even more evident in younger sexual abuse victims. In another recent paper, the convergent validity of the CITES-R and the TSCC was studied (Crouch, Smith, Ezzell, & Saunders, 1999). Specifically related to self-report of sexual concerns, TSCC Sexual Distress was significantly correlated with the following CITES-R scales: PTSD, Intrusive Thoughts, Avoidance, Hyperarousal, Sexual Anxiety, Self-Blame/Guilt, Personal Vulnerability, Negative Reactions by Others, and inversely with Empowerment. TSCC Sexual Preoccupation was significantly correlated with the following CITES-R scales: Eroticism, and Negative Reactions by Others.

I sometimes have difficulty understanding why one sexually abused child reports sexual distress on the TSCC and another one does not. The reasons outlined in Chapter 3 about the variability in sexually abused children can certainly illuminate this point. I do believe there are a number of other contributors. I recall a 10-year-old boy who had been molested by three different men over a 4-year period. He responded with a vehement "No" to Item 34, "Not trusting people because they might want sex." His response was as much wish/denial as anything else. He responded in a strikingly different way than a painfully anxious girl with a one-time experience of fondling by a slightly older peer, who endorsed this same item as, "Almost all of the time." I think we would agree that despite the different responses, the first child had the more severe problem.

The 10 items that make up the TSCC Sexual Concerns subscales are a welcome addition to the testing armamentarium. The norms cover a broad age range, but teenagers may chafe at the simple wording of the items. The two subscales are not easy to interpret and usually require a follow-up conversation with the child. For example, I have seen teenage boys with no history of sexual abuse or sexual aggression score high on the sexual preoccupation subscale, and have also seen sexually abused girls score high on both this scale and on sexual distress. High scores on sexual distress are not that common and have proven to be quite a useful set of screening items on the inpatient unit on which I consult. A central problem is that neither the TSCC nor the CITES-R thoroughly addresses the sexually avoidant pattern. Although some of the items are anxiety/distress related, I believe questions directly about avoidant sexual behavior, such as, "The thought of sex is frightening to me," and "I try not to think about sex at all," could nicely augment the scale.

## ❑ Common Clinical Assessment Dilemmas

Referral questions accompanying children who behave in sexually intrusive ways with other children include whether the child has been sexually abused and/or is a danger to other children, and treatment recommendations. Although it is true that sexually intrusive children are likely to be sexually abused, particularly females and younger boys, other forms of maltreatment are likely to characterize the lives of these children as well. Establishing their abuse status is preferably done by the designated local investigative authority, although your test data may also suggest something about their past.

It is best to think about a sexually aggressive child the same way you would a child who has an impulse and anger control problem. What is going on in the family that either drives the behavior or fails to extinguish it? Does the child feel rejected? What resources does the child have, including language skills, that can help him inhibit his behavior and profit from psychotherapy? Has prior maltreatment been openly discussed and resolved? Are there competencies at school or with peers that are positive? What about sexual behavior in general, or is he exhibiting primarily aggressive behavior? Does he have guilt over his behavior? If abused, does he feel guilty about that? What efforts have been made to stop the behavior, and were they successful?

It is even more difficult to establish risk for future offending in a child than in an adult. Most children can inhibit their behavior. Given the low rate of recidivism of adolescent sexual offenders, it is more likely than not that a sexually aggressive child will never offend again (Chaffin & Bonner, 1998). If asked to render an opinion about the child's treatment needs and safety with other children, the Hall and Mathews (1996) risk factors are an excellent place to start.

Another variable to keep in mind in these assessments, particularly with older boys, for example, between 10 and 12, is a prior diagnosis of conduct disorder. You need to assess whether the sexual aggression was a function of their tendency to exploit others or whether it reflected a greater focus on sexuality, and if so, for what reason.

Another referral question pertains to the appropriateness of sexually aggressive children for group therapy. Although there are certainly data supporting group work with children who have sexual behavior problems, particularly in the context of parent therapy (Bonner et al., 2000), there is also clinical lore that suggests that some children are clearly not suited for group work (Friedrich, Berliner, Urquiza, & Beilke, 1988). Children who are problematic for group can sometimes be managed if there is a rigid structure or psychoeducational approaches dominate. However, if the group is small, or the group has a strong process component, then even one inappropriate child can ruin the group. Though these characteristics can be detected through a screening interview, validating them with various psychological measures may be important. The characteristics of children who are poor group candidates include reduced social skills (very low social competence on the CBC), intrusive behavior during the screening interview (boundary problems on the Evaluator Rating Scale, Appendix K), deficient language (low Verbal IQ), and significant sexual aggression (elevated CSBI score). Another factor to consider, though it can be managed, is that children may be still so reactive to the abuse that group becomes aversive (elevated reexperiencing on the PTSD Symptom Scale).

I have also learned that sexual behavior that is self-directed, like masturbation, in the context of a safe and supportive home environment can be easily eliminated with simple behavioral strategies, including token systems and redirection. In the past several years I have met several children with a developing obsessive-compulsive disorder who engage in sexual behaviors, for example, masturbation or insertion of objects into the rectum. None of these children reported sexual abuse, and I had little reason to doubt them. Behavioral strategies were helpful and were augmented with medication.

## ❑ Translating the Evaluation Into Treatment Recommendations

Treatment of children who have sexual behavior problems, even those who are not behaving coercively with other children, is usually aimed at eliminating the behavior or at least teaching the child to refrain from exhibiting the behavior in public. Parents will be critical change agents, and an evaluation of their ability to monitor and respond in an appropriate fashion will be key to the assessment. Data about parents can be used to guide the treatment process and to determine if they have the potential to help change to occur. The results may suggest that the child needs to go into a foster home in order for the behavior to be eliminated.

A recent study found that insecure attachment characterized the parent-child relations in all five of the authors' typologies of children with sexual behavior problems (Pithers et al., 1998). In fact, parental attachment to the child was significantly correlated to treatment success after 16 weeks. The authors recommended that for this reason alone, treatment must involve the child's caregivers.

Children with noncoercive behavior problems, for example, compulsive masturbation, often come from families where the agitation level is higher and prior abuse is being triggered. Poor parental monitoring makes it very hard to correct these problems, since behavior treatment aimed at the target behavior is the treatment of choice to get the symptoms under control. Information from the Safety Checklist can point to specific domains that need to be changed, such as domestic violence. Once children are less reactive, they are more likely to benefit from talking about the abuse experience that is temporally related to the masturbation.

For coercive behavior problems, I usually recommend strategies very similar to those outlined in social learning approaches (Patterson, Reid, Jones, & Conger, 1975). There must be a simultaneous beefing up of parental support and involvement, and age-appropriate variations on the relationship-enhancement portion of Parent-Child Interaction Therapy (PCIT; Hembree-Kigin & McNeil, 1995) are also incorporated at the same time. Multisystemic therapy has a place with these families as well (Brunk, Henggeler, & Whelan, 1987).

An individual or dyadic therapy approach with the child is also recommended. If there is a history of earlier sexual abuse, its discussion and initial resolution are usually made a treatment goal. In the dyad, opportunities for peer problem solving and the practice of more prosocial behaviors become possible. Recruiting the parent into his or her own therapy is optimal, but two appointments a week may already be a huge burden for the system. Other than stimulants, I have rarely found psychiatric medicines truly useful with these children. If you go down this path and fail, the child often is blamed. You also remove the focus on the family issues that must be addressed and blunt the treatment urgency while everyone waits in vain for the medication to take effect. However, there are many times where the parent may benefit from a psychiatric consultation.

## ❏ Summary

This chapter has provided an overview of the assessment of sexual behavior and sexual behavior problems in sexually abused children and teenagers. This is a critically important topic, since sexual behavior problems, more than any other symptom cluster, are characteristic of sexually abused children. This is despite the fact that information about these behaviors typically comes from parents who are poor observers of their child and whose issues with victimization make accurate reporting problematic. However, at this time in the development of evaluation technology, there is no real mechanism other than parent- and, to a lesser degree, self-report to use in allowing children to express their sexual behaviors and concerns.

Sexual behavior in both children and adolescents is strongly related to family context. These context variables include all forms of maltreatment other than sexual abuse, family violence, stress, and family sexuality. Sexual abuse is likely to be the single most important contributor to excessive sexual behavior in young children. There are data that suggest it is not the most critical aspect in teenagers, with the exception of self-destructive and deviant sexual behaviors. In order to understand accurately the emergence of sexual behavior problems in the clients you evaluate, you must also examine for the presence of variables that contribute to dysregulation and consider their relative impact on the emergence of the behavior problems.

Some of the children referred to you have sexual behavior problems combined with generic aggression. The family factors important to the emergence of oppositional behavior are likely to be operative here as well. Treatment recommendations for sexually aggressive children will be similar to those you provide to families where oppositionality is an issue.

I am often asked questions about risk prediction for sexual aggression in young children. Predicting risk for any rare behavior is extremely difficult for psychologists to do accurately. No cross-validated, empirically derived set of risk factors for sexually aggressive children exists at this point. It is likely that the best predictor is the quality of the parent-child relationship.

# 7

# Assessment of Self-Perception

A central focus in this book is on the highly interpersonal process of attachment (Table 7.1). The reader may wonder about including such an intrapersonal process as the self in this book. Although the self is traditionally viewed as an individual formulation, the child does not exist in isolation, and a more accurate phrase for any individual is self-other (Nakkula & Selman, 1991). In keeping with the developmental focus of this book, it is also critical to assert that the self is an active, cognitive construction, continually undergoing developmental change (Harter, 1983). The past decade has witnessed a resurgence of interest in the self, and practitioners have come to appreciate that a positive self-image is part of adaptive functioning (Harter, 1990).

Central to this chapter is the fact that the effects of sexual molestation and related life events are cognitively mediated, that is, there is the formation of negative appraisals such as the perception of physical damage, self-blame, and so on (Spacarelli, 1994). Prior social experiences also affect how information is processed and thus influence

**Table 7.1**    Psychological Assessment of Self-Issues

---

I. Parent Report—Self
   A. Generic Measures
      1. MCMI (Dyer, 1997)
      2. Intelligence
   B. Abuse-Specific Measures
      1. TSI (Briere, 1995)
II. Parent Report—Child
   A. Child Behavior Checklist (Achenbach, 1991a) or BASC
      (Reynolds & Kamphaus, 1998)
      1. School Competence
      2. Somatic Complaints
III. Teacher Report
   A. Teacher Report Form (Achenbach, 1991b) or BASC
      (Reynolds & Kamphaus, 1998)
      1. School Competence
IV. Child Report
   A. Generic Measures
      1. Human Figure Drawing
      2. Sentence Completion
      3. Intelligence
      4. Perceived Self-Competence Scale (Harter, 1982)
      5. BASC Self-Report (Reynolds & Kamphaus, 1998)
   B. Abuse-Specific Measures
      1. CITES-R (Wolfe, Gentile, Michienzi, Sas, & Wolfe, 1991)
         a. Self-blame and guilt
         b. Dangerous world
         c. Empowerment
         d. Personal vulnerability
      2. Children's Attributions and Perceptions Scale
      (CAPS; Mannarino, Cohen, & Berman, 1994)
      3. My Feelings About the Abuse Questionnaire (Feiring, Taska, & Lewis, 1998)

---

cognitions that influence behavior (Gully, in press). Problematic coping strategies, such as cognitive avoidance and wishful thinking, also contribute to distress. It is important to note that wide variability occurs in the development and utility of these cognitive appraisals. In addition, any thinking about self must take into consideration that there are developmental changes that must be addressed in the assessment (Harter, 1990).

If a maltreated individual, of any age, can view herself in a variety of favorable ways that maintain positive self-esteem, promote a favorable self-regard, enhance self-awareness, and foster a stable sense of identity, then she has attributes that contribute to good psychological adjustment (Weiner, 1998). Conversely, a negative self-perception and a reduced or insufficient sense of self are liabilities and the victim is even more likely to have adjustment difficulties.

Harter (1990) urges that the assessment of self-concept flows from a clear framework of the self-concept. The theory, more than the measure, should dictate the assessment of this concept. The degree of self-integrity is related to the damaging effects of trauma and includes the dimensions of efficacy, potency, self-ownership, and shame. Finding a theory that subsumes each of these is not an easy task.

The clinical assessment issues that fall into this category are several. For parents, they include personality features that interfere with their ability to make the necessary and lasting changes to be more effective parents. As for the child or teen victim, this is also the arena to evaluate issues related to self-efficacy, shame, and accuracy of perception of self and others, and the impact of the abuse. Because I consider problem-solving capacity and intelligence as critical aspects of self-development, relevant data from these areas are also presented here.

However, this chapter begins with the final installment of case material on A. B., with the focus on self-perception in both the parent and child.

## ❑ Case Material Related to Self-Perception

### Parent

Mrs. B. completed the Millon Clinical Multiaxial Inventory (MCMI-II) and answered in a manner designed to portray herself in a favorable light. However, the overall profile was deemed valid. She was significantly elevated on four clinical personality patterns, including avoidant, dependent, self-defeating, and schizoid. She was also significantly elevated on two clinical syndromes: dysthymic disorder and anxiety disorder.

Taken together, these results suggest that Mrs. B. has significant problems with issues of closeness/distance in her relationships. One could surmise that her difficulties with personal relationships and her ambivalence about closeness are likely to interfere with her parenting. She also has a pattern of behavior in which she seems to be further victimized in her relationships, and this could serve to solidify her ambivalence. She is responding to these distresses with significant dysthymia and anxiety, which need to be evaluated more specifically with an eye toward treatment recommendations.

### Child

A. B.'s intellectual abilities were assessed with the WISC-III. He obtained a Verbal IQ of 93, a Performance IQ of 100, and a Full Scale IQ of 96. These scores are all within the average range and extend from the 32nd to the 50th percentile. When WISC-III factor scores were calculated, they ranged from 86 on Freedom From Distractibility, to 103 on Perceptual Organization, to 98 on Verbal Comprehension. A relative weakness was noted on short-term memory for digits, which was thought to be related to his difficulties concentrating at this time.

Academic achievement was screened with the WRAT-3, and age-corrected standard scores ranged from 100 on Written Spelling, to 105 on Single Word Reading, to 107 on Computational Arithmetic. Grade equivalencies ranged from the mid-third-grade level to the mid-fourth-grade level.

A. B.'s human figure drawings are inappropriate in that a female was drawn first. His drawing of a female lacked arms and was distorted. His drawing of a male had long hair and could not be discriminated from the female.

Further evidence for A. B.'s difficulties with self-perception is reflected in Rorschach responses that indicate significantly elevated egocentricity, as well as poor judgment. The lack of blended responses is also reflective of reduced psychological complexity.

### Self-Development-Related Treatment Issues

1. Mrs. B. needs to be assisted in exploring her ambivalence about closeness, most particularly as to how it affects the quality of her relationship with her son.
2. Mrs. B. may benefit from a medication that addresses the clinical levels of depression and anxiety she reports. A psychiatric referral is recommended.

3. Although A. B. could be resistant to this in his individual therapy, he needs to be assisted in learning how to take the perspective of the other people to whom he is relating.

## ❑ Overview of Self-Perception Issues

A central tenet of this book is that the impact of trauma is always mediated. Critically important mediators include attachment security and the quality of other interpersonal relationships. Although secure relationships may be a primary mediator, a second constellation of mediators reflects the person. They include the characteristics and belief systems the individual brings to the traumatic situation. Both of these sets of mediating variables must be considered if you are to have an accurate understanding of individuals and their current and future functioning.

Recent research has suggested that there are situations where individual characteristics play a larger role than relationship characteristics. For example, self-efficacy was related to more adaptive coping in maltreated individuals than reliance on closeness to the parent (Cicchetti & Rogosch, 1997). Successful individuals turned away from the negative relationship and relied more on their own attributes, including intelligence. Presumably, a continued dependence on the abusive parent would have undermined an individual's forward progress.

The degree to which children, teenagers, and parents can view themselves both accurately and positively is a reflection of the self-derived mediator. The self-related dimensions that warrant assessment include perceptions of self-efficacy; the attributions individuals make about their successes and failures, including abuse-specific attributions; and the degree to which individuals experience shame and guilt. These include abuse-specific attributions as well as more generic ones.

Maltreatment types are related to different sequelae. For example, neglected children were found to have the lowest overall levels of positive self as measured by a story-stem task, whereas physically abused individuals had the highest levels of negative self (Toth, Cicchetti, Macfie, & Emde, 1997).

Self-perception represents a culmination of the child's prior experiences, including attachment and dysregulating experiences. The development of the self is tantamount to the aggregation of experiences of self in relationships (Fonagy & Target, 1997). Self-development and the early integration of affect become intertwined with the concepts of the self and the capacity to self-regulate (Miller, 1996). The self is also a reflection of the internalized working model that develops in direct relation to the child's attachment quality. In this fashion, the self is interpersonal and reflects both attachment history and coherence in the face of dysregulation. Quite logically, it is the last assessment area to be reviewed.

In addition, self-perception reflects the often-noted "false self" or "disguised presentation" that develops in abuse survivors (Gelinas, 1983). These phenomena reflect persons who present with superficially positive veneers that are far removed from their underlying feelings of inadequacy and of having been damaged. Evidence of a false self may manifest behaviorally, where the success the 14-year-old has at school seems unrelated to his or her self-description as inadequate and stupid. For example, Trickett (1993) found that physically abused girls, unlike boys, were unusually quiet, wary, and compliant compared to controls.

Winnicott (1965) has written about the continuum of the false self, ranging from the healthy, polite aspect of the self to the truly split-off, compliant, false self that is mistaken for the whole person. This self emerges as the child learns to comply with parenting that is "not good enough."

The manner in which adversity leads to distress is not easily understood. Equally misunderstood is the manner in which the individuals arrive at the biased belief systems they often vigorously maintain regarding the blame and responsibility they have about the traumatic event. Changing these negative self-perceptions seems to require guided self-examination, usually in the form of therapy. I have found that when traumatic impact seems to persist despite solid therapeutic efforts, it is important to revisit issues such as shame, guilt, brokenness, and self-loathing. Early efforts at repair are likely to have been insufficient.

Dissociation is also relevant in a chapter on self-perception. Dissociation can imply the fragmentation of the self on the one hand, or a dynamic adaptation to overwhelming experiences on the other (Fischer et al., 1997). Dissociation reflects the integrity of the developing self and the degree to which thinking, awareness, and memory are connected (Braun, 1988). It is also related to how the individual manages the dysregulating experience of extreme stress and hence was discussed in Chapter 5.

Distortions in body image, often related to trauma, and the closely related issue of self-injurious behavior (SIB) are also appropriate topics for this chapter. Body image and the person's sense of sexual self are reviewed here; SIB was a focus in Chapter 5. SIB has a clear role as a tension-reducing behavior and is probably related as much to one's capacity for self-regulation of overwhelming emotions as it is to negative self-perception.

At one time, most of the patients I was seeing were sexually abused preteens and their parents. Helping preteens think about themselves and report accurately seemed to be a waste of therapeutic time and effort. It was easy to dismiss self-perception in light of these experiences. But gradually I began to listen to the self-loathing that parents would admit to, usually after some extended time in therapy. And as I began to work more and more with teens, I was struck both by their increasing ability to think about themselves and by the attendant inaccuracy about their self-related thoughts. Consequently, I began to see self-perception as a crucial therapy component (Friedrich, 1995a).

I continued to maintain some resistance to individual processes, such as self-perception, however. This was in response to therapists tossing around words like *shame* too loosely. Some clinicians spoke as if shame, an often vague notion, constituted the central therapeutic issue. The words *shame* and *enabling* activated a knee-jerk reaction against them.

A paper by Schore (1996) linked the concept of shame to both attachment security and dysregulation. He stated that shame is a "primary social emotion" (p. 69) and makes its appearance at 14 to 16 months. Schore attributes its emergence to a break in affective attunement with the primary caregiver and elaborates further when he writes, "shame represents this rapid state transition from a preexisting positive state to a negative state" (p. 69). Shame, then, becomes an attachment emotion and is the reaction "to an important other's unexpected refusal to enter into a dyadic system that can recreate an attachment bond"

(p. 69). How long and how frequently a child remains in this state is an important factor in the child's ongoing emotional development.

The concept of shame became worthwhile once I realized how shame was tied to both attachment and self-regulation. It needs to be carefully assessed, along with related abuse-specific attributions as well as other person-specific issues. In addition, there are now data suggesting the relationship of shame and guilt in the emergence of postabuse sexual behavior problems (Hall & Mathews, 1996) and the persistence of symptoms in victims (Deblinger & Hefflin, 1996). In addition, appreciating Schore's (1996) concept of shame sharpens my perception that children and teenagers who cannot view their trauma accurately, and who attribute much self-blame, will have a history of impaired attachment and a lack of training/modeling of self-regulation. In addition, children's ability to talk about emotions is tied to the maturity of their interpersonal interaction (Bretherton, Fritz, Zahn-Waxler, & Ridgeway, 1986).

In summary, the underlying constructs for this book are inextricably linked. Attachment results in an internal working model, which is a major component of the relational self. The ability to register internal states and affective cues accurately, a self-function, is related to the emergence of panic disorders, a dysregulation symptom (Fonagy & Target, 1997).

This chapter is a bit of a potpourri, because included in the list of topics reviewed are issues as divergent as IQ and shame. However, even these two divergent topics are linked, although how they are linked deserves an explanation. Both are related to the accuracy of self-perception and the degree to which individuals can marshal their personal resources to resolve their victimization.

## ❑ Parent Report—Self

### GENERIC MEASURES

Intelligence is directly related to self-efficacy and problem solving. Parenting also involves significant cognitive activity (Azar, Lauretti, & Loding, 1998). It is also an important predictor of resilience from maltreatment (Cicchetti & Rogosch, 1997). Consequently, if you are performing a parenting evaluation, a measure of intelligence must be obtained. You may work with many clients of color or others who have been disadvantaged in one way or the other, and thus have concerns about the validity of IQ scores with these parents. However, parenting has a huge cognitive component, and this information must be available to understand if parents can implement a protection plan, advocate for their child, manage a complex medication regiment, and respond to verbally based psychotherapy.

At a recent APSAC workshop, Kerry Drach (1998) reported that the majority of the parents referred for parental competency evaluations at his program in Portland, Maine, were of low average intelligence. This corresponds to what I have found in more than 20 years of performing court-ordered parenting competency evaluations.

Why do I think a measure of intelligence is important to parenting evaluations? Intelligence is related to problem-solving capacity. It is related to the person's ability to carry out complex tasks such as parenting. It has something to say about one's ability to benefit from experience, including psychotherapy and parent-training approaches. I think it is also related to the degree that parents can accurately report their child's behavior to you. In light of earlier comments about reflective functioning and self-perception (Fonagy, 1998), intelligence is likely to be related to this critical task of self-perception as well. Data on recidivism in criminal populations indicate that IQ scores in the low average range and lower are associated with higher rates of repeat offenses (Holland, Beckett, & Levi, 1981). I suspect that the same holds true in cases of child maltreatment.

There will be times when you are asked to evaluate children whose abuse is related to parental neglect. Parenting competence will definitely be one part of the issue, for example, the capacity to monitor the child's behavior. A quick screen of parents' cognitive abilities, and preferably a more formal, standardized assessment with the Wechsler Adult Intelligence Scale (WAIS; Wechsler, 1997) or related measure of adult intelligence, like the Kaufman Brief Intelligence Test (Kaufman & Kaufman, 1990), can help to answer questions about competence. With limited parents whose strength is nonverbal, a nonverbal measure may be more appropriate and more respectful (Test of Nonverbal Intelligence [TONI-3]; Brown, Sherbenou, & Johnsen, 1997).

The results of the cognitive assessment must be interpreted with care. Issues of race and cultural background need to be considered as well as parents' practical intelligence, for example, problem-solving abilities (Azar et al., 1998). One parent's low average IQ may reflect across-the-board impairment in intellectual functioning and be closely related to problems in child rearing, including monitoring. Another parent with a similar IQ may actually be far more capable, given a higher level of practical intelligence but a substandard education. In addition, it is imperative always to remember that although intelligence is a very important consideration, how and whether it directly impacts the parenting of the individual in front of you can be difficult to decipher.

It is quite likely that personality disorders are present to a greater degree in the parents of maltreated children than in the general population. A closer link between personality disorder and both treatability and parenting quality exists than for intelligence and these same two variables. If the referral issue is related to parenting quality, and the parent's ability to take the child's perspective and provide safety is paramount, a valid measure of ongoing personality functioning is needed. This is even more the case when the court is considering whether parental rights should be terminated. I have found that using both the MMPI-2 and the MCMI (Millon, 1987), or one of its variations like the MCMI-II, is very useful for assessing personality functioning. By using both, I obtain two perspectives, something that is very critical when an evaluation can influence something as life-altering as termination of parental rights. Other options for one of the above include the NEO Personality Inventory-Revised (NEO-R; Costa & Widiger, 1994) and the Sixteen Personality Factors Questionnaire (16 PF; Cattell, Eber, & Tatsuoka, 1970).

Although the Millon scales tend to overpathologize if used with nonreferred patients, the circumstances of the parents referred for this type of evaluation necessitate determining what personality characteristics are operative. My experience in the assessment of personality disorders in these parents is primarily with the MMPI-2, the Millon scales, and the NEO-R. Interpretation of these scales is augmented by an excellent text by McCann and Dyer (1996). In fact, McCann and Dyer (1996) devote several pages and an equal number of cases to the issue of Millon scales and parental competence issues.

My view on parental competence in these cases pertains to the resolution of prior victimization, their openness to change, and their ability to be protective of their vulnerable children. For example, I evaluated a mother referred by social services because of repeated reports that a relative was chronically molesting her daughter. This mother apparently could not realize how inappropriate it was that her daughter was sleeping in the same bed as the man who had molested her (the mother) as a child. The county had tried a number of interventions to prevent this from happening and finally removed the girl from the home. However, she was due to return home since the mother had completed parenting classes and a CD evaluation had not recommended treatment.

An earlier assessment with an MMPI resulted in a normal limits profile, and this had also been used to argue for the girl's return home. However, I interpreted this profile as largely due to the lack of distress the mother felt in her life. The fact that she was not upset with her situation and her daughter's plight was in itself a poor prognostic sign. In addition, her MCMI-II profile had very significant elevations on Dependent, Avoidant, Self-Defeating, and Passive-Aggressive, and her Rorschach also suggested a significant dissociative element. The information was useful in supporting further treatment before the daughter returned home.

Parents who have been sexually abused and received treatment for it have probably adapted relatively well if their personality disorder falls into the mildest category, Cluster C. This includes avoidant, dependent, and obsessive-compulsive personality disorders. The anxious-fearful underlay of many of these styles will often be reflected in parents' efforts to keep their children safe. Typically, they also lead a life that is calmer and more sedate. However, a significant percentage of parents with unresolved victimization are more malignant. Their behavior suggests Cluster B personality disorders, for example, aggressive-sadistic, narcissistic, and borderline. These are parents who don't show up for visits; who stir up their children at visitation; and who view the world, including therapists, as a war zone. The court needs to be informed of the poor prognosis of these individuals.

A large proportion of patients with borderline personality disorder have a history of childhood sexual abuse, but the experience of sexual abuse is neither necessary nor sufficient in the etiology of borderline personality disorder (Zanarini, 1996). Parents with a sexual abuse history, and who present as intense, angry, and variable, do not automatically qualify for this "prize-winning" diagnosis. Careful assessment is still needed to arrive at the most appropriate diagnosis.

When I am referred parents in whom the possibility of a serious Axis II diagnosis has been raised, a thorough review of their trauma history and prior therapy experiences is needed. Denise Gelinas (1983) summarized the differences between women with a sexual abuse history who were and were not borderline. A critical issue pertains to the stability of mood, albeit depressed, and relative absence of anger in the latter group. The presence of eroticizing and/or idealizing transference is more likely present in the former group, and interpersonal wariness is actually a positive in the latter. Frequently incest victims who are not borderline are overresponsible, with acting out occurring in someone else in the family.

Gelinas (1983) introduces the term *disguised presentation* in her paper. This is defined as "a characterological depression with complications and with atypical impulsive and dissociative elements" (p. 326). The victim has a long history of role reversal with her parent(s). Out of loyalty and relational imbalances, she is overly concerned with the welfare of others. However, this does not prevent her children from being victimized, nor does it guarantee that she approaches caring for her children with empathy and nurturance. In these circumstances, the mother's initial presentation is likely to be of someone who is quite competent. In fact, she may appear completely at odds with the child's sexual victimization by a father or other ongoing maltreatment like domestic violence.

Although Gelinas does not equate her "disguised presentation" with Winnicott's (1965) concept of "false self," I believe these constructs overlap significantly and are responsible for many misjudgments by clinicians about victims, both child and adult. The typical initial and cursory interview finds them to be competent individuals, but formal assessment would suggest the defects in their self that interfere with them taking their child's perspective.

Many parents of sexually abused children, with and without a personal history of sexual abuse, will have an elevation on scale 7 (Compulsive) of the MCMI. This is frequently the only significant elevation, although some of the relational subscales—Avoidant, Dependent—may be moderately elevated and capture their ambivalence with close relationships. If a parent is not answering in a socially desirable manner, the scale 7 elevation is associated with inhibition of affect, reduced psychological mindedness, and conflict about autonomy (McCann &

Dyer, 1996). This elevation reflects the trouble many parents have tolerating day-to-day affective displays in their children. It also seems to be related to their lack of comfort with physically touching their children.

*False self* is Winnicott's (1965) very useful term for that structure formed in response to frustration of the "real self." It is a compromise of all of the demands and blocks of the environment (Johnson, 1985) and is the self presented to the world. Winnicott believed that a continuum of awareness existed with the false self. This awareness reflected what the individuals knew about themselves apart from that false presentation. Individuals with no awareness beneath this mask will experience any challenge to this version of themselves as extremely threatening.

My experience with parents of sexually abused children is that the emergence of their real self has been frustrated. They now present to the clinician unaware of their prior hurts and how these affect their difficulties with affect and making a genuine connection. It can be manifested in a number of ways on psychological testing, including the previously mentioned elevation on scale 7 (Compulsive) of the MCMI. Rorschach variables include the avoidance of affect reflected in an elevated lambda, emotional constriction manifested in their form-dominated color ratio, a surprisingly low egocentricity index given their competence, and excessive conventionality, such as a high number of Popular responses.

There are several other self-related issues that deserve mention. These include a parent's body image and sexual self. Both have a relationship to trauma and form a dimension of the personality. For example, body image distortion is an essential feature of eating disorders. It reflects the individual's inaccurate perception of who they are. Bulimia in the parents of sexually abused children was my introduction to this disorder back in 1982. Selected questions about body image, eating problems, and so on, are often illuminating when there is unresolved abuse.

The same is true for the parent's sexual sense of self. It is important to screen for marital satisfaction in the parents of sexually abused children and teenagers. Separate from that issue, sexuality is typically not addressed, and this is regrettable. I have found it useful to ask about satisfaction with sexual relations since that is one indicator of whether these parents have resolved their own abuse.

For example, you might begin by stating, "Parents with a child who has been sexually abused are often affected indirectly by the abuse. Sometimes it shows up as an increase in generalized anxiety. Other times it can be more specific and affect your own sexuality." You are then in a better position to ask a question such as, "Have you found that you are enjoying sexual relations less?"

## ABUSE-SPECIFIC MEASURES

The TSI (Briere, 1995) contains several self-related subscales, including one titled Impaired Self-Reference. The motivation behind the creation of this subscale is reflected in Briere's (1992) statement that "severe child maltreatment may interfere with the child's access to a sense of self" (p. 43). Without this access, problems with identity confusion, boundary issues, and feelings of personal emptiness arise. Self-soothing capacities are reduced because victims don't know when they are in need of them, or, as one parent informed me, "I don't deserve it."

Individuals who score high on the Impaired Self-Reference scale "often appear to have less self-knowledge and self-confidence than others, may be more easily influenced by individuals or groups, and may present as easily excitable and less functional under stress" (Briere, 1995, p. 14).

Another relevant TSI subscale is Tension Reduction Behavior. High scores come from individuals who report numerous attempts to avoid and interrupt negative internal states. A critical item on the scale pertains to self-mutilation, and this is endorsed in over 40% of the parents of sexually abused children that I have assessed with the TSI. In fact, persisting self-injury can be equated with unresolved maltreatment or trauma, particularly Type II PTSD (Kelly, 1999).

Briere's contributions to the assessment of sexually abused children and adults are enormous. Although I have had minimal experience with one of his latest adult measures, the Inventory of Altered Self-Capacities (IASC; Briere, 2001a), it deserves mention. The underlying dimensions of the 63-item IASC mimic the three constructs of this book: capacity to form and maintain meaningful relationships, capacity to modulate and tolerate negative affect, and capacity to maintain a stable sense of personal identity. The two identity scales that are most relevant to this chapter are titled Identity Impairment, with the related subscales of Self-Awareness and Identity Diffusion, and Susceptibility to Influence. The IASC was extremely helpful in a recent case where trauma and borderline issues were being considered in the young mother of a child sexually abused by her boyfriend. The TSI, which indicated unresolved PTSD, was very useful next to the IASC, which suggested relatively better skills in the areas of relatedness and identity. The treatment has since focused on trauma, with positive results.

## ❑ Parent Report—Child

Adequate self-development is reflected in academic and social competence and the capacity for self-reflection. The Child Behavior Checklist (CBCL; Achenbach, 1991a) allows for parental input related to self-perception. One area is school competence, which is directly related to the child's self-efficacy. Doing well in school becomes an even more critical arena if school achievement is one of the few sources of positive input to the child. However, the Adaptive Behavior subscales of the Behavior Assessment System for Children (BASC; Reynolds & Kamphaus, 1998) assess competence more thoroughly. The very brief Strengths and Difficulties Questionnaire, which has some clear strengths over the CBCL, has a scale labeled Prosocial Behavior (Goodman, 1997).

In a different vein, somatic complaints are related to maturity of self-perception and the capacity for self-reflection (Fonagy & Target, 1997). Although unusual somatic complaints in children may reflect a conversion disorder (a symptom cluster more appropriately discussed in Chapter 5), somatizing children and teens have both an impaired self-reference and reduced psychological mindedness (Kelly, 1999).

There are reasons why the sexually abused child may report somatic complaints. The first is the obvious relationship of abuse to subsequent pain and nausea. Two separate studies illustrate the association of sexual abuse with somatic complaints (Fisher & Friedrich, 2001; Friedrich & Schafer, 1995). The second study found that somatic complaints are also related to the child's secretiveness (the absence of self-reflection), overall life stress, and comorbid maltreatment, including physical abuse. Relatively little unique relationship to sexual abuse severity was noted.

## ❑ Teacher Report—Child

The Teacher's Report Form (TRF; Achenbach, 1991b) also includes a measure of academic competence, the Academic Performance scale. Comparing this to parental input can be quite informative, particularly when the discrepancy suggests that the parent views the child more negatively than the teacher. Positive data from teachers can be used in cognitive behavior therapy (CBT) to correct negative self-percepts in latency-aged and teenage victims, for example, "Is it rational to think you are stupid when your teacher says you . . . ?"

## ❑ Child Report—Generic

Questions to children are often met with blank stares and "I don't know" responses. This is frustrating but understandable. The structure of the self is built on self-awareness (Westen, 1991). Self-awareness is reduced by a number of factors. These include, but are not limited to, the child's cognitive developmental level, expressive language problems, chronic avoidance of self-monitoring related to PTSD, and the lack of "training" in self-perception—children have been given few words for their thoughts and feelings.

Psychological assessment becomes extremely helpful in the evaluation of children with reduced self-awareness. A comprehensive evaluation can circumvent the problems with face-valid tools that are rendered useless by reduced self-awareness. Treatment recommendations that have not considered children's capacity to accurately self-report become questionable (LaGreca, 1990).

*Intelligence.* Intellectual capabilities are part of self-efficacy, and the relationship of maltreatment to reduced intellectual competence and reduced school performance is well established (Einbender & Friedrich, 1989; Eckenrode, Laird, & Doris, 1993; Perez & Widom, 1994; Trickett, McBride-Chang, & Putnam, 1994). Neglect has been shown to have a causal effect on decreased cognitive performance, with developmental scores steadily decreasing with repeat testing, dropping from average to low average and lower (Egeland & Erickson, 1987; Egeland, Sroufe, & Erickson, 1983). In addition, there are data that children who are psychiatrically referred differ from their siblings in having a higher percentage of language disorders than would be expected, and in 24% of the cases these disorders had not been suspected prior to assessment (Cohen, Barwick, Horodezky, & Isaacson, 1996).

The increased frequency of language disorders is very important to the topics included in this chapter. For example, the child's ability to talk about emotions permits a different level of intersubjectivity than nonverbal communication of emotion, even in the here and now (Bretherton et al., 1986).

Whenever the opportunity presents itself, I try to assess the child's cognitive and academic competence. Important treatment recommendations may result and generate broader based advocacy for the child and parent in school settings. A child's learning disability becomes one more issue for a marginally competent parent to manage. If your assessment can increase access to school resources, both the child and parent benefit.

The assessment of cognitive capacities doesn't need to be a time-consuming process, given the availability of many valid short forms of the WISC-III (Campbell, 1998) and the Wechsler Abbreviated Scale of Intelligence (WASI; 1999). The developmental level of preschool children can be validly assessed with caregiver input like the Child Development Inventory (CDI; Ireton, 1992)

A valid measure of intelligence can yield data that are useful for treatment planning. For example, children with limited expressive language are more vulnerable to further abuse. These children also have a more difficult time with conventional therapies. It can be nearly impossible for children with a reading disability, who also have problems with written language, to complete workbook-based group therapy interventions, and their therapists need to know this.

Female victims may be compulsively compliant and draw little negative attention in school. Consequently, their academic struggles garner little help from school, whereas acting-out boys may have already been evaluated by the school psychologist and already be receiving services.

A study with direct implications for therapy found that an abbreviated Wechsler IQ score was positively correlated with overall internalizing problems in a sample of sexually abused black girls (Shapiro, Leifer, Martone, & Kassem, 1992). This same relationship did not exist for externalizing behaviors. The authors explained the relationship between well-developed thinking capacities and emotional distress as reflective of self-blame: Girls who blamed themselves for their victimization were both brighter and more distressed. Since this is not the relationship that exists in nonabused populations (Anastasi & Urbina, 1996), the authors suggested that the relationship reflected the more active and less avoidant processing that brighter girls will do in order to understand their victimization. Further research is clearly needed to understand this link, and it would serve us well if cognitive capacity were measured along with coping style.

*Projective Drawings.* Human figure drawings have long been used to evaluate the level of self-development in children. Although their utility is the object of debate, there are several features of drawings that have some reported validity. These include whether the gender matches the child, the presence of distortions or of missing body parts, the nature and quality of the affect, and the immaturity of the drawing related to the child's developmental age (Malchiodi, 1998).

Four of the "serious seven" criteria outlined by Peterson and Hardin (1997) in their book on utilizing drawings as a screen for sexual abuse are related to sexual detail. The fifth is also related, since it pertains to opposite sex drawn by the child. Sexual detail in drawings is more common in sexually abused children, but it is also more common in children who have psychiatric problems and who have been exposed to adult sexuality (Chantler, Pelco, & Mertin, 1993).

Sometimes a distorted view of self emerges only in drawings of the children in their families. For example, the human figure drawing is well done, but the child in the family is drawn very small or very large relative to the other family members. The latter is possibly reflective of an exaggeratedly precarious view the child has of his or her efficacy.

The interpretation of drawings is best done idiographically, with interpretations reserved only if there is independent corroboration from other test or interview data. Signs and features in the drawing may have unique importance to the child. For example, although an exaggerated mouth is not a "sign" of sexual abuse (Peterson & Hardin, 1997), nor is it one of the emotional indicators according to Koppitz's scoring criteria (Koppitz, 1968), it made perfect sense in a drawing by an 8-year-old boy. Although he was exhibiting no significant behavior problems, he had been forced to perform oral copulation. The presence of these details, in combination with high levels of shame on the CITES-R, prompted me to recommend a few supportive sessions addressing these perceptions.

*Projective Tests.* Other projective devices that can be useful in self-assessment include the Rorschach, Sentence Completion Test, Thematic Apperception Test, and the Roberts Apperception Test for Children. The Rorschach has several variables that are related to self-esteem, self-regard, and self-integrity. For example, the egocentricity index can suggest deflated, inflated, or adequate self-esteem (Weiner, 1998). Imagine the differences in two boys, both with an elevated egocentricity index, which is suggestive of exaggerated and rather brittle self-esteem. The first boy was self-absorbed and relied on blaming of others to divert attention from his misdeeds. The second boy, who shared many of these features, was also self-injurious, preoccupied with "what he should have done" to prevent the abuse, and worried obsessively that his growth was forever stunted from taking Ritalin. He also had numerous morbid responses (negative attitudes about one's bodily integrity) and both a Vista response (painful feelings) and a color-shading blend (self-loathing) that were consistent with his worries.

The egocentricity index is suggestive of the degree to which the child is developing the capacity for accurate self-reflection and accurate interpretation of other people's behavior and intentions through his or her eyes. To some degree this is similar to the developmentally appropriate egocentricity seen in children and that has a resurgence in adolescence (Elkind, 1967, 1985).

The lambda index is also indicative of the degree to which children can consider their emotions and the meaning of them. Higher scores suggest that they hold feelings at a distance and hence are less likely to integrate appropriate emotionality into their developing self. On the other hand, children with very low lambdas are often overwhelmed by their feelings and are far too easily caught up and permeable to those around them.

The Rorschach is often challenged as to its utility, but a brief case example can highlight how it was useful to long-term management of a very difficult child. The patient was a 7-year-old child with a history of physical abuse by her mother. A child psychiatrist referred her because she reported visual hallucinations of blood dripping, was scratching herself to get the "worms out," and heard a voice say, "You should be dead." The brief evaluation I completed found above-average intelligence, high levels of agitation and accompanying distractibility, and a Rorschach protocol that indicated significant problems with coping and numerous unusual content scores of blood, sex, anatomy, and special scores of morbid.

Because of this pattern of results and of research that indicates this pattern is consistent with sexual abuse (Friedrich, Einbender, & McCarty, 1999), I spoke to the mother, who agreed that she had concerns about two paramours who had lived with her in the past 3 years. Using their names as a point of reference, I had the child draw both men for me, and this evoked a spontaneous mention that they had molested her. A more formal interview by the local authorities later validated these statements. With the mother's assistance, the police established that the abuse could have lasted for as long as 3 months each episode, the first when the child was 4, and the second 6 months prior to the time of the evaluation.

More relevant to the issue of self-development was the fact that the Rorschach did not find the child psychotic, which had been the original assumption. It suggested symptoms more consistent with chronic PTSD and raised concerns about her intense avoidance of affect that would make direct therapy of the abuse difficult. That in fact was the case, and the child refused to talk about the victimization for the next several months despite the direct support of her mother. I directed the therapist to speak indirectly about the abuse each session—tell a story about a child to whom some scary event had occurred and describe the child's responses to the tragedy with some detail. The therapist was told to preface the story with, "I'm going to talk about someone who had some strong feelings. I know you don't like to have these feelings so you only have to listen to half of it."

This stage of therapy was quite helpful and resulted in better sleep, urinary continence, and a drop-off in unexplained rage outbursts. The Rorschach contained many contradictions, however: intensity versus constriction, dependency versus avoidance, and so on. I suggested that the next phase of therapy help the child talk about the "feelings war" going on inside. The goal was for her to articulate the internal polarities as well as those characterizing her relationship with her mother. This consisted of drawings with a line demarcating the page, and the child drawing herself happy and sad, loving and mean, and so on. Her mother was struggling with depression at this time and there was ample fodder for each session.

When the elementary teacher told the mother at conferences that the child was so much different from before and seemed so "solid and settled," I knew that this therapy tack had been the correct course. The Rorschach helped to rule out psychosis; identify intense, free-floating agitation akin to PTSD; direct the therapy to respect her avoidance of affect; and then redirect the therapy to explore the numerous contradictions her emerging identity contained.

Loevinger's work with the sentence completion test, available for both children and adults, is based in ego-psychology and is also directly relevant to the issue of self-reflection (Loevinger & Wessler, 1970). The responses are scored across seven categories reflecting ego development: presocial/symbiotic, impulsive, self-protective, conformist, conscientious, autonomous, and integrated. Quite relevant to the topic above are conformist responses, which reflect issues of shame and guilt.

For example, one of the sentence stems is, "I am." Let's suggest that we have completions from three female teens. The first one completes the stem by writing in her age, "16." The second one completes the stem with "a victim of sexual abuse." The third one writes "very confused about life and upset that I blame myself all the time." These would be scored by the Loevinger system as varying across a continuum of conformity and complexity. The first response is likely to be scored as conformist, the second conscientious, and the third one autonomous. They are clearly indicative of the degree to which individuals are able to describe themselves and to entertain conflicting thoughts.

The capacity of children to step out of their situation and accurately observe other people is something that the Roberts or the TAT can assess well (Westen, Lohr, Silk, Gold, & Kerber, 1990). A child whose worldview contains only images of darkness and despair may produce only stories that are dark and pessimistic in response to the stimulus pictures. The children in his stories may be threatened, treated unfairly, and victimized. This is quite different from a child with similar circumstances who gives trite, predictable stories avoidant of feelings. The first child seems to have more language for feelings, whereas the second one may not.

A highly aggressive boy gave stories dominated by an overall theme of the male child "doing something wrong." This suggested an underlying dysphoria and negative self-view suggestive of the mix of affective distress and aggression often seen in younger oppositional children and is far different from another aggressive boy whose stories contained no self-recrimination or self-criticism (Kelly, 1999). Treatment approaches more sensitive to his dysphoria were quite helpful and certainly different from a behavior management approach.

The Roberts has an easily accessed scoring system described in the manual, but recent research has suggested that the norms are outdated and need revision (Bell & Nagle, 1999). I score Roberts protocols in four steps. The first is to examine responses to Cards 5 and 15 for sexual comments or avoidance of the sexual aspects of the pictures. Second, I look for the accuracy of the story and its direct relationship to the picture. Third, I check whether the child can go beyond a simple description of the illustration. The last step is to add up the dominant emotional themes, for example, loss, doing something wrong, and so on.

Measures that purportedly assess self-esteem are pertinent to this section. I have used several with sexually abused children and adolescents to no avail. The same is true for other clinician-researchers (Kendall-Tackett, Williams, & Finkelhor, 1993). How one defines self-concept will dictate the particular strategy adopted to assess this potentially important but frustrating area (Harter, 1990). It is most appropriate to view children's self-perceptions as multidimensional. The dimension that is most related to the sexual abuse experience, such as shame, is the one I choose to assess, and this can be done quite well in the measures described below. As support for my contention, I quote from Harter (1990), who has developed two of the most useful measures in this domain. She writes, "In all likelihood, assessments of self-concept alone are not that interesting, nor are the correlations of self-concept with other variables in the absence of any thoughtful set of hypotheses about the underlying nature of such relationships" (p. 318).

## ❑ Child Report—Abuse Specific

The Children's Attributions and Perceptions Scale (CAPS) was developed in response to criticism that global measures of psychopathology in children may not be as sensitive to abuse-specific or abuse-related assessment strategies (Mannarino, Cohen, & Berman, 1994). A number of clinicians have observed the unique attributions and perceptions that victims generate and that are related to their victimization. These attributions include feeling different from peers, feeling that other people do not believe what they say, blaming themselves for the abuse, and reduced interpersonal trust.

In a fashion similar to but narrower than the CAPS, the My Feelings About the Abuse Questionnaire (Feiring, Taska, and Lewis, 1998) also measures children's beliefs about their victimization. It is quite brief, but still a very important predictor of the sexually abused child's self-report of symptoms. See Appendix N for a copy of the measure.

The Trauma Symptom Checklist for Children (TSCC) has an item (Item 26, "Washing myself because I feel dirty on the inside") that is on the Depression Scale. It is very similar to one of the items on the Shame Questionnaire. In a study using the TSCC, this was one of the TSCC items that differed significantly between a sexually abused sample and one that was not abused but was psychiatrically impaired (Friedrich, Jaworski, Huxsahl, & Bengston, 1997). Taken together, these are a validation of the need to assess attributions.

There are also several CITES-R subscales that are relevant to self-perception. These include Self-Blame and Guilt, Empowerment, Personal Vulnerability, and Dangerous World. A recent study found that the first three of these CITES-R scales correlated significantly with the majority of the clinical scales of the TSCC; for example, there was a correlation of .56 between TSCC Anxiety and CITES-R Personal Vulnerability. However, the scale labeled Dangerous World was not related to any of the TSCC scales. The items on the Self-Blame and Guilt subscale transfer directly into the therapist's office and open the child up for a discussion of shame. If the child seems ready to address this topic, and other aspects of the child's life are stable, the evaluator should send along a copy of the measure to the therapist for review and follow-up with the child.

## ❏  Common Clinical Assessment Dilemmas

The most intriguing puzzle for me in this assessment domain are those people who are best described as "disguised presentations" or as having adopted a false self (Gelinas, 1983). Most often these are parents, although compulsively compliant and compulsively caregiving children and teenagers (usually reflecting defended attachment) seem well on their way to the development of a false self. Evaluation can be very useful, since it serves to determine if the parent's false self is malignant, or possibly contributes to the child's own difficulties, or both.

An elegant paper by Calverly and colleagues illustrates the fact that sexually abused adolescent girls rate themselves far more negatively than they do other people (Calverly, Fischer, & Ayoub, 1994). This is a frequent facet of the false self phenomenon.

Both parents and teens with a false self may present in a number of ways on the MMPI-2. For example, the K scale is often elevated relative to their score on Ego Strength. This suggests that they are reasonably good at presenting well but have reduced resilience. In terms of clinical scale elevations, you are likely to see several two-point codetypes. These include 2-3/3-2, "smiling depressives"; 4-3/3-4; and 3-6/6-3. The latter two may behave more provocatively with you in the session. A fundamental feature is their inability to know who they are and accurately describe what they are feeling. These people are a puzzle to you, and as parents they are a puzzle to their children. Often there is a compulsive aspect to them that works both to help them appear competent and to keep them buffered from too many feelings (this explains the often elevated Compulsive scale on the MCMI-II).

Projective testing can also help to illustrate underlying feelings of inadequacy, despite a superficial competence. The self-perception cluster from the Rorschach is one example (Exner, 1991). For example, the presence of morbid content in a sexually abused teen who was also a straight A student led to a suggestion that the therapist address the ways the person "hated herself." This proved to be a useful avenue of intervention.

If their child gets into therapy as needed and makes improvements, and parents can keep their house safe from further abuse, I usually recommend support for these "false self" parents rather than therapy. They may express interest in improving the relationships they often end up in, but follow-through is often poor. These parents have a hard time being helpful to themselves, finding therapy interesting and pertinent, and tolerating the tedious task of character change.

## ❑  Translating the Evaluation Into Treatment

Treatment goals for parents are several and can include a better understanding of their emotions so they can be more consistent in their response to their child. It is also useful for those with victim histories to understand better their reactions to their child, including feelings of rejection and a reactivation of their PTSD as well as depression. Some parents who are at least trying to be better parents than their own were can benefit from treatment that affirms these positive aspects of theirs. Suggesting some affirmations of their own parenting as part of their treatment could be warranted.

Targeting shame in the therapy of the victim is important, but I expect that simple reassurances from the therapist that "it was not your fault" are not valuable and can discount the child (Friedrich, 1995a). Addressing this very important emotion can proceed if the home can provide both support and safety. Premature focus on shame is likely to create a rift between patient and therapist. It communicates to clients that the therapist does not understand them.

## ❑ Summary

The psychological evaluation of children's or teenagers' self-perception includes an assessment of the integrity of the self because trauma can have a fragmenting effect and result in the victims' having difficulty combining their thoughts and feelings. Other issues are related to the blame, guilt, and shame that might be experienced and that is related to the victimization. This is true for all parties involved, including victims and parents. Related to self-perception are the issues of accurate self-perception and the capacity for self-reflection. Individuals who grow up in chaotic households with little opportunity to think about their feelings and who have a limited vocabulary for feelings are going to have a distorted self-perception. Being competent may not be a possibility they entertain. A life of victimhood may be the only one they see for themselves.

Included in this chapter is my polemic for the importance of measuring intelligence and academic competence in the patients that you see. Intelligence is tied to several critical prognostic factors, including ability to respond to therapy, use language to inhibit behavior, talk about feelings, possess feelings of accurate self-competence, and problem solve in the manner that parents must do.

One of the most frequent therapy goals therapists have for their patients is to help them understand that they are still good people and that what happened to them is not their fault. A careful assessment of this domain and the possible mediators of blame, including secure attachment, is important in order to provide the most appropriate guidance for therapists working with shame and self-blame. Besides being important, an evaluation can suggest the best timing for the intervention.

# 8

# *Screening*

The chapters up to this point have focused on the more complex evaluation strategies that rely heavily on psychological measurement tools. However, I am acutely aware that the majority of maltreated children who enter therapy are never assessed, even minimally. This is despite the well-known fact that young children who enter foster care often present with a variety of mental health conditions that are both undiagnosed and untreated (Dale, Kendall, Humber, & Sheehan, 1999).

There are many occasions when brief screening is quite useful to the process of monitoring and investigation. For example, an in-home therapist may have questions about the true difficulties a child is having in school and choose to use a teacher rating scale. A parent raises concerns about sexual behavior in a preschooler, and the therapist uses the Child Sexual Behavior Inventory (CSBI; Friedrich, 1997) to establish the range and context of these behaviors. Both of these measures are likely to be more valid than a series of questions delivered over the phone, and the results from each of these two very brief screening measures can quickly reveal both the extent and the range of the child's behavior difficulties and guide the direction of intervention.

A welcome addition to the investigative literature is a recent paper from individuals who work at the National Children's Advocacy Center (Carnes, Wilson, & Nelson-Gardell, 1999). Carnes and colleagues (1999) outline an eight-session extended interview format that utilizes brief parent ratings and self-report. It has been found to be useful in cases where there is no immediate disclosure following the legally mandated interview. All of the measures utilized are brief screening tools that rely on self- or parent report.

This chapter articulates a process whereby a more valid and standard assessment of underserved children can occur. The process utilized may follow either the model described in Carnes et al. (1999) or it may be individually tailored by therapists who desire to practice in an informed and accountable fashion. No child should be kept from safety or treatment simply because we are not sure what to look for.

Psychological assessment does not have to be an either-or situation, that is, comprehensive psychological evaluation versus no assessment. In fact, there are countless times when the child and family are best served by brief screening. Agencies and therapists who lack access to mental health professionals skilled in the area of trauma assessment still serve their clients better if they systematically evaluate for several key symptom clusters: PTSD, sexual behavior problems, family safety, and risk factors, including the quality of the parent-child relationship. In addition, a functional screening evaluation can still serve to bring together disparate pieces of information, such as background, number of foster care placements, and health-related concerns that illustrate who this child is and what he is facing.

Screening can serve several functions. These include quickly identifying problems, determining the need for treatment, evaluating the degree of risk to the child from either remaining in or returning to the home, whether the child has been affected by contact with the perpetrator, and finally, to document progress for the court and/or social services. There are times when screening identifies issues that are better served by a more comprehensive assessment, but again, that may not be possible.

The techniques outlined below are designed to enhance the practice of professionals and move them beyond simple subjective input to something that is more quantifiable, reliable, and valid. The use of reliable and valid measures can help to standardize practice, validate intuition, gain accurate and additional information, and enable the use of scientific procedures that are defensible in forensic settings. For example, you are on the witness stand, testifying about a child who was diagnosed with a sexually transmitted disease. The child, however, is nondisclosive. Valid, standardized information from a care provider that indicates behavioral responses that are also consistent with sexual victimization can help the court move for protective custody of the child that can increase the likelihood of continued safety down the road (Hewitt, 1999). This chapter will suggest a framework and then outline screening techniques that can be used with sexual behavior, PTSD, and needs for both protection and treatment.

## ❏  Framework

The three-part model that is at the core of this book can also guide the screening process. However, for the sake of parsimony, the strategies outlined are best at identifying overt behavior problems and risk factors. These fall most naturally into the dysregulation domain and consequently include PTSD and sexual behavior problems. Another common screening question with traumatized children is related to the question of ADHD versus PTSD.

Psychotherapy with children who continue to live in chaos or who are in foster care can be a frustrating experience for both the child/teen and therapist. Loyalty to the family may interfere with any exploration of the maltreatment experience or of feeling unloved or of the shame subsequent to abuse by a family member (Friedrich, 1990). However, it is probably deleterious not to intervene in ongoing behaviors that reflect feeling out of control, or that solidify behavioral patterns, such as sexually intrusive behaviors.

Consequently, if screening identifies problems with sexual behavior, PTSD, or risk for future sexual behavior problems, and the child's family is safe enough not to retrigger the child, and the family can set limits on the child's behavior, treatment can move forward.

Screening doesn't just magically yield useful data. The information you obtain is only as good as the reporter, and you must pay close attention to this fact. Carnes et al. (1999) found that parental support of the child, separate from belief in the child's statements, was the key variable contributing to accurate disclosure in extended forensic evaluations. This suggests that you need to figure out ways to solidify your relationship with the parent so she or he can trust you enough to answer honestly.

How is this done? Help the caregiver appreciate that the child's safety is the paramount need. Children who make ambiguous reports, about either what happened or how they are feeling, will directly reflect caregiver uncertainty and anxiety. Sensitive attending to parents may reduce their uncertainty, help them be more accurate reporters, and in turn, allow their child to be more forthcoming.

## SCREENING FOCI

The most common calls I receive from caseworkers regarding screening fall into seven categories. The first raises questions about a child or teen in suspicious circumstances. The caseworkers are asking for help in determining the likelihood of abuse and the need for protection. The second is whether a child needs treatment and, if so, for how long. The third is related to the second and typically goes, "When is the therapy going to be over?" This usually comes after a child has been in treatment far in excess of the usual 8 to 10 sessions that children seem to receive. The fourth is related to the above but more specifically is a question about the most appropriate treatment modality—individual, abuse-focused, family, supportive, and so on. The fifth referral is in response to a sexually aggressive child and whether he or she is in danger of further inappropriate behavior. The sixth pertains to understanding a child's behavioral response to a caregiver, usually when the child is in foster care and reunification is beginning. The last issue is related to the parents' long-term viability as the child's parents. This includes both the offending and nonoffending parents.

Although many of the above referral questions seem to be related only to the child or teen, it bears repeating that both children and their context will dictate treatment needs for the children you see. A child can appear asymptomatic in foster care but then display many symptoms when contact with the parent(s) resumes. Consequently, screening must include some review of the parent-child relationship and the safety of the home environment.

Before each of the above foci is examined in more detail, a clinical example will be presented that illustrates some of the points to be made.

## ❑ Case Example

Caitlin is a girl, 4 years and 2 months old, who has been in foster care for the past 3 months. Her biological mother and half-brother are living together. Caitlin was removed from the home following disclosure by the mother and Caitlin that her brother was molesting her. The 9-year-old half-brother has Fetal Alcohol Syndrome and is in a self-contained classroom for children with severe behavior problems. The reason the mother gave for why Caitlin was removed rather than her brother is that she felt that her son needed her more, and she believed that Caitlin was the more resilient of her children. The biological mother was afforded liberal, unsupervised visitation in the home.

The guardian ad litem (GAL) called me because the foster mother, described as excellent, was on the verge of asking that Caitlin be removed from her home. The GAL vouched for the foster mother's concerns and stated that only occasionally could the foster mother count on even one day per week being free of major behavioral outbursts. Caitlin was compulsively masturbating, touching the foster mother sexually, having bowel movements outside of the toilet, wetting herself both at night and during the day, and having tremendous sleep difficulties. The GAL believed that the child was seriously reaffected by contact with the mother and brother during the unsupervised visits that were occurring typically at least once per week. The county of custody did not wish for an assessment, and the GAL desired to bring the child into therapy in order to reduce her symptoms.

Prior to the first appointment both the foster mother and the GAL, who saw the child weekly for at least 2 hours, separately completed the CBCL and the CSBI. Caitlin was above a $T$ of 70 on the majority of the CBCL subscales (Internalizing, $T = 76$; Externalizing, $T = 78$; Total, $T =$

**Table 8.1** Screening Results from 4-Year-Old Girl (Reported in *T* Scores)

| Measure | Time 1 | | Time 2 | | Time 3 | |
|---|---|---|---|---|---|---|
| | Foster Mom | GAL | Foster Mom | GAL | Foster Mom | GAL |
| CBCL | | | | | | |
| Internalizing | 76 | 70 | 63 | 61 | 59 | 56 |
| Externalizing | 78 | 76 | 68 | 66 | 61 | 60 |
| Total | 79 | 78 | 68 | 65 | 62 | 60 |
| CSBI | | | | | | |
| DRSB | 89 | 89 | 89 | 73 | 67 | 73 |
| SASI | 110 | 110 | 90 | 82 | 77 | 69 |
| Total | 110 | 110 | 82 | 71 | 67 | 65 |

79 for the foster mother; Internalizing, $T = 70$; Externalizing, $T = 76$; and Total, $T = 78$ for the GAL). Both the foster mother and GAL had identical scores on the CSBI (Total, $T = 110$; DRSB, $T = 90$; SASI, $T = 110$). These are summarized under Time 1 in Table 8.1.

Because developmentally delayed children can be more behaviorally reactive than nondelayed children, I also asked the foster mother to complete the Child Development Inventory (CDI; Ireton, 1992). This developmental screening tool is superb with preschoolers, and its use with maltreated preschoolers is reported in Hewitt and Friedrich (1991). Caitlin's General Development Index on the CDI was at the 4-year, 8-month level with relative strengths in self-help skills (5-4; a frequent strength in neglected children who have learned to fare for themselves), gross and fine motor skills (5-3), and expressive and receptive language (5-1 and 5-2, respectively). She was slightly below her age level in the preacademic areas and also social development. Consequently, her behavioral dyscontrol could not be attributed to cognitive delay.

I interviewed both the foster mother and the GAL with the Safety Checklist. Very few safety concerns were identified in the foster home, but the GAL reported numerous concerns in the natural mother's house. These were primarily in the areas of nudity, PTSD triggers, violence, and poor monitoring. Further evidence of this child's poor boundaries and related vulnerability occurred in my brief play interview with Caitlin. During the 25 to 30 minutes we were together, she hugged or touched me several times, despite redirection; touched herself sexually twice; attempted to kiss me once; spontaneously mentioned that her brother "had a wiener"; and then drew a "wiener" when asked to draw a picture of her family.

On the basis of the behavioral ratings completed by the caregivers, and quantifying the information from my play interview on the Evaluator Rating Scale (Appendix K), I concluded that this child was most likely being overwhelmed in her contacts with her mother and brother. I believed that they were continually retriggering her and that this directly led to her inappropriate behavior. I recommended that it was in the child's best interests to change the visitation to include only the mother, preferably in a neutral setting.

In cases like this, where the child is living in an unstable environment, therapy is likely to be frustrating to all parties. I typically do not recommend therapy at this time, and if pressed, use it to monitor the situation. The therapist is better served by consultation with the foster parent and conferencing with county social services about the child's behavior problems and possible triggers that need to be corrected before therapy can begin.

Using the information from my brief consultation/assessment, the GAL was able to get visitation restricted so that it occurred only with the mother and in a nonhome setting. Refer to Time 2 in Table 8.1 to see how sharply the behavior problems dropped off over the next 2 months when the child was rated again on the same measures. The decrease in behavior problems suggested clearly that continued interaction with her brother was too much for her to manage.

It is clear from the table that the decrease in behavior problems was most clearly evident in terms of her more positive mood and reduced agitation. Aggressive behavior remained in the clinical range and so did her overall sexual behavior. She continued to exhibit numerous self-stimulating behaviors but was no longer masturbating herself to sleep and had stopped touching her foster mother's breasts. She was also making far fewer random comments about either her or her brother's genitalia.

This was documented at Time 3 in Table 8.1. In a follow-up meeting with the GAL, which occurred 10 weeks after the change in visitation structure, I agreed to help install a behavior management plan around the angry outbursts, poor boundaries, and self-stimulating behavior exhibited by Caitlin. The goal was to reduce these behaviors and then teach her mother the same strategies. The Weekly Monitor Sheet (Appendix O) was used, and two behaviors were initially targeted: angry outbursts and self-stimulation.

A behavioral intervention of this sort, which requires daily ratings and reinforcements, also constitutes an active screening process and provides information on how amenable this very young child is to treatment. I simply requested the foster mother to count the frequency of behavior on the daily rating sheet. These data served as a baseline. Because the foster mother had a positive and rewarding relationship with Caitlin, there was no need to enhance that relationship further prior to starting the behavioral consequences, for example, use of a brief time-out when there was aggression, and redirection when self-stimulation was noted.

Reducing the frequency of these two behaviors proved to be quite difficult. It was only when the biological mother was hospitalized for 3 weeks for alcohol treatment and no visits occurred that any gains were noted. However, as soon as the mother returned from the treatment center, the behaviors resumed and reached a level that was close to the previous frequency.

This information told me quite clearly that this was a very troubled mother-daughter relationship. In addition, the data strongly suggested that the mother could not be a secure base for her daughter. Rather, she served as a stimulus that further agitated Caitlin, making her more reactive. Caitlin also associated her mother with out-of-control feelings and behavior, similar to her association with her brother.

I was able to work with the GAL to present these data very clearly to the local authorities. A court hearing resulted in the presiding judge ordering a more extensive assessment of the mother and her treatability.

In summary, a combination of valid screening tools with more than one informant, that is, CBCL, CSBI, and Safety Checklist, in combination with daily ratings resulted in data that clearly illustrated the needs of this child in terms of safety. This objective information impressed the court and was very useful in creating the momentum needed to develop a plan to more hopefully intervene in the life of this child.

## SEXUAL BEHAVIOR

The valid screening of sexual behavior is an obvious necessity. As one of the most salient and frequently observed symptoms subsequent to sexual maltreatment, the CSBI (Friedrich, 1997) is the most obvious measure, and it is useful for 2- to 12-year-olds. The parent can fill it out while you meet with the child. However, it works best as a structured interview with parents. Not only do you get an opportunity to ask parents about their emotional and behavioral responses to any behaviors that are identified, you are also able to identify the context in which the behavior is exhibited. For example, a child who masturbates before going to sleep at night is different from a child who masturbates during the day, at school, in the backseat of the car, and so on.

For teens, the Adolescent Sexual Behavior Inventory (ASBI; Friedrich, 1996a) can be used and allows for information from both the parent and the teen. With a recent referral of a teenage girl who was raped at a party, I had both the parent and self versions of the ASBI available. The mother's answers were markedly different from the daughter's, and the teen's responses suggested a pattern of prior risky sexual behavior. In a separate session with the teen, I asked questions prompted by her responses, for example, "When I meet with girls who have run away from home at night, stayed overnight in unsafe places, etc., I wonder what is making them take these risks?" Although she did not admit to anything at this time, she did agree that a few additional sessions could be helpful for understanding her motivations. Eventually she reported that she felt quite unloved in her home, and risky contacts with boys were a chance to feel important.

It is also useful to inquire about several context features that seem to coexist with the display of sexual behavior, at least in preteens. These include domestic violence, physical abuse, family nudity, overt sexuality in the home, recent stressful events, and sexually provocative peers. These topics are included in the Safety Checklist and can be screened using that as an interview (refer to the section, "Parent Rating—Family" in Chapter 6, for the introduction to use with the Safety Checklist).

Sexual behavior problems in children are the driving force for many referrals these days (Gil & Johnson, 1993). These referrals bring with them questions about the child's risk for acting out sexually with other children. Questions of risk are difficult to answer about adults, and even more so about children. History is the best predictor of acting-out behavior; consequently, a child who has acted out sexually is more likely to behave in this way than a child who doesn't have this history.

Children and teenagers with externalizing behavior problems, for example, ODD, CD, and ADHD, are also more likely to act on their impulses. Consequently, information from parents and teachers about externalizing symptoms is very useful in these cases. The quickest way to access this information is with either the parent and teacher versions of the BASC (Reynolds & Kamphaus, 1998) or the CBCL (Achenbach, 1991a). A history of unresolved sexual abuse in a child with an externalizing behavioral pattern will make the child more at risk for sexual behavior problems. In addition, the use of a risk factor checklist (Hall & Mathews, 1996; see also Chapter 6), while only rudimentary and in need of cross-validation, can guide your thinking and organize your thoughts about risk for future sexual behavior problems.

## POSTTRAUMATIC STRESS DISORDER

As the other feature most commonly associated with sexual abuse, PTSD can be validly assessed with younger children using a combination of self-report and parent or caregiver input. As mentioned in Chapter 5, the symptom presentation of young traumatized children is likely to be different from that of older children or teenagers. For example, it is quite difficult for young children to report flashbacks accurately. They may not know if they feel more agitated now than before, since their capacity for self-observation is reduced.

There is reference to several child-specific manifestations of PTSD in *DSM-IV,* including repetitive play, frightening dreams without recognizable content, and trauma-specific reenactment (American Psychiatric Association [APA], 1994). The first does not seem different from the third symptom, but all three of these are symptoms of reexperiencing, and only one is needed for this component.

All 17 of the PTSD symptoms have been incorporated into several checklists available from the National Center for PTSD-Behavioral Science Division at the Boston VA Hospital. With teenagers and adults, the Posttraumatic Diagnostic Scale (Foa, 1995) is quite useful and is available commercially. In addition to these possibilities, I have found it useful with older children and teens to identify the traumatic event(s) and then use the items from the PTS scale of the TSCC (Briere, 1996) as a structured interview to assess the syndrome. As children get older, self-report of these symptoms is the most accurate strategy to use, given not only the often poor observation capacities of their parents but also the highly private nature of the syndrome.

The diagnostic dilemma of ADHD versus PTSD deserves comment. The first consideration is age of onset. If the child is just now distractible and impulsive, at the age of 8, and after a sexual assault, ADHD is not a correct diagnosis. Information from both parents and teachers may show elevation on Attention Problems on the CBCL (Achenbach, 1991a, 1991b) after sexual abuse. However, if you have the CBCL, also use it to examine the items that correspond to the PTSD items in Table 5.2. You may then be able to see both inattentiveness and elevated PTSD-related symptoms, and you can use that information to arrive at which of these symptom clusters is primary.

If the child can validly self-report, then questions about reexperiencing and avoidance can help with the diagnostic dilemma. The differential diagnosis of ADHD and PTSD is a common dilemma in child psychiatry clinics, and the efficacy of stimulants with children elevated on both has not been adequately studied.

## OTHER SYMPTOMS

The above two clusters, sexual behavior and PTSD, don't account for every child who comes into your office. However, a careful screening of the areas of concern will make you more systematic than most and will allow for a treatment plan that is more specific, focused, and friendly to the child. Screening usually implies brevity, and the shortest and most valid behavior checklist for children and teens that I am aware of is the 25-item Strengths and Difficulties Questionnaire (Goodman, 1997). It comes in self-report, teacher-report, and parent-report versions. It contains five 5-item scales generating scores for conduct problems, hyperactivity- inattention, emotional symptoms, peer problems, and prosocial behavior. In fact there are data to suggest that even with fewer items, it has more discriminating ability for several externalizing dimensions than the CBCL (Goodman & Scott, 1999). The addition of a prosocial scale that measures competence in the child is an excellent feature. (The measure is available from Dr. Robert Goodman, Department of Child and Adolescent Psychiatry, Institute of Psychiatry, De Crespigny Park, London SE5 8AF, U.K.).

Kay Hodges (1995) has developed the Child and Adolescent Functional Assessment Scale (CAFAS) as a mechanism to organize level of impairment objectively across the areas of school/work, home, community, behavior toward others, moods/self-harm, moods/emotions, substance use, and thinking. These problems are then placed in the context of caregiver resources, including material needs and family/social support. It functions as a much more precise and ecologically useful Global Assessment of Functioning (Axis V) from the *DSM-IV* (APA, 1994). For example, if no problems are reported by the parent on the rating scales, but the CAFAS identifies problems based on objective data from the caseworker or the case file, you are likely to be working with a defensive parent whose home environment is not conducive to the child's resolution of the abuse.

Lastly, parental monitoring with the Weekly Monitor Sheet (Appendix O) can help to determine the frequency and impact of the behavior on the child. In addition, it is an excellent test of parental cooperation and treatment readiness. Those parents who complete the measure are signaling that they are ready to work with you.

## DETERMINING LIKELIHOOD
## OF SEXUAL ABUSE

The model suggested by Carnes et al. (1999) has a battery of screening measures. These include a parent report general behavior problem measure, the CBCL (Achenbach, 1991a); a measure of sexual behavior problems, the CSBI (Friedrich, 1997); and for older children, the TSCC

(Briere, 1996). This brief battery coincides with my experience in using these measures (along with the ASBI; Friedrich, 1996a) as a screen on every child and adolescent inpatient at my clinic. Elevations on the Sexual Distress Subscale of the TSCC, in combination with either the CSBI or the ASBI, are particularly noteworthy. High scores on these scales in children/teenagers for whom there is at most suspicion of abuse, and in many cases not even suspicion, are more often than not illuminating of prior sexual maltreatment in the patient. Follow-up interviews with these patients have led to disclosures of sexual abuse for roughly half of the patients with this pattern of elevations. Given the fact that patients were in an inpatient setting, they may have finally been ready to disclose. However, the added utility of these measures has kept them part of my intake screening battery.

By themselves, these scales are not proof of abuse. But they have proven very useful at case-finding in a busy clinical practice where every parent and patient is asked about prior maltreatment.


## TREATMENT NEEDS

The second question identified in this chapter is whether the child needs treatment and, if so, for how long. For example, let's suggest that your role is the child's case manager or in-home therapist. During your interactions with the child, you keep the items on the Evaluator Rating Scale (Appendix K) in mind. This gives you a system to quantify child's behavior along the dimensions of boundary permeability and overt sexual focus. Red flags from this measure—the child keeps touching you—strongly suggest that some intervention is needed. Because children will reflect their home environment, it is important to begin by helping to create greater safety in the home. Here the Safety Checklist (Appendix G) can be your guide.

Once you have arranged for individual therapy to begin, you certainly can use your role as case manager to ask the child's new therapist to obtain generic behavior and sexual behavior checklists from both the parents and the teacher. This can inform the therapist how the child is doing in other settings. Other problems related to learning, attention, aggression, or social withdrawal and anxiety might then be identified.

Because you are working with a sexual abuse victim, screening for sexual behavior will be important, and the CSBI is useful to assess these behaviors. If the child is a teenager, inquire from either the victim directly or from the parent whether the individual is engaging in any risky sexual behavior, is being used sexually, or seems unusually sexually focused (these are items from the ASBI (Appendix L and M) that discriminate abused from nonabused teens (Friedrich, Lysne, et al., 2001).

A related question pertains to how much longer a child who already is in therapy will need to continue therapy. Again, the focus begins on the behaviors the child is exhibiting in the most relevant arenas: in the home, in school, and—for teenagers—with peers and at work. Data suggest that internalizing symptoms, that is, anxiety and depression, are the most immediately addressed in therapy and drop out the quickest from the symptom picture (Berliner & Saunders, 1996). If these behaviors are no longer present, then the victim has made progress.

Aggression and sexual behavior take longer to treat and are variably related to maltreatment. An aggressive boy in a self-contained classroom for behavior disordered kids, who also was sexually abused after he had already started an aggressive pattern, needs help with his aggression vis-à-vis his parents, for example, family therapy. However, it is unlikely that abuse-specific therapy will be as helpful prior to his and his parents' getting their anger under control.

Therapy needs to be sensitive to the needs and resources of the child. Prolonged therapy that leaves the child feeling confused about what is going on is contraindicated. Sometimes shorter blocks of therapy can be the most sensitive to the child, and if the immediate symptoms have dropped out, and the family is safer, then it makes sense to stop the therapy, knowing that later it can start up again if needed.

## TREATMENT TYPE

Increasingly, the data point to the need for abuse-specific therapy. Children and teenagers will typically have more of an internalizing or externalizing presentation. If screening with parent and teacher ratings suggests that they are asymptomatic, and you are reasonably assured that the caregiver has been open and is a good observer, then educating the victim and caregiver about what to watch for in the future is probably the most appropriate initial strategy. Symptom patterns of anxiety and/or simple acute stress disorder (ASD) or PTSD are most sensibly addressed with cognitive-behavioral strategies or with supportive play-based sessions combined with parent education/support. Aggressive responses, self-injurious behavior, or sexual behavior problems suggest that the maltreatment was more forceful and of longer duration, and the family context is less supportive and more aggressive as well. A key lesson from the two projects funded by the National Center on Child Abuse and Neglect with children with sexual behavior problems was the importance of a family focus to the therapy (Bonner, Walker, & Berliner, 2000). Parent-Child Interaction Therapy (Hembree-Kigin & McNeil, 1995) is an excellent place to begin with preteens. It will assist in repairing the parent-child relationship and empower the parents to use more appropriate discipline strategies.

## RISK TO REOFFEND SEXUALLY

I expect that risk prediction in sexually abused children will consume a great deal of time and energy over the next few years. I don't know what the outcome of these efforts will be. However, this question increasingly comes up, and clinicians of all types must be in a position to answer risk questions intelligently and in a fashion that is fair and sensitive to the child in question.

The variables that have emerged as the most important in my research include comorbid conduct disorder or oppositional behavior, harsh family discipline, elevated levels of family sexuality, unresolved maltreatment, and a chaotic rearing experience (Friedrich, Drach, & Wright, 2001). These also coincide with the 25 risk factors identified by Hall and Mathews (1996).

I have used this information to advocate for 9- to 12-year-olds to be seen in outpatient and not residential treatment. I have also used it to lobby for a 12-year-old to be sent to residential treatment. In the latter case, data from the CAFAS (Hodges, 1995) clearly demonstrated the enormous problems in the caregiver and the child. Up-to-date screening from school personnel indicated his predatory and sexual focus.

He also obtained 16 of the 25 risk factors from the Hall and Mathews (1996) study. The recommendation seemed the most humane to him at the time, given the complete absence of foster care capable of handling him. I believe the data I assembled helped to make the case much more clearly to the caseworker and judge, who were now able to realize how far from the norm he was.

His case was in marked contrast to that of an 11-year-old boy who was being unnecessarily treated in a teenage perpetrator group. The CAFAS revealed no problems; school problems were relatively nil; and although he exhibited excessive sexual behavior, his single parent was committed to closer monitoring, the one problem identified on the Safety Checklist. The parent readily agreed to follow a behavioral plan and bring him to therapy that was both individual and family-based. At the hearing in front of the same judge who had heard the earlier case, the contrast was enormous, and the judge greatly appreciated the clarity the data brought to the situation.

## MONITORING BEHAVIOR
## WHILE IN FOSTER CARE

The case presented earlier in this chapter is applicable to this last question that can be answered with screening. I routinely work with foster children, and they can have variable responses in care. Some will exhibit improved behavior in foster care, others revert to previous behavior after a short "honeymoon," and still others exhibit a more variable course, for example, initial improvement followed by a long, slow deterioration. Children's behavior reflects how their biological parents treat them, and foster parents can have the same influence. The data derived from occasional screening can demonstrate why children need care, when they are ready to return home, and what to watch for after they return home. This information can also be used to raise concerns when a previously well-adjusted foster child shows deterioration in one or more settings. When case managers turn over rapidly, a long-term perspective can be lost. Screening data may be a constant that serves to mark a child's progress or deterioration in care. It can also indicate the need for therapy at critical points along the way.

❑  **Case Example**

A second, more straightforward case can help illuminate the concepts presented above. A mother brings in her 9-year-old daughter, Sarah, asking whether treatment is needed. Sarah's teenage sister observed Sarah on one occasion with Tim, a 12-year-old neighbor boy. Both were naked, Tim was on top simulating intercourse, and both were extremely embarrassed at the discovery. Tim is described as a "good kid," and the girl has no prior history of sexual abuse or behavior problems. However, the boy's mother has questioned him, and he reported that it had happened several times. Sarah has refused to talk about the event in any detail with her mother, claiming that it happened only once. The mother has asked her several times why it occurred, but the girl claims she can't remember. Sarah and Tim can have no unsupervised contact, and she has been compliant with this request. You obtain this history from the mother, and when you speak to Sarah, she states she is there to talk about "what happened with Tim," but reports no detail and continues to say that it happened only one time. Other than that area of defensiveness, she exhibits appropriate affect and good eye contact when talking about any other topic. She denies that she has any intrusive recollections of the event with Tim, and says that she likes both of her parents and gets along with her sisters. Her mother validates these comments. Sarah exhibits none of the behaviors rated on the Evaluator Rating Scale.

The mother continues to be concerned, since she has a psychologically disturbed niece who was molested. You decide to be more thorough and interview the mother with the Safety Checklist. None of the safety categories is elevated. She also completes the CBCL and the CSBI, with normal ratings across all scales. She takes a TRF with her for the teacher to complete and mail back to you. When scored, it comes back with positive reports about this child, and no behavior problems are reported.

At your second visit with the mother you share these results, mention that peer sexuality at this age does occur, and that it does not have to be deleterious. You inform her about possible behaviors to watch for that would suggest that Sarah is distressed, you praise her for the reasonable limits they have set regarding contact with Tim, and she is much more reassured given these objective perspectives on her daughter.

This screening process, which generated normal scores on a child who most likely is well-adjusted, is not separate from your clinical observations and training. The mother's prompt attention to the situation, the sensitivity she exhibited toward her daughter in the waiting area, the ease with which the mother spoke of her feelings, and the fact that she was nondefensive in response to the questions of the Safety Checklist are all positives that are also considered along with the screening data.

## ❏ Summary

In summary, clinicians, no matter their level of skill, can enhance the accuracy with which they view the child and family by utilizing a range of standard measures. Not only do the data illuminate the child, but they can lead to treatment targets and elucidate the accuracy with which the parent sees the child and the child sees herself. However, screening data are still blended with clinical wisdom to arrive at an overall perspective, with each aspect enhancing the other. Even brief assessment will balance the therapy process so that it combines the best of subjectivity and objectivity.

# 9

# A Case Example for the Psychological Assessment of Teens and Their Families

## DIANA M. ELLIOTT

## ❏ Introduction

This chapter illustrates some of the principles outlined in this book as they relate to the assessment of a teenager and her family.[1] It is outlined as follows. First, a summary of the background information received by me prior to seeing the client and her family is reviewed. Second, a summary of the assessment process with a particular focus on the areas discussed in this book is presented: attachment, dysregulation, sexual problems, and self-perception. The psychological test results are provided, followed by information obtained through the interviews with all parties and the results of various rating scales completed by them. Finally, a template of the actual report is provided at the end of this chapter. The assessment process and report were designed to be responsive to the specific referral questions in this case.

## ❏ Background Information

Catherine A. is a 14-year-old female. She and her family were referred for a psychological evaluation by child protective services (CPS) following sustained allegations of sexual abuse by her brother and neglect by her parents. Catherine first came to the attention of CPS 4 months earlier. At that time, she went to the school nurse with an infection in her upper thigh where she had recently had the word *TORTURE* tattooed. In a conversation with the nurse, Catherine disclosed a 4-year history of physical and sexual abuse by her brother. The sexual abuse was alleged to have occurred between the ages of 8 and 12, and to have included penile-vaginal penetration and the use of force during the incidents. The physical abuse was reported to have been ongoing since the age of 10, and included being shoved, punched, and kicked. The court sustained the allegation of sexual (but not physical) abuse of Catherine. A neglect charge was also sustained against the parents based on their failure to protect Catherine from her brother.

Catherine is the youngest of three children, raised in a two-parent home. At the time of the initial referral to CPS, all members of the family resided in the home: Mr. A., 45; Mrs. A., 44; Mary, 18; Jonathan, 16; and Catherine, 14. Both parents were working full-time in manual labor jobs, with the father working the graveyard shift, and the mother working the swing shift. All three children attended the same Catholic high school and were reported to be average students. Catherine was a freshman, involved in no extracurricular activities. Jonathan was a junior and was reported to be out with his friends when not in school. Mary was in her senior year and worked part-time. After the allegations were made, CPS filed the petition on only Catherine. They did not perceive Jonathan to be a victim of, or at risk for, abuse in his home, but required that he leave the home in order to ensure Catherine's safety. No allegations were investigated regarding Mary because she had already reached the age of majority. CPS required that the parents seek treatment for Catherine, which they did. She had been seeing a master's level intern for the 3 months prior to my evaluation. According to a letter to the social worker, the therapist indicated that Catherine was diagnosed with a conduct disorder and that she was doing adequately in treatment. She voiced no particular concerns in her 3-month update to CPS.

At the time of my evaluation of the family, Jonathan was living with a family from their church but allowed liberal visitation with the family if the parents supervised his time there. All other family members resided in the home. To the social worker, Jonathan acknowledged "sex play" with Catherine when she was between 8 and 10 years of age and he was between 10 and 12. By his report, the sex play was mutual. He denied any contact with her since he was 12 and Catherine was 10.

After the court sustained the allegations of sexual abuse of Catherine by Jonathan, but before my evaluation of the family, CPS became aware that the father had pled guilty to a single count of a lewd and lascivious act with a child under the age of 14. When asked by the CPS worker about the conviction, Mr. A. reported that he had been masturbating in a bathroom at home while his nieces were over, and that he didn't realize the door was opened. He reported that a niece came to the door and saw him. He told the worker that, "I tried to stop, but I couldn't." He reported that he pled guilty to make it easier on everyone in the family, but that his only requirement for probation was that he attend counseling, which he did. Mrs. A. provided a similar account to the worker, but added that since that time, there had been no contact with her extended family, stating that she "was too embarrassed by it all." Other than this incident, there were no other investigations for child abuse. No other family member had any history of involvement with the legal system.

CPS had monitored the family over the 4 months prior to my evaluation. They were planning on terminating their supervision of the case, perceiving the parents to have been completely compliant with social worker's requests that Jonathan be out of the home and that Catherine enter counseling. However, as a precautionary measure, at the suggestion of a CPS supervisor, the social worker requested the current evaluation to assist in determining the following: (a) the risk of physical, sexual, or emotional abuse of Catherine in her parents' home; (b) the appropriateness of Catherine's placement with her parents; (c) recommendations for visitation between Catherine and Jonathan; and (d) an evaluation of the family's treatment needs. My evaluation of the family was conducted over a 2-week period in which Mr. and Mrs. A. and Catherine were each seen on three separate occasions for a total of approximately 12 hours per individual, including interviews and psychological testing. Mary was interviewed on one occasion for 2 hours and completed a packet of questionnaires about her family but did not complete psychological tests. Jonathan refused to participate in the evaluation.

## ❏ Psychological Assessment of Catherine and Her Parents

Psychological tests administered to members of the family were chosen to answer the specific questions outlined by CPS. If the referral questions had been different, alternate tests would have been chosen.

### TESTING OF CATHERINE

Catherine's level of distress was assessed using the Adolescent Sexual Behavior Inventory (ASBI), Dissociative Experiences Scale for Adolescents (DES-A), Minnesota Multiphasic Personality Inventory for Adolescents (MMPI-A), Rorschach (Exner Scoring), Self-Injurious Behavior Questionnaire (SIBQ), Trauma Symptom Checklist for Children (TSCC), and the Youth Self-Report (YSR). Mrs. A. also completed the Child Behavior Checklist and the ASBI with reference to Catherine.

The results of the TSCC were valid and revealed significant elevations in all areas of psychological distress: Anger ($T = 70$), Anxiety ($T = 73$), Depression ($T = 70$), Dissociation ($T = 72$), Posttraumatic Stress ($T = 71$), and Sexual Concerns (specifically, the Sexual Distress subscale, $T = 76$). The clinical interview revealed that the symptoms of PTSD were primarily in category B: intrusive images including nightmares of the sexual and physical abuse, flashbacks, and sudden disturbing memories. Catherine reported having few symptoms of active (conscious) avoidance. Rather, she appears to engage in more of an unconscious process of dealing with the intrusion through dissociation. This hypothesis is supported by her score of 4.1 on the DES-A. In the clinical interview, the intrusive symptoms were related to her sexual and physical abuse by her brother, as well as to an incident of rape when she was 13 years of age by another teen.

Catherine's MMPI was valid. She was frank about her difficulties (F+ K/ L#, 4" 2+ 56389/701:). She obtained a moderately elevated scale 4 ($T = 81$) caused by elevations on Family Discord, Social Alienation, and Self-Alienation subscales. Important for treatment and prognosis, neither the Authority Problems or Social Imperturbability subscales were elevated. She produced a mildly elevated scale 2 ($T = 67$) caused by Subjective Depression, Mental Dullness, and Brooding subscales. In addition, MAC-R ($T = 65$), PRO ($T = 79$), FAM ($T = 84$), and R ($T = 66$) were elevated. The overall clinical picture suggests a sad, lonely, moody, pessimistic teen who defends against her distress by portraying an angry, rebellious exterior. The data also suggest that she is at high risk for engaging in self-defeating, sensation-seeking, and tension-reducing behaviors, all of which are supported by a review of her recent history and the 11 items endorsed on the SIBQ. In the clinical interviews, Catherine acknowledged alcohol abuse, self- mutilatory behavior, prostitution, starting arguments and physical fights to get her anger out, and running away from home to unsafe places after fights with family members. Of note, her parents denied any knowledge of the runaway behavior, even though CPS later confirmed there were nights the minor was away from the home without the parents' apparent knowledge.

The Rorschach indicated that under most conditions, Catherine's internal capacities and tolerance for stress were similar to most teens (AdjD = 0, EA = 8.5). However, the data also suggest she was experiencing a significant increase in stress (D = –2) that was impacting her capacity for control. This creates the potential for increased impulsiveness and poor judgment in her thinking and behavior, especially in complex or ambiguous situations. She experiences intense depression and emotional turmoil (DEPI = 5; C' = 6). She appears reluctant to express or process her emotions openly, except in an unmodulated form (PureC = 3). This may be because of her general confusion in the context of emotional situations, with a strong tendency to experience both positive and negative feelings in the context of the same situation (with three chromatic-achromatic blends). Consistent with the MMPI and TSCC, the Rorschach suggests she harbors a very negative, angry attitude toward the world (S = 5; Xu% = .41). This is likely to be a chronic attitude that has a significant impact on all aspects of her psychological functioning. Given that her emotional responses are not well modulated, highly negativistic attitudes are likely to be manifested in various arenas. Interpersonally, she appears to be as interested in people as most teens (Hcont = 8; PureH = 3; M = 3); however, she has little expectation for closeness or cooperation in relationships ($t$ = 0; COP = 0). In addition, she is an underincorporator (Zd = –4) who has some pervasive problems with perceptual accuracy (Xu% = .41; X – % = .30). The data suggest she will overlook critical pieces of interpersonal information available to her and misinterpret the actions and intentions of others.

Mrs. A. completed the Achenbach Child Behavior Checklist on Catherine. The only scale significantly elevated at a $T$ score of 70 or greater was Delinquent Behavior ($T$ = 70). Mrs. A. indicated "0" or "not true" on all questions in the experimental PTSD and Dissociation subscales. By way of contrast, Catherine completed the Achenbach Youth Self Report. By her report, she was significantly elevated on the scales measuring Anxious/Depressed, Attention Problems, Delinquent Behavior, and Aggressive Behavior. In addition, her raw score on the experimental PTSD scale was 10. Although there are no normative data on this scale for the youth report, it points to the significant difference between Catherine's perception of her difficulties and that of her mother. Catherine's classroom teacher completed the Teacher Report Form of the Achenbach. The results were more similar to Catherine's self-report than Mrs. A.'s report. Significant elevations were reported on the Anxious/Depressed, Withdrawn, Social Problems, and Delinquent Behavior.

Both Catherine and her mother also completed Friedrich's (1996a) ASBI. Although there are no normative data available on this scale, important qualitative information was obtained. Catherine received a score of 14 on the form completed by Mrs. A., and a 29 on her self-report. For several items, Mrs. A. indicated a zero (not true), while

Catherine reported a 2 (very true). These items included: knows more about sex than others their age; staying away from home overnight without permission; spends a lot of time in front of the mirror; has many boyfriends; gets used sexually by others; runs away from home to unsafe places; and has been caught in a sexual act. In addition, Mrs. A. believed Catherine to have had no sexual partners, while Catherine reported having more than six. Mrs. A. indicated it was unlikely that Catherine had been physically or emotionally abused, but probable that she had been sexually abused, while Catherine indicated that she had definitely been sexually, physically, and emotionally abused. In the interview, Catherine reported that the physical and sexual abuse were by her brother, while the emotional abuse was by her brother and father. She also reported an incident of rape at school and two incidents of prostitution when she had run away from home.

Responses to the questions pertaining to sexuality on the TSCC as well as to questions in the interview suggest that Catherine was not preoccupied with sex, per se, but was highly distressed around sexual issues. For example, she indicated that she did not trust people because they might want sex; and almost always felt confused about her sexual feelings, and had bad thoughts or feelings during any sexual contact. She indicated that although she had been quite sexually active, "I don't go out looking for it, it just seems to happen, whether I want it or not, and I don't really know sometimes whether I want it or not. Even when I did the guys [prostitution], I didn't go out to do that, it just happened. And why not? At least I got paid for it. Better than nothing."

TESTING OF MRS. A.

Mrs. A. completed the following psychological tests: Minnesota Multiphasic Personality Inventory-2 (MMPI-2), Millon Clinical Multiaxial Inventory-II (MCMI-II), Rorschach Inkblot Test (Exner Scoring), and the Trauma Symptom Inventory (TSI). Mrs. A. produced a somewhat defensive but valid MMPI-2. None of the clinical scales were elevated above a $T$ score of 60. Only two supplementary scales were elevated above 65, R and O-H, both suggesting an inability to deal with emotions directly and an unconscious processing of anger.

Mrs. A.'s MCMI-II was also somewhat defensive, but valid. Two scales were mildly elevated: Dependent (BR = 79) and Schizoid (BR = 76). No other scale was elevated above a BR of 60. The results are quite consistent with my clinical impressions of Mrs. A., a quiet, reserved, if not stoic, woman. Although her life and family were in a great deal of turmoil, she appeared affectless much of the time. In addition, although above average cognitively, she orchestrated her life such as to have few responsibilities, demands, or interactions with others. It was my clinical impression that this interpersonal reserve was Mrs. A.'s defense for dealing with her dependency conflict. It is likely that the circumstances in which she finds herself fortify patterns formulated in her family of origin in the context of her own abuse (discussed in the clinical interview) and reinforce her desire to withdraw from interpersonal relationships. Her fear of independence and belief that a connection to others results in disappointment or rejection leads to an undercurrent of anger that is rarely seen. She would be described by others as introverted, passive, quiet, dependent, self-sacrificing, and uncommunicative.

Mrs. A.'s TSI was valid. She had a single scale elevation on Sexual Concerns ($T = 67$). She reported being unsatisfied with her sex life, having intrusive thoughts during sex, being confused about her sexual feelings, and having problems related to various aspects of sexuality.

Mrs. A. produced a very conservative Rorschach. She provided only 15 responses with a very high lambda. She produced no color responses and few movements, all of which were animal rather than human content. The data raise no concern about perceptual inaccuracies or problems in her thinking, but the Depression and Coping Deficit Index were elevated. Overall, the data suggest that this is a depressed woman who has few resources, no access to her feelings, and who, in response to stress, narrows or restricts her input from the environment. She has little interest in others and little expectation of cooperation or emotional closeness between people (COP = 0; Texture = 0).

## TESTING OF MR. A.

Mr. A. produced a valid, moderately distressed MMPI-2 (F+ LK#, 827″ 546031′ 9/). Scales 8, 2, and 7 were within one point of one another

($T$ = 84, 83, and 82, respectively). Only scale 9 was in the normal range. The overall clinical picture suggests a chronically distressed man who is dysphoric, agitated, apprehensive, fearful, and socially very uncomfortable. It is likely that he obtains little pleasure in life, is easily hurt by others, and is socially withdrawn. He acknowledges a history of engaging in unusual sexual practices and being bothered by his sexual thoughts. Although not overtly psychotic, he has some peculiarity in his thinking and is likely to ruminate obsessively over his problems and/or feelings.

Mr. A.'s MCMI-II was also valid and indicated severe personality disturbance in the same scales elevated by Mrs. A.: Schizoid (BR = 109) and Dependent (BR = 111). Additionally, Avoidant is elevated at a BR of 94 and Anxiety Disorder is elevated at a BR of 83. This is consistent with his clinical presentation in my office—a quiet, affectless, introverted man who has little capacity for intimacy. He is likely to have oddity in his thinking and behavior and to have a very active fantasy life. The data suggest that when he is in a relationship, he fears being engulfed, but would experience intense aloneness if separated from significant others. To deal with his conflicts, he will typically placate others, acting passive and submissive, in order to maintain a sense of security and support he has in his relationships.

Mr. A.'s TSI was valid, and also moderately distressed. Scales elevated above a $T$ of 65 were Anxious Arousal ($T$ = 65), Intrusive Experiences ($T$ = 67), Dissociation ($T$ = 67), Sexual Concerns ($T$ = 92), and Dysfunctional Sexual Behavior ($T$ = 71). In my clinical interview with him, Mr. A. acknowledged a history of child sexual abuse by an aunt. A review of the symptoms he endorsed on the TSI is summarized in the "Interview" section below.

The Rorschach also raised concerns about Mr. A.'s current functioning. Mr. A. has little capacity to tolerate stress and few emotional resources (D = –2; AdjD = –1). At the time of testing he appeared more stressed than usual, which may reflect the CPS's involvement in his life. As well, he is experiencing emotional distress often associated with loneliness or loss (Y = 7). Consistent with the MMPI, the Rorschach suggests Mr. A. may have chronic problems with reality testing (X – % = 31; Xu% = 12), but is not psychotic (Wgtd Sum6 = 0; SCZI = 2). The data suggest that he is highly influenced by his emotions but not very careful about how he displays his feelings (PureC = 3). All of his color responses were of blood content. More typically, however, Mr. A. avoids emotionality altogether. Consistent with the MCMI, the data suggest that he is a lonely, isolated man with intense needs for closeness (Texture = 4), but who has a poor understanding of others, with negative form quality on his only two human movement responses. In addition, four of his contents were of sexual material, two of which were also morbid responses. His only aggressive response was also a human movement response, with sexual and morbid content.

## ❑ Information Obtained in the Interviews

Mr. and Mrs. A. were high school sweethearts. After high school, they worked at the same factory but on different shifts. They dated for 9 years prior to their marriage when he was 25 and she was 24. Both parents reported that they were not sexually active prior to their marriage and that Mary was a "honeymoon baby." The father continued to work full-time after her birth, while the mother stayed at home with her children until Catherine entered kindergarten. The family moved only once during the 20-year marriage. This followed the father's guilty plea for child molestation and coincided with the timing of the mother's return to the workforce. Upon moving, the parents once again began working at the same factory but on different shifts. The parents have a very stable work history, both having been employed in only two jobs since graduating from high school.

### INTERVIEW WITH MRS. A.

Among other approaches, Mrs. A. was interviewed with the Attachment Interview developed by Friedrich (see Appendix A). She described a stable relationship with her husband during their dating and in the early part of their marriage. Both individuals were described as being quite shy and reserved and only minimally involved in social activities through their church. The couple became pregnant with Mary immediately after their marriage. She reported being glad about the pregnancy. "I always wanted to be a mother." There were no complications with that or the two subsequent pregnancies and births. There were no spontaneous or planned abortions. She was highly descriptive of her three pregnancies and births, using warm, endearing language, but quite noticeably talked as though she were in a dream-like state.

When asked about her parents' reaction to her pregnancy, she indicated that she had not seen her parents since she left home at the age of 18. She reported a childhood history of chronic physical abuse by her mother and a "few" incidents of sexual and physical abuse by her father. Her parents had never met her children. "I always wanted to be a good mother and protect them from anything bad or evil." When asked what she learned about parenting from her mother, she stated, "To do nothing like her." She reported feeling unloved by her mother but "extremely" loved by her father. "He was my rescuer." She stated that "he showed me his love when he tried to protect me from her, but he couldn't." She believed her physical and sexual abuse by her father was "because of how stressed he was because of my mom. We were both just trying to survive her. I think when he hit me it was because she was making him or telling him he wasn't a man. I think that's why he turned to me sexually too. But it just happened a few times."

When asked about various aspects of her relationship to her children when they were young, Mrs. A.'s description suggested good initial bonding and subsequent attachment to Catherine (as well as the two older children). Her description of Catherine as a toddler and pre-schooler was animated and full of pride, which was the only affect she displayed during the evaluation. It was clear from the conversation that she enjoyed being with her young children.

Mrs. A. reported that after the allegations of abuse arose against her husband (when Catherine was 5), "things weren't the same." Although Mr. A. had pled guilty to one count of molestation, Mrs. A. reported that

> three of my nieces had seen it. He told me it was accidental. He didn't know the girls were there when he was masturbating. I believe him. He didn't mean to hurt anyone. But after that, there wasn't as much fun in the family. It was like a black cloud was over us all the time. Probably because we left the area and I had to go back to work. Those years all seem like a dream. Hard to believe we are the same family. It seemed as though I was doing everything right until then. I had the perfect family and I was doing everything my mom never did for me. Now, I don't know. Maybe I didn't do anything right.

Mrs. A.'s description of Catherine during elementary school years was quite vague with few specific positive or negative memories. Throughout Catherine's school years, Mrs. A. saw her daughter only on the weekends due to her work schedule. Although there has been no time when any of the family has lived apart from each other, the amount of interaction between mother and children has been quite limited.

Mrs. A. was aware of some of the effects of the physical abuse she experienced as a child. She made a firm commitment neither to engage in nor to allow the physical discipline of her children by her or her husband. However, she reported that

> I hear there were a lot of spats between the kids, but they are kids. Kids fight. Mary tells me it never happened when I was home because Jonathan wouldn't do it in front of me, but he did whatever he wanted in front of his father. My husband's not a very strong man and never took charge in the home. That was always something he left for me. Maybe I should have worked graveyard and my husband worked swing.

When asked why she thought that didn't happen, she stated, "He wanted the night shift. He said he liked being awake at night. I hated it. Convenience I guess." When asked if there were any changes planned for either her or her husband's work schedule, she stated that there were not.

Mrs. A was also aware of her sensitivity around sexual issues due to her sexual abuse history. She indicated that she was attracted to her husband, but that they had not been sexually active with each other for more than 5 years. She attributed this to their work schedules. "I don't really need it. I guess he doesn't either. He never initiates. I would do it if he wanted."

When asked to describe each of her children currently, Mrs. A. described Mary as a quiet, reserved teen,

> very naive, but she never gets into any trouble. She's nearly the perfect child. She's been like that her whole life, not so much as a tardy or absentee from school. She's going for the record. I think she's smarter than she lets on. She reads all the time, a real home-body.

She indicated that Mary reminded her of herself (Mrs. A.).

Mrs. A. described Jonathan as an angry child, who's

> been angry his whole life. Never in any big trouble, but always trying to
> prove himself, especially with the other kids and his father. He's
> quick-tempered but he's not home much. That's why this is all so hard to
> believe. I don't know when it could have happened. He's always out
> with his friends. Always has been.

Although Mrs. A. initially denied being aware of any "real" violence between the children, she acknowledged that she was sometimes afraid
of her son. She stated,

> He's always letting me know about his size and strength. Maybe it's my
> imagination. Maybe he's not doing anything. Maybe it's accidental. But
> sometimes I feel like he's trying to intimidate me, standing over me,
> pushing into me, shoving me. But really, I think I'm just sensitive to these
> things. I know he'd never hurt me.

She reported that Jonathan reminded her of her (Mrs. A.'s) father.

Regarding Catherine, Mrs. A. stated, "She was my baby. I don't
know what happened. I don't know how we got here." She perceived
Catherine as relatively symptom free, but in need of attention,

> maybe because I wasn't available to her enough. I think she's saying all
> this stuff because she gets the attention she didn't get from me. Every-
> one's calling it abuse, but he's only two years older than her. How could
> it be abuse? I think a lot of brothers and sisters do this sort of thing, don't
> they? That's what I've heard at least.

She indicated she didn't know who to believe about the allegations: "He's
my son. He says it was mutual." I commented, "She's your daughter.
What does she say?" Mrs. A. responded,

> She won't talk to me about it anymore. She did the first day the social
> worker was there, but not anymore. She just acts angry now, or like a lit-
> tle child. I don't know what to believe. She lies all the time. How can I be-
> lieve everything she says. I was abused. I told myself I'd never let it hap-
> pen to my kids. I don't know what to believe. She doesn't act sad or
> anything.

When asked of whom Catherine reminded her, she stated, "I don't like
to think about that. Sometimes I see my mother in her eyes."

Catherine's behavior in the interviews was suggestive of a very angry, needy, sad teen who was dealing with moderate levels of post-traumatic sequelae. Much of the time with me and in the waiting area, she was quite provocative. For example, she made statements like, "You can't make me do this" (referring to the evaluation). To such comments, where I could, I joined her in the process with responses such as, "Nope, and neither can your mother or your father, or even the judge for that matter." With these responses, she joined in whatever task was necessary at the time.

Although the weather was quite cold at the time of the evaluation, she wore shorts to the interview, allowing her TORTURE tattoo to be seen while she was sitting. When asked about her choice of tattoo, she stated she chose it because "it just looked cool." Also apparent were self-inflicted cuttings in various stages of healing on her inner thighs. She explained in great detail how she inflicted each one. As she did this, her tone of voice was upbeat and she had a smile on her face. However, when I asked her what was going on before she cut, her affect and demeanor changed markedly. She became obviously anxious, at times teary-eyed. She indicated these incidents were typically triggered before, after, or during visits from her brother. For example, she initially described one incident in an almost gleeful manner, stating she was "digging a pen deeper and deeper into my thigh. I couldn't even feel it. Bet you can't do that." When asked what was happening in her home when this occurred, she stated that her brother had come over for dinner.

> They were just talking normal crap. I didn't want to be around it. I went to my room. He whistled at me as I walked by. I heard him laugh. I couldn't stand it. I tried to block my ears. They just kept at it. I started reading. I had a pen in my hand. When I looked down, there was blood.

At that point, she grabbed her shorts and tried to pull them over the scabs, teary-eyed as she sat there in silence for several seconds. She then flopped into the sofa and said, "They are all jerks. I don't care. What shall we talk about now, Doc?"

Because the allegations of sexual abuse had been sustained, there was not a need to review in detail what had occurred. However, certain information about when and under what conditions it occurred were important to assess Catherine's current level of safety in the home. She indicated that no sexual abuse by her brother had occurred since she was 12. She did not believe that any incident had occurred when her mother was in the home, but that all of them had occurred with her father there. "I don't know how he [father] didn't know about it. He had to have heard me. I was screaming for christ-sake." She reported that although there was no contact after the age of 12, Jonathan continued to make sexual comments at her, such as, "You miss it, don't you." When asked what she did when this occurred, she stated that she did nothing and explained, "I told my mom the first time he did it on a visit. He laughed, saying I took the comment out of context, and made up a story about what he meant. She believed him."

Regarding the physical fights, she reported, "I was his punching bag. Mary too. He'd beat on us for fun. He'd never do it in front of mom. He cusses us out in front of her and she gets all over him" (referring to her mother yelling at, rather than physically disciplining, Jonathan). When asked about any injuries that might have occurred during the fighting, Catherine lifted up various parts of her clothing to show me scars where Jonathan had hurt her.

When asked how she felt about being in her home, she reported, "It's better than a foster home. I can make my own space. I just stay away from them all. They want him home. I don't care if he is. He won't dare come near me again. He knows I'll tell the worker in a second. Let him try. I dare him." She indicated that whenever Jonathan was in the home, she went to her bedroom and put a chair in front of the door. When asked why she did that, she stated, "I think he's going to kill me one day, really, I'm not kidding. I really think he'll do it."

Her description of her relationship with her mother was highly ambivalent. At times, Catherine appeared to feel protected by her, as in the situation with Jonathan "cussing" at her. At other times, she was protective of Mrs. A.:

> She has too much to take. All the stuff from when she was a kid. Her family was so screwed up. And dad is such a wimp. I don't know why she stays with him. She's too good for him.

Still, at other times, her anger toward her mother was obvious. She was aware that her mother did not believe that she was abused by her brother, but that "we were just fooling around." As she discussed this in the interview, she began to gouge her nails into her skin. When I commented on it, she immediately pulled her hand away, stating, "Geez, I didn't even know I was doing that," and then became very nonchalant about her mother's reactions. Still later, she stated, "I don't know who I'd believe either. I lie to her so much. I steal stuff from her. Jonathan doesn't do that stuff."

When asked more about her father, Catherine stated, "He's sick." When asked why she thought so, she reported that "he jerks off all the time. Man, can't he keep it to himself. He's a f—ing pervert!" When asked how she knew he "jerked off all the time," she screamed, "Because I seen it! My friends friggin' saw it. Can't he shut the f—ing door?!" She reported numerous times when she slammed the door to the bathroom shut because she'd see her father masturbating. She indicated that everyone in the family had told him to shut the door, "but he keeps forgetting . . . ya, right! Who forgets to close the door when they're doing that. That is soooo disgusting!" When asked what her mother did about this, Catherine stated, "She yelled at him and told him to shut the door." She denied any contact sexual abuse by her father.

Catherine described thoughts about suicide and provided several potentially lethal plans, but glibly stated she'd never actually do it. When asked why she wants to live, she teared up and stated, "It would give my brother too much satisfaction. If I'm going to suffer, so is he. I'm just so mad. I feel like I'm going to explode all the time," and then let out a very loud, long scream in my office. She also reported engaging in very dangerous behavior, both for the sake of excitement and in the service of tension reduction. These behaviors included, for example, cutting on herself, driving the family car without any parental permission or knowledge (although she was only 14), staying out all night (even after CPS involvement), having unprotected sex with strangers, and playing with a loaded handgun (not in the family home).

When asked about her therapy, Catherine stated, "It's fun. We just shot the breeze. At least it gets me away from the house." She could not discuss anything she had learned during the treatment. When asked if she ever talked with her therapist about what happens in her home, she indicated that she did not: "I go there to get a break from it. We just talk about boys and school and shit."

Consistent with the psychological testing, Catherine's self-report indicated that posttraumatic intrusion was frequently triggered in her day-to-day activities. She met the criteria for PTSD and four other diagnoses: Major Depressive Disorder, Dissociative Disorder NOS, Oppositional Defiant Disorder, and Alcohol Abuse.

### INTERVIEW WITH MARY

I was somewhat taken aback when I met 18-year-old Mary. She looked like a child who had barely reached puberty in her physical appearance, dress, and interpersonal style. She reported that she had never been on a date, let alone engaged in any sexual activity. She was straightforward but quite naive in her view of life and interpretation of interpersonal matters. Despite this, she also appeared parentified and exhibited caretaking behaviors toward all members of the family except Jonathan.

When asked about sexual abuse of Catherine, she reported that she had no idea if anything was going on, but stated that the two of them were frequently alone in Jonathan's bedroom. She confirmed the frequent use of physical violence by Jonathan toward Catherine and herself. She indicated that she was bruised by her brother's aggression toward her many times, and sometimes she bled because of where she had been pushed or shoved. As with Catherine, she believed that Jonathan might one day kill her.

Mary also reported seeing her father masturbating in the bathroom "when he forgets to close the door. But he's better about that since we told him to remember." When asked how old she was the first time she saw this, she reported that she didn't know for sure, but knew it was before she was nine—"that was when my cousins made such a big deal about it. It was only an accident. He didn't know we were all around. But it freaked them out." She also believed that a couple of her friends had "accidentally seen him." She denied any behavior that was suggestive of contact sexual abuse by her father. When asked why she thought her father masturbated in the bathroom with the door open, she stated, "Because that's where he keeps his [pornographic] magazines, I guess." When asked why she thought they weren't kept in a more private place, she stated, "I guess because they are easier to get there."

When asked about the home since Jonathan had left, Mary reported that "he still is there a lot. Catherine doesn't like it. But mom or dad is always there. Usually, she just goes to her room." She reported that Jonathan continues to try to intimidate her (Mary) but has not physically touched either of the girls since the social worker was to the home. "I think someone told him he could go to jail. I don't know for sure, but I think he's a little scared even though he'd never admit it."

### INTERVIEW WITH MR. A.

Mr. A. presented as a very compliant individual who was willing to participate fully in the evaluation, at least in terms of providing information. The possibility of some secondary gain in his presentation could not be ruled out. His description of himself was consistent with the test data and his clinical presentation. He reported being a socially awkward, shy individual who was easily frightened by anything new. He indicated that he felt constantly tense, worried about the future, and confused about the past.

Mr. A. reported regret over his behavior: "I don't know what I've done wrong exactly, but I know this is all somehow related to my behavior. I don't know what went wrong with Jonathan." He reported being angry at his son for abusing his daughter. Unlike, Mrs. A., he was quite clear that Jonathan's behavior toward Catherine was sexually abusive. In addition, he reported that he was aware of the physical abuse Jonathan perpetrated on Catherine. "I saw what was happening. Maybe I should have stopped it. But I would just get so mad at him it would scare me. I froze. I was afraid to do anything." When asked what he thought he might have done, he stated, "I don't know. That's just the thing. I did tell him to stop. But he didn't. If I had moved toward him, I would have hurt him. I don't know what else I could have done. I was an only child. I didn't know kids fought that much. But my wife told me siblings do that kind of thing."

When asked why he thought he'd done something wrong, Mr. A. stated, "They are telling me it's wrong." When asked what he was referring to, Mr. A. stated, "I don't know. I mean, I've always masturbated a lot. I thought it was normal—a guy thing? My wife doesn't understand that." When asked to describe his masturbatory activity, he indicated that he has done so for "as long as I can remember. I was a little kid in the bathroom doing it. My mom would walk in and just turn around and shut the door." He reported that his abuse by his aunt began when he was 7 and included oral copulation and manipulation of his genitals by her. He was not sure if his masturbatory activities began before or after his abuse. He reported that as a teenager at school, he would intentionally masturbate in front of other teenaged girls.

> I liked the rush from doing it, from getting psyched up to do it and following through. But one time, one of the girls told their mom, and I thought I was going to be arrested. I decided I had to be more careful about how I masturbated and I never did it in a public place again.

When asked to explain that further, Mr. A. stated, "After that, any time I did it, I was at home and I'd make it look like an accident." He provided elaborate details on how he accomplished this. When asked about the last time it had occurred, he stated, "I'm not sure when it was—probably before the social worker came out. I'm not sure. I don't think it's a good idea to do it now. I don't think there's anything wrong with it. It's natural to do. But they don't like it. So I guess I shouldn't do it."

When asked about specific questions he had endorsed on the TSI, his responses were reflective of concerns about abuse he had perpetrated on others, rather than reflective of his own history of trauma. This included such things as "bad dreams about masturbating in front of girls," stopping thoughts "about what I did before," sudden memories "of those girls," getting in trouble because of sex, worrying "about what's going to happen to me and my family," "flirting with kids to get attention," and sexual feelings about "girls that I shouldn't have, at least people tell me I shouldn't. I think about having sex with them. I think I'm obsessed with it. But I don't know. I think they [the fantasies] are probably okay if I don't act on the feelings."

When asked about the treatment received after he pled guilty to child molestation, Mr. A. reported that he had been given referrals from his probation officer. He picked a male therapist "because I thought he would understand better. I went a couple of times and he said I was fine and didn't need to come back. He wrote a letter to the court and I was done with it." Mr. A. stated that when he talked to the therapist about his fantasies about masturbating in front of girls, the therapist told him that his fantasies were normal, but it's the acting on them that was not. Mr. A. stated he was relieved to find out it was normal. He further stated that he thought if it was normal to fantasize about it, "it must be normal to act on it, but people just don't do it because they are so uptight. It's not morally wrong, just socially inappropriate."

## PARENT-CHILD INTERACTION

I make a case-by-case decision about whether to conduct conjoint sessions between parents and their teenaged children in evaluations such as these. Based on information obtained from interviews and testing, I judged the conjoint session between Mr. A. and Catherine to be unnecessary. I had already decided against the placement of Catherine in the same residence as her father, and the treatment needs were clear. No other issues relevant to the referral questions from CPS could be clarified by seeing the two in a conjoint session. It was my opinion that to conduct a conjoint session with the two might needlessly traumatize Catherine.

Catherine and Mrs. A. were seen together for one hour because the crux of the safety issues for Catherine revolved around the mother-child relationship. I was not using this time to assess the attachment per se, but rather to examine issues related to communication and compliance, and to feelings of affiliation and affection. The session occurred following the completion of the individual evaluations of mother and child. The decision whether to discuss the abuse in such interactions is based in part on the support expressed by the mother and experienced by the minor, as well as the specific referral questions.

Mrs. A. and Catherine were told that I wanted to meet with them together to hear about how things were going in the home since Jonathan left. However, when the two entered the room and for the 40 minutes following, this issue was not specifically addressed by either party. All of the interactions witnessed between the mother and child suggested a great deal of tension between the two. Catherine wavered between acting quite immature (e.g., talking in a high-pitched voice, flopping about in the sofas, whining, asking for her mother's assistance fastening a button), to demonstrating her anger toward her mother (e.g., speaking to her in a provocative tone, stating she wasn't going to participate in the evaluation, and saying the beginning of words such as bi—, fu—, shi—). The mother most typically ignored her daughter's provocations or looked to me to intervene. When not ignoring her, Mrs. A. spoke at her daughter in an affectless, dissociated manner. Toward the end of our time together, I specifically asked them what it had been like at home since Jonathan had left the home. The following brief conversation occurred before I terminated the session:

| | |
|---|---|
| **C:** | Ha!! Left?!?!? He's there every day. (pause) But I don't care, I just go to my room and close the door. |
| **Mrs. A.:** | You could try. You could join us. You don't have to eat in your room. |
| **C:** | No thank you. |
| **Mrs. A.:** | (to the evaluator)   This is what I mean. I try. I want her to feel a part of the family, but she doesn't want to. She rejects us. I don't know what else to do. |
| **C:** | Ya, it's all my fault. He's such the perfect child! |
| **Mrs. A.:** | No, he's not. You know he's not. But you could try. We're family. |
| **C:** | Ya, such a close family. Couldn't get much closer! |
| **Mrs. A.:** | Catherine, it's not happening any more. We just have to get things back to normal. |
| **C:** | Ya, I'm the picture of normal, right? We're such a normal family. |
| **Mrs. A.:** | We're all we have. |
| **C:** | Lucky me. |
| **Mrs. A.:** | We've got to make this work. |
| **C:** | No mom, you've got to make it work. That's what you want. I don't care if it works. You don't even believe it happened. I heard what you told the social worker. You think this was all fun and games. Well, he's had his fun, hasn't he?!? |
| **Mrs. A.:** | I didn't say I didn't think it happened. I know it happened. But it's over. Kids do things and then they grow up. We have to grow up. |
| **C:** (angrily) | Tell me mom, why do you let him in the house? |
| **Mrs. A.:** | Because he's my son. I love him. |

C:          That says it all. (Turning to me) See why I hate this place?
            Geez, she's so stupid. She just doesn't get it. (Turning to mom)
            You don't have a clue! You live in your own world. We aren't
            the perfect family you wanted. We are all screwed up. You
            sleep with a man who masturbates in front of your kids for
            christ-sake!

Mrs. A.:    Catherine! Watch your language! And he doesn't masturbate
            in front of you. And he's doing a lot better at closing the door.
            Don't you give anyone second chances?

After the conjoint session, I processed the time with both individuals
to ascertain their perspective on the time. As well, I use the time to de-
brief a client when necessary. This was especially important for
Catherine, given her propensity to inflict pain on herself following
such interactions.

## RATING SCALES

Catherine, Mary, and both parents completed the Family Relations
Index and the Conflict Tactics Scale. The parents also completed the
Child Abuse Potential Inventory (CAP). With regard to the Family Relations Index, all four members of the family described their family in
the average range for Expression. It was clear from all reports that everyone in the family felt that they say what they want and can openly
express their feelings. While Mrs. A. rated her family in the average
range for Conflict and Cohesion, the children and Mr. A. rated Conflict
above average and Cohesion below average. In all interviews except
that of the mother, family members reported that tempers often flare,
people hit each other, and the prevailing emotion is that of anger. They
reported virtually no cohesion within the family. The overall sense
conveyed was that of five separate people, whose primary interactions
were volatile, living solitary lives in the same household.

Mrs. A.'s CAP was valid and completely within the normal range.
Quite remarkable to me was the lack of elevations on scales measuring
Unhappiness, Problems with Child and Self, and Problems With Family, given the circumstances in which she finds herself, and the history
she reported. The Conflict Tactics Scale was completed by all parties
twice, once related to the mother and again related to the father. The re-

sults of this measure related to Mrs. A. by all parties were consistent with Mrs. A.'s CAP as related to her child abuse potential. No one reported any physical discipline by Mrs. A., either in the current time or in prior years.

Mr. A also produced valid results on the CAP. In contrast to his wife's, Mr. A.'s results revealed scores above the cutoff of scales measuring Distress (score = 166), Problems With Child and Self (score = 27), and Problems With Family (score = 38). As well, he obtained a total score on the Abuse scale well above the cutoff (score = 278), suggesting his responses are like those of individuals known to have physically abused a child. According to all parties' report on the Conflict Tactics Scale, Mr. A. had used no physical discipline during the 12 months prior to the evaluation. However, everyone except Mrs. A. reported that Mr. A. had insulted or sworn at the children, stomped out of the room, done things to spite them, thrown things, and threatened to hit. All parties reported that in the past he had slapped the children, but denied any incident of physical abuse (e.g., no marks, bruises, blood, etc.).

The Safety Checklist (developed by Friedrich, 1996c) was completed by both the mother and the father. There were several areas of concern. Although both parents reported no cosleeping behaviors, there were no locks on any bedroom doors. Both parents reported that cobathing had occurred between the father and the girls until they were both approximately 11 years of age. Although not acknowledged by the mother, the father reported that currently he regularly walks into the bathroom while the girls are dressing or applying makeup "for convenience." The father bathes or uses the toilet with the girls present "so we can get through the morning routine more rapidly." The father reported that he frequently spoke of sex with the two girls "just to get them used to talking about this stuff, so they won't have a hard time when they marry." Mrs. A. was unaware of any such conversation. There is no public display of affection between the parents in front of the children. Both parents reported being unaware of any sexual contact between Catherine and Jonathan prior to the current CPS involvement. All members of the family were aware of the father's collection of pornography kept in the only bathroom in the household. By all reports, there was no incident of physical abuse of any child by either parent, or domestic violence between the parents, but regular fighting between the kids. However, the family lived in a safe, virtually violence-free, neighborhood. Both parents reported several potential PTSD triggers for Catherine in that Jonathan was frequently at the home, eating meals with the family, having his mother help him with homework, and so on. The monitoring of the children prior to CPS involvement was rather atypical. Because the mother worked the swing shift, she did not see the children except for about 30 minutes in the morning getting them off to school and on the weekends. The father was in the home whenever the children were home after school and on the weekends. Mr. A. saw no problem with this arrangement. Mrs. A. reported that "in retrospect, I guess it would have been a good idea to work days." She reported feeling uncomfortable with some of her husband's behavior (e.g., his masturbation), "but he [Mr. A.] thinks I'm too uptight because of what happened with my dad."

Based on the Risk Factor Checklist, there are numerous areas of concern in this family (10 out of 21). Both parents had a childhood history of sexual abuse—Mrs. A. by her father and Mr. A. by an aunt. Mrs. A. was also physically abused by her parents, while Mr. A. was raised in an emotionless home, with little access to his parents physically or emotionally. Currently, there were no interactions with extended family members. Neither parent reported having a "best friend" or a social support system, but both occasionally attended social functions at church. Although there was not a lot of time when Catherine was not monitored, the supervision was being provided by a man who pled guilty to a sexual offense of a minor and who continued to perpetrate that same offense against numerous individuals. Catherine's sexual abuse was long-standing and included physical abuse as well. Her disclosure was met ambivalently by the mother, who, while confident the sexual contact occurred, did not believe it had been abusive. The parents' marital relationship was strained, with no reported sexual contact during the past 5 years.

**APPENDIX: Case Report on Catherine A.**

**CONFIDENTIAL INFORMATION—FOR PROFESSIONAL USE ONLY**

*THE FOLLOWING REPORT IS A SUMMARY OF AN EVALUATION OF*
*FAMILY MEMBERS WHERE A MINOR IS IN THE PROTECTIVE CUSTODY OF*
*CHILD PROTECTIVE SERVICES (CPS). IT CONTAINS INFORMATION THAT*
*IS SUBJECT TO MISINTERPRETATION BY UNTRAINED, NONPROFESSIONAL*
*PERSONS. THE REPORT WAS RELEASED DIRECTLY TO CPS. ANY FURTHER*
*RELEASE OF THIS REPORT IS GOVERNED BY WIC SECTION 827 AND THE*
*JUVENILE COURT. IT CANNOT BE RE-RELEASED WITHOUT A COURT ORDER.*

TO:      _____

Child Protective Services

FROM:  Diana M. Elliott, Ph.D.
Clinical Psychologist

RE:      Catherine A.

CPS Case #:

D/Birth:
D/Petition:
D/Evaluation:
D/Report:

Dear Mr. _____:

On the above dates, I evaluated Catherine A. and her family at your request. Catherine and her parents were seen for approximately 12 hours each in face-to-face interviews and psychological testing. A list of the tests administered each party is provided below:

**Psychological Testing:**

*Client Name*                                    *Test Name*_____

*(Client and test information would be inserted here.)*

Jonathan A., Catherine's brother, was contacted by my office regarding an appointment, but refused to take the phone call. Additionally, I attempted to contact him through his parents, but Mr. & Mrs. A. informed me that Jonathan was refusing to participate in the evaluation. Mary A. (Catherine's sister), Mrs. B. (Catherine's teacher), and Ms. C. (Catherine's therapist) were also interviewed, solely for the purposes of providing collateral information relevant to CPS concerns. In addition to these contacts, I reviewed the following records provided by your office:

**Records Reviewed:**

*(Document name and date would be inserted here.)*

**Reason for Referral:**

This family was referred for an evaluation by your office on —/—/—. They came to the attention of CPS four months earlier, when 14-year-old Catherine reported that she had been physically and sexually abused by her 16-year-old brother. CPS is considering terminating supervision of the family because of the cooperativeness of the parents with the department's plan for the family, but requested an evaluation to assist in answering the specific concerns listed below:

1. The likelihood that Catherine would be physically/emotionally abused by a member of the household;
2. The likelihood that Catherine would be sexually abused by a member of the household;
3. Recommendations for placement of Catherine;
4. Recommendations regarding visitation between Catherine and Jonathan;
5. Recommendations for therapy.

**Informed Consent:**

This evaluator explained to all five evaluees in separate interviews the purpose of the evaluation and the likely uses of its results. I explained the psychological issues that would be addressed, that the report would be sent to the CPS worker, and that the court controlled any further release of the report to additional parties. Specifically, they were told that this report was being generated for the purposes of child protection, and was not intended to be used in any other legal proceedings. However, they were told that the court ultimately determined if the contents of the report could be released, should other proceedings occur. They were told that they would be interviewed and would complete psychological tests. It was explained that the purpose of the face-to-face contacts was to respond to specific questions posed by CPS. Mr. & Mrs. A. and Mary A. were told that they were not obligated to participate or to answer any questions, but if they chose to do so, their answers could appear in the report or be stated by the evaluator under oath in any subsequent CPS hearings. Catherine was told that CPS had ordered her participation, but that it was her choice about the extent to which she participated. She was told about the relative benefits (and potential problems) of participating. All parties were told that at any point in time that they chose, they could terminate the evaluation. All five parties stated that they understood the limits of confidentiality to the evaluation and agreed to participate. Mr. & Mrs. A. and Catherine also signed a release of information form, allowing me to speak with Catherine's therapist and teacher.

### Background Information:

The following is a summary of the background information obtained through the documents and interviews with all parties. The opinions contained in this report are based in part on the accuracy of the information I have received. Were new information available in contrast to the information provided heretofore, or if any of the data contained in the documents reviewed were found to be inaccurate, any opinions expressed below based on that data would need to be reconsidered.

> *(Inserted here are the paragraphs from the Background Information section of this chapter. It was followed by a summary of the clinical interviews in this chapter. When writing a report, I often include lengthy write-ups of the interviews with numerous quotes in order that the reader be able to understand how my opinions were reached).*

*Collateral Contacts:* The CPS worker indicated that the parents were compliant with the court orders that Jonathan not sleep overnight in the home, that he not be in the home if one of his parents were not present, and that Catherine be in psychotherapy. He perceived the family to be relatively stable and capable of following these requirements without the system's involvement. The case was nearing a 6-month review, and his plan was to close it at that time.

Catherine's teacher reported that Catherine was having numerous problems in the classroom and in peer relations. She reported that Catherine "is a scared, angry, withdrawn girl who's going to lash out against someone. I don't know if it will be herself or someone else." She reported problems with lying and stealing in the classroom, but added, "I don't want you to think she's a bad kid. I don't think she is. But she thinks she is, and she sure wants the world to think she's the baddest of the bad."

Catherine's therapist had seen Catherine 13 times, brought to sessions by her mother. The therapist found Mrs. A. to be cooperative with the treatment process—"She's not intrusive like many parents; never asks what Catherine is talking about." When asked her understanding of the case, she provided an account similar to the CPS worker's. She believed Catherine was an angry child but could not articulate what she thought the source of her anger to be. When asked of any symptoms that might be of particular concern to her, she reported that both Catherine and her mother had talked about Catherine's lying, stealing, and alcohol use, and indicated that these things were being worked on in treatment. She reported that Catherine's primary diagnosis was Conduct Disorder. When asked if she had considered PTSD or any mood disorder, she indicated that she did not see any evidence of them. When asked if the abuse had been discussed in session, she responded, "I'm not really sure if it was abuse. Catherine is such a mature young lady. It's hard to imagine it happened without some participation on her part. But she doesn't want to talk about it, and I don't make her. We'll get to it when she's ready. There might be too much ambivalence about her part in it for her to deal with it right now." Because the release of information was only for Ms. C. to provide information to me, there was no discussion of the contents of this report. However, Ms. C. appeared unaware of the extent of the abuse by Jonathan, the masturbatory behavior of the father, the lack of supervision in the home, and the potentially dangerous behavior or suicidal ideation in Catherine.

## Results of Evaluation as Related
## to Issues Presented by CPS:

*1. What is the likelihood that Catherine will be physically/emotionally abused by a member of the household?*

With regard to physical abuse, it is my opinion that the presence of Jonathan in the home creates a physical risk for Catherine (and Mary). There is a long history of violence between the siblings. All parties described Jonathan as a boy who is full of rage. Both girls have been physically injured by him and fear that he might kill them. Even Mrs. A. acknowledged that she felt physically intimidated by her son. Mr. A. feels he has no ability to control Jonathan. Thus, it is my recommendation that the current arrangement, which allows Jonathan to be in the home if the parents supervise him, be discontinued immediately.

With regard to emotional abuse, it is my opinion that Catherine is at risk for such abuse by her brother and that all of the children are at risk for such abuse by their father. Related to Jonathan, it is sometimes difficult to discern when arguments and name-calling between siblings should be viewed as normal versus pathological. This is not such a case. Jonathan has verbally and physically intimidated all members of the family. He regularly insults and taunts the girls such that both fear for their lives. He has threatened to kill them. Whether or not this is a real threat is beyond the scope of my evaluation, but both girls perceive it to be real. He engages in various types of emotionally abusive behavior such as rejecting, degrading, terrorizing, and exploiting Catherine, despite the very small age difference between the two.

All parties except Mrs. A. reported that Mr. A. regularly yells at, insults, intimidates, and threatens to inflict harm on the children. Although there is no reported history of physical abuse by Mr. A., he harbors a great deal of anger and has few resources for dealing with it. Additionally, his test data are similar to those of individuals who are known to have physically abused their children. It is likely that when Mr. A.'s anger is expressed, it is in an unmodulated fashion that frightens even Mr. A. Additionally, Mr. A.'s sexual behavior, which he has framed as "accidental" to his family but clearly understands is not, is, at best, emotionally exploitive.

2. *What is the likelihood that Catherine will be sexually abused by a member of the household?*

It is my opinion that Catherine is at great risk for continued sexual abuse in her home. This is based on the prior reported behavior of Jonathan and Mr. A. Although there has been no incident of contact sexual abuse perpetrated against Catherine by her brother since she was 12 years of age, the physical intimidation and sexualized comments continue. In addition, Mr. A. has been perpetrating sexually abusive behavior over the past 25 years. This abuse has caused significant emotional damage to his children. He admitted to being "obsessed" with masturbating, having continued fantasies of doing so in front of the girls, and has used chronic deception in the perpetration of the abuse. The risk for abuse remains high until he is treated for his offenses.

3. *What are my recommendations regarding the placement of Catherine?*

It is my recommendation that this minor be removed from her parents' home as soon as possible. She is at risk for abuse and self-harm in her home. Jonathan is regularly in the home being supervised by his mother, whom he physically intimidates, and his father, who reports no ability to control his son's behavior and who was responsible for the supervision of the minors when the abuse occurred. The fact that Jonathan does not appear to have physically or sexually abused Catherine since CPS investigation is insufficient to assure Catherine's safety. She is engaging in numerous high-risk behaviors, many of which occur while she is under her parents' supervision. These behaviors appear to be motivated both for the purpose of excitement and in order to reduce her internal pain related to various aspects of her history. Some of these behaviors are potentially lethal. In addition, she reports fairly chronic suicidal ideation and lethal plans, although she reports no intent to kill herself. However, the probability of self-harm increases in the presence of stress. Having her father or brother in or around the home increases the risk for such behavior. She is constantly reminded of the potential threat of danger in her home, and may continue to have been exposed to Mr. A.'s masturbatory activity.

While I believe Mrs. A. desires to keep her child from harm, I do not believe she has the ability or resources to do so. She has allowed the children to be exposed to numerous incidents of sexual abuse by her husband. She failed to make any logical connection between his prior and current behavior and accepts his interpretation of reality. As well, she does not appear to have the ability to read the less-than-subtle cues that her daughters have communicated to her in the past with regard to her son's and husband's behavior. It is clear that her own history prevents her from being able to discern her husband's intentions or the appropriateness of his behaviors.

Even with the elimination of these interpersonal stressors, Catherine's psychological status will remain fragile for some time. It is my opinion that at this time, the appropriate placement is in a psychiatric residential treatment facility. Her placement in such a unit would allow for an assessment of her risk for significant self-harm in a safe environment, the need for psychotropic medication, and allow for the necessary time to find a less restrictive, out-of-home placement.

Ultimately, if Catherine is to be reunified back into this family, it is my opinion that the father will need to leave the home. The fact that he may not have masturbated in front of Catherine since CPS involvement does not negate the damage that has occurred by his presence in the home. His continued presence there prevents the children from beginning to deal openly and successfully with their feelings related to their father. This family has no sense of appropriate boundaries either at an individual level or as a family unit. His presence in the home as an untreated offender allows for the dynamics and behaviors of sexual abuse to continue. It is my opinion that any interactions between the children and their father should occur only in the context of clinical intervention (i.e., conjoint therapy) as discussed below.

### 4. What are my recommendations regarding visitation between Catherine and Jonathan?

Catherine reports no desire to see her brother and is obviously uncomfortable when he is in the home. By a finding of the court, she is a victim of sexual abuse by him. Any visitation that occurs between Catherine and Jonathan should occur with the consent of Catherine. It should be monitored by a professional, and occur outside the home, in order that some sense of safety and personal boundaries be established in this home. This visitation arrangement should not be liberalized unless Jonathan becomes involved in the therapeutic interventions being provided this family, and until both Jonathan's and Catherine's therapists indicate both are ready.

### 5. What are my recommendations for therapy?

A. As previously stated, I recommend that Catherine be placed in a residential treatment center (RTC) based on her potential for significant self-harm, suicidal ideation, and her high level of depressive and posttraumatic symptomatology. It is likely that after a relatively brief stay she could be released to a therapeutic foster home while her parents complete their treatment plans. Catherine is currently in psychotherapy with a master's level trainee who appears to have limited understanding of the case. Because of the complex issues involved in this case, as well as the coordination of treatment that will be required between the various providers for the family, I recommend that she be referred to a licensed clinician who has significant experience in the treatment of adolescent abuse survivors. Ideally, her individual therapist could begin therapy with Catherine while she is in the RTC, with transportation to the therapist's office provided by the department or RTC. Such continuity of care, while difficult to manage logistically, will be particularly important for this child. Additionally, I recommend that she be in group treatment with other teens who are dealing with the effects of abuse. This girl is having significant difficulties in her peer relationships and has no good model of social relatedness in her family. Group treatment will allow her the opportunity to obtain some of the social skills necessary for her to form meaningful relationships. The individual and group therapists' treatment planning would be facilitated by receiving a copy of the portions of this report that relate to Catherine.

B.  Mr. A. should be required to attend a treatment program for sex offenders. Specifically, I recommend that he be referred to the _____ treatment program. He has a 25-year history of numerous sexual offenses against multiple victims. As well, he has pervasive psychological and personality problems evidenced in the psychological testing that will make his recovery a long and difficult process. It is recommended that his treatment providers be given those portions of this report relevant to Mr. A. to facilitate their treatment planning for him.

C.  Mrs. A. should be required to attend _____'s treatment program for nonoffending mothers. While it may seem logical to also refer her to an individual therapist, it is unlikely that she will be able to benefit from it at this time. Rather, I would recommend that she initially engage in the group process with other mothers. As she sees other mothers struggling with similar issues, she may become less defensive and experience more anxiety. At that time, a referral to individual therapy should be made.

D.  Although Mary is not a part of the CPS case, it is clear from my conversation with her that she would benefit from individual treatment. She has been subjected to numerous physical assaults by her brother and has been sexually violated by her father at least since the age of 9. Because of her level of repression and sexual naïveté, she has yet to realize some of what has occurred between her and her father. Her reactions to him are likely to become more intense as she gains insight into his behavior and as she begins to be sexually active with peers. She would benefit from the provision of services through the department in the context of the family reunification plan. Specifically, I would encourage her involvement in the _____ group treatment program for teenaged victims of sexual abuse.

E.  Jonathan's treatment needs, and the potential danger he poses to various members of the family, cannot be fully understood without his participation in an evaluation. CPS should continue to seek his participation in the evaluation/treatment process. It may be necessary to find some alternative means for motivating his involvement in the family reunification plan.

F.  Both parents reported to me that it is against their religious beliefs to consider any separation or divorce. At some point, marital therapy will be necessary in order for this couple to repair the damage from the deception that has been going on between them for nearly two decades. Although Mr. A. has acknowledged his behaviors to his wife, he has not been forthright with his intentions or arousal patterns and has, in essence, used her trust in him to facilitate his abusive behavior toward their children. As Mrs. A. begins to deal with this, her sense of betrayal is likely to intensify. Marital therapy is apt to be most effective after the couple has had some time in the respective group programs mentioned above.

G.  As previously stated, I recommend that the only contact between Mr. A. and his minor children (and Mary) occur in a therapeutic context. Each child has major issues that directly relate to their father's ongoing violation of them. It is my opinion that neither the children nor Mr. A. is ready for contact at this time. The onset of conjoint therapy should be at the recommendation of the children's and Mr. A.'s therapist.

If you have any further questions, please feel free to contact me.

## Note

1. The data are a composite of families who presented for an evaluation with similar histories and levels of functioning. However, the composite history and test data have remained faithful to the original dynamics of a specific case.

# 10

# *The Language of Distress:*

## *The Role of Ongoing Assessment in Understanding True and False Allegations of Sexual Abuse*

*W. HOBART DAVIES*
*MOLLY MURPHY GARWOOD*
*ANITA R. O'CONOR*
*ANGELA CARRON*

The following case illustrates the value of carefully assessing the interconnected areas of attachment, dysregulation, and self-perception (Friedrich, 1990, 1995a, 1996b), and particularly the synergy that can be created between this psychological assessment and the process of forensic investigation of child sexual abuse. The girl whose case is presented here appeared with allegations of new sexual assaults on several occasions; one was believed to be accurate, two were eventually admitted to be fabricated, and one could not be determined. She had obviously learned that making allegations was a powerful way to get attention from caregivers and other significant others, and was a way for her to express distress for which she had no other outlet. Fortunately, the integration of forensic and psychological services allowed the repeated disclosures to be used as important information in guiding treatment planning without jeopardizing the consensus assessment that the original allegation was credible.

Linda was a 10-year-old African American female referred to a multispecialty child advocacy center by her caseworker from Child Protective Services. She had reported to her foster mother and guardian ad litem that she had been sexually abused 3 months earlier by three same-aged boys while visiting the home of her paternal step-grandmother. She said she had reported the incident to this grandmother, but was told not to tell anyone about it. She had told her foster mother that the assault included penile-anal penetration, oral-penile contact, insertion of an object into her vagina, and fondling of her breasts.

Initial background information included that she had been removed from her biological mother's care at age 3½ because of neglect. She had been in her current foster home for 3 years. Her 8-year-old half-sister and 6-year-old half-brother lived in the foster home with her. The 8-year-old's paternal grandmother has been pursuing placement of all three children, and they all had been having visitation with her every other weekend. At about the time the incident is alleged to have occurred, Linda began expressing reluctance to go on these visits. Her teachers also began raising concerns about declining academic performance and problems with self-esteem. There had been no previous experience in psychotherapy.

At the child advocacy center, Linda received a forensic medical examination and was interviewed by a forensic interviewer using the Step-Wise interview protocol (Yuille, Hunter, Joffe, & Zaparniuk, 1993). She engaged easily with the interviewer and quickly demonstrated the ability to provide detailed narrative about events not related to the abuse. She was cooperative and maintained her attention on the task at hand. Her affective presentation shifted markedly as the interview turned to discussion of the alleged abuse. She covered her face with a stuffed bear and was reluctant to answer questions. Asked if she would rather write out the story, she said she would. She wrote:

> I have been hurt and it was [date] I guess? I was watching TV when my cousins brought up this game called "come and get at it." I said "I don't want to play" but they forced me into it.

Asked to tell more about the game, she wrote:

> You have to get even boys and girls then the girls hide and the boys have to find them and pull down their pants and stick their penis in the girls.

Linda was then able to continue with a verbal account. She reported that her cousins threatened to hit her with a dog collar if she did not co-operate with the game. She said that she tried several times to pull up her pants, and also tried hiding in another room. She began to describe a portion of the assault in which her cousin penetrated her vagina with a pencil, then covered her face again and said that she needed a break. After the break, she again asked to write:

> Then he pulled down my pants and he broke the lead off that pencil, then he stuck it in my private.

She reported that later that night, at bedtime, her cousin snuck into her bed. Again, she returned to writing:

> Then he pulled down his pants and pulled up my nightgown and stuck his penis in my *butt*, then he stuck his penis in my *private*.

Linda reported that she talked to her grandmother in the morning about the incident. The grandmother got mad at her first, then talked to the boys. The boys claimed that Linda had made up the game.

At this point, Linda suddenly stopped and said she had forgotten something. She requested another break, and then asked to write again:

> And then they told me to suck their penis or they will hit me with that belt more times then you could ever amagin so I told them no, then I ran and ask my auntie could I take a nap, she said "Fine" and told the boys to get out of the room and then I took a long nap trying to forget about what

had happened. Then Sunday when it was time for me to leave my grand-mother said "You bet not tell anyone about what happened." I said "I promise I won't" but I guess I broke that promise.

The interviewer reassured her that it was all right to break that kind of promise, which she seemed to accept. The interviewer then contin-ued to collect further details about each incident. Linda periodically became uncomfortable, but she did not request to write again and managed to complete the interview without needing any more breaks.

The interview was judged to be highly credible, given the large amount of detailed description and idiosyncratic detail. The central story of the assault emerged in free response (both spoken and written) from her. She was quite creative in self-regulating her own state by ask-ing to write or take a break when she was uncomfortable. Perhaps most impressive was how freely she was able to move from one self-defined context to another as her level of distress dictated. Of course, such an interview requires a highly skilled interviewer, an appropriate inter-view context, and a willingness to let the interview take as long as it needs to take.

The medical exam followed the interview. Linda presented to the pe-diatrician as slightly anxious and agitated, but was cooperative throughout the exam. Her general exam was unremarkable. She was seen to be at early to mid-puberty (Tanner II-III) in her physical devel-opment. Her genital exam was abnormal. The hymen showed a dis-ruption in a localized area. Although now fully healed, its origin was from a tear at some time in the past. Such a tear is consistent with sex-ual abuse involving vaginal penetration, and certainly could have healed in the time period since the incident was alleged to have oc-curred. Her anal exam was normal, which does not rule out the alleged anal contact and penetration. She tested negative for sexually trans-mitted diseases.

Bringing together all of the forensic information, the evaluation team rated the allegation as highly credible and referred it back to Child Protective Services for further investigation. A referral was made to the in-house mental health services for evaluation and treat-ment.

An intake session was completed with Linda and her foster mother. Linda's relationship with the foster mother and with members of her biological family was explored. The foster mother has made a commitment to Linda and would like her to remain in her home until age 18. The biological mother continues to make intermittent attempts to have Linda returned home. Linda said she was very comfortable in the foster home, but was obviously ambivalent about the idea of never returning home. The foster mother appeared very connected and had spent considerable time talking with Linda about her reactions to the sexual assault. There continued to be some concerning symptoms since the time of the assault, including frequent nightmares and periodic neglect of personal hygiene. Linda and her foster mother reported that the biological family has called Linda and told her that she is to blame for the incident and for the family's reinvolvement with CPS.

Psychological testing was initiated to obtain a standardized assessment of her functioning and to clarify directions for treatment. Seen alone for the testing sessions, Linda appeared quite sad, never smiling, and speaking in a monotone voice. The ambiguous demands of the testing tasks frequently elicited abuse-related responses. For example, she drew and named her primary perpetrator on the Draw-a-Person task.

Cognitive screening with the Peabody Picture Vocabulary Test and the Developmental Test of Visual-Motor Integration suggested intellectual functioning in the average to below-average range. Symptom self-reports indicate an extreme level of distress. The clinical scales on the Revised Children's Manifest Anxiety Scale were all above the 95th percentile, and her total score on the Reynolds Child Depression Scale (RCDS) was at the 99th percentile. She also endorsed two critical items on the RCDS, responding "never" to "I feel loved" and "almost always" to "I feel like running away." Thus despite reports of a positive emotional connection to the foster mother, she presented with feelings of disconnection, an extreme level of stress, and thoughts of making an impulsive escape from her problems. On follow-up she reported that the running away fantasy related to wanting to run "back home," but she said she knew that it was not a good place for her. This was clearly a wish for having a safe and secure home base, despite knowing that her own home could not be that for her.

Projective assessment was completed using the Draw-a-Person, the Roberts Apperception Test for Children, and the Rorschach Inkblot Test. These results echoed many of the impressions formed already. She showed extreme distress, both sadness and anxiety. She had a negative view of herself and as a result tended to isolate herself from others, including potentially important sources of support. She was highly critical of herself, seeing most problems as her fault. This included her recent sexual assault, as well as the removal from her family. Similarly, she felt responsible for the fact that visits with her mother and step-paternal grandmother were terminated after she made the rape allegation. She also showed signs of thinking that being in foster care was a status that automatically reflected poorly on her as a person. This interfered with her ability to form a strong attachment to the foster mother and heightened her ambivalence regarding her biological family. Themes of sexual abuse were rampant throughout her projective responses, suggesting both preoccupation and the possibility that the abuse material had become a "language of distress" with which she could communicate her needs to other people.

On the basis of the psychological evaluation, Linda was referred for group therapy with the goals of better understanding her emotions, challenging distorted attributions related to sexual abuse and personal responsibility, and allowing her to learn to benefit from group support. We were also concerned about the possibility that she was developing a "false self" presentation style and thought the group format would allow us to assess that most efficiently. Our group therapy program for school-aged victims of sexual abuse is a 10-week program adapted from the more extensive program of Mandell and Damon (1989). Areas covered are recognizing, expressing, and responding to emotions; creating and maintaining friendships; misconceptions about sexual abuse; sharing one's story with the group; and identifying further needs.

During a semi-structured pretest for the group, Linda reported she "always" wants to hide so she doesn't have to talk about the abuse; she "always" wants to cry; she "always" thinks she should have been able to stop it; she "always" believes that the boys who assaulted her really did care about her; and "never" understands why the abuse happened. Linda participated well in group, engaging with the other four girls and especially with the two female group leaders. She showed the ability to identify emotions correctly based on experience and context, but seemed better able to do so for others than for herself. She was able to tell her story with minimal distress and shared an appropriate level of detail. Toward the end of the group, she began expressing a wish that the group could continue longer than its scheduled length. She expressed relatively low frequencies and intensities of distress, apparently continuing her pattern of being able to maintain a positive presentation, especially in front of peers. She often tried to mediate tensions and conflicts between group members or took on a caregiving role. At the time of the posttest, she continued to state that she believed the perpetrators cared for her and that she should have been able to stop it. However, she now said that she "sometimes" wants to hide, "sometimes" wants to cry, and "sometimes" understands why it happened.

The group leaders recommended that a second round of group would be beneficial (not an uncommon recommendation given the relatively short length). There were about 3 months off between the groups. During this break, we received a call from the foster mother indicating that Linda had been the subject of an attempted rape. She reported that a boy from school chased her down an alley behind the school, caught up to her, and pulled her pants down. She reported that Linda was able to escape and run home before anything else happened. Linda was scheduled for an urgent appointment. It became clear that this allegation had none of the specific details, consistencies, or coherence of the allegation against the cousins. With only gentle questioning, Linda admitted that she had fabricated the report. As she talked with the therapist about this, she expressed serious concern for her foster mother. She reported that the foster mother was convinced that she herself was soon to be raped. As a result, the foster mother was staying up all night in a chair positioned in the middle of the living room with all the lights on. She was walking the children around in the street, avoiding all sidewalks because she had been previously raped on a sidewalk. Linda described the foster mother's symptoms of hyperresponsiveness, affective blunting, irritability, and possible flashbacks, compounded by the sleep deprivation.

When the therapist spoke with Linda and the foster mother together, the foster mother acknowledged all of these symptoms, and confirmed a level of distress verging on panic. She reported that she had received no therapy after either of two previous rapes and that she always experienced some intrusive thoughts and affective dysregulation. These symptoms had been greatly increased by her awareness that she would soon have a child in the house who was the age that her older children were at the time of the two previous rapes. She acknowledged that she needed to get assistance with the posttraumatic stress disorder, but reported that she was doing all she could do to get through the day. When the therapist offered to help arrange the first appointment at an appropriate clinic, the foster mother was quite agreeable. She did follow through on therapy and responded very well to trauma-focused survivor therapy.

Linda reported that she made up the abuse allegation because she was too afraid to bring up her concerns with the foster mother directly and could think of no other pretense that would reliably lead to an appointment with one of the therapists or another helping professional. She was very worried that the foster mother or the therapist would be angry with her and that she would not be able to complete group. The foster mother was, in fact, openly grateful, although this caretaking role reversal was of some concern in the context of Linda's relationship history. The therapist spent considerable time with them, exploring other avenues Linda might have used to try to make people aware of her foster mother's distress. She was able to participate in identifying other strategies but unable to choose any that she wished she had used instead.

At the first group meeting, Linda immediately reported that she needed to talk about something. The previous day, she told her foster mother that she had been raped by a boy at school. She was taken to a different sexual assault evaluation center, where she eventually admitted during a 2-hour interview that she had made up the story. Her motivations for this appeared to come at several levels. Linda had been trying to develop a friendship with a classmate. The girl reported that she had "gotten away" with making up a molestation story and dared Linda to come up with something "more outrageous." She was trying to create a stronger connection with this friend, but also was clearly envious of the attention and concern that had come to the girl in the wake of the false allegation. Linda was very distressed, saying she felt guilty and ashamed, and was remorseful that she had betrayed her foster mother's trust. She was also worried that she would be moved to a different foster home (she was not).

As the group moved toward discussing their own abuse histories, Linda now began talking about having been sexually abused by her biological father. This allegation had come up in vague terms in the past, but the lack of detail and context surrounding this allegation stood in contrast to that seen for the allegation involving her cousins. Her story included an incident of discovering that a young neighbor girl had been raped and believing (but not wanting to) that her father was the perpetrator. In light of the recent fabricated allegations, her caseworker declined to investigate formally anything new regarding the father. The group leaders were concerned that this was largely a joining tactic, as this story would be much more in line with the abuse stories being told by the other girls in the group. At the end of one session, Linda handed a contraception brochure to one of the group leaders. She said she had picked it up at a doctor's office but emphatically stated that she "had no interest in it," then refused to discuss it any more.

At the conclusion of group, a decision was made to refer Linda for individual therapy. We believed she had made progress in group therapy in self-perception (especially in not blaming herself) and to some extent with self-regulation as we discussed her fabricated allegations. However, abuse-related themes continued to be a frequent language in expressing herself, in joining with others, and in asking for help. We were quite concerned about this well-developed style of self-perception and saw this as a primary goal of individual therapy. We also continued to be concerned about her relationship with her foster mother. This was clearly her most consistently positive and supportive relationship, yet Linda was unable to express her concerns directly when the foster mother's PTSD symptoms escalated. Even more concerning was that Linda kept engaging in behaviors that after the fact she realized were hurtful to the foster mother and even betraying of her trust.

In light of these specific concerns, we elected to refer Linda for individual therapy to the same agency that was providing services to the foster mother. Our established relationship with that agency allowed us to express these explicit goals based on our experiences, and we knew that the family systems orientation that was adopted throughout the agency would enable them to work toward filial therapy in an integrated way.

This case highlights the value of ongoing psychological assessment in a complicated forensic case that might well have ended up with no clarity regarding the abuse issues *and* a treatment dropout. Our developing understanding of Linda's functioning and the ability to work in close collaboration with forensic colleagues allowed us to manage the riptides that repeat allegations often become. Often the consequences include a decision that all the allegations are not credible, leading to reinitiating contact with the perpetrators. Our model of brief intervention coupled with careful reassessment allowed us to begin intervening on common areas of difficulty following sexual abuse (e.g., cognitive misunderstandings, self-blame, interpersonal isolation), while clarifying the areas of functioning that demand more intensive or extensive treatment (in this case, Linda's perception of herself as a victim and using that role to meet other psychological needs).

Obviously, the sheer volume of sexual abuse cases in our society prevents us from providing this level of truly integrated service to all children and adolescents who have been sexually abused. This case highlights the need to work toward this ideal through ensuring that child advocacy centers have ready access to psychological consultation; ensuring that child psychologists are adequately trained in issues of child sexual abuse and its sequelae; ensuring that the lines of communication remain open between forensic and therapeutic professionals, and working on making those boundaries more permeable; and aggressively working to develop better models for dealing with children and families who present with repeated allegations of sexual abuse.

This case provides a clear example of the benefits to a careful assessment of the child's functioning in the interrelated areas of attachment, dysregulation, and self-perception, and the important role this can play in informing the ongoing forensic process. Viewed in this context, new allegations are able to be simultaneously evaluated forensically and integrated into treatment planning and process.

# Appendixes A Through S

A. Parent Interview
B. Rating of Parent-Child Interaction
C. Family Evaluation Checklist
D. Marital/Significant Other Relationship Checklist
E. Attachment-Related Interview Questions to Use With Children
F. Attachment Story Stems
G. Safety Checklist
H. Preschool Structured Interview
I. Risk Factor Checklist
J. Checklist of Factors to Assess With the CSBI
K. Evaluator Rating Scale
L. Adolescent Sexual Behavior Inventory—Self Report
M. Adolescent Sexual Behavior Inventory—Parent Report
N. My Feelings About the Abuse Questionnaire
O. Weekly Monitor Sheet
P. Victimization Screen: Problems In Your Family Growing Up
Q. Self-Injurious Behavior Checklist
R. Self-Injurious Behavior Interview
S. Alternate PTSD Criteria for Early Childhood

## Appendix A
## Parent Interview

### Pregnancy/Delivery

1. Who is the biological father of your child?
2. What type of relationship do you now have with him?
3. What was it like to be pregnant with _____?
4. What events were going on in your life that made being pregnant difficult?
5. Did you want to get pregnant with this child by that man _____ at this time _____ in your life?
6. What percentage of you was completely ready to get pregnant at this time?
7. What were your feelings when you found out you were pregnant?
8. What were your hopes and feelings during your pregnancy?
9. How would you describe your delivery?
10. What were your feelings when you first saw your child?
11. Did you smoke _____ Drink _____ Use drugs _____ Make your prenatal visits _____?

### Grand-Parental Acceptance/Rejection

1. Do you remember your parents ever talking about your becoming a parent?
2. What specifically did they say?
3. What kind of parent did they think you would become?
4. What did your parents think about the pregnancy?
5. Does any relative tell you how to raise your child?
6. Do you ask for their input?
7. Do you need their input?
8. Does anyone butt in when you are trying to discipline _____ and tell you how to do it differently?

### Acceptance of Child

1. Was anything happening in your other relationships that made it hard to get connected with _____?
2. What was your impression of _____ as a baby?
3. What are three words that describe _____ now?
    a.
    b.
    c.
4. What is a specific example that backs each of those up?
    a.
    b.
    c.

5. Who in your family does _____ remind you of in the way he/she acts?
6. Who does _____ look like?
7. Is there any part of your personality in _____?
8. What is it like to live with _____?
9. Is there anything about _____ that makes him/her hard to like?
10. Is _____ helpful around the house? In what ways?
11. How do you think _____ will turn out?
12. Do you ever worry that _____ will turn into a criminal? A prostitute?
13. Does _____ expect you to give him/her anything he/she wants?
14. Is _____ like a bottomless pit about wants and wishes? Never satisfied?

## Secure Base
1. If _____ was hurt or in trouble, what would he/she do?
2. Who would _____ turn to?
3. Describe a time when _____ came to you for help.
4. How does it feel to be needed/not needed in this way?

## Ruptures in Parenting
1. Have there been any times when you were not living with your child?
2. When?
3. How long?
4. Why was that?
5. How did these times apart affect _____?
6. How did these times apart affect your relationship with _____?

## Abuse-Related Acceptance
1. Do you believe what _____ said about the abuse?
2. Is there any part about what _____ said that you don't believe?
3. Why did _____ wait to tell you?
4. Sometimes parents get mad at their child when things like this happen. When have you gotten mad?
5. How did you let _____ know that whatever happened you stand by him/her?

## Perspectives on Their History of Being Parented
1. Are you the type of parent you want to be?
2. What do you think you learned about mothering from your mother?
3. What about how your parents raised you has made it hard to be as good a parent as you want to be?
4. Did you feel loved by your mother?
   In what ways was this shown?
   a.
   b.

5. Did you feel loved by your father?
   In what ways did he show this?
   a.
   b.
6. To whom did you really matter when you were growing up? Who made
   you feel special? Who in your life was always concerned about you?

## Trauma/Abuse Interruptions

1. Were you sexually abused as a child or teen?
2. Physically abused?
3. Does this still affect you?
4. When did you first talk about this with your parent(s)?
5. Did they believe you?
6. As an adult, have you talked about this with your parents?
7. What do they say (would they say) when (if) you bring this up?
8. How about your siblings? What is their response?

## Current Attachments

1. Do you have a partner/significant other/spouse?
2. What words describe this relationship?
3. Give an example of how you are close.
4. How many close friends do you have?
5. Are any of them the type of person to whom you could say anything?
6. Could you turn to them for "real help in time of need"?
7. Do you feel you get used in relationships?

## Appendix B
## Rating of Parent-Child Interaction

| Behavior | T1 | T2 | T3 | T4 | T5 |
|----------|----|----|----|----|----|
| Observation Times | | | | | |
| Positive Verbal | | | | | |
| Positive Physical | | | | | |
| Parent Initiate | | | | | |
| Child Initiate | | | | | |
| Parent Comply | | | | | |
| Child Comply | | | | | |
| Criticize | | | | | |
| Teach | | | | | |

Rate the following Maternal Behavioral Features

    Supportive Presence

    Quality of Assistance


Rate the following Child Features

    Enthusiasm

    Persistence

    Self-Reliance

    Affection

    Negativity

    Avoidance

    Controlling Behavior

    Anxiety

    Compliance With Parental Requests

## Appendix C
### Family Evaluation Checklist

1. Can the parent(s) get the children to talk about uncomfortable topics?
2. Who is in charge of the family? The discussion?
3. Are there scapegoats in the family?
4. Safety review:
   a. Open at talking about the problems?
   b. What are the identified problems?
5. Abuse review: Who in the family knows about what has gone on?
6. Determine the amount of time parent spends in the home
7. Family conflict: Query about yelling and hitting, particularly when the parents are not home.
8. Discipline: Who gets it the most, what types are used, ask about verbally abusive strategies
9. Parentified child: Who is the kid who bails out the parent?
10. By the end of the interview, did you feel as if this was an enjoyable family to be with, and why?

## Appendix D
### Marital/Significant Other Relationship Checklist

1. Determine who is the parent's significant partner.
2. How did they meet? Have them tell the story behind this.
3. Does the partner help with parenting?
4. Are they involved with discipline? Even physical discipline? Are there conflicts around discipline?
5. How often is the partner around?
6. Does the partner have a criminal history?
7. What is it like to live with the partner?
8. Sex life—frequency, satisfaction, unusual aspects.
9. Is there coercive/atypical sex?
10. Is there sexually provocative behavior in front of the kids?
11. Domestic violence—include yelling, hitting, threatening
12. In-law relationships—permission to get married, have children, etc.
13. Do his/her parents approve of this individual?
14. Would they get married/involved again if they had the choice?

## Appendix E
## Attachment-Related Interview Questions to Use With Children

(Start with a Kinetic Family Drawing to learn
about the family and have a point of reference)

1. Of all the kids in this picture, who likes being in your family the most?
2. What do they like about it?
3. Who's the favorite kid in the family?
4. What is it about you that your mom likes the most? Your dad?
5. Who is it easiest to be alone with? Your mom? Your dad?
6. Who yells the most? Hits the most?
7. Who in your family doesn't really like you?
8. If you were feeling sad, who in your family would help you the fastest? The slowest?
9. Who in your family is having the hardest time being in foster care?
10. What does it feel like inside to see your mom on a visit? Your dad?
11. Can you tell your mom anything? Even embarrassing stuff? Your dad?
12. What does your teacher like about you? Think about you?
13. What can you do that makes other people want to be with you?
14. Are other kids ever mean to you? Do they take advantage of you?

## Appendix F
## Attachment Story Stems

Begin by informing children that you wish for them to make up interesting stories. They can use the dolls and props that you will provide to act out the stories. Indicate to them that you will give them an idea and they will finish it so it has an ending. Then indicate the various characters for each scene, read the beginning of the story, and then ask them to "tell me and show me what happens next." Write down the child's story verbatim. When the child appears to be done, be sure to ask, "Anything else?"

1. (Spilled juice)  While the family is seated at the dinner table, the younger child accidentally spills juice on the floor, and then . . . (issue: an attachment figure is authority relation to the child).

2. (Hurt knee)  While the family is taking a walk in the park, the younger child climbs a rock, falls off, hurts a knee, and cries. And then . . . (issue: pain as an elicitor of attachment and protective behavior)

3. (Monster in the bedroom)  After the child is sent upstairs to go to bed, the child cries out about a monster in the bedroom. And then . . . (issue: fear as an elicitor of attachment and protective behavior)

4. (Departure)  The parents leave for an overnight trip, with grandmother remaining behind to look after the two children. And then . . . (issue: separation anxiety and coping ability)

5. (Reunion)  Grandmother looks out of the window the next morning and tells the children the parents are coming back. And then . . . (issue: welcoming vs. avoidant, resistant, or disorganized reunion behavior)

## Appendix G
## Safety Checklist

Name of Child _____

Age _____    Sex _____

Who is living in the home and what are their ages? _____

_____

Who visits the home? _____

_____

Check all that apply about the child in question. Please rate the frequencies as precisely as possible, for example, how many times per week.

**Cosleeping.** I am going to begin by asking you questions about the sleeping arrangements in your home. These pertain to the child we named above. First, who is usually home when your child is sleeping? _____

1. _____ **Sleeps every night in own bed in private bedroom**
2. _____ Sleeps in same bed as sibling
   How often _____    Age of Sibling _____
   Sexual Abuse Hx of sibling _____
3. _____ Sleeps in same room as sibling, but not in same bed
   How often _____    Age of Sibling _____
   Sexual Abuse Hx of sibling _____
4. _____ Sleeps in parents' bed    How often _____
5. _____ Parents have had sex while child is in bed    How often _____
6. _____ **Parents never behave sexually while child is in bed**
7. _____ Sleeps in parents' bedroom but not in their bed    Where _____
8. _____ **Child's bedroom is next door to the parents' bedroom**
9. _____ Parents' bedroom door is left open
10. _____ **Parents have a lock on their bedroom door**
11. _____ **Child has a lock on his or her bedroom door**
12. _____ **Absolutely no cosleeping occurs**

_____

**Cobathing.**   I am now going to ask you about who your child bathes/showers with. Where is the bath tub/shower located in your house? _____

13. _____ **I can hear what is going on in the bathroom from where I usually am**

14. _____ Bathes/showers together with mother          How often _____

15. _____ Bathes/showers together with father          How often _____

16. _____ Bathes/showers together with sibling          How often _____

17. _____ **Absolutely no cobathing occurs**

**Family Nudity.**   Now let's discuss your family's attitudes about nudity. Every family is going to be different. Some are more relaxed. Others are more strict.

18. _____ Father is nude in the home                      How often _____

19. _____ Mother is nude in the home                     How often _____

20. _____ Siblings are nude in the home                  How often _____

21. _____ Father wears underwear in the house          How often _____

22. _____ Mother wears underwear in the house         How often _____

23. _____ Teenage sibling wears underwear in the
             house                                                 How often _____

24. _____ Parent(s) sleeps in the nude                     How often _____

25. _____ **Absolutely no nudity occurs in the home**

**Family Sexuality.**   Families vary as well as how affectionate they are in front of each other.

26. _____ Parents grab each other's breasts/butt/crotch
             (even when clothed)

27. _____ Parents French kiss

28. _____ Teenage siblings grab each other's breasts/butt/crotch
             (even when clothed)

29. _____ Teenage siblings French kiss

30. _____ Parents talk about sex acts in front of the child

31. _____ Teenage siblings talk about sex acts in front of the child

32. _____ Farm animals are having sex on the property

33. _____ **Absolutely no opportunities to witness sexual behavior**

**Pornography/Witnessing Sexual Intercourse.**   Here are some more questions about sexual materials and behavior in the house.

34. _____ Magazine pornography is in the home
    Where kept _____     Accessible _____     What magazines _____
35. _____ Video pornography is in the house
    Where kept _____     Accessible _____
    What are the titles _____
36. _____ Has unlimited access to TV, including sexually explicit shows
37. _____ Has access to Internet, including pornographic Web sites
38. _____ Has seen intercourse
    Live _____     Video/movie _____     How often _____
39. _____ **Absolutely no opportunities to see pornography or witness intercourse**

**Family Violence.**   Some families are more open about violent behaviors in the home.

40. _____ Child is hit/slapped
41. _____ Child is punched/beat
42. _____ Parents hit each other
43. _____ Child hits parents
44. _____ Child is yelled/screamed at
45. _____ Parents yell/scream at each other
46. _____ Siblings punch each other
47. _____ Siblings hit/slap each other
48. _____ Parent is intoxicated
49. _____ Guns are displayed in the home
50. _____ Guns are waved around in a threatening manner
51. _____ Guns are discharged in the house
52. _____ Violent/horror videos are available
53. _____ Drug dealing occurs in the house
54. _____ **Absolutely no family violence of the physical or verbal types**

**Community Violence.**   Some families live in dangerous settings, crowded buildings, and so on

55. _____ Drive-by shootings occur in the neighborhood
56. _____ Drug dealing occurs in the neighborhood
57. _____ Child is beaten up by peers
58. _____ Child has no age-appropriate peers
59. _____ House is unsafe or unclean and you wish you lived elsewhere
60. _____ **Absolutely no community violence**

**PTSD Triggers.** Sometimes we forget that there are things that trigger our child's behavior. Sometimes these are reminders of bad things from the past.

61. _____ Reminders of the perpetrator are in the house
62. _____ Pictures of the perpetrator are in the house
63. _____ There are other sexually abused children in the house
64. _____ There is a sexually abused child at my child's day care
65. _____ Sexually abused adults live in the house
66. _____ Sexually abused child/adolescent/adult is involved in baby-sitting the child
67. _____ Sexual perpetrators live in the house or in the neighborhood
68. _____ Child has visual contact with the perpetrator
69. _____ **Absolutely no triggers or past events are around our house**

**Monitoring.** It's important for me to get an idea of how easy it is for you to keep track of your child and whether anything from your own past gets in the way of you keeping him/her safe.

70. _____ Number of hours/day the child is not being visually or auditorially monitored by the parents or another adult
71. _____ Parents would have a hard time objectively seeing sexual behavior (due to depression, cognitive limitations, sexual abuse history, rejection of the child, neglectful pattern of parenting, etc.)
72. _____ Parents would have a hard time objectively seeing rule violations
73. _____ Parents would have a hard time being consistent
74. _____ **Absolutely no problems monitoring their child's behavior**

Positive Safety Points
  (Sum up Items **1, 6, 8, 10-13, 17, 25, 33, 39, 54, 60, 69, 74**)
  **Total** _____

Negative Safety Points
  (Sum up Items 2-5, 7, 9, 14-16, 18-24, 26-32, 34-38, 40-53, 55-59, 61-68, 70-73)
  **Total** _____

**Problem Areas** (Check all that apply)
    _____ Cosleeping
    _____ Cobathing
    _____ Family Nudity
    _____ Family Sexuality
    _____ Pornography
    _____ Family Violence
    _____ Community Violence
    _____ PTSD Triggers
    _____ Monitoring

## Appendix H
### Preschool Structured Interview

William N. Friedrich, PhD                    Sandra Hewitt, PhD
Mayo Clinic                                  St. Paul, MN

**Administer a CSBI prior to intake.**

Please complete the following structured interview. Some of this material will emerge naturally during the course of an interview, but please pay extra attention to covering each of the details included here. We anticipate that some of the demographic information (items with asterisks) could be obtained directly from the Child Sexual Behavior Inventory, particularly if that is administered ahead of time.

BACKGROUND INFORMATION

*1. Birth date of child          _____
*2. Age in months               _____
*3. Race _____
*4. Gender    male _____    female _____
 5. Birth order          _____ of _____
 6. Gender of other siblings _____
 7. How did this child get to you:
        self-referral by parent          _____
        referral by pediatrician         _____
        referral by social services      _____
        referral by attorney             _____
 8. Is this part of a contested custody situation?      yes _____ no _____


DEVELOPMENTAL INFORMATION ON THE CHILD

1. Was this a wanted child?                          yes _____ no _____
2. How long did labor last? _____ hours
3. Were there any delivery complications?            yes _____ no _____
4. Was the child medically normal at birth?          yes _____ no _____
5. Was there any placement in intensive care?        yes _____ no _____
6. Have there been any medical complications since birth?
   Please list _____
   _____
   _____

POTENTIATING FACTORS

*1. What is the education level of the mother in years?  _____
*2. What is the education level of the father in years?  _____
*3. What is the gross annual income of the family?  $_____
 4. Does either parent have a history of chemical dependency or abuse?
    yes _____ no _____ don't know (dk) _____
 5. Have either or both parents been physically aggressive with each other?
    yes _____ no _____ dk _____
 6. Have they been physically aggressive in front of the child?
    yes _____ no _____ dk _____
 7. Does the child have opportunities to sleep with the parent(s)?
    yes _____ no _____ dk _____
 8. Does the child have opportunities to bathe with the parents?
    yes _____ no _____ dk _____
 9. Has the child witnessed intercourse?
    yes _____ no _____ dk _____
10. Has the child seen X, XXX, or pornographic movies?
    yes _____ no _____ dk _____
11. With what regularity does the child see the parents without clothes?
    _____/week dk _____
12. Does the mother have a history of sexual abuse?
    yes _____ no _____ dk _____
    Did this involve penetration? _____ Force? _____
13. Does the mother have a history of physical abuse?
    yes _____ no _____ dk _____
14. Does the father have a history of sexual abuse?
    yes _____ no _____ dk _____
15. Does the father have a history of physical abuse?
    yes _____ no _____ dk _____
16. Has the mother ever been arrested?
    yes _____ no _____ dk _____
    If so, for what? _____
    Time in jail? yes _____ (# of months)  no _____
17. Has the father ever been arrested?  yes _____ no _____ dk _____
    If so, for what? _____
    Time in jail?        yes _____ (# of months)   no _____
18. Does the mother feel supported by her own mother?
    yes _____ no _____ dk _____
19. Does she visit with her mother regularly?
    yes _____ no _____ dk _____

20. Was there ever a period of time in which she did not feel supported by her mother?

yes _____ no _____ dk _____    When? _____

21. Has the child ever been separated from the mother for more than a weekend?

yes _____ no _____ dk _____

Please describe _____

_____

## PRIOR INCIDENTS OF CONCERN

1. What was the first behavior/statement that made you suspect sexual abuse? Describe the child's behavior/statement, its context, and the child's affect at the time.

_____

_____

_____

2. What other behaviors/statements have you or others seen that might indicate sexual abuse? Describe the behaviors/statements and the child's affect for each one.

_____

_____

_____

3. What behavior suggesting problems with sleeping has the child exhibited in the past?

| | | |
|---|---|---|
| Problems getting to sleep | yes _____ | no _____ |
| Waking up | yes _____ | no _____ |
| Nightmares | yes _____ | no _____ |
| Night terrors | yes _____ | no _____ |

4. What behavior has the child exhibited regarding toileting in the recent past?

| | | |
|---|---|---|
| Wets during the day | yes _____ | no _____ |
| Wets at night | yes _____ | no _____ |
| Soils | yes _____ | no _____ |
| Afraid of the bathroom | yes _____ | no _____ |

5. Has the child shown any problems with separation lately?                 yes _____ no _____

Describe _____

_____

PRECIPITATING INCIDENT
1. What behavior prompted you to report? Describe the behavior/
   statement, its context, and the child's affect at the time. _____

   _____

   _____

   _____

2. Are there any other incidents since this report? Describe the behavior/
   statement, its context, and the child's affect at the time. _____

   _____

   _____

   _____

DISCLOSURE CONTEXT
1. Where did the behavior/statement occur?
   Provide the number of disclosures in the appropriate category.
       diapering            _____
       bathing              _____
       toileting             _____
       bedtime             _____
       while playing with toys      _____
       out of the blue          _____

RESPONSE BY PARENTS
1. How did the parent respond when the child exhibited the
   behavior or made the statement?
   For the mother, check all that apply, including frequency
   the response occurred if more than once:
       blaming             _____
       angry              _____
       shaming             _____
       a calm recipient of the news    _____
       anxious, sad, decompensates    _____
       immediate provision of support   _____
2. For other reporters, check all that apply, including the frequency
   the response occurred if more than once:
       blaming             _____
       angry              _____
       shaming             _____
       a calm recipient of the news    _____
       anxious, sad, decompensates    _____
       immediate provision of support   _____

3. Has the parent done any further questioning?        yes _____ no _____
4. Has the parent tape-recorded or videotaped any
   disclosures?                                        yes _____ no _____
5. Have there been any prior accusations?              yes _____ no _____
   How many? _____


BACKGROUND EVIDENCE

1. Has there been any medical evidence reported?
   If so, what kind? _____

   _____
   _____

   Were there any significant behaviors during the exam? _____

   _____
   _____


2. Is there any supporting data from CPS, police, and day care provider?
   If so, what type? _____

   _____
   _____


3. What is the time elapsed from the alleged incident until now?
   _____ weeks


4. What do other people in the child's life say with regard to this
   behavior? _____

   _____
   _____


5. Have they seen any of the behavior being described? _____


WHAT CAN THE CHILD SAY OR SHOW YOU?

Please indicate what the child was able to say or demonstrate in your
interview. _____

_____
_____

Observation of the child and the alleged perpetrator (if done). _____

_____
_____

NATURE OF ABUSE

1. From the above information, what are you able to state about possible or probable victimization?

   (A) Who was involved?

   _____

   (B) How many years separate the child from the alleged offender?

   _____

   (C) Where did this occur?

   _____

   (D) What type of abuse?

   _____

   (E) Level of force?

   _____

   (F) Number of incidents

   _____


DISPOSITION

Please choose a category.
The preponderance of the evidence would not support abuse          _____
The preponderance of the evidence supports abuse                   _____
It is impossible to say                                            _____

*Available from CSBI

## Appendix I
### Risk Factor Checklist

1. _____ Disruption(s) in child's parenting (parent in psychiatric hospital or CD treatment for more than 1-2 weeks; formal or informal foster care of more than 1-2 weeks cumulative; cared for extended periods by relatives, neighbors, etc.)

2. _____ Maternal History of Sexual Abuse
   _____ has received treatment for abuse
   _____ has not received treatment for abuse

3. _____ Child is poorly monitored during the day (extended periods where adult is not present)

4. _____ Rejection of the child (child is often criticized; parent sees few positives; child reminds parent of perpetrator or other disliked adult)

5. _____ Abuse had a duration of more than one month

6. _____ Child's report of abuse not believed by parent

7. _____ Parent has not obtained a high school diploma or equivalency (GED) or reports other educational problems, for example, slow learner, special education

8. _____ Employment problems in parent

9. _____ Child has experienced other abuses, for example, physical, emotional, neglect

10. _____ Criminal history in either parent

11. _____ Substance abuse in either parent

12. _____ Conflict with extended family (lack of support by in-laws, extended family; parent reports being criticized in her parenting by family members; reports emotional abuse as a child)

13. _____ Marital instability, for example, separations, divorce, multiple marriages/liaisons

14. _____ Pregnant prior to age 18

15. _____ Family lives in high crime neighborhood, for example, drug houses, drive-by shootings, other abusive families next door

16. _____ Poverty (receives subsidy; income below poverty level)

17. _____ Inconsistent parenting (indulgence or permissiveness followed by rejection)

18. _____ Parent cannot use child management skills (can't explain how to use or can't demonstrate the successful use of time out, consequences, limit setting)

19. _____ Mother reports no close friends (has no one who can provide real help in time of trouble)

20. _____ Physical abuse of mother   (_____ resolved   _____ unresolved)

21. _____ Violence in the home, for example, adults hitting each other, siblings fighting physically

## Appendix J
## Checklist of Factors to Assess With the CSBI

|  | Yes | No |
|---|---|---|
| Factors That Increase the Reporting of Sexual Behavior | | |
| 1. Spousal battering | ___ | ___ |
| 2. Pornography in the home | ___ | ___ |
| 3. Family nudity/sexuality | ___ | ___ |
| 4. Recent stressful events | ___ | ___ |
| 5. Physical abuse | ___ | ___ |
| 6. Modeling of sexuality by peers | ___ | ___ |
| Factors That Decrease the Reporting of Sexual Behavior | | |
| 1. High school education or less | ___ | ___ |
| 2. Income below middle class | ___ | ___ |
| 3. Parent is a poor monitor of the child | ___ | ___ |

## Appendix K
## Evaluator Rating Scale

|  | Yes | No |
|---|---|---|
| Boundary Variables | | |
| 1. Child physically touches you | ___ | ___ |
| 2. Child is physically destructive of objects in office | ___ | ___ |
| 3. Child moves about the office without permission | ___ | ___ |
| 4. Child hits, kicks, bites, or shoves you | ___ | ___ |
| 5. Child touches objects in office without asking | ___ | ___ |
| Sexual Variables | | |
| 1. Child kisses or hugs you | ___ | ___ |
| 2. Child sits with underwear exposed | ___ | ___ |
| 3. Child touches his or her own sexual body parts | ___ | ___ |
| 4. Child lifts clothing or begins to remove clothing in office | ___ | ___ |
| 5. Child spontaneously talks about sexual acts or sexual body parts | ___ | ___ |

## Appendix L
## Adolescent Sexual Behavior Inventory—Self-Report

Please rate yourself on how frequently you have shown each of the behaviors below in the past 12 months. Circle the number that fits best and *please answer every question.* Thank you.

**0 = Not True**  **1 = Somewhat True**  **2 = Very True**

| | | | |
|---|---|---|---|
| 1. I know more about sex than others my age | 0 | 1 | 2 |
| 2. I am fearful to begin dating | 0 | 1 | 2 |
| 3. I make sexual comments to my friends | 0 | 1 | 2 |
| 4. I am unhappy with my looks | 0 | 1 | 2 |
| 5. I wear clothing that shows off my underwear or skin | 0 | 1 | 2 |
| 6. I stay away from home overnight without permission | 0 | 1 | 2 |
| 7. I spend a lot of time in front of the mirror | 0 | 1 | 2 |
| 8. I flirt with other teens or adults | 0 | 1 | 2 |
| 9. I prefer to socialize with people of the opposite sex | 0 | 1 | 2 |
| 10. I masturbate | 0 | 1 | 2 |
| 11. I stand too close to others | 0 | 1 | 2 |
| 12. I am completely uninterested in the opposite sex | 0 | 1 | 2 |
| 13. I quickly become sexual in relationships | 0 | 1 | 2 |
| 14. I dress modestly | 0 | 1 | 2 |
| 15. Interested in TV, movies, or videos with sexual content | 0 | 1 | 2 |
| 16. I push others into having sex with me | 0 | 1 | 2 |
| 17. I have many boyfriends or girlfriends | 0 | 1 | 2 |
| 18. I make sexual comments to adults | 0 | 1 | 2 |
| 19. I show off my skin or body parts | 0 | 1 | 2 |
| 20. I talk about sexual behaviors | 0 | 1 | 2 |
| 21. I wish I were the opposite sex | 0 | 1 | 2 |
| 22. I have had unprotected sex | 0 | 1 | 2 |
| 23. I get used sexually by others | 0 | 1 | 2 |

24. I have no friends of the opposite sex                              0   1   2

25. I am gay, lesbian, or bisexual                                     0   1   2

26. I run away from home to unsafe places                             0   1   2

27. I am afraid of males                                               0   1   2

28. I am uncomfortable with my own body                               0   1   2

29. I am uncomfortable when people talk or joke about sex             0   1   2

30. I have been involved in prostitution                              0   1   2

31. I do not like to shower or bathe                                  0   1   2

32. I am very interested in the opposite sex                          0   1   2

33. Others are worried about my sexual behavior                       0   1   2

34. I am concerned about looking just right                           0   1   2

35. I own pornography                                                 0   1   2

36. I am not shy about undressing                                     0   1   2

37. I have been caught in a sexual act                                0   1   2

38. I have been sexually abused                                       0   1   2

39. I have been accused of sexually abusing another person            0   1   2

40. I am afraid of females                                            0   1   2

41. I use phone sex lines or computer sex chat rooms                  0   1   2

42. I have had a sexually transmitted disease                         0   1   2

43. I have been pregnant                                              0   1   2

44. I peep into windows or try to see others in the bathroom          0   1   2

45. I seek information about sex from adults that I trust             0   1   2

46. How many sexual partners, including current partner(s), have you had? (Circle the right answer):

| 0 | 1 | 2 | 3 | 4 | 5 |
|---|---|---|---|---|---|
| None | One | Two | Three or Four | Five or Six | Seven or more |

47. Have you been sexually abused? (been exposed to, touched, or fondled against your will)

| 0 | 1 | 2 | 3 | 4 |
|---|---|---|---|---|
| Not Likely | Possible | Probably | Very Likely | Definitely |

48. Have you been physically abused? (Hit hard, kicked, or punched by an adult)

| 0 | 1 | 2 | 3 | 4 |
|---|---|---|---|---|
| Not Likely | Possible | Probably | Very Likely | Definitely |

49. Have you been emotionally abused? (criticized, put down, ridiculed)

| 0 | 1 | 2 | 3 | 4 |
|---|---|---|---|---|
| Not Likely | Possible | Probably | Very Likely | Definitely |

50. Do you think your sexual experiences are about the same as other kids your age?

| 0 | 1 | 2 | 3 | 4 |
|---|---|---|---|---|
| Not Likely | Possible | Probably | Very Likely | Definitely |

51. Please add any other comments you would like to about yourself related to the above:

## Appendix M
### Adolescent Sexual Behavior Inventory—Parent Report

Please rate your child on how frequently she or he has shown each of the behaviors below in the past 12 months. Circle the number that fits best and *please answer every question.* Thank you.

**0 = Not True**          **1 = Somewhat True**          **2 = Very True**

| | | | |
|---|---|---|---|
| 1. Knows more about sex than others their age | 0 | 1 | 2 |
| 2. Seems fearful to begin dating | 0 | 1 | 2 |
| 3. Makes sexual comments to their friends | 0 | 1 | 2 |
| 4. Is unhappy with their looks | 0 | 1 | 2 |
| 5. Wears clothing that shows off underwear or skin | 0 | 1 | 2 |
| 6. Stays away from home overnight without permission | 0 | 1 | 2 |
| 7. Spends a lot of time in front of the mirror | 0 | 1 | 2 |
| 8. Flirts with other teens or adults | 0 | 1 | 2 |
| 9. Prefers socializing with people of the opposite sex | 0 | 1 | 2 |
| 10. Masturbates | 0 | 1 | 2 |
| 11. Stands too close to others | 0 | 1 | 2 |
| 12. Seems completely uninterested in the opposite sex | 0 | 1 | 2 |
| 13. Quickly becomes sexual in relationships | 0 | 1 | 2 |
| 14. Dresses modestly | 0 | 1 | 2 |
| 15. Interested in TV, movies, or videos with sexual content | 0 | 1 | 2 |
| 16. Pushes others into having sex | 0 | 1 | 2 |
| 17. Has many boyfriends or girlfriends | 0 | 1 | 2 |
| 18. Makes sexual comments to adults | 0 | 1 | 2 |
| 19. Shows off their skin or body parts | 0 | 1 | 2 |
| 20. Talks about sexual behaviors | 0 | 1 | 2 |
| 21. Wishes they were the opposite sex | 0 | 1 | 2 |
| 22. Has unprotected sex | 0 | 1 | 2 |
| 23. Gets used sexually by others | 0 | 1 | 2 |
| 24. Has no friends of the opposite sex | 0 | 1 | 2 |

25. Describes self as gay, lesbian, or bisexual               0  1  2

26. Runs away from home to unsafe places                      0  1  2

27. Is afraid of males                                        0  1  2

28. Seems uncomfortable with their own body                   0  1  2

29. Uncomfortable when people talk or joke about sex          0  1  2

30. Has been involved in prostitution                         0  1  2

31. Does not like to shower or bathe                          0  1  2

32. Is very interested in the opposite sex                    0  1  2

33. You are worried about their sexual behavior               0  1  2

34. Is concerned about looking just right                     0  1  2

35. Owns pornography                                          0  1  2

36. Is not shy about undressing                               0  1  2

37. Has been caught in a sexual act                           0  1  2

38. Says they have been sexually abused                       0  1  2

39. Has been accused of sexually abusing another person       0  1  2

40. Is afraid of females                                      0  1  2

41. Uses phone sex lines or computer sex chat rooms           0  1  2

42. Has had a sexually transmitted disease                    0  1  2

43. Has been pregnant                                         0  1  2

44. Peeps into windows or tries to see others in the bathroom 0  1  2

45. Seeks accurate information about sex from trusted adults   0  1  2

46. How many sexual partners, including current partner(s), has your child had? (Circle the right answer):

| 0 | 1 | 2 | 3 | 4 | 5 |
|---|---|---|---|---|---|
| None | One | Two | Three or Four | Five or Six | Seven or more |

47. Do you believe your child has been sexually abused? (Been exposed to, touched, or fondled against his or her will)

| 0 | 1 | 2 | 3 | 4 |
|---|---|---|---|---|
| Not Likely | Possible | Probably | Very Likely | Definitely |

48. Do you believe your child has been physically abused? (Hit hard, kicked, or punched by a parent figure, excessive physical discipline)

| 0 | 1 | 2 | 3 | 4 |
|---|---|---|---|---|
| Not Likely | Possible | Probably | Very Likely | Definitely |

49. Do you believe your child has been emotionally abused? (criticized, put down, ridiculed)

| 0 | 1 | 2 | 3 | 4 |
|---|---|---|---|---|
| Not Likely | Possible | Probably | Very Likely | Definitely |

50. Do you think your child's sexual experiences are about the same as other kids'?

| 0 | 1 | 2 | 3 | 4 |
|---|---|---|---|---|
| Not Likely | Possible | Probably | Very Likely | Definitely |

51. Please add any other comments you would like to about your child related to the above:

## Appendix N
### My Feelings About the Abuse Questionnaire
### (Feiring, Taska, & Lewis, 1998)

1. I feel ashamed because I feel that people can tell from looking at me what happened

| 1 | 2 | 3 |
|---|---|---|
| Not True | Somewhat True | Very True |

2. When I think about what happened, I want to go away and hide

| 1 | 2 | 3 |
|---|---|---|
| Not True | Somewhat True | Very True |

3. What happened to me makes me feel dirty

| 1 | 2 | 3 |
|---|---|---|
| Not True | Somewhat True | Very True |

4. I am ashamed because I know I am the only one in my school who this happened to

| 1 | 2 | 3 |
|---|---|---|
| Not True | Somewhat True | Very True |

SOURCE: Feiring, Taska, & Lewis, M. (1998). Used by permission.

## Appendix O
## Weekly Monitor Sheet

Please rate how often you see your child do the behaviors we are watching.

Behavior 1 _____          Behavior 2 _____

| Day 1 | Day 2 | Day 3 | Day 4 | Day 5 | Day 6 | Day 7 |
|-------|-------|-------|-------|-------|-------|-------|
| A.M. | A.M. | A.M. | A.M. | A.M. | A.M. | A.M. |
| Behavior 1 _____ | Behavior 1 _____ | Behavior 1 _____ | Behavior 1 _____ | Behavior 1 _____ | Behavior 1 _____ | Behavior 1 _____ |
| How often: _____ | How often: _____ | How often: _____ | How often: _____ | How often: _____ | How often: _____ | How often: _____ |
| Behavior 2 _____ | Behavior 2 _____ | Behavior 2 _____ | Behavior 2 _____ | Behavior 2 _____ | Behavior 2 _____ | Behavior 2 _____ |
| How often: _____ | How often: _____ | How often: _____ | How often: _____ | How often: _____ | How often: _____ | How often: _____ |
| P.M. | P.M. | P.M. | P.M. | P.M. | P.M. | P.M. |
| Behavior 1 _____ | Behavior 1 _____ | Behavior 1 _____ | Behavior 1 _____ | Behavior 1 _____ | Behavior 1 _____ | Behavior 1 _____ |
| How often: _____ | How often: _____ | How often: _____ | How often: _____ | How often: _____ | How often: _____ | How often: _____ |
| Behavior 2 _____ | Behavior 2 _____ | Behavior 2 _____ | Behavior 2 _____ | Behavior 2 _____ | Behavior 2 _____ | Behavior 2 _____ |
| How often: _____ | How often: _____ | How often: _____ | How often: _____ | How often: _____ | How often: _____ | How often: _____ |

## Appendix P: Victimization Screen:
## Problems in Your Family Growing Up

I. I now want to ask some sensitive questions about things that happen in families. Some families do a lot of yelling and arguing. Verbal arguments and punishment can range from quiet disagreement to yelling, insulting, and more severe behaviors. *How often did the following happen to you in an average year while growing up in your family?* and *How often did the following happen in the past year?* Answer these questions for your mother, father, or other parent figure(s) (e.g., foster parents) with the following codes:

0 = Never
1 = Once a Year
2 = Twice a Year
3 = 3-5 Times a Year

4 = 6-10 Times a Year
5 = 11-20 Times a Year
6 = More Than 20 Times a Year

| | Average Year | | | | | | | | This Past Year | | | | | | |
|---|---|---|---|---|---|---|---|---|---|---|---|---|---|---|---|
| | 0 | 1 | 2 | 3 | 4 | 5 | 6 | | 0 | 1 | 2 | 3 | 4 | 5 | 6 |
| Yelled at you | | | | | | | | | | | | | | | |
| Insulted you | | | | | | | | | | | | | | | |
| Criticized you | | | | | | | | | | | | | | | |
| Tried to make you feel guilty | | | | | | | | | | | | | | | |
| Ridiculed or humiliated you | | | | | | | | | | | | | | | |
| Embarrassed you in front of others | | | | | | | | | | | | | | | |
| Made you feel like you were a bad person | | | | | | | | | | | | | | | |

Was the person who did this mainly your father (F), mother (M), Both (B), or Other (O)

_____ F _____ M _____ B _____ O  (Please specify _____ )

309

II. Here are some questions about hitting and physical violence. Everyone gets into conflicts with other people, and sometimes these lead to physical blows or violent behavior. *When you were 18 or younger, at the worst point, how often did the following happen to you in an average year?* and *How often have the following occurred in the past year?* Answer these questions for your mother, father, or other parent figure(s) (e.g., foster parents) with the following codes:

0 = Never
1 = Once a Year
2 = Twice a Year
3 = 3-5 Times a Year

4 = 6-10 Times a Year
5 = 11-20 Times a Year
6 = More Than 20 Times a Year

|  | Average Year | | | | | | | This Past Year | | | | | | |
|---|---|---|---|---|---|---|---|---|---|---|---|---|---|---|
|  | 0 | 1 | 2 | 3 | 4 | 5 | 6 | 0 | 1 | 2 | 3 | 4 | 5 | 6 |
| Slapped you |  |  |  |  |  |  |  |  |  |  |  |  |  |  |
| Hit you really hard |  |  |  |  |  |  |  |  |  |  |  |  |  |  |
| Beat you |  |  |  |  |  |  |  |  |  |  |  |  |  |  |
| Punched you |  |  |  |  |  |  |  |  |  |  |  |  |  |  |
| Kicked you |  |  |  |  |  |  |  |  |  |  |  |  |  |  |

Was the person who did this mainly your father (F), mother (M), Both (B), or Other (O)?

____ F   ____ M   ____ B   ____ O   (Please specify _____ )

III. Now I am asking some questions and would like for you to describe any *unwanted* sexual experiences you may have had with people such as strangers, friends, or family members like cousins, uncles, siblings, mother, or father. I would like you to be as open about this as you can, even though it could be a bit scary. *If you have had such experience(s), please complete the following items (A-K) for at least two of the experiences.* If you have had no such experience, check the box below.

|  | Experience #1 | Experience #2 |
|---|---|---|
| ☐ *No such experience* | | |

A. About how old were you at the time?  _____    _____

B. How many people were involved in being sexual with you? (1 = one person, 2+ = two or more people)  ☐ 1 ☐ 2+   ☐ 1 ☐ 2+

If you answered 2+ to (B), please answer C-I for the most significant person involved.

C. About how old was the other person?  _____    _____

D. Was the other person male (M) or female (F)?  ☐ M ☐ F   ☐ M ☐ F

E. Was the other person a(n) (check only one for each experience):

|  | Experience #1 | Experience #2 |
|---|---|---|
| 1. Stranger | 1. _____ | 1. _____ |
| 2. Person you knew but not a friend | 2. _____ | 2. _____ |
| 3. Friend of yours | 3. _____ | 3. _____ |
| 4. Friend of your parents | 4. _____ | 4. _____ |
| 5. Cousin | 5. _____ | 5. _____ |
| 6. Uncle or aunt | 6. _____ | 6. _____ |
| 7. Grandparent | 7. _____ | 7. _____ |
| 8. Brother or stepbrother | 8. _____ | 8. _____ |
| 9. Sister or stepsister | 9. _____ | 9. _____ |
| 10. Father | 10. _____ | 10. _____ |
| 11. Stepfather | 11. _____ | 11. _____ |
| 12. Mother | 12. _____ | 12. _____ |
| 13. Stepmother | 13. _____ | 13. _____ |
| 14. Mother's boyfriend | 14. _____ | 14. _____ |
| 15. Father's girlfriend | 15. _____ | 15. _____ |
| 16. Foster father | 16. _____ | 16. _____ |
| 17. Foster mother | 17. _____ | 17. _____ |
| 18. Other | 18. _____ | 18. _____ |

F. What happened (check all that apply):

  1. They asked you to do something sexual      1. _____   1. _____

  2. Kissing and hugging in a sexual way      2. _____   2. _____

  3. Other person showing his or her sex parts to you      3. _____   3. _____

  4. You showing your sex parts to the other person      4. _____   4. _____

  5. Other person touching you in a sexual way      5. _____   5. _____

  6. You touching the other person in a sexual way      6. _____   6. _____

  7. Other person touching your sex parts      7. _____   7. _____

  8. You touching other person's sex parts      8. _____   8. _____

  9. Attempted intercourse      9. _____   9. _____

10. Intercourse (oral, anal, or vaginal)      10. _____   10. _____

11. Insertion of an object in the vagina or anus      11. _____   11. _____


G. Did the other person(s) threaten or force you?

  1. No force      1. _____   1. _____

  2. Bribed me with candy, clothes, special privileges,      2. _____   2. _____
     and so on.

  3. Threatened to harm me or someone I cared about      3. _____   3. _____

  4. A little force      4. _____   4. _____

  5. A lot of force      5. _____   5. _____


H. About how many times did you have a sexual      _____     _____
   experience with this person?

I. Over how long a time did this go on?    _____ days    _____ days
  (Indicate the number of days, months,    _____ months   _____ months
   or years)    _____ years    _____ years

J.  Who did you tell about this experience?
    (Check all that apply)

    1. No one                          1. _____    1. _____

    2. Mother                          2. _____    2. _____

    3. Father                          3. _____    3. _____

    4. Other adult                     4. _____    4. _____

    5. Brother/sister                  5. _____    5. _____

    6. Friend                          6. _____    6. _____

    7. Male physician                  7. _____    7. _____

    8. Female physician                8. _____    8. _____

    9. Law enforcement                 9. _____    9. _____

    10. Minister                       10. _____   10. _____

    11. Counselor                      11. _____   11. _____

    12. Teacher                        12. _____   12. _____

    13. Other _____                    13. _____   13. _____

K. Did you feel emotionally supported        ☐ Yes ☐ No    ☐ Yes ☐ No
   by those you told?

# Appendix Q
## Self-Injurious Behavior Checklist

Please read the list of behaviors below. Circle all of the behaviors you have ever done to yourself. Then put a check mark next to the behaviors you have done most often. Underline your most recent behavior.

|  | | |  | | |
|---|---|---|---|---|---|
| Wrist cutting | Y | N | Overeating to the point of pain | Y | N |
| Scratching self | Y | N | Vomiting | Y | N |
| Burning skin | Y | N | Refusing to eat when hungry | Y | N |
| Nail biting | Y | N | Holding breath | Y | N |
| Hair pulling (hair/eyebrows) | Y | N | Choking self | Y | N |
| Scab picking | Y | N | Swallowing poison | Y | N |
| Head banging | Y | N | Hitting/poking self with sharp objects | Y | N |
| Biting tongue | Y | N | Picking fights | Y | N |
| Punching walls | Y | N | Excessive drinking of alcohol | Y | N |
| Unsafe driving | Y | N | | | |
| Jumping out of moving vehicle | Y | N | Taking drugs to: | | |
| Cutting skin with sharp objects (other than wrists) | Y | N | (a) hurt self | Y | N |
| Overexertion (to the point of injury or exhaustion) | Y | N | (b) get high | Y | N |
| Rubbing skin so it leaves a mark | Y | N | (c) calm down | Y | N |
| Refusing to take prescribed medication | Y | N | Other (please describe) | | |
| Exceeding prescribed medication levels | Y | N | _____ | | |
| Not getting help when in pain | Y | N | _____ | | |

## Appendix R
## Self-Injurious Behavior Interview

*Instructions.* After you feel you have established some rapport with the individual, present the list of self-injurious behaviors that is presented below. You will review these with the individual as part of your interview.

*Directions.* Present the sheet of behaviors and then ask the individual to draw a circle around all of the behaviors he or she has ever done. Then ask which behaviors were done the most frequently. Have the individual underline the most recent behavior(s).

| | | | | | |
|---|---|---|---|---|---|
| Wrist cutting | Y | N | Overeating to the point of pain | Y | N |
| Scratching self | Y | N | Vomiting | Y | N |
| Burning skin | Y | N | Refusing to eat when hungry | Y | N |
| Nail biting | Y | N | Holding breath | Y | N |
| Hair pulling (hair/eyebrows) | Y | N | Choking self | Y | N |
| Scab picking | Y | N | Swallowing poison | Y | N |
| Head banging | Y | N | Hitting/poking self with sharp objects | Y | N |
| Biting tongue | Y | N | Picking fights | Y | N |
| Punching walls | Y | N | Excessive drinking of alcohol | Y | N |
| Unsafe driving | Y | N | | | |
| Jumping out of moving vehicle | Y | N | Taking drugs to: | | |
| Cutting skin with sharp objects (other than wrists) | Y | N | (a) hurt self | Y | N |
| Overexertion (to the point of injury or exhaustion) | Y | N | (b) get high | Y | N |
| Rubbing skin so it leaves a mark | Y | N | (c) calm down | Y | N |
| Refusing to take prescribed medication | Y | N | Other (please describe) | | |
| Exceeding prescribed medication levels | Y | N | _____ | | |
| Not getting help when in pain | Y | N | _____ | | |

315

Name of Patient _____ Date _____

Age _____          Male _____ Female _____          MC# _____

1. When did you first begin doing things to yourself that were harmful or painful?

    Age in years _____

2. How often did you do any of these behaviors per month? (circle one)

| Daily | More than 1x/week | Weekly | Several times a month | Less than 1x/month |
|---|---|---|---|---|
| 1 | 2 | 3 | 4 | 5 |

3. Do you know any other people who injure themselves?

    Yes          No
    1            0

    a. How many do you know?                    _____ (number)

4. Had you heard about this behavior from someone before you started?

    Yes          No
    1            0

    a. Do you think knowing that other people do this played a role in what you do now?

    Yes          No
    1            0

5. Which pattern are you most likely to use when you hurt yourself?

| Out of the blue | Fairly continuously | Once and stop for awhile | Do it a number of times only, then stop | Other |
|---|---|---|---|---|
| 1 | 2 | 3 | 4 | 5 |

6. When you do (identify behavior), does it hurt from the moment you start?

    Yes          No
    1            0

7. Do you always feel pain?

    Yes          No
    1            0

8. Does it ever stop hurting? Do you become numb even though you may still be doing something to hurt yourself?

    Yes          No
    1            0

9. When do you usually stop?

| When I see blood | When I feel pain | When I get scared | Other |
|---|---|---|---|
| 1 | 2 | 3 | 4 |

10. Do you ever injure yourself in front of other people?

        Yes               No

         1                0

11. Can other people see where you have hurt yourself or do you keep it invisible?

| Always hidden | People can usually see it | Sometimes hidden |
|---|---|---|
| 1 | 2 | 3 |

12. Which part or parts of your body do you favor to injure yourself? (circle all mentioned)

| breasts | close to genitals | genitals | wrists | arms | legs | chest | abdomen | thighs | feet |
|---|---|---|---|---|---|---|---|---|---|
| 1 | 2 | 3 | 4 | 5 | 6 | 7 | 8 | 9 | 10 |

13. Where have you hurt yourself? (circle all mentioned)

| breasts | close to genitals | genitals | wrists | arms | legs | chest | abdomen | thighs | feet |
|---|---|---|---|---|---|---|---|---|---|
| 1 | 2 | 3 | 4 | 5 | 6 | 7 | 8 | 9 | 10 |

14. If you have ever cut or scratched yourself, do you have a favorite tool, such as a knife, to use?

        Yes     No     Use whatever is available

         1      0            2

    a. What is it? _____ (name)

15. Have you ever tried to stop your pattern of self-injurious behavior?

        Yes               No

         1                0

16. How many times have you tried to stop? _____ (number)

17. Has your use of self-injurious behavior expanded over time? For example, are you now doing more things to hurt yourself than you used to do?

        Yes               No

         1                0

18. Has your self-injurious behavior become more restricted over time? For example, did you used to do it more and now do it less?

        Yes               No

         1                0

19. Do you mainly hurt yourself when you are intoxicated, or do you typically do it when you are completely sober?

        Sober        Intoxicated        Varies

         1            2           3

20. Are you typically feeling numb when you begin to hurt yourself?

| Yes | No |
|-----|-----|
| 1 | 0 |

21. Do you tend to feel numb afterward?

| Yes | No |
|-----|-----|
| 1 | 0 |

22. Are you always aware you are doing it from the moment you start?

| Yes | No | Varies |
|-----|-----|--------|
| 1 | 0 | 2 |

23. Have you ever scratched words or symbols onto your body?

| Yes | No |
|-----|-----|
| 1 | 0 |

24. Have you ever put yourself in a life-threatening situation due to your self-injurious behavior?

| Yes | No | Unsure |
|-----|-----|--------|
| 1 | 0 | 2 |

25. Have you ever hurt yourself after remembering bad things from your past?

| Yes | No |
|-----|-----|
| 1 | 0 |

26. Do you have to do the behavior a certain number of times or a certain length of time before you let yourself stop?

| Yes | No |
|-----|-----|
| 1 | 0 |

27. Do you usually hurt yourself in pretty much the same way each time?

| Yes | No |
|-----|-----|
| 1 | 0 |

28. Do you ever plan ahead to cut yourself or is it usually a very impulsive act?

| Plan ahead | Varies | Impulsive |
|-----------|--------|-----------|
| 1 | 2 | 3 |

29. Which of the following are your predominant emotions at the time you start your self-injury? (Read them slowly and check the ones selected.)

_____ overwhelmed by feelings
_____ self-hate
_____ anger at others
_____ loneliness
_____ hopelessness
_____ emptiness
_____ suicidal
_____ numb
_____ other (describe)

30. What is your main feeling when you stop? (Read the following slowly and check the ones selected.)

_____ overwhelmed by feelings

_____ self-hate

_____ anger at others

_____ loneliness

_____ hopelessness

_____ emptiness

_____ suicidal

_____ numb

_____ physical pain

_____ other (describe)

31. What is your physical pain threshold? How much pain can you tolerate compared to other people?

| Less pain than others | The same as others | More pain than others |
|:---:|:---:|:---:|
| 1 | 2 | 3 |

32. Are there times of the day that you are more vulnerable to hurting yourself?

Yes            No

1               0

a. If so, when? _____

33. Are there certain times of the week where you are more vulnerable to hurt yourself?

Yes            No

1               0

a. If so, when? _____

34. How many total body piercings, including ears, do you have?
_____ (number)

35. Has anyone asked you to stop (identify the predominant self-injury)?

Yes            No

1               0

36. Who are they? (list)

_____

_____

_____

37. What is your emotional reaction when someone asks you to stop?

| Anger | Shame | Sadness | Loss | Misunderstood |
|---|---|---|---|---|

38. How do you feel after talking in this way about self-injury?

_____ overwhelmed by feelings
_____ self-hate
_____ anger at others
_____ loneliness
_____ hopelessness
_____ emptiness
_____ suicidal
_____ numb
_____ physical pain
_____ other

39. Has talking about it right now brought any relief?

Yes                No
1                  0

## Appendix S
### Alternate PTSD Criteria for Early Childhood
### (Scheeringa, Peebles, Cook, & Zeanah, 2001;
### Scheeringa, Zeanah, Drell, & Larrieu, 1995)

| | | |
|---|---|---|
| **Criterion A.** | **The traumatic event** | Response to the event |
| **Criterion B.** | **Reexperiencing** | Recurrent recollections<br>• not necessarily distressing<br>Increased nightmares<br>• Objective features of a flashback<br>Psychological distress from reminders<br>Physiological reactivity to reminders |
| **Criterion C.** | **Avoidance/Numbing** | Avoidance of any type of reminder<br>• Constriction of play<br>• Social withdrawal<br>Restricted affect<br>• Loss of developmental skills |
| **Criterion D.** | **Hyperarousal** | Sleep disturbance<br>Irritability, labile, temper tantrums<br>Decreased concentration<br>Hypervigilance<br>Exaggerated startle response |
| **Criterion E.** | **New fears & aggression** | • New fears<br>• New separation anxiety<br>• New aggression<br>• Not redundant with *DSM-IV* |

# References

Abidin, R. R. (1995). *Parenting Stress Inventory* (3rd ed.). Odessa, FL: Psychological Assessment Resources.

Achenbach, T. M. (1991a). *Manual for the Child Behavior Checklist/4-18 and 1991 Profile.* Burlington: University of Vermont, Department of Psychiatry.

Achenbach, T. M. (1991b). *Manual for the Teacher's Report Form and 1991 Profile.* Burlington: University of Vermont, Department of Psychiatry.

Achenbach, T. M. (1991c). *Manual for the Youth Self-Report and 1991 Profile.* Burlington: University of Vermont, Department of Psychiatry.

Achenbach, T. M., McConaughey, S. H., & Howell, C. T. (1987). Child/adolescent behavioral and emotional problems: Implications of cross-informant correlations for situational specificity. *Psychological Bulletin, 101,* 213-232.

Ainsworth, M. D. S. (1979). Infant-mother attachment. *American Psychologist, 34,* 932-937.

Ainsworth, M. D. S. (1985). Patterns of infant-mother attachment: Antecedents and effects on development. *Bulletin of the New York Academy of Medicine, 61,* 771-791.

Ainsworth, M. D. S., Blehar, M. C., Waters, E., & Wall, S. (1978). *Patterns of attachment: A psychological study of the Strange Situation.* Hillsdale, NJ: Lawrence Erlbaum.

Aldridge, M., & Wood, J. (1997). Talking about feelings: Young children's ability to express emotions. *Child Abuse & Neglect, 21,* 1221-1233.

Alexander, P. C. (1992). Application of attachment theory to the study of sexual abuse. *Journal of Consulting and Clinical Psychology, 60,* 185-195.

Allan, W. D., Kashani, J. H., & Reid, J. C. (1998). Parental hostility: Impact on the family. *Child Psychiatry and Human Development, 28,* 169-178.

323

Almqvist, K., & Brandell-Forsberg, M. (1997). Refugee children in Sweden: Post-traumatic stress disorder in Iranian children exposed to organized violence. *Child Abuse & Neglect, 21*, 351-366.

American Academy of Child and Adolescent Psychiatry. (1997). Practice parameters for the forensic evaluation of children and adolescents who may have been physically or sexually abused. *Journal of the American Academy of Child and Adolescent Psychiatry, 36*(Suppl. 10). 37S-56S.

American Academy of Child and Adolescent Psychiatry. (1998). Children and adolescents with posttraumatic stress disorder. *Journal of the American Academy of Child and Adolescent Psychiatry, 37*(Suppl. 10), 1-24.

American Professional Society on the Abuse of Children. (1990). *Guidelines for psychosocial evaluation of suspected sexual abuse in young children.* Chicago: Author.

American Psychiatric Association. (1994). *Diagnostic and statistical manual of mental disorders* (4th ed.). Washington, DC: Author.

American Psychological Association. (1992). *Ethical principles of psychologists and code of conduct.* Washington, DC: Author.

American Psychological Association. (1998). *Guidelines for psychological evaluations in child protection matters.* Washington, DC: Author.

Anastasi, A., & Urbina, S. (1996). *Psychological testing.* Englewood Cliffs, NJ: Prentice Hall.

Archer, R. (1992). *MMPI-A: Assessing adolescent psychopathology.* Hillsdale, NJ: Lawrence Erlbaum.

Armsden, G. C., & Greenberg, M. T. (1987). Inventory of Parent and Peer Attachment: Individual differences and their relationship to psychological well-being in adolescence. *Journal of Youth and Adolescence, 16*, 427-454.

Armstrong, J. (1991). The psychological organization of multiple personality disordered patients as revealed in psychological testing. *Psychiatric Clinics of North America, 14*(3), 533-546.

Armstrong, J., Putnam, F., & Carlson, E. (1993). *Adolescent-Dissociative Experiences Schedule* (Version 1.0). Unpublished test. (Available: Judith Armstrong, Suite 402, 501 Santa Monica Blvd., Santa Monica, CA 90401)

Azar, S. T. (1997). A cognitive behavioral approach to understanding and treating parents who physically abuse their children. In D. A. Wolfe, R. J. McMahon, & R. D. Peters (Eds.), *Child abuse: New directions in prevention and treatment across the lifespan.* Thousand Oaks, CA: Sage.

Azar, S. T., Lauretti, A. F., & Loding, B. V. (1998). The evaluation of parental fitness in termination of parental rights cases: A functional contextual perspective. *Clinical Child and Family Psychology Review, 1*, 77-100.

Bandura, A. (1977). *Social learning theory.* Englewood Cliffs, NJ: Prentice Hall.

Barbaree, H. E., Marshall, W. L., & Hudson, S. M. (1999). *The juvenile sexual offender.* New York: Guilford.

Barkley, R. A. (1991). *Attention-deficit hyperactivity disorder: A clinical workbook.* New York: Guilford.

Barrios, B. A., & Hartman, D. P. (1988). Fears and anxieties. In E. J. Mash & L. G. Terdal (Eds.), *Behavioral assessment of childhood disorders* (2nd ed., pp. 196-262). New York: Guilford.

Beck, A. T. (1996). *Beck Depression Inventory-II.* San Antonio, TX: Psychological Corporation.

Beeghly, M., & Cicchetti, D. (1994). Child maltreatment, attachment, and the self-system: Emergence of an internal state lexicon in toddlers at high social risk. *Development and Psychopathology, 6*, 5-30.

Beitchman, J. H., Cohen, N. J., Konstantareas, M. M., & Tannock, R. (1996). *Language, learning, and behavior disorders*. New York: Cambridge University Press.

Beitchman, J. H., Zucker, K. J., Hood, J. E., Da Costa, G. A., & Akman, D. (1991). A review of the short-term effects of child sexual abuse. *Child Abuse & Neglect, 15*, 537-556.

Beitchman, J. H., Zucker, K. J., Hood, J. E., Da Costa, G. A., Akman, D., & Cassavia, E. (1992). A review of the long-term effects of child sexual abuse. *Child Abuse & Neglect, 16*, 101-118.

Bell, N. L., & Nagle, R. J. (1999). Interpretive issues with the Roberts Apperception Test for Children: Limitations of the standardization group. *Psychology in the Schools, 36*, 277-283.

Bellak, L. (1986). *The TAT, CAT, and SAT in clinical use* (4th ed.). Orlando, FL: Grune & Stratton.

Belsky, J., Rosenberger, K., & Crnic, K. (1995). The origins of attachment security: "Classical" and contextual determinants. In S. Goldberg, R. Muir, & J. Kerr (Eds.), *Attachment theory* (pp. 153-184). Hillsdale, NJ: Analytic Press.

Bene, E., & Anthony, J. (1976). *Manual for the Family Relations Test*. Windsor, England: NFER Publishing.

Berliner, L., & Saunders, B. E. (1996). Treating fear and anxiety in sexually abused children: Results of a controlled 2-year follow-up study. *Child Maltreatment, 1*, 294-309.

Bernstein, E. M., & Putnam, F. W. (1986). Development, reliability, and validity of a dissociative scale. *Journal of Nervous and Mental Disease, 174*, 727-735.

Beutler, L. E., & Berren, M. R. (1995). *Integrative assessment of adult personality*. New York: Guilford.

Biederman, J. (1998). Resolved: Mania is mistaken for ADHD in prepubertal children, Affirmative. *Journal of the American Academy of Child and Adolescent Psychiatry, 37*, 1091-1093, 1096-1098.

Bodiford-McNeil, C., Hembree-Kigin, T. L., & Eyberg, S. M. (1996). *Short-term play therapy for disruptive children*. King of Prussia, PA: Center for Applied Psychology.

Boney-McCoy, S., & Finkelhor, D. (1995). Psychosocial sequelae of violent victimization in a national youth sample. *Journal of Consulting and Clinical Psychology, 63*, 726-736.

Bonner, B., Walker, E., & Berliner, L. (2000). *Children with sexual behavior problems*. New York: Guilford.

Borrego, J., Urquiza, A. J., Rasmussen, R. A., & Zebell, N. (1999). Parent-child interaction therapy with a family at high risk for physical abuse. *Child Maltreatment, 4*, 331-342.

Bowlby, J. (1969). *Attachment and loss: Vol. 1. Attachment*. New York: Basic Books.

Boyle, M. H., & Pickles, A. R. (1997). Influence of maternal depressive symptoms on ratings of childhood behavior. *Journal of Abnormal Child Psychology, 25*, 399-412.

Bradley, S. J. (2000). *Affect regulation and the development of psychopathology*. New York: Guilford.

Brand, E. F., King, C. A., Olson, E., Ghaziuddin, N., & Naylor, M. (1996). Depressed adolescents with a history of sexual abuse: Diagnostic comorbidity and suicidality. *Journal of the American Academy of Child and Adolescent Psychiatry, 35*, 34-41.

Braun, B. G. (1988). The BASC model of dissociation. *Dissociation, 1*, 4-23.

Bretherton, I., Fritz, J., Zahn-Waxler, C., & Ridgeway, D. (1986). Learning to talk about emotion: A functionalist perspective. *Child Development, 57*, 529-548.

Bretherton, I., Ridgeway, D., & Cassidy, J. (1990). Assessing internal working models of the attachment relationship: An attachment story completion task for 3 year olds. In M. T. Greenberg, D. Cicchetti, & E. M. Cummings (Eds.), *Attachment in the preschool years* (pp. 273-308). Chicago: University of Chicago Press.

Briere, J. (1991). *Childhood Maltreatment Interview Schedule.* Los Angeles: University of Southern California, Department of Psychiatry.

Briere, J. (1992). *Child abuse trauma: Theory and treatment of lasting effects.* Thousand Oaks, CA: Sage.

Briere, J. (1995). *Trauma Symptom Inventory.* Odessa, FL: Psychological Assessment Resources.

Briere, J. (1996). *Trauma Symptom Checklist—Children.* Odessa, FL: Psychological Assessment Resources.

Briere, J. (1997). *The psychological assessment of adult posttraumatic states.* Washington, DC: American Psychological Association.

Briere, J. (2001a). *Inventory of Altered Self-Capacities.* Odessa, FL: Psychological Assessment Resources.

Briere, J. (2001b). A self-trauma model for treating adult survivors of severe child abuse. In J. E. B. Myers, L. Berliner, J. Briere, C. T. Hendrix, C. Jenny, & R. Reid (Eds.), *The APSAC handbook on child maltreatment* (2nd ed.). Newbury Park, CA: Sage.

Briere, J., & Gil, E. (1998). Self-mutilation in clinical and general population samples: Prevalence, correlates, and functions. *American Journal of Orthopsychiatry, 68,* 609-620.

Briere, J., & Runtz, M. (1989). Trauma Symptom Checklist (TSC-33): Early data on a new scale. *Journal of Interpersonal Violence, 4,* 151-163.

Brown, L., Sherbenou, R. J., & Johnsen, S. K. (1997). *Test of Nonverbal Intelligence—3rd edition.* Austin, TX: Pro-Ed.

Brunk, M., Henggler, S. W., & Whelan, J. P. (1987). A comparison of multisystemic therapy and parent training in the brief treatment of child abuse and neglect. *Journal of Consulting and Clinical Psychology, 55,* 311-318.

Burgess, A. W., Hartman, C. R., & McCormack, A. (1987). Abused to abuser: Antecedents of socially deviant behaviors. *American Journal of Psychiatry, 144,* 1431-1436.

Burgess, R. L., & Conger, R. D. Family interaction in abusive, neglectful, and normal families. *Child Development, 49,* 1163-1173.

Burkett, L. P. (1991). Parenting behaviors of women who were sexually abused in their families of origin. *Family Process, 30,* 421-434.

Burns, R. C., & Kaufman, S. H. (1972). *Actions, styles, and symbols in Kinetic Family Drawings (K-F-D).* New York: Brunner/Mazel.

Burton, D. L. (2000). Were adolescent sexual offenders children with sexual behavior problems? *Sexual Abuse: A Journal of Research and Treatment, 12,* 37-48.

Butcher, J. N., Dahlstrom, W. G., Graham, J. R., Tellegen, A., & Kaemmer, B. (1989). *Minnesota Multiphasic Personality Inventory-2 (MMPI-2). Manual for administration and scoring.* Minneapolis: University of Minnesota Press.

Caldwell, A. B. (1997). *Forensic questions and answers on the MMPI/MMPI-2.* Los Angeles: Caldwell Report.

Calverly, R. M., Fischer, K. W., & Ayoub, C. (1994). Complex splitting of self-representations in sexually abused adolescent girls. *Development and Psychopathology, 6,* 195-213.

Campbell, J. M. (1998). Internal and external validity of seven Wechsler Intelligence Scales for Children—Third edition short forms in a sample of psychiatric inpatients. *Psychological Assessment, 10*, 431-434.

Carlson, E. (1997). *Trauma assessments*. New York: Guilford.

Carlson, E. A., Jacobvitz, D., & Sroufe, L. A. (1995). A developmental investigation of inattentiveness and hyperactivity. *Child Development, 66*, 37-54.

Carlson, V., Cicchetti, D., Barnett, D., & Braunwald, K. (1989). Disorganized/disoriented attachment relationships in maltreated infants. *Developmental Psychology, 25*, 525-531.

Carnes, C. N., Wilson, C., & Nelson-Gardell, D. (1999). Extended forensic evaluation when sexual abuse is suspected: A model and preliminary data. *Child Maltreatment, 4*, 242-254.

Caruso, K. R. (1987). *Basic manual (version 1): Projective storytelling cards*. Redding, CA: Northwest Psychological Publishers.

Cassidy, J., & Shaver, P. R. (1999). *Handbook of attachment*. New York: Guilford.

Cattell, R., Eber, H., & Tatsuoka, M. (1970). *Handbook for the Sixteen Personality Factors Questionnaire*. Champaign, IL: IPAT.

Ceci, S. J., & Bruck, M. (1993). Suggestibility of the child witness: A historical review and synthesis. *Psychological Bulletin, 113*, 403-439.

Ceci, S. J., & Hembrooke, H. (Eds.). (1998). *Expert witnesses in child abuse cases*. Washington, DC: American Psychological Association.

Chaffin, M., & Bonner, B. (1998). "Don't shoot, we're your children": Have we gone too far in our response to adolescent sexual abusers and children with sexual behavior problems? *Child Maltreatment, 3*, 314-316.

Chaffin, M., & Friedrich, W. N. (2000, November). *Developmental-systemic perspectives on children with sexual behavior problems*. Keynote presented at the annual meeting of the Association for the Treatment of Sexual Aggression, San Diego, CA.

Chantler, L., Pelco, L., & Mertin, P. (1993). Psychological evaluation of child sexual abuse using the Louisville Behavior Checklist and Human Figure Drawing. *Child Abuse & Neglect, 17*, 271-279.

Cicchetti, D. (1989). How research on child maltreatment has informed the study of child development: Perspectives from developmental psychopathology. In D. Cicchetti & V. Carlson (Eds.), *Child maltreatment* (pp. 377-431). Cambridge, UK: Cambridge University Press.

Cicchetti, D., & Olsen, K. (1990). The developmental psychopathology of child maltreatment. In M. Lewis & S. M. Miller (Eds.), *Handbook of developmental psychopathology* (pp. 261-279). New York: Plenum.

Cicchetti, D., & Rogosch, F. A. (1997). The role of self-organization in the promotion of resilience in maltreated children. *Development and Psychopathology, 9*, 797-816.

Cicchetti, D., & Toth, S. L. (1995). A developmental psychopathology perspective on child abuse and neglect. *Journal of the American Academy of Child and Adolescent Psychiatry, 34*, 541-565.

Cohen, J. A., & Mannarino, A. P. (1988). Psychological symptoms in sexually abused girls. *Child Abuse & Neglect, 12*, 571-577.

Cohen, J. A., & Mannarino, A. P. (1996). The Weekly Behavior Report: A parent-report instrument for sexually abused preschoolers. *Child Maltreatment, 1*, 353-360.

Cohen, J. B., Deblinger, E., Maedel, A. B., & Stauffer, L. B. (1999). Examining sex-related thoughts and feelings of sexually abused and nonabused children. *Journal of Interpersonal Violence, 14*, 701-712.

Cohen, N. J., Barwick, M. A., Horodezky, N., & Isaacson, L. (1996). Comorbidity of language and social-emotional disorders: Comparison of psychiatric outpatients and their siblings. *Journal of Clinical Child Psychology, 25,* 192-200.

Colligan, R. C., Davis, L. J., & Morse, R. M. (1988). *The Self-Administered Alcoholism Screening Test (SAAST): A user's guide.* Rochester, MN: Mayo Foundation.

Costa, P., & Widiger, T. (1994). *Personality disorders and the 5 factor model of personality.* Washington, DC: APA.

Crittenden, P. M. (1994). Peering into the black box: An exploratory treatise on the development of the self in young children. In D. Cicchetti & S. L. Toth (Eds.), *Disorders and dysfunctions of the self* (pp. 79-148). Rochester, NY: University of Rochester Press.

Crittenden, P. M. (1995). Attachment and psychopathology. In S. Goldberg, R. Muir, & J. Kerr (Eds.), *Attachment theory: Social, developmental and clinical perspectives* (pp. 367-406). Hillsdale, NJ: Analytic Press.

Crittenden, P. M., & DiLalla, D. (1988). Compulsive compliance: The development of an inhibitory coping strategy in infancy. *Journal of Abnormal Child Psychology, 16,* 585-599.

Crnic, K. A., & Greenberg, M. T. (1990). Minor parenting stresses with young children. *Child Development, 61,* 1628-1637.

Crouch, J. L., Smith, D. W., Ezzell, C. E., & Saunders, B. E. (1999). Measuring reactions to sexual trauma among children: Comparing the Children's Impact of Traumatic Events Scale and the Trauma Symptom Checklist for Children. *Child Maltreatment, 4,* 255-263.

Crowell, J., Feldman, S., & Ginsburg, N. (1988). Assessment of mother-child interaction in preschoolers with behavioral problems. *Journal of the American Academy of Child and Adolescent Psychiatry, 27,* 303-311.

Cull, J. G., & Gill, W. S. (1982). *Suicide Potential Scale.* Los Angeles: Western Psychological Services.

Dale, G., Kendall, J. C., Humber, K. I., & Sheehan, L. (1999). Screening young foster children for posttraumatic stress disorder and responding to their needs for treatment. *APSAC Advisor, 12*(2), 6-9.

Dancu, C. V., Riggs, D. S., Rothbaum, B. O., & Foa, E. B. (1991, November). *A clinician-administered vs. self-report instrument to measure post-traumatic stress symptoms: The PTSD Symptom Scale.* Paper presented at the 25th Annual Convention of the Association for the Advancement of Behavior Therapy, New York.

Dansky, B. S., Brewerton, T. D., Kilpatrick, D. G., & O'Neil, P. M. (1997). The National Women's Study: Relationship of victimization and posttraumatic stress disorder to bulimia nervosa. *International Journal of Eating Disorders, 21,* 213-228.

Daro, D. (1988). *Confronting child abuse.* New York: Free Press.

Davidson, J. R. T., Smith, R. D., & Kudler, H. S. (1989). Validity and reliability of the DSM-III criteria for posttraumatic stress disorder: Experience with a structured interview. *Journal of Nervous and Mental Disease, 177,* 336-341.

Deblinger, E., & Hefflin, A. H. (1996). *Treating sexually abused children and their nonoffending parents.* Thousand Oaks, CA: Sage.

Deblinger, E., Lippman, J. T., & Steer, R. (1996). Sexually abused children suffering post-traumatic stress symptoms: Initial treatment outcome findings. *Child Maltreatment, 1,* 310-321.

Dembo, R., Williams, L., LaVoie, L., Barry, E., Getreu, A., Wish, E., Schmeider, J., & Washburn, M. (1989). Physical abuse, sexual victimization, and illicit drug use: Replication of a structural analysis among a new sample of high-risk youths. *Violence and Victims, 4,* 121-138.

Derogatis, L. R. (1983). *SCL-90-R: Administration scoring and procedures manual-II for the revised version and other instruments of the psychopathology rating scale series.* Baltimore, MD: Clinical Psychometrics Research.

Dishion, T. J., & McMahon, R. J. (1998). Parental monitoring and the prevention of child and adolescent problem behavior: A conceptual and empirical formulation. *Clinical Child and Family Psychology Review, 1,* 61-75.

Dodge, K. A., Pettitt, G. S., McClaskey, C. L., & Brown, M. M. (1986). Social competence in children. *Monographs of the Society for Research in Child Development,* 51(2, Serial No. 213).

Down, W. R. (1993). Developmental considerations for the effects of childhood sexual abuse. *Journal of Interpersonal Violence, 8,* 331-345.

Drach, K. M. (1998). *Evaluating parenting competence.* Workshop presented at APSAC National Colloquium, July, Chicago.

Dyer, F. J. (1997). Applications of the Millon Inventories in Forensic Psychology. In T. Millon (Ed.), *The Millon Inventories: Clinical and personality assessment* (pp. 124-139). New York: Guilford.

Eckenrode, J., Laird, M., & Doris, J. (1993). School performance and disciplinary problems among abused and neglected children. *Developmental Psychology, 29,* 53-62.

Edelbrock, C., Costello, A. J., Dulcan, M., Kalas, R., & Conover, N. C. (1985). Age differences in the reliability of the psychiatric interview of the child. *Child Development, 56,* 265-275.

Edelbrock, C. S. (1991). Children's Attention Profile. In R. A. Barkley (Ed.), *Attention-deficit hyperactivity disorder: A clinical workbook* (pp. 50-51). New York: Guilford.

Egeland, B., & Erickson, M. F. (1987). Psychologically unavailable caregiving. In M. Brassard, B. Germain, & S. Hart (Eds.), *New directions for child development: Developmental perspectives in child maltreatment.* San Francisco: Jossey-Bass.

Egeland, B., Jacobvitz, D., & Sroufe, L. A. (1988). Breaking the cycle of abuse: Relationship predictors. *Child Development, 59,* 1080-1088.

Egeland, B., Sroufe, L. A., & Erickson, M. F. (1983). Developmental consequence of different patterns of maltreatment. *Child Abuse & Neglect, 7,* 459-469.

Einbender, A. J., & Friedrich, W. N. (1989). Psychological functioning and behavior of sexually abused girls. *Journal of Consulting and Clinical Psychology, 57,* 155-157.

Eisman, E. J., Dies, R. R., Finn, S. E., Eyde, L. D., Kay, G. G., Kubiszyn, T. W., Meyer, G. J., & Moreland, K. L. (2000). Problems and limitations in using psychological assessment in the contemporary health care delivery system. *Professional Psychology—Research & Practice, 31,* 131-140.

Elkind, D. (1967). Egocentrism in adolescence. *Child Development, 38,* 1025-1034.

Elkind, D. (1985). Egocentrism redux. *Developmental Review, 5,* 218-226.

Elliott, D. M. (1994). Impaired object relations in professional women molested as children. *Psychotherapy, 31,* 79-86.

Elliott, D. M., & Briere, J. (1994). Forensic sexual abuse evaluations of older children: Disclosures and symptomatology. *Behavioral Sciences and the Law, 12,* 261-277.

Elliott, D. M., Kim, S., & Mull, S. (1997). *Impact of pornography on sexually abused and unabused children.* Paper presented at the annual meeting of the American Psychological Association, Chicago.

Erickson, M. F., & Egeland, B. (1987). A developmental view of the psychological consequences of maltreatment. *School Psychology Review, 16,* 156-168.

Erickson, M. F., Sroufe, L. A., & Egeland, B. (1985). The relationship between quality of attachment and behavior problems in preschool in a high-risk sample. In I. Bretherton & E. Waters (Eds.), *Monographs of the Society for Research in Child Development, 50*(1-2), 147-166.

Everson, M. D., Hunter, W. M., Runyon, D. K., Edelsohn, G. A., & Coulter, M. L. (1989). Maternal support following disclosure of incest. *American Journal of Orthopsychiatry, 59*, 197-207.

Exner, J. E. (1991). *The Rorschach: A comprehensive system: Vol. 2. Interpretation* (2nd ed.). New York: John Wiley.

Faller, K. C. (1996). *Evaluating children suspected of having been sexually abused.* Thousand Oaks, CA: Sage.

Famularo, R., Fenton, T., Augustyn, M., & Zuckerman, B. (1996). Persistence of pediatric post traumatic stress after two years. *Child Abuse & Neglect, 20,* 1245-1248.

Famularo, R., Fenton, T., Kinscherff, R., Ayoub, C., & Barnum, R. (1994). Maternal and child post-traumatic stress disorder in cases of child maltreatment. *Child Abuse & Neglect, 18,* 27-36.

Farmer, E., & Pollock, S. (1998). *Sexually abused and abusing children in substitute care.* New York: John Wiley.

Feiring, C., Taska, L., & Lewis, M. (1998). The role of shame and attributional style in children's and adolescents' adaptation to sexual abuse. *Child Maltreatment, 3,* 129-142.

Fergusson, D. M., Horwood, L. J., & Lynskey, M. T. (1997). Childhood sexual abuse, adolescent sexual behaviors, and sexual revictimization. *Child Abuse & Neglect, 21,* 789-803.

Fergusson, D. M., & Mullen, P. E. (1999). *Childhood sexual abuse.* Sage: Thousand Oaks, CA.

Finch, A. J., Nelson, W. M., & Ott, E. S. (1993). *Cognitive-behavioral procedures with children and adolescents.* Boston: Allyn & Bacon.

Finkelhor, D. (1995). The victimization of children: A developmental perspective. *American Journal of Orthopsychiatry, 65,* 176-193.

Finkelhor, D., & Browne, A. (1985). The traumatic impact of child sexual abuse: A conceptualization. *American Journal of Orthopsychiatry, 55,* 530-541.

Fischer, K. W., Ayoub, C., Singh, I., Noam, G., Maraganore, A., & Raya, P. (1997). Psychopathology as adaptive development along distinctive pathways. *Development and Psychopathology, 9,* 749-780.

Fisher, J. L., & Friedrich, W. N. (2001). *Maltreatment and somatic symptoms in children.* Manuscript under review.

Fletcher, K. E. (1996, November). *Measuring school-aged children's PTSD: Preliminary psychometrics of four new measures.* Paper presented at the Twelfth Annual Meeting of the International Society for Traumatic Stress Studies, San Francisco.

Foa, E. B. (1995). *Posttraumatic Stress Diagnostic Scale.* Minneapolis, MN: National Computer Systems.

Fonagy, P. (1998). An attachment theory approach to treatment of the difficult patient. *Bulletin of the Menninger Clinic, 62,* 147-169.

Fonagy, P., & Target, M. (1997). Attachment and reflective function: Their role in self-organization. *Development and Psychopathology, 9,* 679-700.

Ford, J., Racusin, R., Ellis, C. G., Daviss, W. B., Reiser, J., Fleischer, A., & Thomas, J. (2000). Child maltreatment, other trauma exposure, and postraumatic symptomatology among children with oppositional defiant and attention deficit hyperactivity disorders. *Child Maltreatment, 5,* 205-218.

Foy, D. W., Madoig, B. T., Pynoos, R. S., & Camilleri, A. J. (1996). Etiologic factors in the development of posttraumatic stress disorder in children and adolescents. *Journal of School Psychology, 34,* 133-145.

Fraiberg, S., Adelson, E., & Shapiro, V. (1975). Ghosts in the nursery: A psychoanalytic approach to the problems of impaired infant-mother relationships. *Journal of the American Academy of Child Psychiatry, 14,* 387-421.

Freud, A. (1966). *The ego and the mechanisms of defense.* New York: International Universities Press.

Friedrich, W. N. (1988a). Behavioral problems in sexually abused children: An adaptational perspective. In G. E. Wyatt & G. J. Powell (Eds.), *Lasting effects of child sexual abuse* (pp. 171-191). Beverly Hills, CA: Sage.

Friedrich, W. N. (1988b). Child abuse and sexual abuse. In R. L. Greene (Ed.), *The MMPI: Use with specific populations.* Philadelphia: Grune & Stratton.

Friedrich, W. N. (1990). *Psychotherapy with sexually abused children and their families.* New York: Norton.

Friedrich, W. N. (1991a). *Casebook of sexual abuse treatment.* New York: Norton.

Friedrich, W. N. (1991b). Mothers of sexually abused children: An MMPI study. *Journal of Clinical Psychology, 47,* 778-783.

Friedrich, W. N. (1994). Assessing children for the effects of sexual victimization. In J. Briere (Ed.), Assessing and treating victims of violence [Special issue]. *New Directions for Mental Health Services, 64,* 17-28.

Friedrich, W. N. (1995a). *Psychotherapy with sexually abused boys.* Thousand Oaks, CA: Sage.

Friedrich, W. N. (1995b). Review of Children speak for themselves, by C. Haynes-Seman & D. Baumgartner. *ASPAC Advisor, 8*(8), 7-8.

Friedrich, W. N. (1996a). *Adolescent Sexual Behavior Inventory: Parent and Teen Reports.* Unpublished test. (Available: W. N. Friedrich, Mayo Clinic, Rochester, Minnesota 55905)

Friedrich, W. N. (1996b). An integrated model of psychotherapy for abused children. In J. Briere, L. Berliner, et al. (Eds.), *The APSAC handbook on child maltreatment* (pp. 104-118). Thousand Oaks, CA: Sage.

Friedrich, W. N. (1996c). *Safety Checklist.* Unpublished test. (Available: W. N. Friedrich, Mayo Clinic, Rochester, Minnesota 55905)

Friedrich, W. N. (1997). *Child Sexual Behavior Inventory.* Odessa, FL: Psychological Assessment Resources.

Friedrich, W. N. (1998). Behavioral manifestations of child sexual abuse. *Child Abuse & Neglect, 22,* 523-532.

Friedrich, W. N., Ascione, F. R., Heath, J., & Hayashi, K. (2001). *Cruelty to animals in normative, sexually abused, and outpatient psychiatric samples of 6-12 year old children.* Manuscript in preparation.

Friedrich, W. N., Berliner, L., Urquiza, A. J., & Beilke, R. L. (1988). Brief diagnostic group treatment of sexually abused boys. *Journal of Interpersonal Violence, 3,* 331-343.

Friedrich, W. N., Drach, K., & Wright, J. (2001). *Predictors of sexually aggressive behavior in children.* Manuscript in preparation.

Friedrich, W. N., Einbender, A. J., & Luecke, W. J. (1983). Cognitive and behavioral characteristics of physically abused children. *Journal of Consulting and Clinical Psychology, 51,* 313-314.

Friedrich, W. N., Einbender, A. J., & McCarty, P. (1999). Sexually abused girls and their Rorschach responses. *Psychological Reports, 85,* 355-362.

Friedrich, W. N., Fisher, J., Broughton, D., Houston, M., & Shafran, C. R. (1998). Normative sexual behavior in children: A contemporary sample. *Pediatrics, 101,* 1-9.

Friedrich, W. N., Fisher, J., Dittner, C., Acton, R., Berliner, L., Butler, J., Damon, L., Davies, W. H., Gray, A., & Wright, J. (2001). Child Sexual Behavior Inventory: Normative, psychiatric and sexual abuse comparisons. *Child Maltreatment, 6,* 37-49.

Friedrich, W. N., Gerber, P. N., Koplin, B., Davis, M., Giese, J., Mykelbust, C., & Franckowiak, D. (2001). Multimodal assessment of dissociation in adolescents: Inpatients and sex offenders. *Sexual Abuse, 13,* 19-29.

Friedrich, W. N., Grambsch, P., Broughton, D., Kuiper, J., & Beilke, R. L. (1991). Normative sexual behavior in children. *Pediatrics, 88,* 456-466.

Friedrich, W. N., Grambsch, P., Damon, L., Hewitt, S., Koverola, C., Lang, R., Wolfe, V., & Broughton, D. (1992). The Child Sexual Behavior Inventory: Normative and clinical contrasts. *Psychological Assessment, 4,* 303-311.

Friedrich, W. N., Jaworski, T. M., Huxsahl, J., & Bengston, B. (1997). Dissociative and sexual behaviors in children and adolescents with sexual abuse and psychiatric histories. *Journal of Interpersonal Violence, 12,* 155-171.

Friedrich, W. N., & Luecke, W. J. (1988). Young school-age sexually aggressive children. *Professional Psychology, 19,* 155-164.

Friedrich, W. N., Luecke, W. J., Beilke, R. L., & Place, V. (1991). Psychotherapy outcome of sexually abused boys: An agency study. *Journal of Interpersonal Violence, 7,* 396-409.

Friedrich, W. N., & Lui, B. (2001). *Behavior of sexually abused children during intake evaluations: Boundary problems and sexual comments.* Manuscript in preparation.

Friedrich, W. N., Lysne, M., Shamos, S., & Kolko, D. (2001). *The Adolescent Sexual Behavior Inventory: Reliability and validity.* Manuscript under review.

Friedrich, W. N., & Reams, R. A. (1986). *Parentification of Children Scale.* Unpublished manuscript. (Available: W. N. Friedrich, Mayo Clinic, Rochester, Minnesota 55905)

Friedrich, W. N., & Schafer, L. C. (1995). Somatic complaints in sexually abused children. *Journal of Pediatric Psychology, 20,* 661-670.

Friedrich, W. N., & Share, M. C. (1997). The Roberts Apperception Test for Children: An exploratory study of its use with sexually abused children. *Journal of Child Sexual Abuse, 6,* 83-91.

Friedrich, W. N., Lengua, L., Trane, S., Fisher, J., Davies, W. H., Pithers, W., & Trentham, B. (2001). *Parent report of PTSD and dissociation symptoms: Normative, psychiatric, and sexual abuse comparisons.* Manuscript under review.

Friedrich, W. N., Trane, S., & Wright, J. (2001). *Factor analysis of sexual behavior in children.* Manuscript in preparation.

Fury, G., Carlson, E., & Sroufe, L. A. (1997). Children's representation of attachment relations in family drawings. *Child Development, 68,* 1154-1164.

Garb, H. N., Wood, J. M., & Nezworski, M. T. (2000). Projective techniques and the detection of sexual abuse. *Child Maltreatment, 5,* 161-168.

Garbarino, J. (1999). *Lost boys.* New York: Free Press.

Garner, D. M. (1991). *The Eating Disorder Inventory-2 Professional Manual.* Odessa, FL: Psychological Assessment Resources.

Gelinas, D. J. (1983). The persisting negative effects of incest. *Psychiatry, 46,* 312-332.

Gelles, R. J., & Straus, M. A. (1988). *Intimate violence.* New York: Simon & Schuster.

Gil, E., & Johnson, T. C. (1993). *Sexualized children.* Rockville, MD: Launch Press.

George, C., Kaplan, N., & Main, M. (1985). *Adult Attachment Interview.* Unpublished manuscript, University of California, Berkeley.

Goldberg, S. (1995). Introduction. In S. Goldberg, R. Muir, & J. Kerr (Eds.), *Attachment theory* (pp. 1-15). Hillsdale, NJ: Analytic Press.

Goodman, R. (1997). The Strengths and Difficulties Questionnaire: A research note. *Journal of Child Psychology and Psychiatry, 38*, 581-586.

Goodman, R., & Scott, S. (1999). Comparing the Strengths and Difficulties Questionnaire and the Child Behavior Checklist: Is small beautiful? *Journal of Abnormal Child Psychology, 27*, 17-24.

Goyette, C. H., Conners, C. K., & Ulrich, R. F. (1978). Normative data on the revised Conners Parent and Teacher Rating Scales. *Journal of Abnormal Child Psychology, 6*, 221-236.

Gray, A., Busconi, A., Houchens, P., & Pithers, W. D. (1997). Children with sexual behavior problems and their caregivers: Demographics, functioning, and clinical patterns. *Sexual Abuse, 9*, 267-290.

Green, A. H. (1985). Children traumatized by physical abuse. In S. Eth & R. S. Pynoos (Eds.), *Posttraumatic stress disorder in children* (pp. 207-212). Washington, DC: American Psychiatric Press.

Greenberg, M. T., Speltz, M. L., & DeKleyen, M. (1993). The role of attachment in the early development of disruptive behavior problems. *Development and Psychopathology, 5*, 191-213.

Gully, K. J. (in press). Initial development of the Expectations Test for Children: A tool to investigate social information processing. *Journal of Clinical Psychology*.

Haley, J. (1987). *Problem solving therapy*. San Francisco: Jossey-Bass.

Hall, D. K. (1993). *Assessing child trauma*. Toronto: Institute for the Prevention of Child Abuse.

Hall, D. K., & Mathews, F. (1996). *The development of sexual behavior problems in children and youth*. Toronto: Central Toronto Youth Services.

Hall, D. K., Mathews, F., & Pearce, J. (1998). Factors associated with sexual behavior problems in young sexually abused children. *Child Abuse & Neglect, 22*, 1045-1063.

Hall, G. C. N. (1996). *Theory-based assessment, treatment, and prevention of sexual aggression*. New York: Oxford University Press.

Hare, R. D. (1991). *The Hare Psychopathy Checklist—Revised: Manual*. Toronto: Multi-Health Systems.

Hare, R. D., & Herve, H. F. (1999). *Hare P-SCAN*. North Tonawanda, NY: Multi-Health Systems.

Harter, S. (1982). The Perceived Competence Scale for Children. *Child Development, 53*, 87-97.

Harter, S. (1983). Developmental perspectives on the self-system. In E. M. Hetherington (Ed.), *Handbook of child psychology: Socialization, personality, and social development* (4th ed., pp. 275-386). New York: Wiley.

Harter, S. (1990). Issues in the assessment of the self-concept of children and adolescents. In A. M. LaGreca (Ed.), *Through the eyes of the child: Obtaining self-reports from children and adolescents* (pp. 292-325). Boston: Allyn & Bacon.

Haynes-Seman, C., & Baumgarten, D. (1994). *Children speak for themselves*. New York: Brunner/Mazel.

Hazan, C., & Shaver, P. (1987). Romantic love conceptualized as an attachment process. *Journal of Personality and Social Psychology, 52*, 511-524.

Hembree-Kigin, T. L., & McNeil, C. B. (1995). *Parent-child interaction therapy*. New York: Plenum.

Henderson, O. (1990). The object relations of sexually abused girls. *Melanie Klein and Object Relations, 8*, 63-76.

Hewitt, S. K. (1999). *Assessing allegations of sexual abuse in preschool children.* Thousand Oaks, CA: Sage.

Hewitt, S. K., & Friedrich, W. N. (1991). Effects of probable sexual abuse on preschool children: In M. Q. Patton (Ed.), *Family sexual abuse: Front line research and evaluation* (pp. 57-74). Thousand Oaks, CA: Sage.

Hinshaw, S. P. (1994). *Attention deficits and hyperactivity in children.* Thousand Oaks, CA: Sage.

Hodges, K. (1995). *Child and Adolescent Functional Assessment Scale (CAFAS).* Ann Arbor, MI: Author.

Holland, T. R., Beckett, G. E., & Levi, M. (1981). Intelligence, personality, and criminal violence: A multivariate analysis. *Journal of Consulting & Clinical Psychology, 49*, 106-111.

Horn, J. L., & Dollinger, S. J. (1995). Sleep disturbances in children. In M. C. Roberts (Ed.), *Handbook of pediatric psychology* (2nd ed., pp. 575-588). New York: Guilford.

Horner, T. M., Guyer, M. J., & Kalter, N. M. (1993). Clinical expertise and the assessment of child sexual abuse. *Journal of the American Academy of Child and Adolescent Psychiatry, 32*, 925-933.

Hussey, D. L., & Singer, M. I. (1989). Innovations in the assessment and treatment of sexually abused adolescents: An inpatient model. In S. Sgroi (Ed.), *Vulnerable populations* (Vol. 2, pp. 43-64). Lexington, MA: Lexington Books.

Hussey, D. L., Strom, G., & Singer, M. I. (1992). Male victims of sexual abuse: An analysis of adolescent psychiatric inpatients. *Child and Adolescent Social Work Journal, 9*, 491-503.

Ireton, H. (1992). *Child Development Inventory: Professional manual.* Minneapolis, MN: Behavior Science Systems.

Jacobvitz, D., & Sroufe, L. A. (1987). The early caregiver-child relationship and attention-deficit disorder with hyperactivity in kindergarten: A prospective study. *Child Development, 58*, 1488-1495.

James, B. (1994). *Handbook for treatment of attachment-trauma problems in children.* Lexington, MA: Lexington Books.

Johnson, J. H. (1986). *Life events as stressors in childhood and adolescence.* Thousand Oaks, CA: Sage.

Johnson, S. M. (1985). *Characterological transformation.* New York: Norton.

Johnson, T. C. (1988). Child perpetrators: Children who molest other children: Preliminary findings. *Child Abuse & Neglect, 12*, 219-229.

Johnson, T. C. (1989). Female child perpetrators: Children who molest other children. *Child Abuse & Neglect, 13*, 571-585.

Jones, D. P. H. (1987). Untreatable families. *Child Abuse & Neglect, 11*, 409-420.

Jones, L., & Finkelhor, D. (2000). *The decline in sexual abuse cases.* Paper presented at the Office of Juvenile Justice and Delinquency Prevention, November 3, 2000, Rockville, MD.

Kaplan, S., Pelcovitz, D., Salzinger, S., Mandel, F., & Weiner, M. (1997). Adolescent physical abuse and suicide attempts. *Journal of the American Academy of Child and Adolescent Psychiatry, 36*, 799-808.

Kaufman, A. S., & Kaufman, N. L. (1990). *Kaufman Brief Intelligence Test: Manual.* Circle Pines, MN: American Guidance Service.

Kazdin, A. E. (1990). Assessment of childhood depression. In A. M. LaGreca (Ed.), *Through the eyes of the child: Obtaining self-reports from children and adolescents*. Boston: Allyn & Bacon.

Kegan, R. (1982). *The evolving self*. Cambridge, MA: Harvard University Press.

Kelly, F. D. (1999). *The psychological assessment of abused and traumatized children*. Hillsdale, NJ: Lawrence Erlbaum.

Kendall-Tackett, K., Williams, L. M., & Finkelhor, D. (1993). Impact of sexual abuse on children: A review and synthesis of recent empirical studies. *Psychological Bulletin, 113*, 164-180.

Kihlstrom, J. F., Glisky, M. F., & Anguilo, M. J. (1994). Dissociative tendencies and dissociative disorders. *Journal of Abnormal Psychology, 103*, 117-124.

Kolko, D. J. (1996). Individual cognitive behavioral treatment and family therapy for physically abused children and their offending parents: A comparison of clinical outcomes. *Child Maltreatment, 1*, 322-342.

Koppitz, E. (1968). *Psychological evaluation of children's human figure drawings*. New York: Grune & Stratton.

Kovacs, M. (1991). *Child Depression Inventory*. North Tonawanda, NY: Multihealth Systems.

LaGreca, A. M. (Ed.). (1990). *Through the eyes of the child: Obtaining self-reports from children and adolescents*. Boston: Allyn & Bacon.

Leifer, M., Shapiro, J. P., & Kassem, J. (1993). The impact of maternal history and behavior upon foster placement and adjustment in sexually abused children. *Child Abuse & Neglect, 17*, 755-766.

Levin, P., & Reis, B. (1997). Use of the Rorschach in assessing trauma. In J. P. Wilson & T. M. Keane (Eds.), *Assessing psychological trauma and PTSD* (pp. 529-543). New York: Guilford.

Liotti, G. (1995). Disorganized/disoriented attachment in the psychotherapy of the dissociative disorders. In S. Goldberg, R. Muir, & J. Kerr (Eds.), *Attachment theory: Social, developmental and clinical perspectives* (pp. 343-363). Hillsdale, NJ: Analytic Press.

Locke, H. J., & Wallace, H. M. (1959). Short marital adjustment and prediction tests: Their reliability and validity. *Marriage and Family Living, 21*, 251-255.

Loevinger, J., & Wessler, R. (1970). *Measuring ego development: Vol. 1. Construction and use of a sentence completion test*. San Francisco: Jossey-Bass.

Loney, J., & Milich, R. (1982). Hyperactivity, inattention, and aggression in clinical practice. In M. Wolraich & D. Routh (Eds.), *Advances in behavioral pediatrics* (Vol. 2, pp. 113-147). Greenwich, CT: JAI.

Lyon, T. D., & Koehler, J. J. (1998). Where researchers fear to tread: Interpretive differences among testifying experts in child sexual abuse cases. In S. J. Ceci & H. Hembrooke (Eds.), *Expert witnesses in child abuse cases* (pp. 249-263). Washington, DC: American Psychological Association.

Maddock, J. W. (1990). *Family Events List*. Unpublished test, Department of Family Social Science, University of Minnesota.

Main, M. (1995). Recent studies in attachment. In S. Goldberg, R. Muir, & J. Kerr (Eds.), *Attachment theory: Social, developmental and clinical perspectives* (pp. 407-474). Hillsdale, NJ: Analytic Press.

Main, M., & Hesse, E. (1990). Parents' unresolved traumatic experiences are related to infant disorganized attachment status: Is frightened and/or frightening parental behavior the linking mechanism? In M. T. Greenberg, D. Cicchetti, & E. M. Cummings

(Eds.), *Attachment in the preschool years* (pp. 161-182). Chicago: University of Chicago Press.

Malchiodi, C. A. (1998). *Understanding children's drawings*. New York: Guilford.

Mandell, J. G., & Damon, L. (1989). *Group treatment for sexually abused children*. New York: Guilford.

Mannarino, A. P., & Cohen, J. A. (1996). Family related variables and psychological symptoms found in sexually abused girls. *Journal of Child Sexual Abuse, 5*, 105-120.

Mannarino, A. P., Cohen, J. A., & Berman, S. R. (1994). The Children's Attributions and Perceptions Scale: A new measure of sexual abuse related factors. *Journal of Clinical Child Psychology, 23*, 204-211.

Marshall, W. L., & Barbaree, H. E. (1990). Outcome of comprehensive cognitive-behavioral treatment programs. In W. L. Marshall, D. R. Laws, & H. E. Barbaree (Eds.), *Handbook of sexual assault* (pp. 363-385). New York: Plenum.

Mash, E. J., Johnston, C., & Kovitz, K. (1983). A comparison of the mother-child interactions of physically abused and nonabused children during play and task situations. *Journal of Clinical Child Psychology, 12*, 337-346.

Mash, E. J., & Terdal, L. (1988). *Behavioral assessment of childhood disorders* (2nd ed.). New York: Guilford.

Mash, E. J., Terdal, L., & Anderson, K. (1981). The Response-Class Matrix: A procedure for recording parent-child interactions. In R. A. Barkley (Ed.), *Hyperactive children: A handbook for diagnosis and treatment* (pp. 419-436). New York: Guilford.

Maughan, B., & Pickles, A. (1990). Adopted and illegitimate children grown up. In L. N. Robins & M. Rutter (Eds.), *Straight and devious pathways from childhood to adulthood* (pp. 36-61). New York: Cambridge University Press.

McArthur, D. S., & Roberts, G. E. (1982). *Roberts Apperception Test for Children*. Los Angeles: Western Psychological Services.

McCann, J. T. (1999). *Assessing adolescents with the MACI*. New York: John Wiley.

McCann, J. T., & Dyer, F. J. (1996). *Forensic assessment with the Millon Inventories*. New York: Guilford.

McGee, R. A., Wolfe, D. A., & Wilson, S. K. (1997). Multiple maltreatment experiences and adolescent behavior problems: Adolescents' perspectives. *Development and Psychopathology, 9*, 131-149.

McLeer, S. V., Deblinger, E., Henry, D., & Orvaschel, H. C. (1992). Sexually abused children at high risk for posttraumatic stress disorder. *Journal of the American Academy of Child and Adolescent Psychiatry, 31*, 875-879.

McMahon, R. J., & Forehand, R. (1988). Conduct disorder. In E. J. Mash & L. G. Terdal (Eds.), *Behavioral assessment of childhood disorders* (2nd ed., pp. 105-153). New York: Guilford.

Meehl, P. E. (1954). *Clinical versus statistical prediction*. Minneapolis: University of Minnesota Press.

Meiselman, K. C. (1980). Personality characteristics with incest history psychotherapy patients: A research note. *Archives of Sexual Behavior, 9*, 195-197.

Meloy, R., & Lewak, R. (1998, January). *The MMPI-2 and Rorschach in court*. Workshop sponsored by the American Academy of Forensic Psychology, Palm Springs, CA.

Melton, G. B., & Limber, S. (1989). Psychologists' involvement in cases of child maltreatment. *American Psychologist, 44*, 1225-1233.

Melton, G. B., Petrila, J., Poythress, N. G., & Slobogin, C. (1987). *Psychological evaluations for the courts*. New York: Guilford.

Miller, S. B. (1996). *Shame in context*. Hillsdale, NJ: Analytic Press.

Miller-Johnson, S., Winn, D. M., Coie, J., Maumary-Gremaud, A., Hyman, C., Terry, R., & Lochman, J. (1999). Motherhood during the teen years: A developmental perspective on risk factors for childbearing. *Development and Psychopathology, 11,* 85-100.

Millon, T. (1987). *Manual for the Millon Clinical Multiaxial Inventory-II* (2nd ed.). Minneapolis, MN: National Computer Systems.

Millon, T. (1993). *Millon Adolescent Clinical Inventory manual.* Minneapolis, MN: National Computer Systems.

Milner, J. S. (1986). *Child Abuse Potential Inventory.* DeKalb, IL: Psytec Corp.

Moffitt, T. (1993). Adolescent-limited and life-course-persistent antisocial behavior: A developmental taxonomy. *Psychological Review, 100,* 674-701.

Moos, R. H. (1990). Conceptual and empirical approaches to developing family-based assessment procedures: Researching the case of the Family Environment Scale. *Family Process, 29,* 199-208.

Moos, R. H., & Moos, B. S. (1986). *Family Environment Scale.* Palo Alto, CA: Consulting Psychologists Press.

Morrey, L. C. (1991). *Personality Assessment Inventory (PAI): Professional manual.* Odessa, FL: Psychological Assessment Resources.

Morrey, L. C. (1997). *Personality Assessment Screen (PAS): Professional manual.* Odessa, FL: Psychological Assessment Resources.

Morton, T. (1987). Childhood aggression in the context of family interaction. In D. H. Crewel, I. M. Evans, & C. R. O'Donnell (Eds.), *Childhood aggression and violence* (pp. 117-158). New York: Plenum.

Myers, J. E. B. (1998). *Legal issues in child abuse and neglect* (2nd ed.). Thousand Oaks, CA: Sage.

Nakkula, M., & Selman, R. (1991). How people treat each other: Pair therapy as a context for the development of interpersonal ethics. In W. N. Kurtines & J. L. Gewirtz (Eds.), *Handbook of moral development and behavior* (pp. 179-211). Hillsdale, NJ: Lawrence Erlbaum.

New, M. J. C., Stevenson, J., & Skuse, D. (1999). Characteristics of mothers of boys who sexually abuse. *Child Maltreatment, 4,* 21-31.

Newberger, C. M., Gremy, I. M., Waternaux, C. M., & Newberger, E. H. (1993). Mothers of sexually abused children: Trauma repair in longitudinal perspective. *American Journal of Orthopsychiatry, 63,* 92-102.

Ogawa, J. R., Sroufe, L. A., Weinfeld, N. S., Carlson, E. A., & Egeland, B. (1997). Development and the fragmented self: Longitudinal study of dissociative symptomatology in a nonclinical sample. *Development and Psychopathology, 9,* 855-880.

Ollendick, T. H. (1983). Reliability and validity of the revised Fear Survey Schedule for Children (FSSC-R). *Behavior Research and Therapy, 21,* 685-692.

Ornduff, S. R., & Kelsey, R. M. (1996). Object relations of sexually and physically abused female children. *Journal of Personality Assessment, 66,* 91-105.

Patterson, G. (1982). *Coercive family process.* Eugene, OR: Castalia.

Patterson, G. R., Reid, J. B., Jones, R. R., & Conger, R. E. (1975). *A social learning approach to family intervention. Vol. 1. Families with aggressive children.* Eugene, OR: Castalia.

Pennebaker, J. W. (Ed.). (1995). *Emotion, disclosure, and health.* Washington, DC: American Psychological Association.

Perez, C. M., & Widom, C. S. (1994). Childhood victimization and long-term intellectual and academic outcomes. *Child Abuse & Neglect, 18,* 617-633.

Perrin, E. C., Stein, R. E. K., & Drotar, D. (1991). Cautions in using the Child Behavior Checklist: Observations based on research about children with a chronic illness. *Journal of Pediatric Psychology, 16*, 411-421.

Peterson, L. W., & Hardin, M. E. (1997). *Children in distress: A system for screening children's art.* New York: Norton.

Phelps, J. L., Belsky, J., & Crnic, K. (1998). Earned security, daily stress, and parenting: A comparison of five alternative models. *Development and Psychopathology, 10*, 21-38.

Pithers, W. D., Gray, A., Busconi, A., & Houchens, P. (1998). Children with sexual behavior problems: Identification of five distinct child types and related treatment considerations. *Child Maltreatment, 3*, 384-406.

Poole, D. A., & Lamb, M. E. (1998). *Investigative interviews of children.* Washington, DC: American Psychological Association.

Pruett, K. D., & Solnit, A. J. (1998). Psychological and ethical considerations in the preparation of the mental health professional as an expert witness. In S. J. Ceci & H. Hembrooke (Eds.), *Expert witnesses in child abuse cases* (pp. 123-135). Washington, DC: American Psychological Association.

Putnam, F. W. (1985). Dissociation as a response to extreme trauma. In R. P. Kluft (Ed.), *Childhood antecedents of multiple personality* (pp. 65-97). Washington, DC: American Psychiatric Press.

Putnam, F. W. (1994). Dissociative disorders in children and adolescents. In S. J. Lynn & J. W. Rhue (Eds.), *Dissociation: Theoretical, clinical, and research perspectives* (pp. 175-189). New York: Guilford.

Putnam, F. W., Helmers, K., & Trickett, P. K. (1993). Development, reliability, and validity of a child dissociation scale. *Child Abuse & Neglect, 17*, 731-742.

Pynoos, R. S., Steinberg, A. M., & Wraith, R. (1995). A developmental model of childhood traumatic stress. In D. Cicchetti & D. Cohen (Eds.), *Developmental psychopathology: Vol. 2. Risk, disorder, and adaptation* (pp. 72-95). New York: John Wiley.

Reams, R. A., & Friedrich, W. N. (1994). The efficacy of time-limited play therapy with maltreated preschoolers. *Journal of Clinical Psychology, 50*, 889-899.

Reid, J. B. (1978). *A social learning approach to family intervention: Vol. 2. Observation in the home settings.* Eugene, OR: Castalia.

Reid, J. B., Kavanagh, K., & Baldwin, D. V. (1987). Abusive parents' perceptions of child problem behaviors: An example of parental bias. *Journal of Abnormal Child Psychology, 15*, 457-466.

Reynolds, C. R., & Kamphaus, R. W. (1998). *Behavior Assessment System for Children.* Circle Pines, MN: American Guidance Service.

Reynolds, C. R., & Richmond, B. O. (1978). What I think and feel: A revised measure of children's manifest anxiety. *Journal of Abnormal Child Psychology, 6*, 271-280.

Rind, B., Tromovitch, P., & Bauserman, R. (1998). Meta-analysis of research with college students on the impact of sexual abuse. *Psychological Bulletin, 124*, 22-53.

Root, M. P. P., & Fallon, P. (1988). The incidence of victimization experiences in a bulimic sample. *Journal of Interpersonal Violence, 3*, 161-173.

Root, M. P. P., & Fallon, P. (1989). Treating the victimized bulimic: The functions of binge-purge behavior. *Journal of Interpersonal Violence, 4*, 90-100.

Root, M. P. P., & Friedrich, W. N. (1989). Heterogeneity in a bulimic sample: A study of MMPI codetypes. *Psychotherapy in Private Practice, 7*(1), 97-113.

Rotheram-Borus, M. J., Mahler, K. A., Koopman, C., & Langabeer, K. (1996). Sexual abuse history and associated multiple risk behavior in adolescent runaways. *American Journal of Orthopsychiatry, 66*, 390-400.

Rutter, M. (1971). Normal psychosexual development. *Journal of Child Psychology and Psychiatry, 11,* 259-283.

Ryan, G. D., & Lane, S. L. (1997). (Eds.). *Juvenile sexual offending.* San Francisco: Jossey-Bass.

Sadowski, C. M., & Friedrich, W. N. (2000). Psychometric properties of the Trauma Symptom Checklist for Children (TSCC) with psychiatrically hospitalized adolescents. *Child Maltreatment, 5,* 364-372.

Saigh, P. A., Yasik, A. E., Oberfield, R. A., Green, B. L., Halamandaris, P. V., Rubenstein, H., Nester, J., Resko, J., Hetz, B., & McHugh, M. (2000). The Children's PTSD Inventory: Development and reliability. *Journal of Traumatic Stress, 13,* 369-380.

Salter, A. (1988). *Treating child sex offenders and victims.* Thousand Oaks, CA: Sage.

Sanders, S. (1986). The Perceptual Alteration Scale: A scale for measuring dissociation. *American Journal of Clinical Hypnosis, 29,* 95-102.

Saunders, B. E., Arata, C. M., & Kilpatrick, D. G. (1990). Development of a crime-related post-traumatic stress-disorder scale for women within the Symptom Checklist-90-Revised. *Journal of Traumatic Stress, 3,* 439-448.

Scheeringa, M. S., Peebles, C. D., Cook, C. A., & Zeanah, C. H. (2001). Toward establishing procedural, criterion, and discriminant validity for PTSD in early childhood. *Journal of the American Academy of Child and Adolescent Psychiatry, 40,* 52-60.

Scheeringa, M. S., Zeanah, C. H., Drell, M., & Larrieu, J. (1995). Two approaches to the diagnosis of post-traumatic stress disorder in infancy and early childhood. *Journal of the American Academy of Child and Adolescent Psychiatry, 34,* 191-200.

Schoentjes, E., Deboutte, D., & Friedrich, W. N. (1999). Child Sexual Behavior Inventory: A Dutch-speaking normative sample. *Pediatrics, 104,* 885-893.

Schore, A. N. (1994). *Affect regulation and the origin of the self: The neurobiology of emotional development.* Hillsdale, NJ: Lawrence Erlbaum.

Schore, A. N. (1996). The experience-dependent maturation of a regulatory system in the orbital prefrontal cortex and the origin of developmental psychopathology. *Development and Psychopathology, 8,* 59-87.

Schore, A. N. (1997). Early organization of the nonlinear right brain and development of a predisposition to psychiatric disorders. *Development and Psychopathology, 9,* 595-632.

Schuengel, C., Bakermans-Kranenburg, M. J., & Van Ijzendoorn, M. H. (1999). Frightening maternal behavior linking unresolved loss and disorganized infant attachment. *Journal of Consulting and Clinical Psychology, 67,* 54-63.

Scott, R. L., & Stone, D. A. (1986). MMPI profile constellations in incest families. *Journal of Consulting and Clinical Psychology, 54,* 364-368.

Seabloom, M. E. (1998). *Crossing boundaries: Family sexual context, family cohesion, intimate communication, and sex role identity in families of males who have engaged in non-societally sanctioned sexual behaviors with a minor.* Unpublished doctoral dissertation, University of Minnesota.

Seligman, L. D., & Ollendick, T. H. (1998). Comorbidity of anxiety and depression in children and adolescents: An integrative review. *Clinical Child and Family Psychology Review, 1,* 125-144.

Shapiro, J. P., Leifer, M., Martone, M. W., & Kassem, L. (1990). Multimethod assessment of depression in sexually abused girls. *Journal of Personality Assessment, 55,* 234-248.

Shapiro, J. P., Leifer, M., Martone, M. W., & Kassem, L. (1992). Cognitive functioning and social competence as predictors of maladjustment in sexually abused girls. *Journal of Interpersonal Violence, 7,* 156-164.

Shaw, D. S., Owens, E. B., Vondra, J. I., & Keenan, K. (1996). Early risk factors and pathways in the development of early disruptive behavior problems. *Development and Psychopathology, 8,* 679-699.

Siegel, D. (1999). *The developing mind.* New York: Guilford.

Singer, M. I., Petchers, M. K., & Hussey, D. (1989). The relationship between sexual abuse and substance abuse among psychiatrically hospitalized adolescents. *Child Abuse & Neglect, 13,* 319-325.

Smith, V. R. (1992). Sexually abused children's performance on the Roberts Apperception Test for Children (Doctoral dissertation, California School of Professional Psychology, 1991). *Dissertation Abstracts International, 52,* 5549B.

Spacarelli, S. (1994). Stress, appraisal and coping in child sexual abuse: A theoretical and empirical review. *Psychological Bulletin, 116,* 340-362.

Spacarelli, S. (1995). Measuring abuse stress and negative cognitive appraisals in child sexual abuse: Validity data on two new scales. *Journal of Abnormal Child Psychology, 23,* 703-727.

Spanier, G. B. (1976). Measuring dyadic adjustment: New scales for assessing the quality of marriage and similar dyads. *Journal of Marriage and the Family, 38,* 15-28.

Spinetta, J. J., & Deasy-Spinetta, P. (1981). *Living with childhood cancer.* St. Louis, MO: C. V. Mosby.

Springs, F. E., & Friedrich, W. N. (1992). Health risk behaviors and medical sequelae of childhood sexual abuse. *Mayo Clinic Proceedings, 67,* 527-532.

Sroufe, L. A. (1997). Psychopathology as an outcome of development. *Development and Psychopathology, 9,* 251-268.

Sroufe, L. A., & Fleeson, J. (1986). Attachment and the construction of relationships. In W. Hartup & Z. Rubin (Eds.), *Relationships and development* (pp. 51-71). Hillsdale, NJ: Lawrence Erlbaum.

Sroufe, L. A., & Ward, M. J. (1980). Seductive behavior of mothers of toddlers: Occurrence, correlates, and family origins. *Child Development, 51,* 1222-1229.

Stauffer, L. B., & Deblinger, E. (1996). Cognitive behavioral groups for non-offending mothers and their young sexually abused children: A preliminary treatment outcome study. *Child Maltreatment, 1,* 65-76.

Steinberg, M. (1996). Diagnostic tools for assessing dissociation in children and adolescents. *Child and Adolescent Psychiatric Clinics of North America, 5,* 333-349.

Stewart, S. H. (1996). Alcohol abuse in individuals exposed to trauma: A critical review. *Psychological Bulletin, 120,* 83-112.

Stoller, R. (1989). Consensual sadomasochistic perversions. In H. P. Blum & E. M. Weinshel (Eds.), *The psychoanalytic core: Essays in honor of Leo Rangell, M.D.* (pp. 265-282). Madison, CT: International Universities Press.

Stone, N. (1993). Parental abuse as a precursor to childhood onset depression and suicidality. *Child Psychiatry and Human Development, 24,* 13-24.

Stone, W. L., & Lemanek, K. L. (1990). Developmental issues in children's self-reports. In A. M. LaGreca (Ed.), *Through the eyes of the child: Obtaining self-reports from children and adolescents* (pp. 18-56). Boston: Allyn & Bacon.

Stovall, G., & Craig, R. J. (1990). Mental representations of physically and sexually abused latency-aged females. *Child Abuse & Neglect, 14,* 233-242.

Straus, M. A., Hamby, S. L., Finkelhor, D., Moore, D. W., & Runyan, D. (1998). Identification of child maltreatment with the Parent-Child Conflict Tactics Scales: Development and psychometric data for a national sample of American parents. *Child Abuse & Neglect, 22,* 249-270.

Swanston, H. Y., Tebbutt, J. S., O'Toole, B. I., & Oates, R. K. (1997). Sexually abused children 5 years after presentation: A case-control study. *Pediatrics, 100,* 600-608.

Terr, L. C. (1981). Forbidden games: Post-traumatic child's play. *American Journal of Orthopsychiatry, 20,* 740-759.

Terr, L. C. (1991). Childhood traumas: An outline and overview. *American Journal of Psychiatry, 148,* 10-20.

Thompson, R. A. (1994). Emotion regulation: A theme in search of definition. In N. A. Fox (Ed.), The development of emotion regulation: Biological and behavioral considerations. *Monographs of the Society for Research in Child Development, 59*(2-3, Serial No. 240), 25-52.

Thompson, R. A., & Calkins, S. D. (1996). The double-edged sword: Emotional regulation for children at risk. *Development & Psychopathology, 8,* 163-182.

Toth, S. L., Cicchetti, D., Macfie, J., & Emde, R. N. (1997). Representation of self and other in the narratives of neglected, physically abused, and sexually abused preschoolers. *Development and Psychopathology, 9,* 781-796.

Trepper, T. S., & Barrett, M. J. (1989). *Systemic treatment of incest.* New York: Brunner/Mazel.

Trepper, T. S., Niedner, D., Mika, L., & Barrett, M. J. (1996). Family characteristics of intact sexually abusing families: An exploratory study. *Journal of Child Sexual Abuse, 5,* 1-18.

Trickett, P. K. (1993). Maladaptive development of school-aged, physically abused children: Relationships with the child-rearing context. *Journal of Family Psychology, 7,* 134-147.

Trickett, P. K., McBride-Chang, C., & Putnam, F. W. (1994). The classroom performance and behavior of sexually abused females. *Development and Psychopathology, 6,* 183-194.

Troy, M., & Sroufe. L. A. (1987). Victimization among preschoolers: Role of attachment relationship history. *Journal of the American Academy of Child and Adolescent Psychiatry, 26,* 166-172.

Tuteur, J. M., Ewigman, B. E., Peterson, L., & Hosokawa, M. C. (1995). The Maternal Observation Matrix and the Mother-Child Interaction Scale: Brief observational screening instruments for physically abusive mothers. *Journal of Clinical Child Psychology, 24,* 55-62.

Urquiza, A. J., & McNeil, C. B. (1996). Parent-Child Interaction therapy: An intensive dyadic intervention for physically abusive families. *Child Maltreatment, 1,* 132-141.

Van der Kolk, B. A., McFarlane, A. C., & Weisaeth, L. (1996). *Traumatic stress: The effects of overwhelming experience on mind, body, and society.* New York: Guilford.

Vaughn, B., Egeland, B., & Sroufe, L. A. (1979). Individual differences in infant-mother attachment at 12 and 18 months: Stability and change in families under stress. *Child Development, 50,* 971-975.

Wachtel, E. F., & Wachtel, P. L. (1986). *Family dynamics and individual psychotherapy.* New York: Guilford.

Wahler, R. G. (1980). The multiply entrapped parent: Obstacles to change in parent-child problems. In J. P. Vincent (Ed.), *Advances in family intervention, assessment, and theory* (Vol. 1, pp. 29-52). Greenwich, CT: JAI.

Wahler, R. G., & Meginnis, K. L. (1997). Strengthening child compliance through positive parenting practices: What works? *Journal of Clinical Child Psychology, 26,* 433-440.

Walker, L. S., Ortiz-Valdes, J. A., & Newbrough, J. R. (1989). The role of maternal employment and depression in the psychological adjustment of chronically ill, mentally retarded, and well children. *Journal of Pediatric Psychology, 14,* 357-370.

Waters, E., & Deane, K. E. (1985). Defining and assessing individual differences in attachment relationships: Q-methodology and the organization of behavior in infancy and early childhood. In I. Bretherton & E. Waters (Eds.), Growing points in attachment theory and research. *Monographs of the Society for Research in Child Development, 50*(Serial No. 209), 41-65.

Wechsler, D. (1997). *Wechsler Adult Intelligence Scale–Third Edition: Administration and scoring manual.* San Antonio, TX: Psychological Corporation.

*Wechsler Abbreviated Scale of Intelligence: Manual.* (1999). San Antonio, TX: Psychological Corporation.

Weiner, I. B. (1998). *Principles of Rorschach interpretation.* Mahwah, NJ: Lawrence Erlbaum.

Weiss, D. S., & Marmar, C. R. (1997). The Impact of Event Scale–Revised. In J. P. Wilson & T. M. Keane (Eds.), *Assessing psychological trauma and PTSD* (pp. 399-411). New York: Guilford.

Weissman, H. N. (1991). Forensic psychological examination of the child witness in cases of alleged sexual abuse. *American Journal of Orthopsychiatry, 61,* 48-58.

West, M. M. (1998). Meta-analysis of studies assessing the efficacy of projective techniques in discriminating child sexual abuse. *Child Abuse & Neglect, 22,* 1151-1166.

Westen, D. (1991). Social cognition and object relations. *Psychological Bulletin, 109,* 429-455.

Westen, D., Lohr, N., Silk, K., Gold, L., & Kerber, K. (1990). Object relations and social cognition in borderline personality disorder and depression: A TAT analysis. *Psychological Assessment, 2,* 355-364.

Wilsnack, S. C. (1991). Sexuality and women's drinking: Findings from a U.S. national study. *Alcohol Health and Research World, 15,* 147-150.

Wilson, J. P., & Keane, T. M. (1997). *Assessing psychological trauma and PTSD.* New York: Guilford.

Winnicott, D. W. (1965). *The maturational processes and the facilitating environment.* New York: International Universities Press.

Wolfe, D. A., & Mosk, M. D. (1983). Behavioral comparisons of children from abusive and distressed families. *Journal of Consulting and Clinical Psychology, 51,* 702-708.

Wolfe, D. A., Sas, L., & Wekerle, C. (1994). Factors associated with the development of post-traumatic stress disorder among child victims of sexual abuse. *Child Abuse & Neglect, 18,* 37-50.

Wolfe, V. V., Gentile, C., Michienzi, T., Sas, L., & Wolfe, D. A. (1991). Children's Impact of Traumatic Events Scale: A measure of post-sexual-abuse PTSD symptoms. *Behavioral Assessment, 13,* 359-383.

Wolfe, V. V., Gentile, C., & Wolfe, D. A. (1989). The impact of sexual abuse on children: A PTSD formulation. *Behavior Therapy, 20,* 215-228.

Wolfe, V. V., & Wolfe, D. A. (1988). The sexually abused child. In E. J. Mash & L. J. Terdal (Eds.), *Behavioral assessment of childhood disorders* (2nd ed., pp. 670-714). New York: Guilford.

Woodward, L. J., & Fergusson, D. M. (1999). Early conduct problems and later risk of teenage pregnancy in girls. *Development and Psychopathology, 11,* 127-142.

Wright, J., Friedrich, W. N., Cyr, M., Theriault, C., Perron, A., Lussier, Y., & Sabourin, S. (1998). The evaluation of Franco-Quebec victims of child sexual abuse and their mother: The implementation of a standard assessment protocol. *Child Abuse & Neglect, 22,* 9-24.

Yuille, J., Hunter, R., Joffe, R., & Ziparniuk, J. (1993). Interviewing children in sexual abuse cases. In G. S. Goodman, B. L. Bottoms, et al. (Eds.), *Child victims, child witnesses: Understanding and improving testimony* (pp. 95-115). New York: Guilford.

Zanarini, M. C. (1996). *Role of sexual abuse in the etiology of borderline personality disorder.* Washington, DC: American Psychiatric Press.

Zeanah, C. H., Benoit, D., & Barton, M. L. (1996). *Working Model of the Child Interview.* Unpublished manuscript, Tulane University Medical School.

Zeanah, C. H., Boris, N. W., & Scheeringa, M. S. (1997). Psychopathology in infancy. *Journal of Child Psychiatry and Psychology, 38,* 81-99.

Zeanah, C. H., Larrieu, J. A., Heller, S. S., Valliere, J., Hinshaw-Fuselier, S., Aoki, Y., & Drilling, M. (2001). Evaluation of a preventative intervention for maltreated infants and toddlers in foster care. *Journal of the American Academy of Child and Adolescent Psychiatry, 40,* 214-221.

# List of Acronyms

AACAP   American Academy of Child and Adolescent Psychiatry
AAI     Adult Attachment Interview
A-DES   Adolescent-Dissociative Experiences Schedule
ADHD    Attention deficit hyperactivity disorder
APSAC   American Professional Society on the Abuse of Children
ASBI    Adolescent Sexual Behavior Inventory
ASD     Acute Stress Disorder
ATSA    Association for the Treatment of Sexual Abusers
BASC    Behavior Assessment System for Children
BDI     Beck Depression Inventory
CAFAS   Child and Adolescent Functional Assessment Scale
CAP     Child Abuse Potential Inventory
CAPS    Children's Attributions and Perceptions Scale
CBCL    Child Behavior Checklist
CBI     Child Behavior Checklist

| | |
|---|---|
| CD | Conduct disorder |
| CDC | Child Disssociative Checklist |
| CDI | Child Depression Inventory |
| CDI | Child Development Inventory |
| CITES-R | Children's Impact of Traumatic Events Scale |
| CPS | Child protective services |
| CSBI | Child Sexual Behavior Inventory |
| CTS | Conflict Tactics Scale |
| CTSPC | Parent-Child Conflict Tactics Scale |
| DES | Disociative Experiences Schedule |
| DRSB | Developmentally related sexual behavior |
| GAL | Guardian ad litem |
| HFD | Human Figure Drawing |
| IOWA | Inattention-Overactivity With Aggression |
| IPPA | Inventory of Parent and Peer Attachment |
| KFD | Kinetic Family Drawing |
| KIA | Kempe Interactional Assessment |
| MCMI | Millon Clinical Multiaxial Inventory |
| MMPI | Minnesota Multiphasic Personality Inventory |
| NOS | Not otherwise specified |
| ODD | Oppositional-defiant disorder |
| PAI | Personality Assessment Inventory |
| PAS | Personality Assessment Screener |
| PCIT | Parent-Child Interaction Therapy |
| PCL-R | Psychopathy Checklist-Revised |
| PERQ | Parental Emotional Reaction Questionnaire |
| PSI | Parenting Stress Index |
| PSQ | Parental Support Questionnaire |
| PTSD | Posttraumatic stress disorder |
| RCMAS | Revised Children's Manifest Anxiety Scale |
| SAAST | Self-Administered Alcoholism Screen Test |

| | |
|---|---|
| SASI | Sexual-abuse-specific sexual items |
| SCL | Symptom Checklist |
| SIB | Self-injurious behavior |
| SIBQ | Self-Injurious Behavior Questionnaire |
| SPS | Suicide Potential Scale |
| TAT | Thematic Apperception Test |
| TONI | Test of Nonverbal Intelligence |
| TRF | Teacher's Report Form |
| TSB | Total sexual behavior |
| TSCC | Trauma Symptom Checklist for Children |
| TSI | Trauma Symptom Inventory |
| WAIS | Wechsler Adult Intelligence Scale |
| WISC-III | Wechsler Intelligent Scales for Children, 3rd Edition |
| WMCI | Working Model of the Child Interview |
| WRAT-3 | Wide Range Achievement Test Revision |
| YSR | Youth Self-Report |

# Index

# About the Author

**William N. Friedrich, PhD,** is a Professor in the Mayo Medical School and a consultant at the Mayo Clinic in Rochester, Minnesota. His position there includes clinical practice with maltreated children and their families, forensic evaluations, and supervision and training, as well as programmatic research in the areas of child and adolescent sexual behavior, the validity of assessment with maltreated and traumatized children, and the function of family environment features in parent-child relations on the short-term and long-term adjustment of sexually aggressive children. He is also a core faculty member of the Eastern European Children's Mental Health Salvation. He is a diplomate in clinical and family psychology with the American Board of Professional Psychology. He is the author of 145 papers and chapters; eight books, including the unpublished *Treating Sexualized Behavior in Children: A Treatment Manual;* and more than a dozen short stories. He is married and the father of two adult children.

# About the Contributors

**Angela Carron** is a pediatrician at the Child Protection Center of Children's Hospital of Wisconsin in Milwaukee. Her interests are in the forensic evaluation of child maltreatment, community pediatrics, and child and family advocacy.

**W. Hobart Davies,** PhD, is Assistant Professor of Psychology at the University of Wisconsin-Milwaukee and Assistant Clinical Professor of Psychiatry and Pediatrics at the Medical College of Wisconsin. His research and clinical work focuses on family response to severe stress, including child maltreatment, community violence, and pediatric illness.

**Diana M. Elliott,** PhD, is in private forensic psychology practice in Los Angeles, California, after having spent many years as the Director of Training and Research at the Harbor-CLA Child Abuse Crisis Center. She is also Assistant Clinical Professor in the Department of Psychology at the University of Southern California. She has published a number of papers and chapters on the impact of sexual abuse in children, adolescents, and adults.

**Molly Murphy Garwood** is Associate Lecturer in the Department of Psychology at the University of Wisconsin-Milwaukee. Previously, she was a Pediatric Psychologist with the Psychiatry Department/ Child Protection Center of Children's Hospital of Wisconsin. Her research interests include the development of parent-child attachment relationships, psychological functioning of children in foster care, and resilience in children who have been physically and sexually abused.

**Anita O'Conor,** MSW, CICSW, has been employed as a forensic interviewer at the Child Protection Center of Children's Hospital of Wisconsin since 1993. She has completed over 650 interviews of children ages 3 to 18 regarding sexual abuse concerns. She is a board member for WIPSAC (Professional Society on the Abuse of Children) and the Milwaukee Commission on Domestic Violence and Sexual Assault and is committed to the development of a coordinated investigative response to child maltreatment.